THE ENCYCLOPEDIA OF
SERIAL KILLERS

Also by Brian Lane

The Murder Club Guides (6 vols., Harrap, 1988–9)
The Murder Guide to Great Britain (Robinson, 1991)
The Butchers (Virgin, 1991)
Murder Update (Robinson, 1991)

THE ENCYCLOPEDIA OF SERIAL KILLERS

Brian Lane & Wilfred Gregg

HEADLINE

First published in 1992
by HEADLINE BOOK PUBLISHING PLC

10 9 8 7 6 5 4 3 2 1

British Library Cataloguing in Publication Data

Lane, Brian
    Encyclopedia of serial killers.
    I. Title II. Gregg, Wilfred
    364.1523

    ISBN 0-7472-0461-6

Typeset by Letterpart Ltd, Reigate, Surrey

Printed and bound in Great Britain by
Richard Clay Ltd, Bungay, Suffolk

HEADLINE BOOK PUBLISHING PLC
Headline House
79 Great Titchfield Street
London W1P 7FN

Contents

Acknowledgements   vii
Introduction   1
Serial Killers A–Z   19
Select Bibliography   285
General Reference Works   295
Alphabetical Index   297
Geographical Index   304

Acknowledgements

Encyclopedias are rarely 'written'; rather, they are distilled and assembled from the accumulated knowledge of countless contributors over a long period of time and a wide geographical area. This is true of *The Encyclopedia of Serial Killers*, for although the words contained in this book are our own they have, in terms of facts and features, relied upon the efforts of a multitude of previous authorities, as well as on our own first-hand researches. In practical terms Wilf Gregg's exhaustive library, supplemented by the cuttings archive of The Murder Club have provided the solid background from which we have composed out cast-list; their characters have been filled out by information from a network of correspondents throughout the world, and we would particularly like to thank John Critchley for being Our Man in New Zealand. Others have taken on the task of elucidating individual crimes, and we are grateful to Susan Dunkley for her contribution to the final text.

But all the words in the world do not necessarily make a book; to do that they need careful crafting, not only by authors, but by editors and publishers. For her imaginative response to the concept of an encyclopedia of serial killers, and for her time and patience in reading and honing the manuscript our grateful thanks to Sally Holloway; as they go also to Jane Carr, who so skilfully steered the project to its final publication.

For the majority of illustrations the authors have drawn on their own archives, and are grateful to those people who have so generously allowed their material to be used. We also thank the following agencies for permission to use their photographs: Associated Press, Popperfoto, Rex Features, Syndication International, Topham Picture Source, Weidenfeld and Nicolson; if we have failed to trace the copyright of any illustration may we apologise in advance.

Brian Lane
Wilfred Gregg

London, 1991

Introduction

The author has been uncomfortably aware while working on this book that to describe it as an 'Encyclopedia' could be seen as somewhat presumptiuous, given the range and complexity of deviant behaviour. Like any thematic 'Who's Who', it will to some extent be out of date as soon as it leaves the printing press, for it is typical of the escalation of the problem of serial murder that even as the book was being prepared for typesetting, three major new cases appeared in the world's press during the course of less than one month. Predictably, perhaps, two of those cases – those of Jeffrey **Dahmer** and Donald **Evans** – occurred in the United States. The third, less predictably, took place in the Soviet Union – Nikolai **Dzhumagaliev**, known as 'Metal Fang'.

Nor is it inconsistent that the serial killer has, in a perverse way, entered the popular consciousness almost as a folk-hero. In the United States the elevation to cult status of Charles **Manson** has extended far beyond the rag-tag remnants of his immediate 'family' so that today youths not even born at the time of the Tate/LaBianca killings are forming their own groups in emulation of the Manson 'tribe'. When David **Berkowitz** was identified as the multicide known as 'Son of Sam' in 1977, his apartment in the Yonkers district of New York was all but torn to pieces by souvenir hunters desperate for some memento of the killer who had already become a cult; eventually his landlord was obliged to change the street number of the block from 25 to 42 in an attempt to discourage sightseers. In England the modest house in Hattersley which was home to the notorious 'Moors Murderers' Ian **Brady** and Myra Hindley had to be demolished before the regular flow of pilgrims to the site dried up. And this fascination does not end with the serial killer in our midst – the monsters of fiction are increasingly cast in the role of multicides. It may be significant that at the time Jeffrey Dahmer was slaying and cannibalising his victims in Milwaukee and Nikolai Dzhumagaliev was doing the same in Kazakhstan, Doctor Hannibal Lecter, fictional multicide and cannibal, was achieving international celebrity in the film of Thomas Harris's novel *The Silence of the Lambs* – not a small-budget cult movie, but a major release that in Britain alone broke all previous box-office records in its first two days, and prompted one critic to ask, 'Since when is a mass murderer a lovable rogue?'*

It is for this reason, then, that a book like this, despite the possible

---

* Stuart Weir, *The Sunday Times*, London, 11 August 1991.

shortcomings of its format, serves not only as a timely and useful reminder of who these 'serial killers' *really* are, but also as an attempt to analyse and explain some of the current work being undertaken with the purpose of understanding and combating the growing menace of serial murder.

The reader will quickly see that those who kill 'serially' are not an entirely recent problem for the world's police forces; indeed, perhaps the best known and most controversial criminal in history was the stereotype sado-sexual serial killer, Jack the Ripper. What is comparatively recent is the identification of a new and increasingly numerous *type* of murderer, who apparently kills randomly and without motive. It is these characteristics that pose the biggest threat to society.

It is customary in cases of murder to categorise the victim according to a clearly identifiable motive – that he or she owned something coveted by the killer, for example, or had been in conflict with him, or had proved to be an unfaithful spouse and so on. For the serial killer the 'motive' is so deeply locked into his inner psyche that a victim need only be of a certain type – to fall into a broad category such as women or children – and to be in the wrong place at the wrong time.

It is true that some serial killers are quite precise in selecting their victims; Joseph Medley, for example, killed only women with red hair. Ramiro **Artieda** killed only girls who 'looked like' the fiancée who had jilted him. Complications arise when a killer's inability to identify members of his target group results in a quasi-random selection: despite his claim that he was benevolently ridding the streets of prostitutes, Peter **Sutcliffe**, by attacking and murdering a number of women who were not, put *all* women who happened to be out at night at risk.

Thus *every* human being is the potential victim of a killer against whom they have no protection, and against whom the traditional means of investigation based on determinable motive are powerless.

Some insight into the scale of the problem posed by the so-called 'stranger-killers', in the United States can be gained from examining the statistics for just one year. In 1989 (the last year for which detailed figures are available*) there were 21,500 recorded homicides, of which some 5000 are unsolved. Unofficial sources believe that as many as a hundred serial killers may be at large at any given time, responsible for the majority of those unsolved murders (some estimates are as high as two-thirds). Add to this the number of *known* victims of serial killers, then between 3500 and 5000 people are killed by serial murderers every year.

Figures for Britain are, for the present, more optimistic, though statistics for the same year (1989)† record 576 homicides (including murder, manslaughter and infanticide) and reveal a five per cent

---

* *Uniform Crime Reports*, US Dept. of Justice, Washington DC, 1990.
† *Criminal Statistics England and Wales*, Home Office, London, 1990.

increase in stranger-oriented homicides. More significant perhaps, is that in England and Wales (Scotland publishes its statistics independently) the clear-up rate for homicide is in excess of ninety per cent, while the overall average for the United States is sixty-eight per cent.

Given these alarming statistics it is not surprising that no effort or expense have been spared by the American law-enforcement agencies to address the problem of serial murder with speed and imagination. It was in the early 1970s that the FBI's Behavioural Science Unit was established to study the techniques of serial killers and to analyse the patterns that emerged. The work of the specialised agencies will be discussed in a later section, but their efforts have resulted in, if by no means a foolproof means of identifying the serial killer, then at least the definition of a set of variable elements all or some of which are possessed by the serial killer and which distinguish him from the single-incident ('normal') murderer and other categories of multicide, the 'mass murderer' and the 'spree murderer'.

'Mass' murder can be conveniently described as an act in which a number of people are slain by a single assassin during a short period of time in roughly the same geographical location. For example, in 1977, Fred Cowan, a Nazi sympathiser, set out with pistols and a semi-automatic rifle to his former place of employment in New Rochelle, New York, where he shot at black and Jewish employees, killing four and a policeman, and wounding several others before turning the gun on himself. In December 1989 a man wearing hunting clothes and carrying a rifle walked into a classroom at Montreal University, Canada, and massacred fourteen women and wounded a dozen more before killing himself; the motive was as simplistic as the crime was appalling – he hated 'feminists'.

With 'spree' murder, the multiple killing takes place over a marginally longer period of time – hours or days. In August 1987, Michael Ryan, armed with a Kalashnikov automatic rifle, terrorised the English town of Hungerford leaving seventeen dead (including his own mother) and fourteen wounded; Ryan shot himself while under siege in a school building. A sinister postscript to the 'Hungerford Massacre' occurred in 1989, when Robert Sartin – a psychotic acting on the instruction of voices – went on a shooting spree in the town of Monkseaton, Tyne and Wear. Sartin had an obsessive admiration for the exploits of Michael Ryan, and had paid a visit of pilgrimage to Hungerford before embarking on his own rampage.

While this introduction was being revised in August 1991, the news was coming in of an Australian named Wade Frankum who had gone berserk in a Sydney shopping mall and shot down seven innocent people before turning the gun on himself. The police chief in charge of the case summed up the frustration and bewilderment of us all in the face of such mindless slaughter when he declared, 'It's a terrible scene in there; there doesn't appear to be any rhyme or reason for it.'

A notable characteristic of both mass and spree killers is their relative unconcern for escape or personal safety. It is not uncommon for these types of killer to commit suicide; psychologist Elliott Leyton refers to 'the mass killer, who no longer wishes to live, and whose murders constitute his *suicide note*'.*

Serial murder – some characteristics

The serial killer exhibits quite separate and distinct characteristics, the main six of which are set out below:

1. *Killings are repetitive ('serial') occurring with greater or less frequency, often escalating, over a period of time, sometimes years; and will continue until the killer is taken into custody, dies or is himself killed.*

This represents the fundamental pattern of the serial killer which distinguishes him or her from other multicides. Clearly there can be no predetermined number of victims at which point the murderer becomes 'serial', nor is there any set frequency of activity required for the term to be applied. For the purposes of this book we have included the South African Ronald **Cooper**, who, although he killed only once before he was apprehended, revealed in his diaries a carefully planned and extensive programme of child murder. The Englishman William **Burkitt** stabbed to death three common-law wives; the first in 1915, the second in 1924, the third in 1939. The reason for the long gaps between crimes was simply that Burkitt spent the intervening years in prison, and had he not finally been incarcerated for life the pattern would almost certainly have continued.

This compulsion to kill is often recognised by the killer himself, and many when arrested have confessed that they would have continued to kill if left at large. William **Bonin**, California's 'Freeway Killer', told a journalist after his trial, 'I'd still be killing. I couldn't stop killing.' William **Heirens** gave advance notice of his own deeply distressed state when he scrawled on his victim's wall: 'For heavens sake catch me before I kill more. I cannot control myself.' Henry Lee **Lucas**, on his own admission one of America's most prolific killers, was so certain of his likely behaviour that, when release from a prison mental hospital approached, he warned the authorities to keep him confined: 'I told them before I ever left prison that I was going to commit crimes, told them the type of crimes I was going to commit, and they wouldn't believe it. They said I was going regardless of whether I liked it or not. And the day I got out of jail is the day I started killing.' And he continued to do so until he was arrested thirteen years later.

To most serial killers, the act of murder – often accompanied by sexual abuse and mutilation – is *of itself* the motive. It was the

---

* *Hunting Humans*, London, 1989.

multicide Ted **Bundy**'s belief that the act of killing generates such a sense of pure pleasure and provides such a psychological 'high' that the murderer is compelled to kill again and again; and as in the case of stimulation by alcohol or drugs, the 'dose' almost always escalates. As an alcoholic or drug abuser will never be cured of his craving while he has access to the stimulant, so will the serial killer continue his course until he either dies, or is himself killed, or until he is caught and removed from the society on which he preys.

2. In common with 'normal' homicides, killings tend to be one-on-one.

The most common form of homicide is the single-incident killing of one person by another. For convenience, criminology puts these into two categories: (i) the 'crime of passion', committed during a moment of intense anger or frustration; and (ii) the 'cold-blooded' murder distinguished by a more carefully planned approach often motivated by hopes of personal gain. Once a perceived objective is realised (the elimination of an unfaithful spouse, say, or of the owner of a coveted object), there is no reason to suppose the assassin will kill again. We can see from a study of crime statistics that the greater proportion of homicides in England and Wales during 1989 were committed by persons known to the victim. Indeed, a startling forty-eight per cent of female victims were killed by husbands or lovers (or ex-husbands/lovers); the corresponding figure for male victims was ten per cent. The most alarming increase was in the percentage of stranger-oriented killings which were up by five per cent. The disproportionately higher figures for the United States have been mentioned above.

There are infrequent instances where a serial killer has struck down more than one victim in a single incident, often members of the same family and in the furtherance of another crime such as theft. The Glaswegian Peter **Manuel** included two such incidents among his series of murders – three members of the Watt family shot dead during a burglary in 1956, and an identical crime committed against the Smart family two years later.

But the most common scenario for the serial killer, as for the single-incident killer, is one-on-one. The reasons for this are to a great extent obvious – it is clearly 'safer' to work alone in the sense that only the killer himself knows about the crime, and to kill a single victim because it reduces the possibility of the perpetrator being overpowered, or of one of the victims escaping to tell the tale. Furthermore the highly individual state of mind of the serial killer makes it unlikely that he will be able or willing to share his compulsions and his pleasures with another. This is borne out by the fact that he is likely also, according to statistical patterns, to be conducting a parallel life as trusted employee, reliable family man and good neighbour.

That said, there is a surprisingly high incidence of killer couples, partnerships and groups, though as the individuals who comprise those pairings are mutually dependent the requirements of security that are felt essential by the lone killer are generally satisfied.

Killer couples
The most common understanding of the phrase is a man and a woman, almost always involved in a sexual relationship, in which the male is generally the dominant party. It is an interesting phenomenon that, while both partners are usually found to have degenerate tendencies as individuals, it is only together that their 'combined personality' proves lethal. It is a phenomenon for which the French have coined the expression *folie à deux* ('a delusion shared by two emotionally associated persons'), and psychology the term *Gestalt* where 'the organised whole is greater than the sum of its parts'.

Among the best known of these killer couples are the English 'Moors Murderers', Ian **Brady** and Myra Hindley, and the Australians David and Catherine **Birnie**. In the case of Brady and Hindley, their relationship was cemented by a mutual fascination with the more loathsome excesses of the Nazis and sexual sadism. Like many other couples who have a fondness for sexual sadism, Brady and Hindley made use of commercially available pornography, but unlike most others they became increasingly hungry for more extreme experiences. This led in the end to the brutal torture and murder of children, given an extra *frisson* by recording their victims' torment on tape and camera. It is significant that, as a couple, Brady and Hindley were entirely secure – it was only when they introduced a third party, in the person of Hindley's brother-in-law David Smith, that safety was breached, leading ultimately to Smith informing the police.

Although the tendency of the male to dominate reflects the traditional pattern of society, there are cases where the female partner exhibits dominance and plays a leading role. Such a partnership was that between Martha **Beck** and Raymond Fernandez. Although Fernandez showed considerable cunning in circumventing Martha's 'rules', it was nevertheless she who directed their murderous activities.

Homosexual partnerships share the same emotional strengths and stresses as heterosexual couples. However, although no rule is without its exceptions, homosexual male partnerships tend to be the most sexually sadistic and to inflict the greatest degree of physical torture upon their victims – Dean **Corll** and Wayne Henley being a classic example. Corll and Henley's systematic abduction, rape, torture and murder of young men ended only when Henley shot his partner dead in 1973.

The Achilles' Heel of any sexually based relationship is infidelity, and there is no more undignified sight than a trial in which each partner, their former love replaced by hate, stands accusing the other of their mutual crimes. Lesbian nurses Gwendolyn **Graham** and

Catherine Wood, for example, were forced to end their regular killing of elderly hospital patients when Graham found herself a new lover, and out of jealous revenge Wood confessed their murders.

Partnerships
These comprise any other coupling that does not have a foundation in sex. Killer cousins are represented by 'Hillside Stranglers' Kenneth **Bianchi** and Angelo Buono, and David **Gore** and Fred Waterfield of Florida. An interesting variation was shown by the brothers Ralph and Tommy **Searl** who killed independently of each other at the same time and in the same area – Kalamazoo, Michigan – from different motives.

Another variant is embodied in the activities of William **Burke** and William Hare, the Scottish body-snatchers. Although Burke and Hare are most frequently viewed as a partnership based on mutual greed and degeneracy, the menage was further embellished by their reliance upon the cooperation and active support of their common-law wives in luring victims to the squalid lodging-house in which they were to meet their death by 'burking'. Not surprisingly these lacklustre characters, when they were finally arrested, fell in a frantic rush to blame each other, resulting in Hare turning King's evidence against his former partner who was subsequently hanged from the gallows.

Group killers
In any discussion of killer groups the name Charles **Manson** is the first to spring to mind, though the Manson 'family' is by no means an isolated phenomenon. Although there is no general pattern, as there may be among killer couples and partnerships, groups have proved very effective instruments of multiple murder, sharing as they most frequently do, a bond created by their mutual fantasies. In fact, quite often the underlying principle of *folie à deux* can be applied to groups, where the individual members may be incapable of forming or carrying out the intent to murder, but as part of a group with a common cause and a dominant leader can be carried along on a wave of shared 'madness'. Some groups, like that responsible for the **'Zebra'** killings, parade their murders as 'political' statements – in this case the cause of Black Power. The gang known as the **'Chicago Rippers'** operated during 1981–82 and used murder and mutilation as part of ritual acts of cannibalism. As recently as 1991 four Austrian nurses were put on trial in Vienna charged with the murder of forty-two of their patients between 1988 and 1989. More extraordinary still was the outbreak of multiple killing which took place in the Hungarian village of Nagyrev between 1914 and 1929, when as many as thirty-eight of the village women were involved in a poison ring that claimed the lives of hundreds.

3. *There is no (or very little) connection between the perpetrator and the*

victim, the persons involved rarely being directly related.

This attribute of serial killers is in a sense a relatively recent phenomenon: there are certainly examples of victims being chosen *because* they are members of the killer's family, as is apparent in cases of systematic familicide in pursuit of financial gain. The majority of such examples occurred, though, at a time when neither policing nor the medical and forensic sciences were sufficiently developed to detect initially what would now be considered obvious homicides. It is really no great surprise, given the comparatively crude state of medical diagnosis, that Mary Ann **Cotton** was able to poison several husbands and all her children and step-children, and have each death registered as 'gastric fever'. However with advances in the techniques of criminal detection and police communications, and a growing understanding of the mind of the murderer, such obvious victim/motive patterns became increasingly difficult to mask.

One of the most alarming characteristics of recent homicide trends is the dramatic increase in stranger-perpetrated murders, and although many are simple felony-related crimes (robbery, rape, etc.), a significant number fall into the 'motiveless' category. Killers in these cases generally exhibit a sociopathic lack of concern or regret over the violence offered to their victims, in some instances expressing great enjoyment in the suffering caused. Gerald Stano, for example, confessed that his killing of thirty-two young women meant no more to him than crushing a cockroach.

4. *Although there may be a 'pattern', or 'victim trait', individual murders within a series rarely display a clearly defined or rational motive.*

We are in the main, then, dealing with what are termed 'psychogenic' explanations for serial murder – reasons that have their origin in an impaired ability to separate right from wrong, an inadequacy at problem-solving, a difficulty curbing desires and so on. Despite this, the individual is often considered to remain responsible for his behaviour; indeed, one of the most chilling observations has been that the serial killer cannot simply be dismissed as a raving psychotic whose observable derangement can be blamed for his manifest violence – frequently he or she can demonstrate a very organised, rational personality, often carefully planning their crimes for some time in advance.

It is this very lack of apparent connection between the serial killer, or 'stranger-killer', and his victim that makes this type of homicide so difficult to detect. It may not be apparent until a killer is apprehended that a series of murders over a wide geographical area are even connected. However, the problem is now being seriously and imaginatively addressed by police forces throughout the world, and by special behavioural and psychiatric units that have been set up to complement the work of the law-enforcement agencies.

> 5. *Increasingly greater spatial mobility since the advent of the automobile has enabled a killer, if he wishes, to move rapidly from one place to another often before a murder has been discovered.*

Just as the absence of apparent motive makes it difficult for an individual police force to build a list of possible suspects, so the nature of stranger-oriented murder makes the interchange of information between police forces very difficult. This is especially true in the United States where the sheer size of the country is complicated by the attitude of many of the state police forces in jealously guarding their own individual patches. Not until a distinct pattern has emerged is it likely that crimes even in bordering states will be compared, and by this time a serial killer could be many murders and several states ahead. An indication of the scale of the problem can be seen in the example of Henry Lee **Lucas** who during thirteen years as a transient killer covered America from coast to coast murdering, it is claimed, in every state but Alaska and Hawaii. It is also significant that it was only when Lucas broke the 'stranger' pattern and murdered his common-law wife and his benefactress that suspicion was aroused.

Predictably, there are notable exceptions to this general observation, and many serial killers have successfully avoided suspicion while operating in a small, stable geographical area – the 'Yorkshire Ripper' Peter **Sutcliffe** was interviewed by the police as many as nine times in connection with the murders of thirteen women in and around Manchester and West Yorkshire between 1975 and 1980. In Australia, Arnold **Sodeman** killed four times almost on his own doorstep but – and this is the secret of the successful home-based killer – his domestic and social respectability put Sodeman above suspicion.

> 6. *There is usually a high degree of redundant violence, or 'overkill', where the victim is subjected to a disproportionate level of brutality.*

The reason for this is again connected with the complex problem of motive. For a large number of serial killers *the act of killing itself* is the whole motivation for the crime – it is not the means to another end, such as robbery, where the essence of operational success is a speedy escape. As the different cases unfold throughout this book many instances arise in which a victim is slowly tortured, sometimes over a period of days, the delay serving to extend the killer's period of pleasure. The cannibal Albert **Fish**, for example, experienced what he described as 'a constant state of sexual ecstasy' over the days during which he cooked and ate the bodies of his child victims. The connection between sado-sexual fantasy and serial murder is very close, and frequently associated with the desire to dominate. All these motives presuppose a total enjoyment of the use of violence, heightened by excess.

The question of motive

An understanding of the phenomenon of serial murder is obscured by any attempt to fit the crimes into a traditionally recognised category of motive, for while all behaviour is, necessarily, 'motivated', it is the lack of *apparent* motive, or any apparent gain to the perpetrator, that is so difficult to fathom.

Patterns of serial killing fall broadly into two centres of motivation: *extrinsic*, where the impulse to kill is located *outside* the killer's psyche – that is, he perceives a rational reason for murder in outside situations and events. Although rare, the extrinsic impulse lies behind such 'political' crimes as the '**Zebra**' murders. More frequently the motivation is *intrinsic* to the psyche of the killer, whether or not that motivation is apparent to an independent observer. Few, for example, who came into contact with Peter **Sutcliffe** saw a man obsessed with the murderous elimination of prostitutes; and few who met a successful ladies' man named Ted **Bundy** would have understood his need to kill – least of all his long-term romantic partners.

However, closer psychological analysis of known cases indicates that serial murderers, with few exceptions, fit into one of four main 'types' according to the predominant homicidal motivation (Visionaries, Missionaries, Hedonists and Power Seakers).

Visionaries

This category includes killers who act in response to 'voices' and *alter egos*, where 'instructions' received serve to justify and legitimise the act of murder. For example, it was Herbert **Mullin**'s conviction – ratified by voices and what he called 'telepathic messages' – that through bloodshed he, and only he, could avert a cataclysmic earthquake that would destroy California. Mullin was assured by other telepathic messages, supposedly from the victims themselves, that they quite understood his need to kill them. Harvey **Carignan** committed all his murders believing that he was acting as an instrument of God ridding the world of sin. Cleo Green, dubbed 'The Red Demon', left four elderly women stabbed to death and decapitated in Louisville, Kentucky. He claimed to be possessed by a red demon who tormented his body and mind and gave him peace only if he killed and allowed the demon to inhabit the victim's body; but the demon always returned, completing an endless cycle of murder that stopped only with Green's arrest.

Because of the psychotic nature of the visionary's behaviour he may belong to a category that is easier to identify among his comparatively sane fellow citizens.

Missionaries

The 'clean-up' killers, who accept a self-imposed responsibility for improving the quality of life and ridding society of its 'undesirable elements'. Of course the world has seen many evangelists – both benevolent and malevolent – who have sought to right individually perceived wrongs and to change society. However, the single-issue fanatic, although his fanaticism may be an impediment to productive dialogue, rarely possesses the sociopathic tendencies required to commit murder, certainly as part of a planned programme.

Almost any category of identifiable appearance, occupation, spiritual or political belief could fall victim to the 'missionary', though most target groups are selected because they are the objects of society's most deep-rooted prejudices – the bugaboos of prostitution, homosexuality and racial minority. While the individual assassin may be aware that killing is wrong, he has so devalued and dehumanised the life of his target that the end appears to justify the crime. No better example could be found than Peter **Sutcliffe**'s explanation to his younger brother that he was 'just cleaning up streets, our kid, just cleaning up streets'. Fanatical Nazi sympathiser Joseph **Franklin** had much in common with his late Führer when he began shooting dead mixed-race couples; and right-wing dreams of a pure race and clean society were at the root of **Abel** and Furlan's crusade against drug addicts, prostitutes, homosexuals and pornographers. Billy **Glaze**, himself a North American Indian, believed that all Indian women should be raped and killed; Carroll **Cole** executed 'loose women'; James and Susan **Carson** rid the world of 'witches'; and unbelievably, the **'Axeman of New Orleans'** appeared to harbour a grudge against Italian grocers.

Hedonists
A complex category incorporating the types of killer for whom, in its broadest sense, 'pleasure' is the reward of murder. Within this heading, there are three sub-types.

Lust killers
Probably the largest sub-section of serial killers, for whom sexual gratification is the primary motivation and whose crimes most frequently exhibit a considerable element of sadism. Quite at variance with the popular misconception of the lust killer (or any serial killer) as a wild-eyed – essentially opportunistic – psychotic, the procedure through which these killers go in planning and executing their crimes is one normally associated with highly organised personalities. Authorities differ in their descriptions of the phases of lust killing, but the following notes are useful:

Fantasy: during which the desire to kill is cultivated, often with the use of pornographic books and films. In this phase, the killer may act out the crime over and over in his head during a greater or lesser period of time – even years – before, like a switch being thrown, phase two is entered and fantasy begins to establish itself as reality.

The hunt: it is possible that during his search the killer has a very clear image of the 'right' victim; a specification such as Ted **Bundy**'s women with straight hair parted in the middle. He may also favour certain locations, such as streets or woods, college campuses or shopping malls. Like the 'fantasy' phase, the hunt may take any length of time and cover many hundreds of miles.

The kill: for the lust killer an intensely personal act – indeed it is his only motivation. As a consequence considerable care is often expended in luring the targeted victim into a situation of apparent safety (John Wayne **Gacy**, for example, used his position as a building contractor to attract young males seeking work). Alone with his victim, the lust killer has the freedom to make real his fantasy. As one might expect, the lust killer favours 'personal' weapons such as hands and knives, and the degree of 'overkill' is extreme – torture, mutilation, necrophilia, dismemberment, even blood-drinking and cannibalism are characteristics. This is the moment of ecstasy, and many serial killers have sought to preserve what they can of the experience by various means. Harvey **Glatman** took photographs of his victims in their death throes and Leonard Lake videotaped his. Jerry **Brudos** kept the foot of one of his victims in the deep-freeze to periodically take out and dress up in one of his collection of black stiletto-heeled women's shoes. Douglas **Clark** kept a victim's head, which he cleaned and made-up with cosmetics in order to use it in sex acts.

Post-kill phase: For most serial killers the passing of the experience of killing results in a feeling of emptiness and depression, often aggravated by a realisation that the primary 'defect' in the psyche (the restrictive childhood, rejection by female peers, etc.) has not been repaired by the act of killing, and that the killer will be obliged to take more and more lives in the search for temporary relief. It is during this phase that, if he intends to do it at all, the serial killer will write confession letters to the police and/or the newspapers, and telephone radio stations. Unless he has been caught at this stage the whole sequence, with tragic inevitability, will start over again.

Thrill killers
A category of serial killers associated in several important respects with lust killers, insofar as pleasure in the act of killing is the primary motive, and consequently results in often sadistic and ritualised torture and mutilation of a victim. What distinguishes the thrill killer is that although sexual abuse may take place, the motivation is not sexual gratification but the desire for an 'experience', a 'thrill'.

Gain killers
Called by Holmes and De Burger* 'Comfort-oriented Killers', gain

* *Serial Murder*, California, 1987.

killers exhibit the comparatively rare motive among serial killers of personal, usually financial, acquisition. For this type of murderer the act of killing is an incidental, often irksome, necessity in the pursuit of some other goal. It is within this division that we find murders occurring within the family and among the wider circle of friends and acquaintances. Clearly a sociopathic outlook which has reduced humankind to 'objecthood' is a prerequisite even for this type of killer, but an outward respectability and believability that will deflect suspicion from a theoretically obvious suspect is essential – exactly the qualities enjoyed by two of Britain's most cynical multicides, John George **Haigh**, the 'Acid Bath Killer', and George Joseph **Smith** of 'Brides in the Bath' fame; both men saw murder as a profitable business venture. Although the greater number of these crimes will be drawn from earlier decades than those associated with serial murder, the increasing availability and use of firearms in robbery and the escalating violence associated with street crime will almost certainly lead to new generations of serial killers for gain.

Power seekers
A common complication among personalities showing low self-esteem is the desire to have control over the life and death of others to such a degree that it serves as an intrinsic motive to murder. It is frequently difficult to distinguish power-oriented killers from the larger group of lust killers for whom domination is also a strong motive force. However, many power seekers are aware of their behaviour and have been able to describe their symptoms while under investigation.

Special means for special needs

An awareness of the need to make positive efforts to analyse and combat the new and baffling phenomenon of serial murder coincided with the establishment in the early 1970s of the FBI's National Academy at Quantico, where senior instructors founded what was called the Behavioural Science Unit.

In response to the virtual impossibility of applying the time-honoured techniques of a traditional homicide investigation, FBI agents began work on a system of 'psychological profiling' which would use the disciplines of the behavioural scientist, the psychologist and psychiatrist (the legendary Dr James Brussel already had an impressive record of criminal profiling) to help analyse evidence, both tangible and intuitive, collected by officers at the scene of the crime.

A profile is built by the careful analysis of elements such as victim trait, witness reports and the method of killing, and will include a detailed list of physical and psychological characteristics, leading to a 'portrait' of the wanted killer and his behavioural patterns. A useful list of elements might be: age group, sex, marital status, race, occupation, criminal record, likelihood of killing again, social class, domestic life, sexual preferences, etc. Clearly, a considerable amount of intuitive guesswork is involved, and no law enforcement agent would dismiss suspects from his investigation simply because they did not fit the profile. However, profiling has proved increasingly accurate in narrowing the field of inquiry.

Following his work on the case of John **Duffy**, the 'Railway Killer', British professor of behavioural science and applied psychology David Canter explained, 'A criminal leaves evidence of his personality through his actions in relation to a crime. Any person's behaviour exhibits characteristics unique to that person, as well as patterns and consistencies which are typical of the sub-group to which he or she belongs.'

In 1985, the enterprising FBI academy introduced an additional investigative tool under the name Violent Criminal Apprehension Program (VI-CAP). The programme is a central information system which collects and analyses reports from all over the United States with the primary objective of revealing early serial killing patterns.

Although the problems of coordination and analysis of information are on a much smaller scale in Britain, the massive and frustrating investigation into the murders of 'Yorkshire Ripper' Peter **Sutcliffe** exposed the inadequacy of a regional police force without access to a central body of information compiled from around the country, and some means of processing it quickly and efficiently. In the wake of the Ripper inquiry, police forces have been offered the use of a computer system developed by the Home Office called HOLMES (Home Office Large/Major Enquiry System) which allows fast search-and-retrieve functions for major cases.

Prevention vs cure

One of the most constructive projects to emerge from the FBI Behavioural Research Unit has been the personality profiles compiled during 1979 to 1983 from the information contained in extensive interviews with some two dozen convicted serial killers with contributions from their families, from doctors, psychiatrists, neurologists and social workers.

The results are profiles of serial killers that may ultimately help in the apparently impossible task of identifying individuals who may be predisposed to deviant behaviour. A list of behaviour patterns has been compiled, and though lack of space in this context precludes extended discussion, the following patterns have been found to recur in the personalities of serial killers examined in this book:

*Patterns of episodic aggressive behaviour**

1. Ritualistic behaviour

---

* Derived from *Serial Killers*, Joel Norris, Arrow Books, London, 1990, where the subject is treated fully. Dr Norris is a counselling psychologist and founding

2. Masks of sanity concealing mental instability
3. Compulsivity
4. Periodic search for help
5. Severe memory disorders and an inability to tell the truth
6. Suicidal tendencies
7. History of committing assault
8. Hypersexuality and abnormal sexual behaviour
9. Head injuries; injuries suffered at birth
10. History of chronic drug or alcohol abuse
11. Parents with a history of chronic drug or alcohol abuse
12. Victim of childhood physical or mental abuse
13. Result of an unwanted pregnancy
14. Product of a difficult gestation for mother
15. Unhappiness in childhood resulted in inability to find happiness
16. Extraordinary cruelty to animals
17. Attraction to arson without homicidal interest
18. Symptoms of neurological impairment
19. Evidence of genetic disorder
20. Biochemical symptoms
21. Feelings of powerlessness and inadequacy

It seems logical in the light of this emerging information – which makes early identification of a potential serial killer more feasible – that a national programme of diagnosis and treatment could be effective. Although there are clearly serious civil liberties' issues involved, the dramatic increase in the problem of serial murder, not only in the United States, may mean that we soon have no other choice.

Equally, there is no doubt that it is in childhood, within the family, that all subsequent behavioural tendencies will have their foundation (for example it is a statistical reality that abused children are more likely to grow up abusers). While examining the cases selected for inclusion in this book there was revealed an appalling level of violence, abuse and neglect in the backgrounds of some of the worst killers. As children they were so regularly exposed to violence that it ceased to be seen as abnormal.

Society will have to address the question of how much freedom, or for that matter obligation, the state, in the persons of educators, social workers and law-enforcement officers should have to interfere in the activities of families and individuals where there is a perceived risk of committing or suffering abuse. In other words, should efforts be more strenuously directed at the early identification of violent behaviour that could escalate?

---

member of the International Committee of Neuroscientists to Study Episodic Aggression.

We must also ask, because of the obvious links between excessive alcohol intake and violence, and between pornography and deviant sexual behaviour, whether similar programmes should be implemented to curb their availability as have been established to combat the menace of drugs.

Debate on the media's contribution to violence has already had some marginal effect on curbing the depiction of violence and unnatural sex on television, and there is some slight indication of a greater responsibility on the part of film-makers to eliminate 'gratuitous' violence from the cinema screen. However, until the unlikely event of direct proof being offered that violence depicted results in violence committed then no very serious attempts are likely to be made. One American source* estimates that, by the time he or she has graduated from high school, the average child has witnessed more than 13,000 real or simulated deaths and more than 100,000 violent scenes on television. The effect, and this does not apply solely to the United States, must be one of giving passive approval to violence which in many cultures is already legitimised by such valued concepts as 'assertiveness', 'standing up for oneself' and 'fighting back'.

The problem, and the question that it poses, is that in order to kill, a person must first dehumanise their victim, must reduce the victim to no more than an 'object', in order to annihilate it. Does constant exposure to real or simulated death have the effect of building up a negative attitude to the value of human life, and an acceptance that the taking of life is part of everyday experience?

In many respects the spread of serial murder is not a problem for the law-enforcement agencies alone; it is a problem for society and the fundamental values and beliefs of that society. Serial murder may be one of the few types of homicide that it is possible to prevent.

---

* *Courier-Journal*, Kentucky, 1986 (News item April 17).

Serial Killers A–Z

A

ABEL, Wolfgang, and **FURLAN, Mario**   Verona was an unlikely sort of city to play host to two of the most grisly serial killers in modern history. A role made that much less likely when one considered the background of this pair of sinister young men whose trial was set to shock Europe when it opened on the first day of December 1986.

Wolfgang Abel, twenty-seven at the time of his trial, was the son of a former managing director of a leading West German insurance company who had settled in Verona's suburb of Monte Ricco – 'Mountain of the Rich'. Twenty-six-year-old Mario Furlan lived with his parents in a new suburban development close to Verona's main hospital where his father was a well-known plastic surgeon and head of the burns unit. The boys had been close friends since school, and at university both were credited as being highly intelligent, if a little weird.

According to the indictment at their trial, Furlan and Abel launched their part-time career in murder by burning alive a gypsy drug addict in his car in August 1977. The victim survived his ordeal just long enough to say that he thought that in this instance there was a third man involved in the attack.

The second killing was in Padua, where a casino employee was knifed to death, and this was followed by the vicious beating and hacking to death of a homosexual waiter in Venice – when his body was found it bore thirty-four separate stab wounds.

A prostitute was axed to death, two priests had their skulls crushed with a hammer in Vicenza, and a sleeping hitch-hiker was burned alive in Verona city centre.

The savagery of this sequence of almost ritualised slaughter was beginning to escalate and the next victim, a homosexual priest of Trento, was 'executed' by having a nail hammered into his forehead followed by a chisel with a wooden cross attached to it.

In Milan, five people were burned to death when Furlan and Abel set fire to a cinema which was showing pornographic films; and in Munich one young woman died and forty other people were seriously injured when, it was alleged, they burned down a discotheque.

On 3 March 1984, Wolfgang Abel and Mario Furlan, dressed in Pierrot costumes, were caught in the act of dousing carpets and furniture with petrol at a discotheque near Mantua. This time the dance floor was crowded with more than four hundred young people.

At each of the murder scenes leaflets were left, written in Italian, explaining the reasons for the killing. The sheets were headed by the name 'Ludwig' over a German Nazi eagle and swastika, and bore such supplementary slogans as 'We are the last of the Nazis', and 'Death comes to those who betray the true god'. The victims, it was made clear, were all carefully chosen to represent what the killers considered 'sub-humans' deserving elimination – homosexuals, prostitutes, drug addicts and so on.

Although Furlan and Abel deny that they had any part in the crimes committed by 'Ludwig', police claim that they found evidence in Wolfgang Abel's flat that he was responsible for writing at least some of the letters. It is also significant that since the two suspects have been in custody 'Ludwig' has committed no more crimes – though a number of copycat leaflets have come to police attention.

After a lengthy trial during December 1986 and January of the following year, both Mario Furlan and Wolfgang Abel were found guilty on ten out of twenty-seven charges of murder, and in February 1987 sentenced to thirty years imprisonment. Acceptance by the court that the pair were at least partially insane saved them from a life sentence.

However, when the appeal procedure began, Furlan and Abel had already notched up three years in gaol – most of it pre-trial – and in an act of what could be seen either as enlightenment or as the benefits of privilege, both men were released to live in 'open custody', Abel in the tiny village of Mestrino, near Padua, Mario Furlan in nearby Casale Scodosia. In effect they are free to live as they choose with the provision that they report regularly to the local police station. Both give periodic interviews to anybody who cares to listen, the main subject of which is that they are completely innocent and merely the scapegoats of a police force unable to bring the real 'Ludwig' to justice.

'ACID BATH MURDERER' *see* **HAIGH, John George**

ALDRETE, Sara Maria *see* **CONSTANZO, Adolfo de Jesus**

'ANGEL MAKERS OF NAGYREV' The small village of Nagyrev is situated some sixty miles to the south-east of Budapest on the river Tisza. At the time of the 'Angel Makers', the village possessed no hospital, nor even a doctor, which left the medical care of the inhabitants pretty much in the hands of the midwife and her assistants. The midwife was Mrs Julius Fazekas.

All manner of ills, rightly or wrongly, are blamed on the Great War, but it would certainly be true to say that without the First World War the phenomenon that occurred at Nagyrev would never have happened. For a start, all the menfolk were away at the front; for another thing, the outskirts of the village were playing host to camps full of prisoners of war. Within no time husbands and fiancés were relegated to history in the face of this new influx of captive males, and it seemed the whole village was about to set up in direct competition with Sodom and Gomorrah. Women of all ages began to consider themselves very badly off if they could not attract at least two or three casual lovers from the camps. In fact the average housewife was having such a good time of it that when husbands did eventually trickle back from the blighted battlefields of Europe demanding their rightful place at the head of the family or in the marital bed, they received a very cool reception. In short, they were superfluous to requirements.

We shall never understand the madness with which their own promiscuity had inflamed these previously virtuous wives and sweethearts. What we know for a fact is that they were forming queues at the door of the midwife Fazekas, who had temporarily taken on the duties of a dispensing chemist and was distributing a steady supply of the arsenic that she boiled off mountains of flypapers. Poisoning became the village's most popular pastime, and the area became known by a new name – 'The Murder District'. What had started as the disposal of a few unwanted spouses had become the accepted means of getting *what*ever you wanted or removing *whom*ever you wanted – parents, children, neighbours, anybody who was in the way. And if these murderesses should quarrel among themselves, then was it not justice that they settle their differences with poison? In all there were about fifty women involved in 'Magyar Murder Incorporated', and they became known as the 'Angel Makers of Nagyrev'. Whenever officialdom got uncomfortably close to examining the uncommonly high death rate in the region, investigators were referred to the impeccably filed death certificates authorised by none other than the midwife's cousin!

And so the deaths continued, hundreds of them, from the first, the murder of Peter Hegedus in 1914, to the last in 1929. It was in July of this latter year that an accusation was made against a Mrs Ladislaus Szabo by a man who claimed she had poisoned his wine. Taken into custody, Mrs Szabo was clearly reluctant to face the music alone and implicated her friend Mrs Bukenoveski. Mrs Bukenoveski made no secret of having poisoned her aged mother, or of throwing her into the river Tisza; in fact she was rather proud of this last deception, because when the old lady was pulled from the water she was certified 'drowned'. Wishing perhaps to share her new found notoriety, Mrs Bukenoveski in her turn pointed the finger in Mrs Fazekas' direction, and the midwife was taken in for questioning. Wiser than her accuser, Mrs Fazekas denied everything, and short of any more concrete evidence than hearsay she was released from custody; and she did exactly as the police had predicted. Officers tailed the midwife while she went about the village warning her customers that the game was up, following behind making the arrests. As a result, thirty-eight women were arrested, twenty-six of whom were later tried at Szolnok – eight were sentenced to death, seven to life imprisonment and the rest to varying terms in gaol.

Among those sentenced to death was the midwife's accomplice, who distributed the poisons for her. Susannah Olah – apparently called 'Auntie Susi' by her regular customers – also had the general reputation of a witch and stories abounded of the menagerie of poisonous reptiles which she had taught to creep into people's beds and kill them.

Aunt Susi's sister, a septuagenarian hag named Lydia, was also given the death penalty, as was forty-five-year-old Marie Kardos who had notched up an impressive record of familicide even by Nagyrev standards, including her husband, her lover and her frail son; she had persuaded her son on his deathbed to sing for her. Mrs Kardos told the court, 'I said "Sing, my boy, sing my favourite song!" He sang with his lovely clear voice, then suddenly he cried out, gripped his stomach, gasped and was dead.'

Rosalie Sebestyen and Rosa Hoyba poisoned their 'boring' husbands, as did Mrs Julius Csaba, though she was treated rather more leniently when it was established that she had been married to a violent drunk. Maria Varga was convicted of killing her blind war-hero husband and her lover – though she denied it to her dying day. Juliane Lipke, described as 'squat and shapeless, with the most evil expression', was responsible for at least seven murders which included her stepmother, aunt, sister-in-law, brother and by way of a novel Christmas present to herself, her husband. Having disposed of most of her own family, Mrs Lipke then offered her wide experience to her neighbour Maria Koteles: 'I was sorry for the wretched woman, so I gave her a bottle of poison and told her that if nothing else helped her marriage to try that.' Mrs Lipke joined the seven others on the gallows, and their bodies were left hanging till they rotted, a reminder of the madness that had gripped the village for almost fifteen years.

As for the ringleader, she had escaped earthly justice by taking poison just as the police arrived to arrest her. If any evidence had been needed, the squalid rooms where she lived were filled with pots of soaking flypapers.

ANN ARBOR HOSPITAL MURDERS As panic spread through the Veterans Administration Hospital at Ann Arbor, Michigan, the body count continued to rise. The year was 1975, and rumour was rife that up to forty patient deaths had resulted from inexplicable respiratory arrest – worse still, it was believed that a single person was responsible.

Because the institution was under the control of the federal government, it was a party of agents from the Federal Bureau of Investigation that moved in to the hospital to lead the inquiry. By August 1975, they had confirmed that at least eight men had died from unnatural causes; it was their belief that a killer was at large in the hospital. Later it was stated that eleven out of fifty-six patients suffering breathing problems had died during the period 1 July to 15 August. FBI experts isolated the cause of death as the drug Pavulon, a muscle relaxant derived from curare which had been added to the dextrose and water solution given to afflicted patients. Curare is a drug extracted from various members of the plant family *Chondodendron* and has been used for centuries by the Indians of South America as an arrow-tip poison for hunting. When the drug enters the bloodstream it interferes with signals from nerves to muscles, and so paralyses the prey. The respiratory muscles are first affected, and cease to work within seven to ten minutes. In fact, curare is not as lethal ingested as injected and is widely used to relax the muscles prior to surgery; nonetheless it is usually kept under lock and key, only to be handled by medical staff, as was the case at Ann Arbor.

As investigations continued into the following year, in June 1976 two nurses, thirty-one-year-old Leonora Perez and Filipina Narciso, one year her junior, were charged with murder and associated offences. Natives of the Philippines, the nurses were said to have been the only people regularly on duty in the immediate area of the victims at the times they were stricken. At their trial in Detroit, the prosecution stressed this coincidence, calling as witnesses relatives of the deceased who testified to seeing the nurses in victims' rooms at the time of the seizures. The case, though, was severely weakened by a complete lack of concrete evidence that the pair had been observed administering drugs; in fact the murder charge against Leonora Perez was withdrawn on instruction from the judge. After a thirteen-week process, Filipina Narciso was acquitted of murder, though both nurses were found guilty of poisoning and conspiracy; these convictions were set aside on appeal. The two nurses were subsequently subjected to psychological testing which proved their behaviour patterns 'normal', and at a second trial, in February 1978, all charges were dismissed.

ARCHER-GILLIGAN, Amy   The Archer Home for the Elderly and Infirm opened at Windsor, Connecticut, in 1907. Amy Archer was its proprietress and her husband put up the funds, after which he passed away unexpectedly in 1910. In 1913 the widow Archer became Mrs Archer-Gilligan, and after Michael Gilligan's sudden and untimely death twelve months later, the widow Archer-Gilligan. Not that husbands proved themselves more vulnerable than anybody else, for it did not go entirely unnoticed in the small local community that the residents of the Archer Home were dropping like flies – in fact, spouses excepted, there had been forty-eight deaths in the space of five years, an alarming statistic even given the customary high rate of mortality among the 'elderly and infirm'. The latest victim had been Franklin R. Andrews, who had enjoyed apparently sturdy health until

30 May 1914, when he quite suddenly expired during the night.

Local residents were beginning to talk, and that kind of talk inevitably attracts the attention of the press who began a discreet investigation into Amy Archer-Gilligan's affairs. This provoked the police into their own inquiry, and between them the representatives of the pen and the 'sword' amassed sufficient incriminating evidence to secure exhumation orders on a selection of the victims of the Archer Home. Post-mortem examinations established that very little of the prodigious quantity of arsenic shown to have been purchased by Mrs Archer-Gilligan to rid the home of rats was ever put to that use – unless, that is, one of those 'rats' was named Michael W. Gilligan and another Franklin Andrews. Charles Smith had been similarly poisoned on 9 April 1914, Alice Gowdy in the early December, Maude Lynch on 2 February 1916, and so on.

During the months of June and July 1917, Amy Archer-Gilligan stood her trial at Hartford court-house, Connecticut, initially on a multiple indictment containing five charges of murder. Objections by the attorney representing her successfully reduced the counts to one – the killing of Franklin R. Andrews. Amy denied the charge of course, claiming that her dedication, in equal proportion, to the welfare of her residents and to following the teaching of the Christian Church automatically precluded such activities as murder. Clearly it was not a view shared by the judge and jury, the latter convicting Mrs Archer-Gilligan of murder and the former passing sentence of death upon her. But in the end Amy did not hang; following an appeal a new trial was ordered at which she pleaded guilty and was sentenced to life imprisonment. She was later certified insane and spent the rest of her days in an asylum, dying in 1928 at the age of fifty-nine.

ARTIEDA, Ramiro   It was no coincidence that all seven of Ramiro Artieda's victims were eighteen-year-old girls, or that each bore a striking resemblance to the others – as well as to Ramiro's former girlfriend.

But it had not started like that at all; these revenge killings were really a postscript. The first murder to be laid to Artieda's account was motivated by the considerably less picturesque motive of sheer greed, made that much worse because the victim was Ramiro's own brother, Luis, from whom he sought to inherit the family estate. Although Ramiro was the chief suspect right from the start, lack of any conclusive evidence precluded his arrest. However, he did not go entirely unchastised, for the girl who had promised to marry Ramiro as soon as he had the money felt disinclined to enter into matrimony with a man suspected of fratricide. In short, she jilted him.

After this setback in his plans for the future, Artieda dropped out of sight for some years, though we do know that he left his native Bolivia and spent a very instructive period in the United States working as an actor. Whether he added to that country's file of unsolved homicides we shall never know; however, when Ramiro returned home, a series of mysterious stranglings began with the death of Margarita Rios in a deserted building in the city of Cochabamba. The killer then struck down Luisita Toranza in Oruro. Rosalino Villavencio was lured to an apartment in the Bolivian capital of La Paz, which had been rented by a man claiming to be a film-company executive; it proved to be one of the many character parts acted out by Ramiro Artieda. Villa Montes on the Pilcamayo river was the scene of Teresa Ardiales' death, and Maria Perez fell victim to a self-styled visiting professor who 'visited' her college at Cucre, and strangled Senorita Perez in one of the classrooms in November 1937. Mariana Aramayo no doubt thought nothing could be safer than walking into the church at Potosi in the company of a 'monk'. Her strangled body was later found hidden behind the altar; 'Father' Ramiro had claimed another victim. Finally it was a 'travelling salesman' who prematurely ended the life of Julia Caceres, throttled in a deserted house in La Paz on 8 December 1938.

Following understandable public concern, the police were obliged to reassess *all* the unsolved strangling cases that had taken place in Bolivia in the previous decade. In this way the still open file on the murder of Luis Artieda reminded the authorities of his elusive brother Ramiro, and a nationwide search was launched. While all this was going on, the strangler attempted to murder another young woman on 9 May 1939, but this time she had outsmarted and outrun him and lived to tell the tale; the frightened young woman identified Ramiro Artieda as her attacker, and the man now living in Cochabamba under the assumed name of Alberto Gonzalez was taken into custody. Under interrogation, Artieda admitted all the murders, including that of his brother.

Ramiro added that it had been his intention to kill as many girls of the same age and appearance as his faithless girlfriend as possible, though it proved too fanciful a motive for the police, who preferred to believe that Artieda was motivated by the desire for power, and that having escaped justice when he murdered Luis, assumed that it would always be as easy. Whatever the true reason, Ramiro Artieda was executed according to Bolivian practice by a firing squad in the courtyard of Cochabamba prison on 3 July 1939.

'AXEMAN OF NEW ORLEANS' On 23 May 1918, an Italian couple named Maggio, who operated a grocery store on the corner of Upperline Street and Magnolia in New Orleans, were attacked during the night by an assailant wielding an axe. Just before dawn somebody had chiselled out a panel from the Maggios' back door to gain entry, and then struck each of the sleeping couple once with the axe before cutting their throats with a razor; Mrs Maggio's head had been severed almost from her shoulders. The razor lay on the bedroom floor, the axe had been discarded on the steps down to the back yard.

On the morning after the murder the police discovered a mysterious message chalked on the pavement a block from the scene of the murder: 'Mrs Maggio is going to sit up tonight just like Mrs Toney.'

Seven years earlier, in 1911, even before the Great War had interrupted everybody's lives, three other Italian grocers and their wives had been murdered by a mad axeman. There were the Crutis, the Rosettis, and Tony Schiambra and his wife (perhaps Mrs Toney?).

Returning to 1918, on 28 June, John Zanca the baker was making his delivery to Louis Besumer the grocer. As the store was closed, Zanca went round to the back of Besumer's shop, where he discovered that a panel had been chiselled out of the door; the baker knocked, and after what seemed an age, the grocer came stumbling to the door bleeding from the head, moaning, 'My God, my God . . .'

Inside the apartment, Zanca found the woman who had been calling herself Mrs Besumer (but was in reality Mrs Harriet Lowe) lying on her bed, terribly injured, unconscious but still alive. On 5 August Mrs Lowe died, but before she did so she murmured that it was Besumer who had hit her with the axe. Besumer was arrested and tried for murder, but in April 1919 acquitted. The very night that Harriet Lowe was mortally wounded the Axeman of New Orleans had struck again.

Edward Schneider arrived home at some time after midnight and found his heavily pregnant wife lying on their bed in a pool of her own blood, her head savagely battered. Mrs Schneider survived the ordeal to give birth to a healthy baby girl, but was never able to describe what had happened to her on that terrible night.

In the early morning of 10 August, Pauline and Mary Bruno were awakened from their sleep by the sounds of scuffling and banging coming from their uncle's room next door. When they crept nervously out to investigate, a man the sisters described as 'dark, tall, heavy-set, wearing a dark suit and a black slouch hat' rushed past them – it seemed to the two girls 'as if he had wings'. Pauline called immediately for help and Joseph Romano was rushed to hospital suffering from axe wounds to his head; he died two days later. As in previous cases, a panel had been cut from his back door, and the axe had been discarded in the yard. The significant difference in this case was that Joe Romano was not an Italian grocer – he was an Italian barber.

Suddenly New Orleans was full of Italians – grocers and other tradesmen – finding panels on their back doors interfered with, sharp implements thrown in their back yards, and reports were coming from every quarter of sightings of shadowy figures wielding axes. One local newspaper reported, 'At least four persons saw the Axeman this morning in the neighbourhood of Iberville and Rendon. He was first seen in front of an Italian grocery. Twice he fled when citizens armed themselves and gave chase. There was something, agreed all, in the prowler's hand. Was it an axe?'

Then, as suddenly as they had begun, the activities of the Axeman stopped, and it was not until March 1919 that he made his continued presence known again. The victims were Charles Cortimiglia, his wife Rosie and their baby daughter Mary – an Italian grocer's family. The pattern of the mutilated back door and discarded axe were awfully familiar, though despite their terrible wounds Mr and Mrs Cortimiglia survived. As soon as she had recovered sufficiently, Rosie told how she had awoken to see her husband struggling with a large white man wearing dark clothes and armed with an axe. When Charles fell to the floor the Axeman swung round and delivered two more blows, the first killing the baby outright, the second splitting Mrs Cortimiglia's skull.

It may have been the blow on the head that unbalanced her, but quite suddenly Rosie began to accuse her two neighbours, Frank Jordano and his father Iorlando – Italian grocers – of being responsible for the attack. Charles Cortimiglia emphatically denied that it was the Jordanos who had tried to kill him, but they were put in jail anyway. When Rosie was released from the hospital she was taken straight to the jail where she again identified Jordano and son as the killers of her baby.

Frank and Iorlando Jordano came to trial on 21 May 1919, for the murder of baby Mary Cortimiglia. Rosie restated her accusation, while Charles Cortimiglia (who had meanwhile left his wife over the disagreement) continued to deny that the Jordanos were responsible – after all, he had also seen the man clearly! On the fifth day of the trial the jury deliberated for forty-five minutes before finding Frank and Iorlando Jordano guilty; Frank was sentenced to death, Iorlando to imprisonment for life.

On 10 August 1919, it became clear to the inhabitants of New Orleans that their Axeman was still among them. Early that morning an Italian grocer, Steve Boca, had his head split open with an axe while he slept. Boca recovered but lost all memory of the attack.

On 3 September, nineteen-year-old Sarah Laumann was found unconscious on her bed with several nasty injuries to the head. A bloody axe was found beneath an open window, though this time the Axeman had not used a door panel to gain entry.

In the early hours of the morning of 27 October, Mrs Pepitone woke to hear a struggle going on in her husband's room next door. She burst in just in time to see a man flee through the door, and then found Mike Pepitone lying on the bed soaked with his own blood – he was dead, killed with the axe that lay where it had been thrown on the back porch by a murderer who had entered the house through a panel cut in the door.

Then the Axeman just melted back into the surroundings, and as the months passed his existence might have become just a horrid memory if it had not been for the drama played out at the newspaper offices of the *Times-Picayune*. On 7 December 1920, Mrs Rosie Cortimiglia burst on to the city desk in great agitation and distress, screaming, 'I lied, I lied, God forgive me, I lied.' Apparently, Mrs Cortimiglia had contracted smallpox in the intervening months, and was convinced that it was divine retribution for falsely accusing her neighbours of murder; she seems to have been avenging some real or imagined grudge and had gone too far. Needless to say, Frank and Iorlando Jordano were released with an embarrassed apology from all concerned with their incarceration.

But what of the Mad Axeman?

The New Orleans police were no nearer a solution to the enigma when they heard a curious snippet of news from their counterparts in Los Angeles. It seems that on 2 December 1920, a man named Joseph Mumfre – a resident of New Orleans – had been walking down a Los Angeles street when 'a woman in black, heavily veiled' stepped out of a doorway and emptied a gun into his body. Mumfre dropped dead on to the sidewalk, and the woman just stood there until the police took her into custody. At first she said her name was Mrs Esther Albano, and refused to account for why she had slain Mumfre. Later she changed her mind and told the police that she was Mrs Mike Pepitone, widow of the Axeman's last victim. 'He was the Axeman,' she said, 'I saw him running from my husband's room.'

As for Mumfre, he had a long criminal record, and had spent a great deal of his time doing short stretches in prison; a quick check revealed that on each of the occasions on which the Mad Axeman struck, Mumfre was free. Still, that is hardly proof that he was the Axeman.

Mrs Pepitone was put on trial in Los Angeles in April 1921, and pleaded guilty; she was sentenced to ten years, but released in just over three.

But still the question remains – what of the Mad Axeman? He never struck again; but does that mean Mumfre was the killer? There are many who think he was not (though there is some evidence that he killed Mike Pepitone); some think that there was more than one Axeman. And if that was true why on earth should so many people have a grudge against Italian grocers? It is rather unlikely at this distance in time, when all the main protagonists have died, that we shall ever know.

B

BALL, Joe To the early American settlers, the alligator was a symbol of manliness – signifying battles to the death between the fearsome reptile and the pioneering boatmen of the Mississippi. Later slang degraded the term 'alligator' to 'a promiscuous male'. It is the latter definition that best described Joe Ball – ex-bootlegger and, in the late 1930s, rumbustuous landlord of The Sociable Inn.

This prosperous Texan roadhouse boasted not only the prettiest waitresses in the state, but a pool of five live alligators out at the back into which Joe would occasionally toss lumps of meat – and now and again even live cats and dogs for his customers' entertainment.

At the age of forty, big muscular Joe still cut a fine figure and was still very definitely a ladies' man. He was also the envy of the local red-blooded Elmendorf males as a succession of dishy waitresses came and left The Sociable Inn – all of them clearly sociably inclined towards their lusty employer.

When the third Mrs Ball left the scene without, it seems, any word of warning, Joe was already heavily involved with twenty-two-year-old Hazel Brown, the latest in a sucession of good-time girls gladdening the eye of The Sociable's clientele.

Then something odd happened. Hazel disappeared too. Elmendorf might not have noticed had it not been for Texas Ranger Lee Miller. Miller wondered why no one had seen Hazel leave town, and why, if she planned to leave, her account with the local bank, so recently and optimistically opened, showed no withdrawals.

A neighbour added to the gathering unease by reporting some foul smell coming from a rain barrel in The Sociable's yard. Joe laughed it all off – the disappearances, these dumb broads! Who knows why they do anything; the rain barrel, just butchers meat for the 'gators. But behind the bluff exterior was a very worried Joe Ball.

During the night of 24 September 1938, a police contingent arrived at The Sociable Inn to ask Joe a few pressing questions. In reply mine host reached behind the till and . . . When the smoke had cleared Joe Ball lay dead on the floor, the bullet fired by his own hand lodged firmly in his skull.

Now gradually the truth of 'Alligator Joe's' fatal affairs was pieced together. The third Mrs Ball had been located, alive but terrified, in San Diego. From her the police learned that Ball had confessed to her the killing off of the waitresses and threatened her with the same if she dared speak a word about it. Not wanting to take the chance of becoming the alligators' next feed, she had fled. Mrs Ball also pointed the investigators in the direction of Clifford Wheeler, The Sociable Inn's handyman and, she alleged, Joe Ball's accomplice. Wheeler was hauled in by the Rangers and finally admitted that Joe *had* killed Hazel Brown and had forced the handyman to dismember the body and store it in the rain barrel prior to burial. He also confirmed the earlier murder of pregnant twenty-year-old Minnie Gotthardt, taking police to where her remains lay in a shallow grave. Searching the roadhouse, detectives uncovered a pack of incriminating letters written to Joe from several former waitresses at the Inn: many had also been pregnant; neither they, nor any trace of them were ever found again.

It was some months after the suicide that an ex-rancher neighbour of Joe Ball's contacted Ranger Lee Miller with a horrifying postscript to the police case. The man's voice quavered as he told how one night in 1936 – a night he had spent the intervening years trying to wipe from his memory – he had come across Joe Ball in the grisly act of dismembering a woman's body and throwing the pieces to the alligators. Ball had terrified the man into silence with threats against his family and the rancher wisely removed himself and his nearest and dearest to California.

The police estimated that at least five murders had been committed at The Sociable Inn, though the true number will never be known. As for the alligators, the creatures were removed to the San Diego Zoo where they were star attractions for many years.

BARBOSA, Daniel Camargo Barbosa had been convicted in his native Colombia of the brutal rape and murder of a nine-year-old girl; in 1986 he escaped from prison, fleeing across the border into Ecuador, where he commenced a nationwide series of sex killings of children. When he was finally arrested, Daniel Barbosa confessed to a total of seventy-one murders.

In the chief port of Guayaquil alone, fifty-five young girls disappeared in a period of fourteen months. The bodies of many remain undiscovered, but those that were found revealed an astonishing degree of brutality inflicted by bludgeoning and by slashing with a machete type of blade. At three of the known murder scenes a similar clue was found – a discarded sweet wrapper, from which police deduced that the killer was luring children with promises of sweets.

In June 1988, the body of twelve-year-old Gloria Andino was discovered on the edge of a mangrove swamp. In her hand, the now familiar candy wrapping, which on this occasion was found to bear a smudged fingerprint – a print belonging to convicted killer Daniel Camargo Barbosa. Soon after this revelation, a police officer on motorcycle patrol arrested a man behaving suspiciously in the general area of Gloria Andino's murder; the man was Daniel Barbosa, and in his pocket was a photograph of one of the missing girls.

Under questioning, Barbosa admitted the killings, and led investigators to the bodies of six of the recent victims. He confirmed earlier police theories that the children had been lured with sweets and ballpoint pens, and gave the cynical explanation for choosing children that he wanted virgins 'because they cried'; this apparently gave him greater satisfaction.

At his trial in Guayaquil in September, 1989, Daniel Barbosa related in detail rape-murders committed in five cities across the country, though incredibly he was sentenced to only sixteen years' imprisonment, the maximum punishment under Ecuador's criminal code.

'BEAST OF THE BLACK FOREST' *see* POMMERENCKE, Heinrich

BECK, Martha and FERNANDEZ, Raymond Martha Seabrook was born in 1920, and had already grown prodigiously fat by the age of thirteen when she was raped by her brother. This unpleasant experience may account for her appetite for the bizarre in sex and her longing for a life of romance. It may also have been at the root of her increasingly callous view of her fellow human beings. Martha trained as a nurse and worked as an undertaker's assistant before being appointed superintendent of a home for crippled children at Pensacola, Florida. Her marriage to Alfred Beck in 1944 quickly ended in divorce, as had two previous marriages.

Raymond Fernandez, six years Martha's senior, was born in Hawaii of Spanish parents, brought up in Connecticut, and had lived for some time in Spain where he had married and fathered four children all of whom he had long since abandoned. During the Second World War Fernandez had served – briefly but apparently with some distinction – with the British Intelligence Service, though a head injury sustained in 1945 seems to have unhinged an already none too stable personality. He began to study black magic and claimed to have an irresistable power over women. Whatever the reason, Raymond Fernandez is thought to have inveigled his way into more than one hundred women's hearts, homes and bank accounts over the next couple of years and swindled them all.

Each of the victims had been selected from notices in newspaper 'Lonely Hearts Clubs'; which is how, towards the end of 1947, Ray met Martha Beck, and together they added murder to fraud and deceit.

Their problem arose from Martha's fanatical demands on Raymond's fidelity, going to extreme and often burlesque lengths to ensure that he did not consummate any of the other lonely-hearts liaisons into which he entered. On one occasion Martha insisted on sleeping with one of the victims herself to make sure there was no nocturnal fun and games. A born philanderer, Fernandez proved a difficult consort to control and, following his frequent falls from grace, became the focus of Martha's violent temper.

In December 1948, Raymond Fernandez made the acquaintance of a sixty-six-year-old widow from New York named Janet Fay. Having plundered her savings via promises of marriage, Raymond invited Mrs Fay to the Long Island apartment which he shared with his 'sister', and strangled and bludgeoned her to death. The body was later buried.

Mrs Delphine Downing, a young widow with a two-year-old daughter was the next victim, only weeks after the disposal of Mrs Fay. Delphine Downing took Fernandez as her lover – much to Martha's annoyance – and moved into the Downing home in Michigan with her child. After robbing her of what money and possessions they could, Beck and Fernandez forced sleeping pills down Mrs Downing's throat and shot the unconscious woman through the head; to stop the child crying, Beck drowned her in the bath. Despite careful burial of the bodies in the cellar under a new covering of cement, suspicious neighbours reported Delphine and little Rainelle Downing's disappearance to the police.

Arrested for the Michigan murders, Beck and Fernandez were extradited to New York when it was realised that Michigan could not implement the death penalty. Both prisoners confessed to the Fay and Downing murders, but stubbornly denied the string of seventeen other deaths of which they were suspected. The trial became a *cause celebre* not so much on account of the murders themselves, but because of Martha Beck's regular dispatches from gaol to the press detailing her and Raymond's sexual exploits. Despite serious doubts as to Raymond Fernandez' state of mind, the 'Lonely Hearts Killers' were judged sane and guilty. Still expressing undying love for each other, Beck and Fernandez were executed in the electric chair at Sing Sing prison on 8 March 1951.

BECKER, Marie Alexandrine In many respects, Marie Becker's discontent was no different from that of many of her peers – not only in her native Liège, but the civilised world over. The years had passed over her in a drab succession, offering an excess neither of joy nor excitement, and the grey vista of mediocrity stretched as far ahead as she dared to look. After fifty-three years, twenty of them spent chained by wedlock to an honest but unromantic and unimaginative cabinet-maker, Madame Becker was desperate for a change. In a word, Marie was looking for the *frisson* of romance; which happened to be what Monsieur Lambert Bayer was also seeking. The passionate affair that followed wrought a change in Marie Becker as dangerous as it was unexpected.

The first casualty, in the autumn of 1932, was Charles Becker who, though previously of stout constitution, could not have been expected to withstand the massive dose of digitalis that his wife administered.

Becker was followed into his grave by Bayer in November 1934, and for the time being at least the widow Becker had a little money and a lot of freedom. It seemed almost as though she had recaptured some of the lost years of youth – she began to dress in gaudy clothes and extravagant make-up, and friends and neighbours were more than a little scandalised by this elderly lady's late-night revelling, and the endless string of lovers half her age, for whose 'services' Marie Becker was obliged to pay. And herein lay the problem – Madame Becker still had the freedom, but was rapidly running out of money with which to buy what passed for romance.

Then in July 1935 a friend, Marie Castadot, was seized with attacks of nausea; she was nursed by Madame Becker, but on the 23rd she died. And so in fairly rapid succession did a number of others among the merry widow's circle of friends and acquaintances. It was not until October 1936, when the police began to receive anonymous letters accusing Marie Becker of poisoning two elderly widows named Lange and Weiss, that investigations uncovered a whole series of similar cases – Julia Bossy, Jeanne Perot, Aline-Louise Damorette, Anne Stevart, Mathilde Bulte and more. All had been nursed in their final days by Madame Becker. A search of her apartment yielded a storehouse of women's clothing and jewellery.

Marie Becker's victims

Date	Name
Autumn 1932	Charles Becker
November 1934	Lambert Bayer
March 1935	Julia Bossy
May 1935	Jeanne Perot
May 1935	Aline-Louise Damorette
July 1935	Marie Castadot
September 1935	Madame Lambert
November 1935	Madame Crulle
May 1936	Anne Stevart
September 1936	Mathilde Bulte
September 1936	Madame Lange
September 1936	Madame Weiss

Marie Becker was taken into custody and when searched a small green flask was found in her handbag, its contents later identified by a chemist as digitalis. The drug was customarily administered in small doses to patients suffering from heart complaints, though in large doses it is a poison as deadly as any. It was to be Madame Becker's consistent claim that she carried the digitalis because she had heart trouble. The problem for her was that all the dead women that she had nursed, when exhumed, also contained fatal residues of the drug.

At her trial, which at times bordered on pantomime, Marie Becker indignantly denied the eleven charges of murder brought against her, though she nevertheless seems greatly to have amused the court with descriptions of her 'patients' as they approached the day of their celestial judgement. One, she thought, 'looked like an angel choked with sauerkraut'. Madame Becker was, predictably, found guilty of murder and routinely sentenced to death. However, in accordance with the established practice in Belgium, the sentence was commuted to life imprisonment*. Marie Becker died some years later in prison.

BERDELLA, Robert On 1 April 1988, officers of the Kansas City police force found a young man wandering the streets naked but for a dog collar round his neck. At the station, the man said his name was Christopher Bryson, and that he had been picked up by a man named Robert Berdella. Berdella had invited him home and after taking him unawares had bound and gagged his guest, and threatened him with sexual assault. When Bryson rejected these indelicate advances and absolutely refused to cooperate, his attacker promised that he would 'end up in the trash like the others'. Taking advantage of Berdella's temporary absence the youth managed to escape.

Robert Berdella was a throwback to the hippie cults of the 1960s, and operated a store which he called Bob's Bizarre Bazaar, specialising in the macabre mumbo-jumbo like replica skulls still so beloved of ageing hippies, pill-poppers, potheads and weekend Satanists. Except that in crazy Bob's case it was all a bit more serious!

When police following Christopher Bryson's directions raided Berdella's home they discovered packs of photographs showing explicit scenes from the bondage and torture of previous victims, and a diary recording details of his captives and the injections of animal tranquillisers used to subdue them. Buried in the yard were a number of skulls – unlike Bob's merchandise, these were the real thing.

Under interrogation, Berdella admitted that between 6 July 1984 and 5 August 1987, he had imprisoned, tortured, sexually assaulted and killed six men, and had dismembered their bodies and disposed of the remains among the garbage. Police investigators piecing together the evidence were able to list the victims as twenty-year-old Larry Pearson, Gerald Howell (nineteen), Robert Sheldon (twenty-three), Walter Ferris (twenty-five), Mark Wallace (twenty) and Todd Stoops (age unknown).

On 13 August 1988, Robert Berdella pleaded guilty to the murder of Larry Pearson, though because of a technical fault on the part of the prosecution in not informing the prisoner that they were seeking the death penalty, Berdella was sentenced only to life imprisonment. On 20 December he officially pleaded guilty to the other five killings and received a further five concurrent life sentences.

---

* Belgium has only once – in 1918 – used the death penalty for civilian crimes since 1863.

Bizarre Bob has now set up a trust fund to help the families of his victims.

BERKOWITZ, David   The terror began in 1976. At one o'clock on the morning of 29 July a young medical technician named Donna Lauria and her friend, nineteen-year-old Jody Valente, a student nurse, were sitting in their stationary car outside Donna's home in the Bronx. As they were talking a man calmly walked out of the darkness, took a gun from a brown paper bag and started shooting; he left Donna Lauria dead and her friend wounded in the thigh.

On 23 October a young couple named Carl Denaro and Rosemary Keenan were shot at and wounded as they sat in their car outside a bar in Queens and, at midnight on 27 November, Donna DeMasi and Joanne Lomino were shot and wounded while sitting on the steps outside Joanne's home in the same district.

Already ballistics had established that the three attacks had been carried out with the same .44 Bulldog – giving the murderer the provisional name 'The .44 Killer'. Then on 30 January 1977, another couple, John Diel and Christine Freund were fired on in their car in Queens – the bullets killed Christine but left her companion unharmed. Further senseless, random attacks were made on 8 March when nineteen-year-old student Virginia Voskerichian was shot dead in the street, and on 14 April when Valentina Suriani and Alexander Esau were both fatally shot as they sat in their car in the Bronx.

Then the letters started arriving. Police officers, members of the 'Operation Omega' team formed to investigate the series of killings, found a letter left by the murderer near the car in which the last victims died. It was addressed to the New York Police Department and read: 'Dear Captain Joseph Borelli, I am deeply hurt by your calling me a woman-hater, I am not. But I am a monster.' He also wrote a letter to New York *Daily News* columnist Jimmy Breslin on 1 June: '. . . Not knowing what the future holds I shall say farewell and I will see you at the next job? Or should I say you will see my handiwork at the next job? Remember Ms Lauria. In their blood and from the gutter, "Sam's Creation" .44.'

'Sam's Creation'? Now the *Daily News* had a new name for the killer, 'Son of Sam'. Breslin, through his column, replied to the letter goading the killer into making another move; it was a dangerous game, and there were still more attacks and one death to come. The first, on 26 June, was in Queens, where Salvatore Lupo and Judith Placido were wounded while they sat in a car. Then on 31 July Stacy Moskowitz and Robert Violante became 'Son of Sam's' last victims; shot in their car, twenty-year-old Stacy died in hospital, Robert Violante was blinded.

Like many before him, the mystery killer known as 'Son of Sam' had made his one big mistake. After the last shooting he walked back to his yellow Ford Galaxie which had been parked blocking a fire hydrant, took a traffic violation ticket off the window and threw it in the gutter. This familiar scene was observed from her car by Cecilia Davis, who might have thought no more of it had she not seen the young man later while she was out walking the dog; this time he was carrying something up his sleeve that Mrs Davis thought might be a gun. When the police were informed, they ran a check on the car that the ticket had been issued to and came up with the name David Berkowitz, resident of the suburb of Yonkers. When police found his car there was a loaded .44 pistol on the seat so they settled down to wait till Berkowitz came out of his apartment to claim it. Now confronted by armed officers, Berkowitz was taken from the car and asked, 'Who are you?' 'I'm Sam,' he replied. David Berkowitz went quietly to the police station where he made a full confession. It was all very much of an anti-climax, with the pudgy twenty-four-year-old postal worker – who was ironically also a former auxiliary policeman – cutting a most unlikely figure as a dangerous multicide.

David Berkowitz had been born in June 1953, a bastard whose mother introduced him early to feelings of rejection and betrayal when she put him up for adoption. Despite a protective braggadocio, Berkowitz was always uncomfortable in female company, and as his paranoia grew over the years he began to entertain the notion that women despised him and thought him ugly. In 1974, so he later claimed, Berkowitz became aware of 'the voices' as he lay there in the darkness of his squalid apartment; the voices were telling him to kill. When police searched the Yonkers flat after his arrest, they found the walls covered with scribbled messages such as 'Kill for My Master'.

The origin of the name 'Sam's Creation' seems to have been Berkowitz' neighbour Sam Carr, whose black labrador kept Berkowitz awake at night with its barking. He began sending a series of hate letters to Carr, and in April 1977 shot and wounded the dog. With his generally peculiar behaviour and fondness for sending anonymous letters to people he believed intent on doing him harm, Berkowitz had already aroused complaints to the police, though such was his otherwise engaging charm that nobody seriously considered him as a candidate for 'Sam'.

An obvious paranoid schizophrenic, Berkowitz was thought sane enough to stand trial, though that process was pre-empted by his pleading guilty. On 23 August 1977, he was sentenced to 365 years, which he serves at the Attica correctional facility.

BIANCHI, Kenneth Alessio, and **BUONO, Angelo** During the period between October 1977 and January 1979, the Los Angeles area of California was plagued by a series of killings attributed to the enigmatic 'Hillside Strangler'; as it was to turn out, the murders were committed not by a single killer, but by two murderous cousins named Bianchi and Buono.

The naked body of a Hollywood prostitute had been found on a hillside near the famous Forest Lawns Cemetery on 17 October 1977; the indications were that the murder had been committed elsewhere and the body dumped. By the end of November five more young women had fallen victim to the 'Hillside Strangler', and a pattern was beginning to emerge. What with the first two victims had started as a hunt for a prostitute killer, was quickly abandoned when of the last four two were students and two were women in regular 'respectable' employment. However, they had all been abducted and bound before being strangled, all had been deposited dead on hillsides with their legs spread in a 'sexual' attitude and all had been raped by two men. Tests on semen deposits proved that one of the rapists was a non-secretor (that is, one of a rare fourteen per cent of the population whose blood group is not contained in their other bodily secretions).

Four more women died in similar circumstances before the police had their first breakthrough. The latest victim had been registered with a modelling agency which kept a record of its clients' assignments; this led police, inconclusively, to an interview with a security guard named Ken Bianchi. The significance of this was not to become apparent until January 1979, when Diane Wilder and Karen Mandic were hired by a young man from a security firm to 'house-watch' a luxury residence in Bellingham, Washington, while, so he said, the alarm system was being repaired. When the girls were found dead in their locked car close to the house, detectives checked with the Coastal Security Company and learned that there had been nothing wrong with the alarm system installed in the house. Again security officer Bianchi's name came up; it had been he who had 'hired' the two girls to look after the house. A check of Bianchi's truck revealed the address of the Bellingham house and a key to its front door. Furthermore, a search of his house provided a number of blood- and semen-stained articles of clothing and Karen Mandic's telephone number. Meanwhile police were painstakingly searching the car in which Karen and her friend were found dead, and forensic experts were busy examining the bodies for transfer clues of hairs and fibres.

Despite the growing body of evidence pointing to his guilt, Ken Bianchi refused to implicate himself in the Washington killings. Police interrogators from the specially formed Hillside Strangler Task Force interviewed him, as did a team of psychiatrists to whom Bianchi confided that he was not one but many people – one of whom was a foul-mouthed, vicious *alter ego* named Steve, who was a sex killer. It is impossible to read or view Bianchi's performance in front of the psychiatrists (the videotaped sessions were later broadcast on television) without being convinced that he is genuinely psychotic, although accusations have been made that the whole show was a cynical charade acted out with a view to escaping the death penalty.

In the end, Bianchi's attorney entered into a plea bargain whereby his client would plead guilty to five of the Hillside Stranglings and also testify in court that his cousin Angelo Buono was the second man involved in the attacks and murders. In return, Bianchi would be given five consecutive life sentences to be served in a Californian prison (which Bianchi thought would be more comfortable than one in Washington). Buono, a sexual degenerate like his cousin, was arrested and charged with murder on the following day.

After one of the longest and most expensive trials in American criminal history, Angelo Buono was convicted of just one of the Hillside murders and sentenced to life imprisonment. In part, the shambling progress of the trial between 16 November 1981 and 14 November 1983, was the result of what Judge Ronald George described as Bianchi's attempts to 'sabotage' the case. He had now begun to protest that he was innocent after all, and such evidence that he did give was described by Assistant District Attorney Kelly as contradictory and little better than useless. As a result Kenneth Bianchi was considered to have broken the terms of his plea bargain and was punished by being sent to serve his sentence in Walla Walla Prison, Washington, where a special protection scheme is in operation to prevent other prisoners attacking him. Angelo Buono serves his sentence in Folsom Prison, California.

'BIBLE JOHN'   On the morning of Friday, 23 February 1968, the body of Patricia Docker was found in the doorway of a lock-up garage in Carmichael Place, Glasgow. Although there was no sign of a ligature, the police surgeon was sure that the victim had been strangled – possibly with a belt. Fixing the exact time of death was difficult owing to the heavy overnight frost interfering with rigor mortis, but again the surgeon offered an informed guess that the woman had been killed late on the previous night; not long, it would be discovered, after she left the Barrowland Ballroom.

Eighteen months on, and with no solution in sight to the first strangling, a second victim was found. On Sunday, 17 August 1969, the body of Jemima McDonald was found, strangled with her own tights, in a derelict building at 23 Mackeith Street. Mima McDonald had also last been seen leaving the Barrowland Ballroom, the city's largest dance hall, at around midnight. She had been seen during the evening with a man described as tall – around six feet to six feet two inches – slim, with reddish hair cut short, and aged between twenty-five and thirty-five. Although the Deputy Director of Glasgow Art School, Lennox Paterson, was called in to compose a sketch from the witnesses' descriptions, and this likeness was published in the press and shown on television, no arrest, of a 'red-headed' man or otherwise, was ever made.

The police did not have long to wait for the third attack. On 30th October 1969, twenty-nine-year-old Helen Puttock and her sister Jeannie Williams were picked up by two young men at the Barrowland Ballroom. Both men, so they said, were called John. Helen's John was, considering the location, a noticeably polite and considerate escort, well spoken, modestly dressed in a well-cut brown suit, and with his hair cut short – not a particularly fashionable length at the time. He had mentioned his surname at one point, but when it became important, Jeannie Williams realised she hadn't really taken it in – it might have been Templeton or Emerson.

As the two couples left the Barrowland, Jeannie lost some money in a cigarette machine, and in trying to get a refund out of the manager, Helen's 'John' became decidedly agitated – not aggressive, but 'very forceful'. It was after they left the building that he turned and remarked, 'My father says these places are dens of iniquity.' In the taxi home he expressed disapproval of married women going to the Ballroom (Helen was married, though he was not aware of it), and referred to them as 'adulterous'. When he was asked how he spent Hogmanay, John said he did not drink, but prayed, and later he made several references to Old Testament stories of Moses – not direct quotations, but recognised by Jeannie, who had enjoyed a Chapel upbringing. So a combination of his strange conversation and his name gave Glasgow 'Bible John'.

When the taxi had dropped Jeannie Williams off at Kelso Street (the other John had taken a bus), it put Helen and John down at Earl Street, Scotstoun; which is where Helen's body was found early the next morning by a man walking his dog.

Despite an impressively large and intense manhunt, 'Bible John' disappeared into the obscurity from which he had emerged to kill three times. In the first year of the inquiry alone, more than five thousand suspects – many of them sharing the wanted man's description – were identified, questioned and eliminated from the investigation. Police were to find to their frustration that there were a great number of people who *looked* like 'Bible John', some of them looked very much like him, a much smaller number were almost identical – but none of them *was* 'Bible John'. Four hundred and fifty hairdressers were visited with the Identikit picture reconstructed by Jeannie Williams, and every dentist in Glasgow was sent a description given by Jeannie of the suspect's slightly overlapping front teeth. Every tailor was visited with a description of 'Bible John's' brown 'Reid and Taylor' cloth suit. It was like looking for the proverbial needle in a haystack.

In 1970, the remarkable Dutch clairvoyant and psychic detective, Gerard Croiset, was called in. Although Croiset had already enjoyed considerable success in the location of missing persons all over the world, and despite a number of tantalisingly accurate predictions, in this present case the Dutchman could not lead police to 'Bible John'.

Although the crime remains unsolved, there was a small spate of killings in Scotland during 1977 and 1978 which led to suggestions that 'Bible John' was back, but the nature of the more recent killings makes it unlikely. One final possibility that has been put forward is that the 'Bible John' murders were, in fact, committed by different people – *that there never was a 'Bible John'.*

BILLIK, Herman   Martin Vzral was an expatriate Bohemian who,
like many of his countrymen, had worked hard and built up a
profitable trade in milk; as a consequence he accumulated a sizeable
nest-egg of six thousand dollars, while at the same time providing a
comfortable home for his wife and seven children in the West
Nineteenth Street district of Chicago. In short, Martin Vzral was a
contented man. That is, he was a contented man until late in 1904,
when his path was crossed by a sorcerer named Herman Billik.

Billik was also an expatriate Bohemian, who had changed his name
from the native Vajicek. Billik could not be said to be hard working,
but had recently arrived from Cleveland and set himself up in
business – 'The Great Billik, Card-reader and Seer' – offering a
sideline in love philtres and such other mumbo-jumbo as his gullible
neighbours would spend hard-earned money on.

Billik's cunning plan to relieve Martin Vzral of his savings began
with a visit to Martin's milk depot where, in the course of buying a jug
of milk, Billik fell to gibbering in tongues and finally blurted out the
warning, 'You have an enemy; he is trying to destroy you.' This was
news to Martin Vzral, who had always got on conspicuously well with
his fellow man. The seer was emphatic; he identified the 'enemy' as a
rival milkman and Martin fell for it. All was not lost, though, for the
Great Billik would work some magic on Vzral's behalf. It proved to be
a long and expensive exorcism.

Billik became a regular visitor to the Vzral home where he went
through the motions of conducting preposterous rituals to ensure the
family's continued good fortune. He also began to tap the family for
small amounts of money. On 27 March 1905, Martin Vzral passed
away after a short illness characterised by intense stomach pains. On
28 July Mary Vzral, the second daughter, perished from a similar
illness. Mary left eight hundred dollars insurance money which was
collected by her mother – as she had also collected her husband's two
thousand dollars. At the end of the year daughter Tilly died leaving
six hundred dollars insurance to be claimed. In August of the
following year, eighteen-year-old Rose Vzral died of stomach trouble
leaving three hundred dollars, and on 30 November twelve-year-old
Ella died, insured for one hundred dollars.

By now people were beginning to talk, and it is a fact that if people
talk long enough and loudly enough their suspicions usually reach the
ears of the police. Detectives arrested Herman Billik and were about
to arrest Martin's widow as an accomplice when she beat them to it
with a self-administered dose of arsenic; the police believed that Billik
persuaded her to commit suicide. He was charged with the murder of
six members of the Vzral family when exhumations and post-mortem
examinations revealed arsenical poisoning. At his trial in July 1907,
Herman Billik admitted swindling the family, but denied any hand in

their deaths. Although there was no direct proof that he had ever possessed arsenic, a jury found Billik guilty and he was sentenced to death. After several stays of execution – brought about mainly by the clamouring of the Great Billik's satisfied customers – the sentence was commuted to life imprisonment. For reasons obscured by time, Herman Billik served only eight years of his sentence before being released in January 1917.

BINGHAM CASE During 1910 and 1911 the gaunt Norman castle of Lancaster was the scene of one of the strangest dramas in its long history. At the centre of the mystery was the family of William Hodgson Bingham, resident custodian and guide to the castle for over thirty years. A widower with several children, his life at the castle was for the most part routine and uneventful; until the winter of 1910, when Death first laid its icy hand on the Bingham family. It was to claim four victims within the space of ten months.

First was William's daughter Annie, thirty years old when she died on 12 November 1910 – certified cause of death: 'hysteria and cerebral congestion'.

Victim number two was William himself, who succumbed in January 1911 at the age of seventy-three. The healthy, active old man was struck down suddenly with vomiting and diarrhoea, and after thirty-six hours of suffering he collapsed and died.

William's son, James Henry, took over as the castle's keeper, and his stepsister Margaret became housekeeper. On 23 July 1911 Margaret became victim number three, from an illness similar to that which had taken her father.

James now needed a new housekeeper, and with some misgivings invited his sister, Edith Agnes Bingham, to step into the breach. Poor Edith, at twenty-nine, was slightly mentally sub-normal and practically illiterate; in addition she and her brother quarrelled frequently about the anything but smooth running of the house. In August 1911, James engaged a housekeeper from outside the family, and Edith was relieved of her duties, though still enjoying the shelter of her brother's home. James eagerly awaited the return of some sort of order to his household; but shortly before the arrival of his new housekeeper, as he was showing a group of visitors around the Castle, James Bingham suddenly doubled up with excruciating pain and violent sickness. Analysis carried out on samples of the sick man's vomit revealed the equivalent of more than four and a half grains of arsenic per pint. Four days later, James died.

At the inquest it was reported that less than an hour before he had been taken ill, James ate some beefsteak which had been cooked by Edith and eaten only by him. When several tins of strong arsenical weed-killer were found in the house, the finger of suspicion began to turn in Edith's direction; she might, it was reasoned, have poisoned her brother in a moment of pique on being replaced as housekeeper.

The case was adjourned while the bodies of the other three deceased members of the family were exhumed, and post-mortems showed that the organs of Annie were free from arsenic, but that those of William and Margaret contained large amounts of the poison. In hindsight, both illnesses had been consistent with arsenical poisoning.

At the reconvened inquest William Edward Bingham, brother of Edith and of the late James Bingham, gave evidence against his sister, saying, 'My sister Edith Agnes Bingham has been a source of trouble for some years, getting into debt, telling lies, and leaving the house untidy.'

After a fifty-minute deliberation the coroner's jury returned the following verdict: 'We are agreed that James Bingham met his death by arsenical poisoning, that the poisoning was not accidental, and also that the poison was not self-administered. And we are agreed that the poison was administered to him by Edith Bingham.'

So Edith was brought to trial at the Lancaster Castle Assizes on 27 October 1911, on charges of murdering her father, her half-sister and her brother.

Amounts of arsenic* found in the organs of the three members of the Bingham family†

	William Bingham	*Margaret Bingham*	*James H. Bingham*
Age	73	48	37
Died	24 January 1911	23 July 1911	15 August 1911
1	36 hours	3-4 days	3½ days
2	8 months	7 weeks	—
Stomach	5.4	0.26	0.16
Intestine	1.62	0.72	—
Liver	64.8	71.28	32.4
Kidneys	0.32	0.5	0.7
Total analysed	72.7	72.7	33.3

1. Length of final illness
2. Period buried before exhumation

* All measurements in milligrams
† The analyst in all cases was W. H. Roberts, and the details derive from Philip Willcox's biography of his father *The Detective Physician*.

From the start, circumstantial evidence pointed to the weeping and hysterical girl in the dock, but still there were large areas of doubt. For example, wasn't Edith too simple-minded to know the poisonous nature of weed-killer, or to carry out the tricky administering of the poison (in the case of William at least it was almost certainly ingested over a period of time). Then there was the testimony of the maid who had witnessed the cooking of the beefsteak and had seen nothing in the least suspicious. Other witnesses testified to the obvious distress of the girl on the deaths of the other members of her family, and even if the slim motive of revenge against her brother for her deposition in the hierarchy of the household were accepted, what possible motive could she have had for the murder of the others? Edith would gain nothing from the murders, and in fact the death of her brother would leave her homeless. The girl might be simple, she might even have a reputation for dishonesty, but was she really capable of multiple and cleverly executed murder? Had the Crown, as it is required to do, proved beyond all reasonable doubt that Edith Bingham was a poisoner?

The jury thought not. They retired for a bare twenty minutes before returning verdicts of 'Not Guilty' on all charges.

Edith Bingham was led weeping from the court, and the mystery of Lancaster Castle has remained one ever since.

BIRNIE, David and Catherine   It was a spree which, but for the courage and determination of the final victim, might have gone on far longer than the four weeks that it did; even then, the month between 6 October and 10 November 1986, left four young women dead.

During the afternoon of 10 November a half-naked teenager rushed into a local supermarket in the town of Fremantle, Australia, and through her anguished tears explained that she had been raped and held captive in a house in nearby Willagee. The house, police discovered, belonged to David and Catherine Birnie, who were soon under arrest. There was no struggle; not so much as a denial, and within hours the Birnies had confessed to four rape-murders and were leading officers to the graves of their victims.

The first had been a twenty-two-year-old student named Mary Neilson, who had come to the Birnie residence to transact the purchase of some car tyres that David Birnie had advertised. In what was an unplanned attack, Birnie raped the young woman at knife-point watched by his wife. They then drove their victim to the Glen Eagle National Park where Birnie raped her again before the couple strangled and mutilated the body and buried it in a shallow grave.

Now the Birnies began actively to seek out prospective victims. The second, a fifteen-year-old hitch-hiker, was kept in the house at Moorhouse Road for several days and was raped repeatedly until Catherine Birnie, perhaps fearing that her husband was becoming too attached to the girl, strangled her. Noelene Patterson, an acquaintance of the Birnies, was forced at knife-point into their car and driven to Willagee where she was subjected to three days of sexual degradation before David Birnie drugged her with sleeping tablets and strangled her. On 4 November Denise Brown was abducted and raped over two days before being stabbed to death in a pine wood at Wanneroo.

Three days later David and Catherine Birnie abducted a fifth young woman, who this time was able to take advantage of an unguarded moment in which to escape from her captors and raise the alarm.

The Birnies represent one of the most difficult categories of serial killer to understand – the killer couple who, although almost always individually degenerate by inclination, only form a *lethal* combination together.

David Birnie, a weak-looking, weasely little man with a background of institutional care was nevertheless possessed of an almost insatiable sexual appetite, and he and Catherine had been lovers since teenage when they had had an unsuccessful burgling partnership. When they were released from juvenile detention David and Catherine each married other people. In 1985 their paths crossed again and Catherine left her husband and five children to live with the now separated David Birnie. Eighteen months later they were stricken with *folie à deux*.

The trial opened on 3 March 1987, and on account of the Birnies pleading guilty to all charges, it lasted barely half an hour. Both defendants were sentenced to life imprisonment – which effectively means a minimum of twenty years, though in David Birnie's case it was Judge Waller's opinion that he 'should not be let out of prison – ever'.

BITTAKER, Lawrence, and NORRIS, Roy Bittaker and Norris, both confirmed psychopaths, met while serving terms in the same prison and discovered that they shared a common interest in dominating, hurting and sexually abusing women. Following close upon their release the two degenerates renewed their friendship at a Los Angeles hotel and between them bought a van which they christened 'Murder Mac'; it was their intention to kidnap a young girl.

The victim was Cindy Schaeffer, sixteen years old, picked up on 24 June 1979, at Redondo Beach. She was bundled into the back of the van and driven up into the mountains where Bittaker and Norris repeatedly raped her before jointly strangling the girl with a coat hanger. Cindy Schaeffer's body was dumped in a nearby canyon.

On 8 July 'Murder Mac' transported another victim, Andrea Joy Hall, along the Pacific Coast highway to where she was subjected to repeated sexual abuse before Bittaker rammed an ice-pick through her ear and into her brain. The beginning of September saw another vicious attack, this time the double murder of fifteen-year-old Jackie Gilliam and her friend Leah Lamp, who was only thirteen years old; after two days of torture, their strangled bodies were thrown over a cliff. At Halloween the same year the pattern of abduction and sexual torture was repeated, this time Shirley Ledford's body was left on the front lawn of a house in Sunland.

But between them, Bittaker and Norris had already made the mistake that would cost them their freedom and, for Bittaker, possibly his life. Between the double murder of September and that of 31 October they had picked up a girl who was raped but unaccountably released. It was this victim that identified Bittaker and Norris as her attackers. At the same time Norris had begun boasting of his exploits to another ex-convict, though clearly one with a sense of moral responsibility, since he reported the conversation to the police.

While in custody Norris confessed to the murders, claiming that he had been led into them by Bittaker. In a further gesture to ingratiate himself with the police, Norris led them to the sites of the murders, and though nothing remained of Cindy Schaeffer or Andrea Hall, the sun-bleached skeletons of Jackie Gilliam and Leah Lamp were found – an ice-pick still protruded from Jackie Gilliam's skull.

Both Bittaker and Norris were charged identically with five counts of murder, robbery, kidnapping, forcible rape, sexual perversion and criminal conspiracy. In the end, the whining Roy Norris exchanged his testimony against Bittaker for immunity from the death sentence or imprisonment without parole. He pleaded guilty and was sentenced to forty-five years to life and will be eligible for parole in 2010.

Bittaker's trial ended on 17 February 1981, in twenty-six guilty verdicts including five for murder. At the separate penalty hearing the jury voted for the death sentence, and Lawrence Bittaker awaits execution on California's densely populated Death Row.

'BLACK PANTHER' see NEILSON, Donald

BLADEL, Rudy Known through his misdeeds as 'The Railway Sniper', Bladel was convicted of three murders and believed to be responsible for a further four around the freight yards of Michigan and Indiana.

On 3 August 1963, two men were found shot dead in the cab of their freight train in the Indiana Harbour Belt railyards. Despite FBI involvement, neither they nor the local police were able to solve the murders of engineer Roy Bottorff and fireman Paul Overstreet.

The 'Sniper' did not reappear for five years, and then, on 6 August 1968, engineer John Marshall was shot dead as he boarded his locomotive in the Elkhart yards in Indiana. Eight more years passed until James McCrory was shot through the head as he sat in his cab at Elkhart; then on New Year's Eve 1978, conductor William Gulak and flagman Robert Blake were waiting in the depot at Jackson, Michigan, for a train to Detroit when a man walked into the room and blasted them with both barrels of a shotgun. A fireman named Charles Burton who was on the platform outside the office was also shot and died later in hospital.

It was obviously more than mere coincidence that all the shootings took place in railroad yards, and that all the victims were railmen, so a check was run on ex-employees who might have left nursing a grudge. This was the first time the name Rudy Bladel appeared in the case. Bladel had been laid off from his job in 1959, when operations at his depot had been relocated to Elkhart. Bladel had subsequently been dismissed entirely from the railways following conviction and imprisonment in 1971 on charges of wounding a fellow railman.

It was the lack of direct evidence that now delayed Bladel's arrest, and he remained at large for a further three months until, quite by luck, a group of hikers crossing a park found a half-buried shotgun. Not only was the gun traceable to Rudy Bladel, but forensic tests established that it was the weapon used in the New Year's Eve slaughter. Bladel was taken into custody and charged with those three killings, to which he initially confessed.

By the time he came to trial, Rudy Bladel had retracted his confession, now claiming that it had been given under duress, adding that as far as the shotgun was concerned, he had sold it long before the killings at Jackson – to a stranger whose name he never knew! Bladel was, nevertheless, convicted and sentenced to three concurrent terms of life imprisonment.

Purely on a technicality – that his confession had been obtained without the benefit of legal advice – Bladel's conviction and sentence were overturned and a retrial ordered. A necessary precaution in the overall cause of justice, but a waste of time in the cause of Rudy Bladel. At a second trial, held in Kalamazoo, he was again convicted and again sentenced to three concurrent terms of life imprisonment – this time without possibility of parole. Despite the unlikelihood of incurring a harsher sentence, Bladel has consistently denied any involvement in the first four of the Railway Sniper's murders.

BODEN, Wayne Clifford Following a series of rape-murders in Montreal and Calgary, Boden was dubbed the 'Vampire Rapist' when all his victims were found with bite marks on their breasts.

Norma Vaillancourt was murdered in her apartment in Montreal in July 1968. Although the twenty-one-year-old school teacher had been found naked, strangled and with severe bite wounds on her breasts – all the features that were to become characteristic of the 'Vampire' murders – it is the one killing that Boden has consistently denied. One of the strange features of the Vaillancourt murder was the absence of any sign that a struggle had taken place. It was to be a feature of future murders also, leading investigators to the conclusion that the assailant was not only known by the victim but, up to a certain point at least, his attentions were not unwelcome.

Just over one year later, twenty-year-old Shirley Audette was found raped, strangled and bitten in a courtyard near the apartment block where she lived in West Montreal. On 24 November 1969, Marielle Archambault, aged twenty, was found in similar circumstances; this time the police were given something to go on. Colleagues at the jewellery store where Marielle worked as a clerk remembered her being met on the evening of her death by a smart-looking young man whom she called 'Bill'. A crumpled photograph recognised by her work-mates as 'Bill' was found in the dead woman's flat, although at the time nobody could put an identity to the face. Another clue of possible significance was the ferocious struggle Miss Archambault had obviously put up. Two months later, in January 1970, the Vampire Killer struck again, and the body of twenty-four-year-old Jean Way was discovered at home by her boyfriend; she had been strangled and bitten.

No doubt reluctant to press his luck any further in Montreal following a massive police investigation, the mystery killer struck next in Calgary, Alberta. On 18 May 1971, Elizabeth Ann Porteous, a teacher at the local high school failed to arrive for classes, and was later found dead at home, her injuries leaving police in no doubt that she was the latest of the Vampire's victims. It did not take investigators long to realise the significance of the fact that Elizabeth Porteous had been dating a young man named Bill. Colleagues at school had seen her with him on the evening of the murder, riding in a blue Mercedes; the same blue Mercedes that had been left parked near the victim's apartment.

When he turned up to remove the car, Wayne Clifford Boden – the man in the crumpled photograph; the man who called himself 'Bill' – was arrested and taken in for questioning. Confronted with a cuff-link left beneath her dead body, Boden admitted having been with Miss Porteous, but insisted that she was alive when he left her.

Wayne Boden was telling the same story when he stood his trial at Alberta Supreme Court, though it was a story whose plausibility quickly evaporated in the face of expert evidence given by a forensic odontologist. The dentist was able to demonstrate, by a remarkable twenty-nine points of similarity, that the bite marks on the last victim's neck and breasts could only have been made by Boden. He was convicted of the murder of Elizabeth Porteous and sentenced to life imprisonment. Boden later stood trial in Montreal charged with the Audette, Archambault and Way murders, pleaded guilty, and was handed down three more life sentences. No charges were ever brought in the case of Norma Vaillancourt.

BOLBER, Dr Morris, and **PETRILLO, Paul and Herman**   Dr Morris Bolber and his two cousins Paul and Herman Petrillo made a very comfortable living from the proceeds of insurance murders among Philadelphia's Italian community during the Depression years.

The enterprise started in 1932 when Dr Bolber and Paul Petrillo conspired for Petrillo to seduce the wife of one of the doctor's patients. The wife entered into the affair enthusiastically and agreed to take out an insurance policy on her husband's life for $10,000. When the unsuspecting man arrived home one night the worse for drink, his wife and Petrillo undressed him and left the man sleeping naked beside an open window; since it was the depth of winter, death from pneumonia was a reasonable consequence.

Bolber and Paul Petrillo recruited another cousin, Herman Petrillo, to their team which effectively increased capacity, having two seduc-

ers now available to lure complacent wives into insuring and afterwards helping to dispose of their unwanted husbands.

After some dozen murders, the trio again increased the number of
their personnel by taking on a new accomplice, Carino Favato, a
faith-healer known locally as the 'Witch'. It was rumoured that Favato
had already disposed of three of her own husbands and assisted
several other ladies to do the same. Bolber pointed out the obvious
error of not having insured the victims first, and eager to learn, Carino
Favato contributed valuable effort to the operation.

The business came to an end following Herman Petrillo's boast to a
former convict about how much money could be made from insurance
murders. Whatever other villainy he got up to, the ex-con obviously
did not approve of murder, and reported the conversation to the
police. The conspirators were arrested together with many of the
women who had been involved; some went to prison, several were
allowed to turn state's evidence.

Following protracted trials, Morris Bolber and Carino Favato were
sentenced to life imprisonment, and the Petrillos were condemned to
death and duly executed in the electric chair.

BONIN, William G. Between 1972 and 1980, a series of homosexual rape-murders known as the 'Freeway Killings' claimed the lives of
some forty-one young men – most had been sodomised and strangled
with their own tee-shirts; in some cases the victims' bodies had been
mutilated with a knife. From the pattern that emerged, it was obvious
that many of the murders had been committed by more than one
person.

In 1974 a fourteen-year-old boy was hitch-hiking home from a party
when he was picked up by one of the other guests; the man pulled a
gun on him and drove to a remote spot where the teenager was
stripped and raped. The boy's life was spared that night because his
attacker feared that they had been seen together at the party.
Nevertheless, the victim did complain to the police and his description led to the arrest of twenty-five-year-old William Bonin, who was
subsequently imprisoned for a period of one to fifteen years; by 1978
he was walking free again.

By 1980, as the 'Freeway' attacks resumed, the police were
reminded of the statement made by Bonin's surviving victim. It seems
that in the car on the way home after the attack, Bonin had confided
in the boy how he loved to pick up young male hitch-hikers and
strangle them. As a consequence, William Bonin was put under
surveillance, and the next time he picked up a young man, on the
night of 11 June 1980, police officers were right behind him. As they
broke into Bonin's parked car he was caught in the act of rape, and he
was put on a holding charge of committing sodomy while detectives
tried to find a link with the freeway killings. In the end, Bonin
admitted the murders, implicating twenty-two-year-old Vernon Butts

as his accomplice. Butts admitted being involved in at least eight of the attacks, claiming that Bonin had a hypnotic effect on him from which he could not escape. In August two nineteen-year-old retards were taken into custody, James Munro and Gregory Miley, who confessed to assisting Bonin in the most recent murders, committed four months before his arrest.

Vernon Butts hanged himself in his prison cell in January 1981. William Bonin stood trial in November of the same year charged on ten counts of murder and an assortment of robberies; Greg Miley had already made a deal to turn state's evidence against him.

The jury was treated to a seemingly endless catalogue of sadistic torture and murder after which, in the words of the prosecutor, the bodies 'were thrown like garbage along the streets and freeways'. Bonin was found guilty on ten counts of murder and sentenced to death. He is said to have told a newspaper reporter afterwards that if he had not been arrested when he was, 'I'd still be killing. I couldn't stop killing.'

BOOST, Werner The illegitimate son of an East German peasant woman, Boost had entered the world of crime early; a child thief who later earned a dishonest pfennig guiding parties of East Germans safely, if illegally, over the border into the West. Only in the light of subsequent revelations were a number of unsolved homicides around the border area at the same time laid to Boost's account. By 1950 Boost had transferred his crooked career to Dusseldorf, where he served a prison sentence for plundering metal fittings from graves. But if he was an indifferent thief, then Werner Boost was at least an accomplished marksman; by the end of the decade his deadly accuracy in firing 'Wild West' style, from the hip, would make headlines throughout both Germanies.

On 17 January 1953, a lawyer named Bernd Serve was sitting with a young male companion in his stationary car on a quiet road leading out of Dusseldorf. As they talked, two masked figures appeared out of the night, one bludgeoning the nineteen-year-old with the butt of his gun, the other shooting Dr Serve through the head. It was later remarked by ballistics experts that the bullet had taken an unusual trajectory, entering the body below the left jaw and leaving through the right temple, seemingly fired from *below* the victim as he sat in the driver's seat of the car.

The crime that was to earn Werner Boost the soubriquet, the 'Dusseldorf Doubles Killer', was discovered in November 1955. A twenty-six-year-old baker, Friedhelm Behre, and his girlfriend Thea had been missing for four weeks when villagers from Kalkum, just beyond Dusseldorf, found two battered bodies trapped in their car in a water-filled gravel pit. Like Dr Serve and his friend, this couple had been robbed.

With no light yet illuminating either case, the second 'doubles murder' was committed on 7 February 1956. A twenty-year-old secretary and her companion, Peter Falkenberg, had been reported missing, and police found their extensively bloodstained car the following day. On the day after that, the 9th, two bodies later identified as the missing couple were found badly burnt in the smouldering remains of a haystack. Both victims had been bludgeoned, and Falkenberg had been shot through the head from the same odd angle that had been observed in the case of Dr Serve. A further abortive attempt at a 'double murder' took place in May of the same year in some woods near Dusseldorf. Luckily for the potential victims the young woman alerted passers-by with her screams for help and the two attackers fled. By plain coincidence, or perhaps divine irony, it was in this same wood at Meererbusch that a forest ranger on patrol saw and apprehended an armed man who appeared to be tracking a young couple. The man's name was Werner Boost.

Boost had surrendered to the ranger without a struggle because, he said, he had been committing no offence. He indignantly denied any part in the recent series of attacks and murders, and defied the police to prove otherwise. And they might have had a much more difficult job doing so if Boost's unwilling partner in crime, Franz Lorbach, had not made a statement in which he confessed his own part in the murders and implicated Werner Boost. Boost, he said, had 'hypnotised' him into complicity on pain of his life. He exposed the bizarre fantasy world into which Boost had dragged him – the drugs and poisons with which Boost dreamed he would find the perfect method of murder; Lorbach told police of one plan to float cyanide-filled balloons into prospective victims' cars. There was also a string of non-fatal rapes and assaults against courting couples who, for reasons best known to himself, Boost considered immoral and degenerate. Werner Boost was eventually brought to trial in 1959, and sentenced to life imprisonment. For his contribution, Franz Lorbach was put away for six years.

'BOSTON STRANGLER' see DE SALVO, Albert

BRADY, Ian, and HINDLEY, Myra More has been written about the Moors Murders than almost any other case in modern criminal history, and their perpetrators have become synonymous with the concept of 'evil'.

Brady and Hindley are typical of the 'killer couple' in that although both had decidedly peculiar tastes and attitudes, it was the reinforcement that each gave the other that escalated their activities in pornography up to child murder. In common with many serial killers, Ian Brady was the product of a disruptive childhood. He was born in 1938, the illegitimate son of a waitress, and spent most of his infancy fostered out to various families. Brady took an early delight in torturing small animals and then small children; he spent many years of his youth on probation for various dishonesties and ended up in Borstal. Myra Hindley showed no strong signs of deviancy in childhood, although she was not particularly bright. Myra was remembered by neighbours as a happy enough child if not very sociable as a teenager. A convert to Roman Catholicism, Myra Hindley held a number of low-grade jobs before joining Millwards chemical suppliers of West Gorton as a junior, and meeting Ian Brady. She was twenty-four, Brady twenty-eight. Before long she was under the spell of Ian and his Nazi heroes, and began to dress and behave as she imagined a concentration-camp commandant might – she was Brady's ideal woman.

They shared a fascination with the worst excesses of the Nazis and a fondness for sado-sexual pornography. In the summer of 1964 the couple went to live with Hindley's grandmother in Hattersley, close to Manchester. During this period they formed a close foursome with Myra's sister Maureen and her husband David Smith. Brady had by this time, predictably perhaps, begun to add a collection of handguns to his store of pornographic books and Nazi memorabilia; he began bragging to Smith that 'I've already killed three or four.'

On 6 October 1965, Ian Brady picked up a seventeen-year-old homosexual named Edward Evans in Manchester and drove him home to Hattersley. Later that night David Smith was invited to the house – he was there to witness a murder. As he walked into the sitting-room he saw Evans sprawled on the sofa and Brady swiping at his head with an axe. Brady was to boast afterwards, 'It's the messiest yet. It normally only takes one blow.'

Brady had been wrong about David Smith. It had been all very well admiring Ian's guns, and his Führer for that matter; it had been fun planning the armed bank raids that they never carried out. But actual and bloody murder had put the fear of the Devil into Smith, and after a sleepless night he contacted the police from a local telephone box.

At 8.40 a.m. a detective disguised as a delivery man knocked on the door of number 16 Wardle Brook Avenue, and when Hindley answered the door forced his way in, admitting other officers. In a locked room they discovered the trussed body of Edward Evans. They also found two left-luggage tickets which corresponded with two suitcases deposited at Manchester Central railway station. The contents of those cases would soon horrify the world, and they would identify Brady and Hindley as two of the world's most callous multicides.

The trial opened at Chester Assizes on 19 April 1966, and lasted until 6 May. Ian Brady and Myra Hindley stood charged with the murders of Edward Evans, John Kilbride, and Lesley Ann Downey; they pleaded not guilty.

In an often harrowing fifteen days the jury was exposed to the contents of Brady's suitcases. Aside from weapons, books and disguises, there were a quantity of photographs and two tape recordings.

Some of the photographs were of ten-year-old Lesley Ann Downey, missing from her home since December 1964. For these pornographic poses Brady claimed that the girl had been paid ten shillings; it was a defence that crumbled before the awful evidence of the tape recording, made at the same time the photographs were taken, of the same young girl pleading not to be undressed, pleading to be allowed to go home. Other photographs were of twelve-year-old John Kilbride – taken of his body as it waited to be buried on Saddleworth Moor just outside Manchester. From landmarks depicted in the photographs, police searchers were able to identify John Kilbride's lonely grave. Just a few hundred yards away officers found the buried remains of Lesley Ann Downey. Myra Hindley was convicted of the murders of Edward Evans and Lesley Ann Downey; Brady of all three murders. Both were sentenced to life imprisonment.

Since the day sentence was passed, hardly a year goes by without some new revelations concerning the iniquities of the 'Moors Murderers'. Hindley has made frequent claims to have reformed, though despite a spirited campaign led by Lord Longford she has not yet been paroled. Ian Brady, his physical and mental health now in ruins, is unlikely to be released from the high-security hospital in which he serves his time, nor, it seems, does he want to be.

In 1986, Myra Hindley confessed to the murders of two other children – twelve-year-old Keith Bennett and sixteen-year-old Pauline Reade. In 1987, almost a quarter of a century after she had disappeared, the body of Pauline Reade was uncovered on Saddleworth Moor. Despite prolonged and extensive searches during which Brady himself was taken up on to the moors as a guide, the remains of Keith Bennett were never found.

'BRIDES IN THE BATH KILLER' see SMITH, George Joseph

BRIGGEN, Joseph Briggen was a farmer in a small way of business, ekeing out a living on his modest Sierra Morena Ranch close to Sacramento, in the Sunshine State. Joe's only claim to celebrity lay in his herd of Berkshire pigs with which he was most always sure to take the Blue Ribbon at the state fair.

His prize pigs, sleek and plump, never failed to fetch the highest prices at auction, but if anyone should ask the secret of his success, Joe Briggen would just wink his eye, put a weatherbeaten finger alongside his nose, and with an utterly guileless grin admit, 'It's all in the feeding.'

Joe always said he could never afford more than one hired hand at a time on the ranch, and even then he was a cheapskate, preferring to ride into San Francisco where he could recruit an endless supply of down-and-outs off the street. Not that they ever stayed long.

'They just up 'n leave,' complained Joe. 'Shiftless bums!' 'Prob'ly the hard work got too much for 'em,' Joe's neighbours would sympathise when yet another ranch hand disappeared.

In 1902, the latest hired hand was a mite put out when he discovered two severed human fingers under the bed in his room. The youth went to the police and when the authorities searched the Sierra Morena they uncovered the bones of at least twelve more bodies. In the pigpen an assortment of gnawed bones was found, including a skull. The secret of Joseph Briggen's success with pigs was explained at last – as was his lack of success in keeping ranch hands. He would keep the men on, hard at work, until they started demanding their back pay, then Briggen killed them, dismembered the bodies, and fed the remains to the Berkshires. In the end he became convinced that it was the diet of human flesh which ensured his continued production of prize winners.

And had he not been careless with a couple of dismembered digits, Joe might have taken the top awards again at the next year's fair. Instead, he had a date with a judge, a jury, and in August 1902, a life sentence.

BRINVILLIERS, Marie Marguerite   Marie Marguerite was born in the year 1630, eldest of five children of the noble French family of d'Aubray. An attractive and precocious girl, Marie was inducted into the joys of sex at a tender age – it is said in company with her brothers. She was married at twenty-one to the Marquis Antoine de Brinvilliers, though her husband made no secret of his preference for the gaming table over the boudoir, and Marie, relieved perhaps to have wealth *and* freedom, took a lover in the person of Gaudin de Sainte-Croix. Sainte-Croix was a friend of the Marquis, though if he knew of the amour at all, Brinvilliers seemed not to care. Which was far from the case with Marie's straitlaced father, one of the Lieutenants-Civil, or Councillors of State, of France; he was so furious that he had Sainte-Croix thrown into the Bastille. Understandably piqued, Gaudin made good use of his incarceration to learn the rudiments of poisoning from an acknowledged master of the science, a fellow-prisoner named Exili. On his release Sainte-Croix found Marie short of money – having decimated her husband's fortune – and between them they plotted to poison her father that she might inherit.

It became clear that Marie Marguerite was a dutiful daughter in many respects, and rather than cause her father the unnecessary pain that an ill-considered concoction might induce – not to mention one that could be detected by the physicians – she and Sainte-Croix experimented with various potions. Marie then tried them out on the patients of the Hôtel Dieu, Paris's public hospital, where she had so charitably volunteered her occasional services. At least fifty of the unlucky inmates died in the cause of 'science' before Dreux d'Aubray was finally dispatched in 1666.

The following is a contemporary translation of the post-mortem report on d'Aubray's death: 'That for the three last days which

Monsieur the Lieutenant-Civil lived, he grew lean, very dry, lost his appetite, vomited often, and had a burning in his stomach. And having been opened . . . they found his stomach all black, the liver gangreen'd and burnt, etc., which must have been occasioned by poison, or a humour which sometimes is so corrupted as to have the same effects as poison.'

Having squandered the resulting inheritance in turn, the Marchioness turned her greedy gaze on the estates of her two brothers, and Sainte-Croix was once again put to work with the box of poisons.

But lest it be thought that Madame confined her motives simply to those of financial advancement, it should be explained that Marie was equally happy to poison people who simply annoyed or disagreed with her – and given an inborn arrogance and shortness of temper it may be imagined how great was her scope for victims. In fact Gaudin de Sainte-Croix is said to have spent so much time mixing poisons that he eventually succumbed to the fumes and died. When officials investigated his sudden death they discovered in his chamber a small cabinet, about a foot square, which contained both a number of incriminating documents and the whole motley apparatus of his and Madame's 'poison factory'.

Marie Marguerite de Brinvilliers was arraigned in 1676. She was found guilty and sentenced 'to be beheaded on a scaffold which shall be erected for that purpose; her body shall be burnt and her ashes thrown in the air. But before her execution she shall be put to the torture, both ordinary and extraordinary, to make her confess her accomplices.'

The following eye-witness account of Madame de Brinvilliers' ignoble death was contained in a letter between Madame de Sévigné and her daughter:

Paris, Friday July 17th, 1676.

. . . It is all over, Brinvilliers is reduced to ashes, her poor little body after her execution was thrown into a very great fire, and her ashes into the air; so that we shall draw them in with our breath, and by the communication of the small particles we shall be seized with an inclination to poisoning, which will do a great deal of mischief.

She was tried yesterday; this morning her sentence was read to her and the torture shown to her, but she said there was no need of it for she would confess everything. And indeed, for four hours together she gave an account of her life which was shocking beyond imagination. Ten times successively did she poison her father, and yet had much ado to kill him. Love and intrigues had always a share in her crimes . . .

At six in the evening she was carried in a cart, without any clothing but her smock, with a halter about her neck, to the church of Nôtre Dame where she made the *Amende honorable*. Then she was put again in the cart, where I saw her lying on some straw that was in it, with the doctor on one side and the executioner on the other. I confess the sight made me tremble . . .

She got upon the scaffold alone and barefooted, and the executioner spent a quarter of an hour shaving and placing her head, which the people complained of as a great cruelty . . .

BROWN, Debra Denise *see* **COLEMAN, Alton**

BRUDOS, Jerry   Brudos has been used by forensic psychiatrists to typify the category of serial murderer called 'lust-killers'. At the age of five, Jerry Brudos was exhibiting the beginnings of a shoe fetishism which would develop in a most macabre direction later in his life. In infancy he would simply play with women's shoes that he had 'borrowed'. In adolescence he became sexually aroused by women wearing black, high, stiletto-heeled shoes. At the age of seventeen he was taken into custody for forcing a young woman at knife-point to take off her clothes while he photographed her; for this he received nine months' confinement in a mental hospital where he was diagnosed as having 'an early personality disorder'.

In fact, considering the underlying problems, Jerry Brudos made a rather promising start to his adult life, graduating from high school and going on to college and vocational training. He joined the army, from which he received a medical discharge, and settled into civilian life as an electronics technician. Jerry's inclination to be 'weird' was confined to the home where, despite her obvious discomfort, he insisted that his wife Ralphene walked about the house naked while he took snapshots of her; he also took to posing himself – in her underwear.

In January 1968, Linda Slawson, selling encyclopedias from door to door, got her addresses mixed up and found herself knocking on the door of the Brudos home in Portland, Oregon. Brudos took her through to the garage, bludgeoned her to death and cut off her left foot. The rest of the body was dumped in the nearby river, while the foot was kept in the freezer in the garage to be taken out on special occasions and dressed up in one of Jerry's growing collection of high-heeled shoes.

The second victim was Jan Whitney, picked up and strangled in his car in November 1968, then taken back to the garage, where Brudos had sex with the corpse before cutting off the right breast and making a plastic mould from it. Her weighted body joined that of Linda Slawson on the river bed.

Four months later, in March 1969, Jerry Brudos strangled nineteen-year-old Karen Spinker, cut off her breasts and disposed of the rest of the body in the river. As well as having sex with this victim before killing her, he committed several acts of necrophilia before getting rid of the corpse. As with many serial killers, the rate of Brudos' murders was accelerating, and it was less than four weeks later, in April, that he picked up Linda Salee from a supermarket by posing as a detective. He took his victim to the garage and strangled her, this time wiring her up in order to experiment by passing currents of electricity through her body. In all three of the later murders, Brudos had photographed the suffering and death of his victims.

Already the disappearances of young women had begun to cause alarm on the nearby Oregon State University campus, where police were told that a man was often to be seen hanging around trying to pick up a date. Next time he appeared, on 25 May 1969, the police were alerted and twenty-eight-year-old Jerry Brudos was taken into custody. Here he eventually told his gruesome tale of rape, murder and mutilation, and the briefest search of his garage confirmed that Brudos was by no means exaggerating.

When he was charged with murder, Jerry Brudos pleaded insanity; when he appeared in court no fewer than seven psychiatrists testified that he was, legally at least, sane and culpable – though none doubted that he had severe personality disorders. Jerry Brudos was convicted of murder and sentenced to life in the Oregon State Prison.

'BTK STRANGLER'   On 15 January 1974, Joseph Otero, his wife Julie and two of their children, Joseph, aged nine, and eleven-year-old Josephine were found strangled at their home in Wichita, Kansas. They had been bound and gagged, and the knots had obviously been tied by an expert. In October, a local newspaper published a long letter, alleged to be from the killer, in which he spoke of 'the monster within': 'When this monster enters my brain I will never know. But it is here to stay. How does one cure himself? I can't stop it, the monster goes on, and hurts me as well as society.'

A woman was stabbed to death in her Wichita home in April 1974, though it is not certain that this was the work of the same killer. And in March 1977, Shirley Vian was strangled after being bound and gagged in the presence of her children who were mercifully spared when their mother's attacker locked them in the bathroom. In December of the same year Nancy Jo Fox was found strangled in the bedroom of her apartment, and the murder was reported to the police by her killer. He then wrote the anonymous letter to a local television station which has given him his pseudonym. Admitting responsibility for the deaths of the Otero family, Shirley Vian and Nancy Jo Fox, the killer signed himself 'BTK' for 'Blind, Torture and Kill'.

Despite the efforts of the special task force set up to investigate the murders, the killings stopped and the identity of 'BTK' remains a mystery.

BUNDY, Carol *see* **CLARK, Douglas**

BUNDY, Theodore Robert ('Ted') Perhaps the most remarkable thing about Ted Bundy was that he seemed to the eyes of a shocked public such an unlikely killer. Most sex murderers exhibit marked emotional repression and sexual inadequacy, which could hardly describe Bundy. A well-educated, good-looking man, Ted Bundy's charm and wit made him an attractive companion, and he experienced no difficulty in his relations with women – except the need to kill them!

Bundy's academic achievements alone placed him in a separate category, having been awarded, among other distinctions, a scholarship in Chinese studies at Stanford University. In 1972 he completed his college programme by receiving a BSc in psychology and he was employed, ironically, as an assistant director of the local Seattle crime commission. Later Bundy was successful in gaining entrance to the University of Utah to study law – it was to be noted later that when he moved to Salt Lake the mysterious spate of killings of young women in Washington State stopped and a new wave of disappearances began in Salt Lake.

Eventually Bundy was arrested and imprisoned for kidnapping an eighteen-year-old named Carol DaRonch. At the same time officers investigating the murder of Caryn Campbell began to take an interest in him, proving eventually that Bundy had been at the location of Caryn's death on the day she was killed. An extradition order was issued, and Bundy removed to Colorado to face a charge of murder. In June 1977, while awaiting trial, he escaped, but was recaptured almost immediately. Six months later he escaped again, this time climbing through the ceiling of his cell, and carried out a further series of robberies, rapes and murders in the Florida area. It was February 1978 before Bundy was finally recaptured, and then by pure luck by officers investigating a minor traffic violation. Under interrogation, Bundy admitted that the number of his killings had reached more than one hundred, though he later withdrew this confession. At his subsequent trial, Ted Bundy was sentenced to death, though the American system of appeals allowed Bundy to remain – prisoner 069063 – on Death Row for a further ten years. It was not until 24 January 1989, that he was executed.

Clearly, a man who over a four-year period rapes and murders no less than forty times over five states is not normal; but nothing in Bundy's background gives any clue to the frightening Jekyll and Hyde personality that developed. Utah State Prison psychologist Dr Al Carlisle, concluded, 'I feel that Mr Bundy is a man who has no problems, or is smart enough or clever enough to appear close to the edge of "normal".' Ted Bundy himself claimed, 'Sometimes I feel like a vampire.'

During his time on Death Row, Bundy proved a cooperative prisoner usually willing – indeed eager – to talk to such police officers and psychiatrists as would listen to him. Over the years he came to be regarded as something of an authority on the personality of the serial killer, and some of his insight found its way into the FBI Behavioural Research Unit's stock of profiling clues. Although Dr Carlisle had earlier sounded a note of caution that Bundy could not always be relied upon to be honest in his responses to questions, Ronald M. Holmes, Associate Professor of Justice Administration at the University of Louisville, and James De Burger, Professor of Sociology, also at Louisville, conducted a lengthy interview with Ted Bundy as part of the research for their own study *Serial Murder* (see Bibliography).

After a few moments spent in small talk and a reassurance from Bundy that he himself was completely innocent of murder, he agreed to pass on to Holmes and De Burger the knowledge that he had picked up, so he said, from being incarcerated with serial killers such as Ottis Toole and Gerald Stano; the descriptions that emerged could equally have fitted Ted Bundy.

Ted Bundy's known victims

Date Missing	Name	Age
1 February 1974	Lynda Ann Healy	21
12 March 1974	Donna Gail Manson	19
17 April 1974	Susan Rancourt	18
6 May 1974	Roberta Parks	22
1 June 1974	Brenda Ball	22
11 June 1974	Georgeann Hawkins	18
14 July 1974	Janice Ott	23
14 July 1974	Denise Naslund	19
2 August 1974	Carol Valenzuela	20
2 October 1974	Nancy Wilcox	16
18 October 1974	Melissa Smith	17
31 October 1974	Laura Aime	17
8 November 1974	Debbie Kent	17
12 January 1975	Caryn Campbell	23
15 March 1975	Julie Cunningham	26
6 April 1975	Denise Oliverson	25
15 January 1978	Lisa Levy	20
15 January 1978	Margaret Bowman	21
9 February 1978	Kimberly Leach	12

In Bundy's opinion there are very few true psychotic killers, that is to say, those driven by voices and visions. The majority are like himself – intelligent people capable of exercising reason and making rational decisions in relation to their crimes. The problem he saw for society, and for law-enforcement agencies, is that the motive for serial murder is most frequently a genuine pleasure in the act of killing that must be endlessly repeated until the perpetrator is caught. Further, the more often he kills the more proficient the serial killer becomes. One thing that Bundy saw as a complication was that overconfidence often caused a killer to become careless; this is at variance with the theory (which Bundy rejected) that the killer secretly *wishes* to be caught.

In the Holmes–De Burger interview Bundy refers to a dimension of the killer's personality that he calls the 'force'; an unstoppable urge that makes a person kill repeatedly and which exists secretly alongside the personality of the kindly family man, or the good neighbour – the outward personality that ensures freedom from suspicion. Perhaps the most revealing observation to emerge from Bundy's discourse on the mind of the serial killer was summed up by Holmes: 'Ted was able to talk about the classic characteristics of serial killers but not able to see the same in his own personality.'

BUONO, Angelo *see* **BIANCHI, Kenneth Alessio**

BURKE, William, and **HARE, William** Like those of Jack the Ripper, the dark deeds of these notorious body-snatchers are almost too familiar to need repeating.

Burke and Hare were Irish immigrant labourers who arrived in Scotland around 1818 and who had worked as navvies on the Union Canal being built between Glasgow and Edinburgh. In 1826 Burke and Hare became acquainted whilst fellow-residents at Logue's lodging-house, a squalid building in Tanners Close in Edinburgh's West Port.

Sharing these same lodgings was an army pensioner known as Old Donald, and in the November of 1827 the old man succumbed to a combination of ill-health, old-age and poverty, which was a source of great distress to William Hare, because the old man had died owing him £4. Between them, Burke and Hare opened Old Donald's coffin and substituted a sack of bark for his body, and sold the latter for seven pounds ten shillings to Dr Knox at the Anatomy School; over the next ten months he was to become a valued customer.

Knox was a brilliant anatomist and head of the successful academy at 10 Surgeon's Square; quite how much he really knew of his suppliers' methods is a matter for conjecture, but with classes of upwards of 500 students, getting hold of bodies for dissection was not always easy in those pre-Anatomy Act days*, and a committed teacher was wise not to ask too many questions.

In fact, most of the trade was done in newly dead bodies 'resurrected' from their graves; Burke and Hare broadened the scope of their craft and created their own fresh supplies. Their *modus operandi* was that a promising 'subject' was lured to Burke or Hare's lodgings either by Maggie Laird – Hare's 'wife' – or Helen M'Dougal –

---

* The Anatomy (or Warburton's) Act of 1830 repealed the existing law that required every corpse to receive a 'Christian' burial, and effectively put a stop to the private trade in dead bodies.

Burke's. Here the victim would be rendered senseless with drink, and then lifeless by means of a blanket over the face (suffocated for preference, to avoid 'spoiling the merchandise').

The shutters were pulled down on Burke and Hare's enterprise at the beginning of November 1828. On the last day of October an elderly beggar named Margaret Docherty fell victim to the demands of medicine, and was lying around awaiting delivery when the body was found under a pile of straw by fellow-lodgers, who summoned the police. Burke and Helen M'Dougal, and Hare and Maggie Laird were arrested, the latter pair escaping prosecution by turning King's evidence. At their trial on 24 and 25 December (at the time the festival of Christmas was not observed in Scotland) at the High Court of Justiciary in Edinburgh, Burke and M'Dougal were charged jointly with the murders of Mary Patterson, a prostitute, James Wilson (called 'Daft Jamie') and Margaret Docherty. After a short deliberation, the jury found the case against Helen M'Dougal 'Not Proven' and against Burke 'Proven'.

In passing sentence, Lord Justice-Clerk Boyle told Burke, 'Rest assured you have no chance of a pardon. The only doubt I have in my mind in order to satisfy the violated laws of your country and the voice of public indignation is whether your body should not be exhibited in chains to bleach in the winds, to deter others from the commission of such offences, but taking into consideration the public eye would be offended by such a dismal spectacle, I am willing to accede to a more lenient execution of your sentence, that your body should be publicly dissected.'

While in Calton Gaol awaiting execution, William Burke is said to have complained bitterly to his warder that Dr Knox still owed him five pounds. He was hanged on the gallows at Liberton's Wynd on 27 January 1829. Helen M'Dougal and Maggie Laird were both mobbed by a blood-thirsty rabble and escaped lynching only through the intervention of the police. William Hare fled to London, where he was recorded as ekeing out an existence by begging in Oxford Street. Dr Robert Knox was also hounded out of Edinburgh, and is said to have ended his days as an obscure general practitioner in Hackney, London.

It will never be known what the full tally of Burke and Hare's murderous career was, but between December 1827 and October 1828 no fewer than sixteen people ended up on a slab at No. 10 Surgeon's Square.

BURKITT, William Unlike most of us, who can expect a fairly even distribution of fair and ill luck, William Burkitt's fortunes tended to swing between the excellent and the terrible. He was unlucky for a start in being born with a wild gene that predisposed him to kill people; on the other hand fortunate, because on each of the three occasions when he was unlucky enough to get caught, he was lucky to be tried in a British court in front of a British jury. When he finally made a little bit of legal history it proved, for Burkitt anyway, to be extremely unlucky.

Burkitt was a Hull fisherman who first achieved local notoriety in 1915. He appeared before the York Assizes charged with murdering his mistress, a Mrs Tyler. Burkitt had stabbed the unfortunate woman several times in the throat, and was now on trial for his life. As it turned out, Burkitt was as lucky as his victim was not, and a sympathetic jury reduced the conviction to twelve years' worth of manslaughter.

With a few years' remission, Burkitt was back on the streets by 1924. He was now living with Mrs Ellen Spencer, who had left Mr Spencer for Burkitt, presumably to effect some kind of change in her fortunes. Although she didn't know it, her luck was running out fast; within the year Mrs Spencer had joined Mrs Tyler, and William Burkitt was back in the dock at York.

Helped by the unfailing fairness of the British legal system in not allowing a prisoner's previous record to be made known to the jury, Burkitt once again had his murder charge reduced to manslaughter; and the hangman's noose exchanged for ten years inside. He was released in August 1935, and for the next few years enjoyed the home comforts of Mrs Emma Brookes.

In the early hours of 1 March 1939, William Burkitt suceeded in frightening the wits out of his sister by arriving at her door, foaming at the mouth and claiming to have swallowed 600 aspirins. Either he had miscounted, or his guardian angel was working overtime, because Burkitt was still active enough by the afternoon to hurl himself suicidally into the cold waters of the Humber.

Such behaviour cannot long go unnoticed, and by the time Burkitt had been tucked into a hospital bed, police officers had broken into his home and discovered the bloody corpse of Mrs Brookes. In May 1939, William Burkitt stood before the bench at Leeds Assizes facing his third trial for murder. Unbelievably, the jury reduced the charge to manslaughter.

It was quite apparent that the judge knew a rogue when he saw one, and was not prepared to share the jury's lenient view. He was, of course, privy to the information from which the jury had been so carefully shielded, and in passing sentence on Burkitt, Mr Justice Cassels gave muted voice to his misgivings when he told the prisoner, 'They did not know what you know and what I knew, and what they were not allowed to know – that this was the third time you have stood in the dock on a charge of murder. Each time it has been the murder of a woman with whom you had been living. Each time the jury have taken a merciful view . . . I can see in your case not one redeeming feature. You will be kept in penal servitude for the rest of your natural life.' Fate had clearly decided that William Burkitt had already enjoyed more than his share of good luck!

BURROWS, Erskine Durrant, and **TACKLYN, Larry Winfield**

During 1972 and 1973 the north Atlantic paradise island of Bermuda, so beloved of vacationing Americans, became the unlikely setting for a series of killings whose victims ranged in social distinction from the Governor himself to two shopkeepers.

The first murder was committed on 9 September 1972, and its victim was police commissioner George Duckett. Duckett had been lured to his back kitchen door and shot from outside the house with a .22 calibre revolver. His daughter who ran to the commissioner's aid was wounded.

Local police, ill-equipped to deal with a major murder inquiry, sought the assistance of Scotland Yard who immediately flew a team of detectives out to the colony. A substantial reward was offered by the government, but neither money nor Murder Squad could raise any clues to the killer's identity.

Following the English detectives' return to the less exotic surroundings of London's Westminster, a sensational double murder took place on the islands. On 10 March 1973, the Governor of Bermuda, Sir Richard Sharples, and his ADC Captain Hugh Sayers were shot dead on the terrace of Government House. Sir Richard's Great Dane was also killed. A serious matter indeed for the British Government and once again a Scotland Yard presence in the persons of Chief Superintendent Wright and Detective Inspector Hadrell returned to head the investigation. With no more evidence than that two black men were seen running from the scene of the latest shootings, and a conviction that the two murders were linked with that of George Duckett, the men from London conceded defeat for a second time and left what investigating could still be carried out to the local police.

Then on 6 April, in the town of Hamilton, two shopkeepers, Mark Doe and Victor Rego, were found dead on the floor of their supermarket; they had been bound hand and foot and shot with a .32 revolver, although some .22 bullets at the scene indicated a link with the previous spate of murders. With what now might seem embarrassing regularity, a new and enlarged police team arrived from London, and in desperation, the Bermuda government offered a reward of three million dollars for information leading to the apprehension of the killers. Once again, two men had been seen leaving the shop after the crime, and this time witnesses were able to put a name to one of them – Larry Winfield Tacklyn. Tacklyn was tracked down and placed under arrest while the inquiry continued to locate his partner. In September, the Bank of Bermuda was robbed of 28,000 dollars by an armed man later identified as Erskine Durrant Burrows, and on 18 October he was arrested. Now that both men were safely in custody, and with a large reward still outstanding, information began to trickle through confirming Burrows and Tacklyn's involvement in the five murders.

At their trial, both Tacklyn and Burrows were charged with the murders of Sir Richard Sharples, Captain Sayers and the two shopkeepers. Burrows alone was indicted for the Duckett killing. It emerged that though the two defendants were simply professional criminals who killed if necessary in the pursuance of theft, they entertained some misguided sympathy with the Black Power movement and this had motivated their political assassinations. At the end of the trial, Burrows was found guilty on all charges, Tacklyn only of the supermarket killings. Both were sentenced to death and hanged.

'BUTCHER OF HANOVER' *see* **HAARMANN, Fritz**

'BUTCHER OF KINGSBURY RUN' This was the soubriquet of an unknown killer responsible for ten brutal murders that terrorised Cleveland, Ohio, during the 1930s.

On 23 September 1935, children playing on the strip of railway wasteland alongside the track between Cleveland and Pittsburgh known as the Kingsbury Run, found the mutilated corpses of two men. Both bodies had been castrated and decapitated. When the missing heads and sexual organs were found, one of the men was identified as Edward Andrassey, a pervert operating on the fringe of the criminal community.

In the first month of the following year, the body of a local prostitute, Florence Polillo, was discovered mutilated on Kingsbury Run, and in the summer another decapitated corpse. Before the start of 1938 further bodies were found, of both sexes, all mutilated in such a way as to suggest the work of a butcher. On 8 April 1938, the last of the estimated twelve victims was found, and the killings stopped as suddenly as they had begun – and as mysteriously.

In July 1939 a private detective working with the police discovered a tavern which had been frequented by Florence Polillo and two other victims. Another customer was Frank Dolezal, who had been an earlier police suspect for the Butcher's killings. Dolezal was taken into custody when stains on the floor of his room and on some knives were thought to be blood. Dolezal was charged with the murder of Florence Polillo, but on 24 August pre-empted his trial by hanging himself in prison.

Frank Dolezal was officially discounted, leaving speculation as to the identity of the 'Butcher of Kingsbury Run' to become almost as popular a pastime as that following in the wake of Jack the Ripper's similar sequence of atrocities a continent away in 1888. Some went so far as to suggest that the Butcher might be a woman, others a tramp riding the box-cars on the Cleveland–Pittsburgh run. And if he served no other useful purpose, the killer at least provided the forces of law and order with a convenient hook on which to hang the area's unsolved homicides!

C

'CANDY MAN' *see* **CORLL, Dean**

'CANNIBAL KILLER' *see* **FISH, Albert**

CARIGNAN, Harvey Harvey Carignan was a veteran of the US Army, in which he had served with no distinction save collecting a conviction for a violent sex murder. It had been in Alaska in 1950, and the victim was Mrs Laura Showalter; Carignan had been sentenced to hang – which could have saved a lot of people a lot of grief. However, due to procedural irregularities in taking down his confession, Carignan's sentence was quashed on appeal, and a fifteen-year term of imprisonment on a separate charge of rape was substituted; he was paroled after nine years.

May 1973 found Harvey busy managing a Seattle filling station – not much in the way of career prospects, but plenty of opportunity to interview prospective employees – young women whose days of pumping gas proved to be tragically short. Fifteen-year-old Kathy Sue Miller went to apply for a job and never returned. Her badly beaten body was found on 3 June at Everett. During the investigation, Seattle police were given one small but significant snippet of information by the Royal Canadian Mounted Police. In October 1972, they had been making inquiries into the murder of Laura Lesley Brock in British Columbia, and a man named Harvey Carignan had received a ticket for a traffic violation in the same area at the same time.

But Harvey Carignan had left Seattle for Minneapolis where on 28 June a woman was raped, battered and left to die by a man answering his description. The body of Eileen Hurley was dumped in a field, and in September 1973, a thirteen-year-old girl was beaten and sexually abused by a truck driver who picked her up. On 17 September the decomposing corpse of a girl who had been assaulted and bludgeoned to death was found in Sherburne County, and four days later eighteen-year-old Kathy Schultz was found dead in Isanti County with similar injuries. Through 1974, in Denver, in Minneapolis, the spate of vicious sexual attacks was terminated only when the sadist who entered contemporary mythology as the 'Want-Ad Killer' was brought in for questioning by officers who had recognised the living picture of a description recently given by a young woman who had been attacked and left for dead on the side of the road outside Minneapolis. When Carignan's car was searched state maps were found marked with red circles at the sites of previous murders and rapes.

As for Harvey Carignan, he was politely and patiently explaining that what the police really had there under arrest was an Instrument of God, one who was acting under His personal instructions – the murder, rape and mutilation were all part of a Grand Plan. Of the survivor whose description had thwarted him, Harvey could only regret: 'I am sorry I didn't kill her – because I was supposed to.' He later described God as a figure who 'has a large hood on and you can't see His face'.

In February 1975, Harvey Carignan was put on trial for attempted murder and attempted sodomy. He pleaded not guilty by reason of insanity, and by way of mitigation explained to the court that God had demanded he attack the girls 'because they were whores'. On 3 March he was convicted on both counts, and in a second trial in April was found guilty of sodomy committed on a thirteen-year-old girl and sentenced to thirty years' imprisonment on each conviction. Next Carignan faced the murder charges, and as the result of a plea-bargain pleaded guilty to killing Kathy Schultz – for which he was sentenced to forty years. He pleaded not guilty to murdering Eileen Hurley, but was found guilty and sentenced to life. Although Harvey Carignan had now received in excess of one hundred years imprisonment, they were to run concurrently, and under Minnesota state law he can serve a maximum of only forty years and is eligible for parole in 1993.

CARPENTER, David J.   Before being identified as California's 'Trailside Killer', David Carpenter had already made the headlines on two previous occasions. First as a participant in the violent Cleveland jailbreak in 1970; and then as a suspect in the notorious **'Zodiac'** killings. In this last case he was cleared twice after both handwriting and fingerprint checks had proved negative in 1970 and 1979 respectively.

The first victim to be linked with the series of murders that came to be known as the 'Trailside Killings' was forty-four-year-old Edda Kane, whose naked and violated body had been found in Mount Tamalpais State Park in August 1979. Evidence seemed to suggest that she had been shot through the head while crouching on her knees. In March 1980, Shauna May was also found dead in the park; she had been stabbed in the chest, again in an unusual kneeling position. Anne Evelyn Alderson was killed in Mount Tamalpais Park on 16 October and on 29 November Diane O'Connell was found; both had been shot in a position which had by now become the signature of Marin County's 'Trailside Killer'. To complicate the already massive investigation, at around this time the decomposed bodies of nineteen-year-old Richard Stowers and eighteen-year-old Cynthia Moreland were discovered.

On 29 March 1981, Ellen Hansen was shot dead and her companion

Gene Blake wounded. Blake was able to describe their assailant with sufficient detail to identify David Carpenter, who already had an impressive record of armed robbery and sexual assault. He was arrested for the murder of Ellen Hansen and also for that of twenty-two-year-old Heather Scaggs, whose badly decomposed body had been found in a San Francisco park. Heather Scaggs, Ellen Hansen and Gene Blake had all been shot with the same gun – David Carpenter's gun.

Carpenter was convicted of the first-degree murder of Ellen Hansen and Heather Scaggs, and sentenced to death. His second trial, for the murders of Anne Alderson, Diane O'Connell, Shauna May, Cynthia Moreland and Richard Stowers, opened in San Diego on 5 January 1988. On 10 May, Carpenter was convicted on all counts, and following a penalty hearing the jury recommended the death sentence.

On 21 February 1989, the trial judge ruled that although he believed Carpenter to be guilty of the crimes of which he was convicted, it had been clearly established that a member of the jury empanelled for the penalty hearing had unlawfully referred to Carpenter's previous convictions for the murder of Ellen Hansen and Heather Scaggs. This left the judge with no alternative but to order a new trial on the later convictions.

CARSON, James and Susan (aka Michael and Suzan Bear)   Like many of their generation, James and Susan Carson were drop-outs from respectable middle-class family backgrounds, who found the overt individual freedom that characterised the decades of the 1960s and 1970s irresistibly beguiling. The couple were first drawn together by a mutual obsession with mysticism and eastern religions, eventually being led by Susan's hallucinatory visions to change their names and declare themselves adherents to the Muslim faith.

So in 1981 they were Michael and Suzan Bear living in the hippie centre of the world, San Francisco, and melting comfortably into the sub-culture of drug dependency and drug dealing. One of their close acquaintances of the time – and a regular customer – was the one-time Hollywood actress Keryn Barnes. When Keryn went missing from the streets and bars, concerned friends asked her landlord if he knew where she had gone. He didn't; until he let himself into her apartment with his pass key and found Keryn's body slumped in the kitchen, her skull smashed and savage knife wounds in her face and neck. There was no evidence of a sexual motive and robbery was ruled out when Keryn Barnes' purse was found near the body with the money intact. When police found the name 'Suzan' scrawled around the flat they put out an alert for the Bears. But by this time the Bears had drifted on.

They had drifted to a pot farm in Humboldt County where Michael encountered Clark Stephens, a friend of a man who had earlier beaten him up. It was a loose connection, but proved motive enough for Bear to shoot him dead. The couple tried to burn Stephens' corpse, and like many before them discovered just how resistant the human body is to fire. Eventually they settled for covering it with rocks and chicken manure. But Clark Stephens was missed and therefore looked for, though by the time he was found in his makeshift cairn, the Bears had moved on once again, resuming a nomadic existence that was to take them into Oregon and then back to California.

In January 1983, the couple were picked up as hitch-hikers by thirty-year-old Jon Hillyar who drove them in his truck to just outside Santa Rosa. Unluckily for him, Suzan Bear had taken it into her drug-dazed head that Hillyar was a witch and must be killed. Suzan proved no match for the job of stabbing him to death and it fell to Michael's lot to deliver the *coup de grâce* with a bullet. But such activity cannot go unnoticed on a public roadside, and Michael and Suzan Bear were overtaken by the police, arrested and charged with murder.

Following their arrest the Bears insisted on holding a press conference from the California jail where they were being detained, and announced to the world that their instructions to kill had been personally given by Allah. Michael Bear admitted murdering Keryn Barnes, a witch who had just put a spell on Suzan and was too dangerous to live. They both admitted complicity in the Stephens and Hillyar killings, but again as a benevolent gesture to rid the world of evil.

Tried in San Francisco first for the Barnes murder, Michael and Suzan Bear were convicted and sentenced to twenty-five years to life. Further trials for the other murders ended in convictions and similar sentences.

'CASANOVA KILLER' *see* **KNOWLES, Paul John**

CHAPMAN, George   He called himself George Chapman, although in his native Poland he had been named Severin Antoniovich Klosowski. After failing to obtain a degree in surgery despite a lengthy apprenticeship in his homeland, Klosowski arrived in England early in 1888 and took up the less exacting trade of assistant to a barber in London's East End. It was the year of Jack the Ripper.

When Mrs Klosowski arrived unexpectedly from Poland she found her position usurped by a bigamously married fellow-countrywoman, Lucy Baderski, though it seems the three of them lived in a kind of precarious unity for a while before Klosowski's legal wife left the house. Klosowski and Lucy left the country for America, and finally Klosowski left both Lucy and the United States to return to England. In 1892 he was living with a woman named Annie Chapman, whose name he adopted as his own.

Walking out on Annie, but keeping her name as a memento, George Chapman attached himself to Mrs Mary Spink, a woman whose husband had walked out on her, and who, with a small private income of her own, proved no end of an attraction when George decided to set up shop as a barber in Hastings. 'Mrs Chapman', as Mrs Spink now called herself, would entertain waiting customers by playing the piano while George snipped; though whether this had any direct influence on the closure of the business we can only guess. Within six months the couple were back in London managing the Prince of Wales pub off City Road.

Towards the end of 1897, Mrs Spink became a martyr to stomach trouble, enduring long bouts of nausea and vomiting until, on Christmas Day, she succumbed to what the doctor certified as consumption – a common enough complaint at the time, and one which guaranteed nothing but sympathy for poor bereft George. 'Mrs Chapman' was buried, nevertheless, in a common grave.

Bessie Taylor took over Mrs Spink's duties behind the Prince of Wales bar and in George's bed. In a trice Bessie and George – now masquerading as 'Mr and Mrs Chapman' – were off to Bishop's Stortford for a brief sojourn running the Grapes before returning to the rigours of London, as represented by the Monument pub and ill-health, for Bessie at least. She followed the previous 'Mrs Chapman' into a premature grave in February 1891. Cause of death: 'exhaustion, from vomiting and diarrhoea'.

Maud Marsh took over Bessie Taylor's duties behind the Monument's bar and in George's bed. In 1902 Mr and Mrs 'Chapman' took over the running of the Crown, a public house not far down Union Street from the Monument. When Maud took sick that year with vomiting and diarrhoea she was removed to hospital where she made an encouraging recovery; back at the Crown Maud relapsed. At this point her mother descended on the sick room to take charge, and in her turn the unfortunate woman took very poorly after drinking a glass of brandy and soda prepared for her daughter by Chapman. This caused the worthy Mrs Marsh to confide to Maud's physician that she believed her daughter was being poisoned. Thus, when on 22 October 1902, Maud Marsh kept her early appointment with the Grim Reaper, the doctor refused to issue a death certificate.

George Chapman's trial opened at the Old Bailey on 16 March 1903. He was charged, convicted and sentenced to death only for the murder of Maud Marsh, though evidence was admitted of the deaths of Bessie Taylor and Mary Spink. The jury were out for only eleven minutes, and Chapman was hanged at Wandsworth Prison on 7 April 1903.

It is worth noting as a postscript that George Chapman was at the time of the 'Whitechapel Murders' strongly suspected of being **Jack the Ripper**. Although this is in hindsight an improbable theory, no less an expert than the redoubtable Chief Inspector Abberline – in charge of the Ripper investigation – commented on Chapman's arrest for an earlier offence, 'You've got Jack the Ripper at last'.

'CHARLIE CHOPOFF' *see* **RIVERA, Miguel**

CHASE, Richard Throughout the early years of his life, the man who was to become notorious as the 'Vampire of Sacramento' had exhibited signs of mental instability, and with the passing of time had withdrawn into a slovenly life-pattern of drug abuse and hypochondria. He was twice admitted to psychiatric hospitals – on one occasion making the preposterous claim that he was suffering from a cardiac arrest induced by somebody stealing his pulmonary artery; on the second his original condition deteriorated dramatically and mysteriously until it was discovered that he had been buying rabbits, killing them and drinking the blood. Richard Chase was weird, but not yet certifiable, and he was discharged from the institution in September 1976.

Free from supervision, Chase experimented further with animals – torturing them, killing them, drinking their blood; all sorts of animals, dogs, cats, more rabbits. In December 1977, Chase escalated the scale of his operation, buying a pistol and, on the 29th, without warning or motive, shooting a stranger dead on the street. On 23 January 1978, he burgled one house, then moved on to another nearby, where he shot dead the occupier Theresa Wallin and eviscerated her body, scattering the intestines around the room and smearing his face with her blood. Theresa Wallin had been three months pregnant.

Four days later Chase was lusting for blood again. He broke into the home of twenty-seven-year-old Evelyn Miroth, and shot her through the head, then he shot her son Jason, aged six, and her boy-friend Daniel Meredith. In another room Evelyn Miroth's twenty-two-month-old nephew was shot dead in the playpen where he slept. Chase then mutilated Evelyn's body while committing sodomy, and had just got around to the sickening business of mutilating the baby when a visitor to the front door caused Chase to flee carrying the infant's corpse away with him. It was found two months later on the vacant lot where he had thrown it.

Following the discovery of this most horrendous crime, widespread police enquiries were rewarded by a tip-off from one of Richard Chase's neighbours who had become suspicious of his peculiar behaviour. When police visited the Chase apartment they found traces of human body tissue and put him under arrest. So great was the ill-feeling in his home town, that the man who had become known as the 'Vampire of Sacramento' was tried in San José, in January 1979. On 8 May of the same year he was found guilty and sentenced to death.

'CHICAGO RIPPERS' In Chicago during 1981 and 1982 women were being kidnapped, raped, mutilated and murdered by a gang who became as notorious in the Windy City as the original Jack the Ripper had been in London a hundred years before.

The first victim, Linda Sutton, was attacked in May 1981, by three men who gang-raped and stabbed her to death, compounding their sickening crime by mutilating her body and cutting off the left breast. Just over a year later in separate incidents, two girls, Lorraine Borowski and Shui Mak disappeared from their homes; it was not until September that their mutilated bodies were found. Meanwhile, in August, the body of Sandra Delaware was found strangled and with the familiar trade-mark of a severed left breast in the north tributary of the Chicago river. With the next victim, the attacks escalated in their savagery and Mrs Rose Beck Davis was found between two apartment blocks in the Gold Coast district; she had been raped, bludgeoned, axed, stabbed, strangled and her breasts had been mutilated.

In September 1982 an eighteen-year-old prostitute was attacked by a client in a red van, raped, slashed and left for dead beside the North Western railroad tracks. The girl was found, miraculously still alive, and rushed to hospital where emergency treatment saved her life – and at the same time the lives of countless potential victims of the 'Chicago Rippers'.

A few nights later a police patrol stopped a red van answering the description given by the victim and took in for questioning the driver Edward Spreitzer, aged twenty-one, and his nineteen-year-old passenger Andrew Kokoraleis. Spreitzer claimed the van belonged to his employer, Robin Gecht, and Gecht was picked up and detained when records revealed convictions for sexual assault and violence. It was Gecht who was later identified by the teenage prostitute as her attacker and he was charged with rape and attempted murder. (A bizarre sidelight to the case was the discovery that Robin Gecht had once been employed by Chicago's most notorious killer John Wayne **Gacy**.)

Under questioning during 5 to 8 November 1982, Spreitzer and Kokoraleis eventually admitted their involvement in the series of mutilation murders and in doing so implicated Thomas Kokoraleis, Andrew's eighteen-year-old brother. Andrew also confessed to the random shooting of a man earlier in the year, and they all described the sickening rituals, including cannibalism, that had been practised with the severed breasts taken from victims. All, that is, except Robin Gecht, who denied having done anything at all.

In view of the lack of direct evidence implicating him in murder, Gecht was put on trial only for attempted murder and rape – enough, though, to earn him a total of 120 years' imprisonment.

Edward Spreitzer was indicted on six murder charges, and after being found guilty in 1986 of the aggravated kidnap and murder of Linda Sutton, he was sentenced to die by lethal injection. In addition each of the other murder charges carried life sentences.

Andrew Kokoraleis was sentenced to death for the murder of

Lorraine Borowski, with thirty years' imprisonment for her aggravated kidnapping, life for the Davis murder, and concurrent terms of sixty and thirty years for rape and aggravated kidnapping.

Thomas Kokoraleis was convicted of the Borowski murder, but won a reversal from the Appeal Court on a technicality. Plea-bargaining before his second trial ensured a lesser sentence of seventy years' imprisonment.

CHRISTIE, John Reginald Halliday   Christie was a stereotypical 'repressed' sex-killer who could achieve satisfaction only through rape, murder and, probably, necrophilia. During the course of thirteen years, Christie killed eight women, including his own wife, without arousing the least suspicion that his quiet respectable manner was anything but what it seemed.

In 1949, Timothy Evans and his wife and baby took over the top flat at 10 Rillington Place where Christie rented the ground floor. On 30 November that year, Tim Evans walked into a police station in Wales and announced that he had found his wife dead at the Rillington Place flat, and had disposed of her body down a drain. Police found not only the body of Beryl Evans but also that of their baby, Geraldine. Tim Evans was arrested and at first claimed to have strangled his own family, then he accused Christie of the crime.

Quiet, respectable Mr Christie of course denied any involvement, and indeed was the chief prosecution witness against Evans, who was found guilty at his trial and hanged on 9 March 1950.

Two years after the murders of the Evans family, John Christie killed his wife. One month later, in January 1953, he killed two prostitutes, Rita Nelson and Kathleen Maloney in quick succession. In March, Hectorina MacLennan became Christie's last victim.

On 19 March, John Christie vacated 10 Rillington Place without notice, leaving the next tenant to trace the source of the unpleasant smell in the kitchen. It seemed to originate behind a section of wall that was hollow, and proved to be a papered-over cupboard door. Tearing off the paper from a cut-out section of the door and looking in with the aid of a torch, Mr Brown, the new tenant, saw the legs of a woman.

After police arrived with pathologist Dr Francis Camps, a total of three bodies were removed from the cupboard, and Mrs Christie's remains were removed from under the floorboards. A search of the back yard revealed skeletal remains of two earlier victims, Ruth Fuerst and Muriel Eady.

Shortly after his arrest on 31 March 1953, John Christie made a detailed confession from which the following extracts describe the killing of six of his victims.

Ruth Fuerst (1943)
One day when this Austrian girl was with me in the flat at

Rillington Place, she undressed and wanted me to have intercourse with her. I got a telegram while she was there, saying that my wife was on her way home. The girl wanted us to team up together and go right away somewhere. I would not do that. I got on to the bed and had intercourse with her. While I was having intercourse with her, I strangled her with a piece of rope. I remember urine and excreta coming away from her. She was completely naked. I tried to put some of her clothes back on her. She had a leopard-skin coat and I wrapped this round her. I took her from the bedroom into the front room and put her under the floorboards. I had to do that because of my wife coming back. I put the remainder of her clothing under the floorboards too . . . during the [next] afternoon my wife went out. While she was out I pulled the body up from under the floorboards and took it into the outhouse. Later in the day I dug a hole in the garden and in the evening, when it was dark, about ten o'clock I should say, I put the body down in the hole and covered it up quickly with earth.

Muriel Eady (1944)
On one occasion she came alone [to the house]. I believe she complained of catarrh, and I said I thought I could help her. She came by appointment when my wife was out. I believe my wife was on holiday. I think I mixed some stuff up, some inhalants, Friar's Balsam was one. She was in the kitchen, and at the time she was inhaling with a square scarf over her head. I remember now, it was in the bedroom. The inhalant was in a square glass jar with a metal screw-top lid. I had made two holes in the lid and through one of the holes I put a rubber tube from the gas into the liquid. Through the other hole I put another rubber tube, about two feet long. This tube didn't touch the liquid. The idea was to stop what was coming from smelling of gas. She inhaled the stuff from the tube. I did it to make her dopey. She became sort of unconscious and I have a vague recollection of getting a stocking and tying it round her neck . . . That night I buried her in the garden on the right-hand side nearest the yard. She was still wearing her clothing.

Ethel Christie (14 December 1952)
On December 14th I was awakened by my wife moving about in bed. I sat up and saw that she appeared to be convulsive, her face was blue and she was choking. I did what I could to try and restore breathing but it was hopeless. It appeared too late to call for assistance. That's when I couldn't bear to see her, so I got a stocking and tied it round her neck to put her to sleep. Then I got out of bed and saw a small bottle and a cup half full of water on a small table near the bed. I noticed that the bottle contained two Phenalbarbitone tablets and it originally contained twenty-five. I then knew that she must have taken the remainder. I got them from

the hospital because I couldn't sleep. I left her in bed for two or three days and didn't know what to do. Then I remembered some loose floorboards in the front room . . . I thought that was the best way to lay her to rest.

Rita Nelson (2 January 1953)
On the way back, in Ladbroke Grove, a drunken woman stood in front of me and demanded a pound for me to take her round the corner. I said, 'I am not interested and haven't got money to throw away.' She then demanded thirty shillings and said she would scream and say I had interfered with her if I didn't give it to her. I walked away as I am so well known round there and she obviously would have created a scene. She came along. She wouldn't go and she came right to the door still demanding thirty shillings. When I opened the door she forced her way in. I went into the kitchen, and she was still on about this thirty shillings. I tried to get her out and she picked up a frying pan to hit me. I closed with her and there was a struggle and she fell back on the chair. It was a deck chair. There was a piece of rope hanging from the chair. I don't remember what happened but I must have gone haywire. The next thing I remember she was lying still in the chair with the rope round her neck. I don't remember taking it off. It couldn't have been tied. I left her there and went into the front room. After that I believe I had a cup of tea and went to bed. I got up in the morning and went to the kitchen and washed and shaved. She was still in the chair. I believe I made some tea then. I pulled away a small cupboard in the corner and gained access to a small alcove . . . I must have put her in there. I don't remember doing it . . .

Kathleen Maloney (12 January 1953)
. . . Some time after this, I suppose it was February, I went into a cafe at Notting Hill Gate for a cup of tea and a sandwich. The cafe was pretty full, and there wasn't much space. Two girls sat at a table, and I sat opposite at the same table. They were talking about rooms, where they had been looking to get accommodation. Then one of them spoke to me. She asked me for a cigarette and then started a conversation. During the conversation I mentioned about leaving my flat and that it would be vacant very soon and they suggested coming down to see it together in the evening. Only one came down [Kathleen Maloney]. She looked over the flat. She said it would be suitable subject to the landlord's permission. It was then that she made suggestions that she would visit me for a few days. She said this so that I would use my influence with the landlord as a sort of payment in kind. I was rather annoyed and told her that it didn't interest me. I think she started saying I was making accusations against her when she saw there was nothing doing. She said that she would bring somebody down to me. I

thought she meant she was going to bring some of the boys down to do me. I believe it was then that she mentioned something about Irish blood. She was in a violent temper. I remember she started fighting. I am very quiet and avoid fighting. I know there was something, it's in the back of my mind. She was on the floor. I must have put her in the alcove straight away.

Hectorina MacLennan (6 March 1953)
I got hold of her arm to try and lead her out [of the house]. I pushed her out of the kitchen. She started struggling like anything and some of her clothing got torn. She then sort of fell limp as I had hold of her. She sank to the ground and I think some of her clothes must have got caught round her neck in the struggle. She was just out of the kitchen in the passage-way. I tried to lift her up, but couldn't. I then pulled her into the kitchen on to a chair. I felt her pulse, but it wasn't beating. I pulled the cupboard away again and I must have put her in there . . .

On 8 June, Christie also confessed to the murder of Mrs Beryl Evans, though not that of her baby. His defence of not guilty by reason of insanity was rejected by an Old Bailey jury, and on 15 July Christie was hanged at Pentonville Prison. It was not until 1966 that Timothy Evans was granted a long-overdue posthumous pardon.

CLARK, Douglas Daniel, and **BUNDY, Carol** Clark, a necrophile, together with his girlfriend Carol Bundy, was responsible for the series of Hollywood murders which became known as the 'Sunset Strip Slayings'.

The first victims were step-sisters, fifteen-year-old Gina Marano and sixteen-year-old Cynthia Chandler, who were found shot dead near the freeway on 12 June 1980. On 24 June two more bodies were found at separate locations – Exxie Wilson and Karen Jones, both prostitutes, both killed with the same gun as the first two victims. In one case the body had been decapitated and the head scrubbed, made-up, deep frozen, then left in a box on a neighbouring resident's driveway. The fifth murder was the shooting of seventeen-year-old Marnette Comer, whose body was found in a ravine in the San Fernando Valley. Another body, of an unidentified girl, was later found near Tuna Canyon.

It was Carol Bundy's role to entice girls into the car so that Clark could force the victim to participate in oral sex and then shoot her through the head during the act. Bundy later described how her companion had kept the severed head of Exxie Wilson at home to be used in sexual acts; it was also his practice to have intercourse with the dead bodies of his victims before disposing of them.

Unwisely, Carol Bundy's former lover, a man named John Robert Murray, confided to her that he thought Clark was the 'Sunset Strip

Slayer'. Murray's decapitated body was later found in his van near Little Nashville; he had been stabbed and slashed and Bundy claimed she had thrown the head into a ravine from whence it has never been recovered.

A former nurse, Carol Bundy confessed her involvement in the murders to a friend who informed the police. They were both arrested, and Clark was charged with six counts of first-degree murder, and Bundy with the murders of John Murray and the unidentified girl.

At Douglas Clark's trial, which ended on 28 January 1983, Carol Bundy was the star prosecution witness against him. Clark was found guilty on all six counts, and at a penalty hearing on 11 February sentenced to die in the gas chamber. Bundy originally entered a plea of insanity, but changed it to one of guilty in the opening stages of her trial. She was sentenced to twenty-seven years to life on one count, and twenty-five years to life on the second, the terms to run consecutively.

CLEMENTS, Dr Robert George   In 1910, this dapper ladies' man embarked on his first marriage, to Miss Edith Mercier; it ended tragically in 1920 when she died from sleeping sickness. Less than a year later he married Mary McCreary, who survived only until 1925, when she succumbed to an inflammation of the heart lining. Miss Kathleen Burke took Clements' name in 1928, and ten years later needed it no more, having become the sad victim of cancer. In all these cases Dr Robert George Clements, Fellow of the Royal College of Surgeons, made out the death certificates himself.

In May 1947 Clements was fifty-seven years old, while his fourth wife Amy Victoria (called 'Vee') was forty-seven – she was fated not to reach forty-eight. On the evening of 26 May, Dr Clements felt constrained to call a colleague to his Southport home to attend Mrs Clements, who on his insistence was removed to a nearby nursing home where she died the following day. It was Clements himself who insisted on a post-mortem. He had already diagnosed myeloid leukaemia, and Dr James Houston, who performed the autopsy, saw no reason to disagree. The vital organs were disposed of and the funeral arranged.

But there is one thing that is not symptomatic of myeloid leukaemia, and that is pinpointing of the pupils of the eyes. Dr Andrew Brown from the nursing home had observed this state in Mrs Clements, and had remarked to himself how indicative it was of morphine poisoning. Now he shared this suspicion with the coroner, who in turn consulted the Chief Constable.

Subsequent inquiries began gradually to implicate Clements in the decease of his wife; people recalled that Vee had for some time been subject to fainting fits and nausea. Further investigation into his practice revealed that the doctor had been prescribing large doses of morphine for patients who never received them.

Such parts of the late Mrs Clements as had not already been disposed of following the first post-mortem were now entrusted to Dr J.B. Firth, Director of the Home Office Forensic Laboratory in Preston, where with immense patience and consummate skill he examined those minute portions that could still bear traces of poisoning. For two weeks the remains resisted tests for virtually every known poison; finally, a microscopic section from the spinal cord responded to the test for morphine. In a formidable feat of scientific deduction, Firth was able to state that not only had Mrs Clements been slowly poisoned, but that the fatal dose had been injected into the spinal region with a hypodermic needle.

Though the noose was already hovering around his neck, still Clements escaped the full weight of justice. When police arrived at his house the doctor was already dead from a self-administered overdose of morphine. Beside him an audacious note: 'To whom it may concern . . . I can no longer tolerate the diabolical insults to which I have been recently exposed.'

There remains the likelihood that perhaps wives one, two and three met their deaths through causes less natural than they seemed. Particularly Kathleen Burke, whose unexpected death from 'cancer' had aroused sufficient suspicion to cause the Chief Constable to order a post-mortem. When the police arrived to claim the body they found that it had just been cremated. The cremation certificate had been signed by Dr Robert Clements.

In a pathetic postscript to the case, the gifted young Dr Houston also took his own life, with cyanide. In a final message he wrote, 'I have for some time been aware that I have been making mistakes.'

CLICK, Franklin *see* **LOBAUGH, Ralph**

CLINE, Alfred Leonard Although convicted forger Cline was linked to the deaths of at least eight elderly people, sufficient evidence was never found to implicate him in any foul play.

In Colorado, in 1929, Cline was found guilty of forging a widow's will and jailed. Between 1931 and 1945, he became associated with the deaths of eight people when it was learned they had all left him large sums of money in their wills. Conveniently for Alfred Cline most of the bodies were cremated, so disposing of any possibly incriminating evidence.

Mrs Carrie May Porter died in a hotel in Reno, Nevada, in 1931, leaving her impressive twenty-thousand-dollar estate to the man who called himself her 'nephew', none other than A.L. Cline, who had been staying with her at the time of her death. In the same year Mrs Laura Cummings, seventy-five years old, who had supposedly eloped with Alfred Cline, died in Winthrop, Massachusetts, leaving him three thousand dollars.

In 1932 Cline was travelling with the Reverend E.F.Jones, a minister from England. Inexplicably, the Rev. Jones died, and even more inexplicably left a will making Alfred Cline the beneficiary of eleven thousand dollars.

Bessie Ann Sickle Cline – Mrs Alfred Cline – died in September 1932 after a short illness, and her condition was certified as heart failure. Later in the year, in California, Cline was taken into custody on charges of theft and the administration of narcotics with intent to commit a felony. He was subsequently clapped in jail for fifteen years, while all the deaths of his previous benefactors were being investigated for any trace of suspicious circumstances; no evidence was ever found which would justify a charge of murder.

In December 1945, Cline was at liberty again and up to his old tricks. He was arrested for a forgery involving the will of his second wife, Delora Krebs Cline, who had recently died at the age of seventy-three. Investigations now commenced into the disappearances of Mrs Isabelle Van Natta, missing since September 1945, and Mrs Elizabeth Hannah Klein, missing since 1943, and the death of Alice Carpenter, who had passed away in Dallas in October 1944. Mrs Carpenter's body had been cremated on the orders of her 'agent' – A.L. Cline.

A formal charge of murder was at one point contemplated in the matter of Mrs Carpenter's death, but in the end lack of evidence made it unsafe to proceed to trial. Nevertheless, Alfred Cline did not go entirely free. He was finally indicted in San Francisco on nine counts of forgery, and on conviction was sentenced to a not-undeserved 126 years' imprisonment. Looking at his record, the Judge described Alfred Cline as 'a one-man Crime Incorporated'.

'CO-ED KILLER' *see* **KEMPER, Edmund Emil**

COLE, Carroll Edward   Carroll Cole admitted to the police that he thought he had murdered thirty-five women, being driven to kill those he called 'loose women' because they reminded him of his mother: 'I think I kill her through them.'

In San Diego, in 1971, he strangled Essie Louie Buck in his car, and although he was questioned about the incident at the time no charges were ever brought. In Las Vegas, in 1977, he strangled Kathlyn Blum in a parking lot; and back in San Diego, in the summer of 1979, he strangled Bonnie O'Neil on the street. In both these latter cases the bodies had been stripped and sexually abused after death.

On a return visit to Las Vegas in 1979, Cole strangled fifty-one-year-old Marnie Cushman in a hotel room. In Dallas, Texas, on 11 November 1980, he strangled Dorothy King in her home and on the following night Wanda Faye Roberts was strangled in a parking lot before Cole returned to Dorothy King's home and slept with her corpse. This time Cole was identified as the man seen in a bar with

Wanda Roberts just before her murder; but by now he had once again dropped from sight. Later in the month of November, Cole strangled thirty-nine-year-old Sally Thompson in her apartment; unluckily for him, while he was about his business, neighbours had called the police to investigate the noise that was going on in Sally Thompson's flat. When they arrived, police officers discovered the body and detained Cole. Unbelievable as it now seems, Cole was initially released, and it was only later under re-arrest that he confessed to his horrific series of killings; he apologised for a certain vagueness of recollection, he was, he said, drunk most of the time.

In April 1981, Carroll Cole went on trial in Dallas for the three Texas killings. He pleaded insanity, and while giving evidence repeated his claim to have killed thirty-five times over nine years – in Texas, Nevada, California, Wyoming and Oklahoma. Perhaps in order to enhance his plea of insanity, Cole claimed to have canniba-lised one of his victims, in Oklahoma in 1976, before dismembering the body and dumping the remains in a trash can. He was convicted on all counts, but at the penalty hearing a jury voted against the death penalty and Cole was sentenced to three life terms, two of which were to be served consecutively.

Following the Texas trial the state authorities of Nevada filed two murder charges against Cole, and he was extradited to face a second trial in Las Vegas. He pleaded guilty to both counts and asked that he be given a non-jury hearing because he wanted to die and thought that judges would be more likely to impose the death penalty than a jury. He was right; the judges ruled that the murder of Kathlyn Blum took place prior to the restoration of capital punishment in Nevada, but sentenced him to death for the murder of Marnie Cushman. Cole smiled and said, 'Thanks, judge'.

He refused to appeal against sentence, and Carroll Cole was executed by lethal injection in Carson City, Nevada, on 6 December 1985.

COLEMAN, Alton, and **BROWN, Debra Denise**   Coleman, who had a previous record for almost every crime it is possible to commit, went on the run from his native Waukegan, Illinois, in company with his girl-friend twenty-one-year-old Debra Brown; he was on bail on a charge of raping a fourteen-year-old girl, and fled following the issue of a warrant for his arrest for the kidnapping of Vernita Wheat, aged nine, who had disappeared on 29 May 1984, after going with a couple calling themselves Paul and Diana Fisher – aliases of Coleman and Brown. The raped and strangled body of the little girl was discovered shortly after Coleman left Waukegan.

Seventy miles south, in Gary, Indiana, on 18 June, seven-year-old Tamika Turks was raped and stabbed, and her nine-year-old cousin raped and beaten after they had been lured into a car by a couple who stopped to ask directions. Tamika Turks died, but her companion was able to give a convincing description of the same couple who had abducted Vernita Wheat. In Toledo, Ohio, Mrs Virginia Temple and her daughter Rochelle, aged ten, were found strangled at their home after a man and a woman pretending to be penniless hitch-hikers asked if they could stay the night. On 11 July in Detroit, Donna Williams, who had been reported kidnapped from Gary by a couple matching the previous descriptions of Coleman and Brown, was found strangled and hidden in a slum building. In Cincinnati, on 13 July, Mrs Marlene Waters and her husband were attacked in their home. Mrs Waters later died from her injuries, but Harry Waters managed to describe their attackers; Coleman and Brown escaped in Marlene Waters' car which they later abandoned. Fifteen-year-old Tonnie Stewart was found raped and strangled in a vacant building, and in Indianapolis, Eugene Scott, a seventy-seven-year-old, was found shot dead in a ditch just outside the city.

Punctuating this catalogue of carnage were a number of cases of assault and kidnapping, and in every instance where victims were able to describe their attackers the descriptions were always of Coleman and Brown.

Alton Coleman and Debra Brown were finally detained in Evanston, Illinois, when an acquaintance of Coleman's recognised him and tipped off the police. When he was arrested, Coleman was carrying two bloodstained knives and Brown a .38 calibre pistol.

As this murderous couple had caused mayhem across no fewer than six states, there was healthy competition as to who should try them first, and there followed a protracted series of trials:

Ohio, Cincinnati: following separate trials in May 1985, for the murder of Mrs Marlene Waters, both were convicted, and Coleman was sentenced to die in the electric chair while Debra Brown was given life imprisonment. They were then tried separately on 8 June of the same year for the murder of Tonnie Stewart and were both convicted and sentenced to death.

Ohio, Dayton: On 1 August 1985, both prisoners received sentences of twenty years' imprisonment for kidnapping.

Indiana: Separate trials were held during April 1986, for the murder of Tamika Turks and the attempted murder and rape of her cousin. On conviction, Coleman was sentenced to death plus one hundred years' imprisonment for attempted murder and rape; Brown was also sentenced to death plus two consecutive forty-year terms.

Illinois: Alton Coleman was convicted in January 1987, of the aggravated kidnap and murder of Vernita Wheat and sentenced to die by lethal injection.

Both Coleman and Brown were last reported to be in custody in Ohio appealing against their sentences.

COLLINS, Norman John What were later called the 'Michigan Murders' were committed in the Ypsilanti area of the state during the period August 1967 to June 1969. The seven victims met their deaths by a variety of weapons – guns, knives, blunt instruments, manual strangulation – and all had been sexually mutilated.

The first was Eastern Michigan University student Mary Fleszar on 10 July 1967. On 7 August, her body was found two miles north of Ypsilanti, badly decomposed and without hands or feet; she had been stabbed to death. As Mary's remains lay in the funeral parlour, a young man arrived claiming to be a close friend of the family and made the bizarre request to take a snapshot of the corpse; the outraged morticians rightly refused.

It was almost one year later, on 6 July 1968, that twenty-year-old student Joan Schell's body was found with forty-seven stab wounds at Ann Arbor; she had last been seen five days earlier getting into a red car containing three young men. She had also, according to fellow students, been in the company of twenty-one-year-old Norman Collins. Collins claimed that he had been with his mother at the time, and there seemed no reason to pursue what was probably a case of mistaken identity.

The third Eastern Michigan student, Jan Mixer, was found dead in a cemetery at Denton Township towards the end of March 1969; she had been shot and strangled. It was known that she had been offered a lift, possibly by a fellow student, to her mother's home at Muskegon. Four days later, on 25 March, the body of sixteen-year-old Maralynn Skelton, known by the police to be involved in drug abuse was found. She had been extensively beaten, probably with a large-buckled belt and her head had been bludgeoned. Just three weeks after Maralynn Skelton's body was found, schoolgirl Dawn Basom, who had disappeared the previous evening, was discovered, strangled; she was just thirteen years old. University graduate Alison Kalom was the 'Michigan Murderer's' sixth victim. She was found by three young boys at the edge of a field in Northfield Township; her body had been stabbed all over and her throat cut; cause of death had been the gunshot wound in her head.

Six corpses, all within the space of two years; six young women, one only just into teenage, molested and murdered within a couple of miles of town – and no suspects. In June 1969, the press took over and invited the successful Dutch psychic detective Peter Hurkos to visit Ypsilanti. The profile Hurkos gave was of a man, under twenty-five years old and strongly built; a description that could have fitted a fair proportion of Eastern Michigan's male student population.

The psychic added that the killer would strike once more; he was right. The victim was student Karen Sue Bieneman, missing from campus since 23 July and found strangled, beaten and sexually abused three days later. This time the police had a break. On the day she disappeared Karen had been in a shop in town, and the manageress had seen her companion waiting outside on a motor-cycle; her excellent description of the young man was identified as Norman John

Collins. Taken into custody, Collins denied having anything to do with murder. But now they had a suspect, the police could start investigating from a position of strength. Collins, it turned out, was an habitual thief, and a number of girl students had complained of being pestered by him. He had also, according to some of his dates, made scary references to the recent murders. Norman Collins was positively identified by the shop owner who had seen him with Karen Bieneman, and more damning still were the clippings of hair that had become attached to the last victim's underwear, and which were a perfect match with hair clippings found in the basement of Collins' aunt's house. He had been feeding Mrs Leik's dog while the family were on holiday, and must have brought the girl back to the house and killed her. Spots of blood on the basement floor which matched Karen's group added to an already strong case. Norman Collins was convicted of murder on 19 August 1970, and sentenced to life imprisonment with hard labour.

CONSTANZO, Adolfo de Jesus, ALDRETE, Sara Maria, et al.
Mark Kilroy, a twenty-one-year-old student at the University of Texas was on spring vacation with three classmates when they decided to take in the Mexican town of Motomoros. They arrived on 14 March 1987, and during a tour of the town's bars, Mark disappeared. Investigations instigated by the Kilroy family seemed to have reached a dead end when drug-squad officers informed the parents that during a recent raid on the remote Rancho Santa Elena they had detained several men, one of whom said that he had seen a 'blond Gringo' bound and gagged in the back of a van parked at the ranch.

As the search of the Santa Elena progressed, large quantities of marijuana and cocaine were found in a shed. The shed itself was dominated by a makeshift altar, and around the building were an alarming number of blood stains, scraps of human hair and a substance only later identified as human brain pulp. In view of this, the least of the horrors was a prominently displayed severed goat's head. Those detained in the drug raid professed allegiance to a Satanist cult loosely based on Santeria and said that Mark Kilroy had been kidnapped and later 'sacrificed' on the orders of the cult's leaders – the man they referred to reverentially as 'The Godfather', born Adolfo de Jesus Constanzo, and Sara Maria Aldrete, the cult's High Priestess. The primary object of the slaughter appears to have been to appease Satan in return for inviolability from police arrest and so that they would not be harmed by bullets in the event of a shoot-out. Whenever a major drug deal was about to take place, a human sacrifice was offered and the victim's heart and brains ripped out to be boiled up in a cauldron as a 'cannibal feast'. Later, the detainees led officers to the graves of fifteen men and boys, including Mark Kilroy. Many of the bodies had been decapitated and all of them had been extensively mutilated.

Needless to say, by this time Constanzo and Aldrete were on the run. On 5 May 1989, they were traced to an apartment in Mexico City. Following a siege, Sara Aldrete fled the building screaming: 'He's dead! He's dead!' Police entering the apartment found three of the cult's members alive, but Constanzo and his homosexual lover had been shot dead, locked in a final embrace in a walk-in wardrobe; they had been killed on their own orders, rather than be taken into custody. Sara Aldrete, not surprisingly, denied any involvement in the killings, but was indicted along with the other survivors of the cult on multiple charges including murder and drug offences.

In August 1990 Sara Maria Aldrete was acquitted of Constanzo's murder, but sentenced to six years imprisonment for criminal association; she awaits trial on charges arising out of the ranch murders. Constanzo's killer, Alvaro de Leo Valdez was sentenced to thirty years for murder, and the two other men taken in the Mexico City apartment await trial for the ranch murders and an assortment of drugs and firearms offences.

COOKE, Eric Edgar At the time of the crimes for which he was arrested thirty-two-year-old Cooke was a truck driver who moonlighted as a burglar and murderer.

During the first eight months of 1963 the inhabitants of Perth, Australia, were put in terror by a spate of brutal and apparently pointless shootings. The first victims, in January, were a couple sitting peacefully in their parked car when a gunman stepped up to the vehicle and shot and wounded them. This attack was followed by the murder of a young man, shot as he slept in his bed. A business man was the next victim, killed as he opened the front door of his house to a stranger, and another youth was shot in his bed; all this activity on a single night.

Despite an enthusiastic response by the Perth police force, the murders were still unsolved in August, when on the 10th a baby-sitter was shot in the suburb of Crawley.

Although local police received assistance from Scotland Yard in London and the United States Federal Bureau of Investigation, it was a piece of gratuitous luck that led to the apprehension of the assassin. A young couple out walking had found a .22 rifle hidden in some bushes which ballistics tests identified as the weapon used in the last shooting. When Eric Cooke went to retrieve his gun from its hiding place on 1 September, he was arrested.

Cooke confessed to all his previous murders, and added another, committed in 1959. His rather obvious explanation was that he wanted to hurt people. A jury rejected Cooke's defence of insanity and he was sentenced to death.

While awaiting execution, Eric Cooke made a further confession – to a murder committed in 1949, for which a deaf mute named Daryl Beamish was already serving time. In one of the most controversial decisions in the history of Australian criminal law, the authorities decided not to accept Cooke's unsolicited admission of guilt, and Beamish remained in prison until he was paroled in 1971. Eric Edgar Cooke was hanged at Fremantle Gaol on 26 October 1964, the last person but one to be executed in Australia.

COOPER, Ronald Frank   Ronald Cooper is rare among the records of serial murder in that although he only killed once, his diaries reveal a carefully prepared plan for an extensive programme of child-murder, aborted only by his early arrest.

Cooper started his belligerent career early, and is recorded as having attempted to kill another child in 1963, when he was only eleven years old. He had still not fully developed the determination of a murderer when in April 1976, while living in Berea, Johannesburg, Cooper forced ten-year-old Tresslin Pohl at gunpoint into a local park. Here he seems to have lost confidence and released the boy; despite a good description, the police failed to trace young Pohl's abductor.

If nothing else, this recent failure seems to have at least slightly strengthened Cooper's resolve, for in a diary entry of 17 March 1976, he clearly states, 'I have decided that I think I should become a homosexual murderer, and shall get hold of young boys and bring them here where I am staying [a hotel in Berea] and I shall rape them and kill them. I shall not kill all the boys in the same way; some I shall strangle with my hands, others I shall strangle with a piece of cord. Others again I shall stab to death, others I shall cut their throats. I can also suffocate or smother others . . .' By way of further variety, Cooper decided to stop at thirty murders of young boys, and then turn his attention to girls and women.

As killers go, we must be thankful that Ronald Cooper was pathetically inept. Less than a week after committing his plan to paper, Cooper tried to stab a ten-year-old boy in the chest, but ran off when the child screamed, leaving him with minor cuts. Courage deserted him again in his attempted strangulation of another youth who also had the sense to start yelling.

Apparently undeterred by his own lack of resolve, Ronald Cooper was out stalking new prey on 16 May, when he came across Mark Garnet, twelve years old, and decided that he should be the one that 'I strangle with my hands'. When the youth lost consciousness and died, Cooper tied a rope round his victim's neck and attempted to commit sodomy – not surprisingly given his previous record, he failed even in this. What was worse, he had at last 'become a homosexual murderer'. Horrified by his own achievement, and overwhelmed by remorse, Ronald Cooper wrote in his diary, 'It's a really dreadful thing that I did; I only wish I could undo it. I never want to do such a thing again.'

He never got the chance. By happy coincidence Mark Garnet had been a school-friend of Cooper's first attempted victim, Tresslin Pohl.

Pohl had in the meantime seen Cooper in the street and followed him back to the hotel. For reasons not entirely clear he had kept the news of his attacker's whereabouts to himself – until his friend was killed.

After a half-hearted attempt to resist arrest, Ronald Cooper was taken into custody, tried, convicted (mostly on the evidence of his own diaries), sentenced to death, and on 16 January 1978, hanged.

COPELAND, Michael Michael Copeland hated homosexuals. He brutally murdered two men in England for that reason, and, inexplicably, a young man out walking with his girlfriend in Germany.

On 12 June 1960, a cyclist found the shoeless body of a man on an isolated moor path near Baslow, outside Chesterfield. The man's head had been badly battered and he had been dead for some hours. The Chesterfield police were less surprised than they might have been because earlier in the day a two-seater 'bubble-car' was found which had collided with a lamp-post. Inside the car had been a pair of men's shoes and copious bloodstains. In fact, the police were looking for the victim of a traffic accident. The man was identified as William Elliott, a sixty-year-old bachelor and resident of Baslow. The post-mortem report suggested that Elliott's head wounds could have been caused by a boot.

A week later, a Mrs Gladys Vickers of Chesterfield told police officers that she had been out late on the night of the murder and saw a man she thought was Mr Elliott being chased along a dark alley by a man she described as dark-haired, swarthy, with thin features; he caught up with Elliott and there was a scuffle.

Among those questioned in connection with the murder was Michael Copeland, a twenty-one-year-old conscript on home leave in Chesterfield from the British Army in Germany. Copeland, who already had a criminal record, had confided to a girlfriend that he had killed a man, but there was no direct evidence to connect the youth with the 'Bubble-Car Murder', and he was released and allowed to return to his unit.

In November 1960, Gunther Helmbrecht, sixteen years old, was stabbed to death while walking with a girl in the forest near the town of Verden in Germany. That same night Copeland staggered into the guard room at his barracks with a knife wound in his leg and explained that he had been attacked by two German civilians. An obvious suspect, he was intensively questioned, but nothing concrete could be found to link him with the death of Helmbrecht.

Copeland completed his army service and returned to Chesterfield. On 29 March 1961, the body of chemist George Stobbs was found in almost the exact spot where William Elliott had been found dead the previous year. As in the earlier case, Stobbs' car was found abandoned and he had died from head injuries probably inflicted with a boot.

The similarity with the Elliott murder was obvious, and led to local newspapers calling it the 'Copy-Cat Murder'. Copeland became a suspect again, and he was detained and questioned. As before, there was no shred of evidence on which to detain him, and Copeland was released but put under strict surveillance. Nevertheless, over the period of the next two years, Inspector Bradshaw of the Chesterfield force built up a relationship of sorts with Michael Copeland, and in November 1963, Copeland telephoned Bradshaw and confessed to the three murders. He refused to make a formal statement, but told the Inspector that he killed Elliott and Stobbs because they were homosexuals: 'It was something I really hated.' He also said he regretted killing the German boy.

At his trial in March 1965, Copeland said that he had made the confession in order to force a trial, establish his innocence and so have the surveillance lifted. The court did not believe a word of it, and Michael Copeland was found guilty and sentenced to death. As capital punishment was at the time under review in England, his sentence was later commuted to life imprisonment.

CORLL, Dean Allen, and HENLEY, Elmer Wayne   It was around 8.30 a.m. on 8 August 1973, that the telephone rang in the Pasadena Police Department and the officer answering the call heard a voice at the other end of the line announce, 'I just killed a man . . .'

Within minutes a patrol car had been dispatched to the address given as Lanar Street, Pasadena, where the patrolman was greeted by two teenage boys and a girl. One of the boys identified himself as seventeen-year-old Wayne Henley, the source of the telephone call; Henley led the officers into the house where the body of Dean Corll lay on the floor, face down, with six bullets in him.

For Henley it was the end of a nightmare in which he was a leading participant. With Corll, he had raped, tortured and killed thirty-two young men, most of them hitch-hikers or vagrants, and most of them procured by Henley at around $200 a head. The victims had been taken up to Corll's house where the genial host – the man described as 'a real good neighbour and a real good guy' and whose largesse with sweets had earned him the nickname the 'Candyman' among local children – would wine and dine his new guests until they passed out through drink or drugs. The unconscious victims were then handcuffed to the plank of wood Corll referred to as his 'torture board', sodomised and subjected to other painful indignities before – sometimes days later – being killed. At the subsequent trial of Wayne Henley, one of the investigating officers described some of the tortures: '. . . pulling out their pubic hairs one by one, shoving glass rods up their penis and shoving a large bullet-like instrument in the victim's rectum'.

Henley implicated another youth in the conspiracy, David Owen Brooks, who had introduced him to Corll. Although they both denied involvement, it became clear to interrogators that Henley and Brooks had participated actively in the torture and murders.

Following Wayne Henley's directions a police search team investigated a boat shed which Dean Corll had rented in south-west Houston. Officers had dug no deeper than six inches before encountering the first of seventeen bodies – that of a young man wrapped in a clear plastic sheet, the noose still around his neck. Henley next led the team to Lake Sam Rayburn where he identified the sites of four more burials, then on to High Island where six more corpses were unearthed. According to Henley there should have been four more, perhaps in the boat shed or on High Island. A total of thirty-two young males between the ages of thirteen and twenty.

In the early morning of 8 August 1973, Wayne Henley had gone to Corll's house with two teenage friends, a girl and a boy, for a glue-sniffing session. The three visitors eventually passed out from the effects of the solvents and Henley awoke to find himself attached to the 'torture board'. Corll made it clear that he was particularly angry that Wayne had brought a female into his home, and pointed a gun at him threatening death as a punishment. Pleading as he never had before, Wayne Henley promised his pal that he would rape and torture the girl for him while Corll 'took care of' the boy. Still half-conscious from the glue-sniffing the two youngsters offered little resistance when they were strapped to the boards. At this point – and it is difficult to know why it was at this point – Wayne Henley decided that he had had enough. Grabbing Corll's gun, he pumped six bullets into him. When he had released the two captives, still groggy enough not to notice that anything was wrong, Henley called the Pasadena police.

Henley was put on trial for murder in July 1974 and found guilty; he was sentenced to six terms of ninety-nine years' imprisonment. For his part, David Brooks was jailed for life.

CORONA, Juan Vallejo   Corona first went to the United States and California as a migrant worker picking fruit in the 1950s, and within ten years had built up his own very successful labour-contracting business, hiring out Mexican migrants to Californian fruit-growers on commission. Juan Corona, if not entirely a pillar of society, had at least earned the respect of people around Yuba County for his hard work and honesty.

Then in 1971, alerted by an anonymous tip-off, a squad of police officers arrived to make a search of his home and the old bunkhouse in which Corona's work-force slept. Here in shallow graves the search team found the remains of twenty-five men, some migrants, some just passing vagrants. All of them had been stabbed to death and their heads hacked with a heavy, sharp implement; in Corona's house was found the bloody machete with which the mutilation was carried out.

Juan Corona was indicted in the California Supreme Court on twenty-five charges of murder, and the most incriminating evidence against him proved to be a ledger, in Corona's own hand, listing several of his victims' names, their dates of arrival and 'departure'. All the victims had died in a single six-week period – a remarkable average of one death every forty-odd hours, presumably stopped only by Corona's arrest.

Although he pleaded not guilty, the jury after a forty-five-hour retirement found otherwise and Juan Corona was sentenced to twenty-five life terms. At the time he held the US record for murder, being toppled from his position at the head of the table in the same year by Dean **Corll** and Wayne Henley.

The motive for the murders appeared to be sexual as many of the victims had been buried either without trousers or with their trousers pulled down. However, it could not be denied that Corona seemed to be happily married and had fathered several children. This dichotomy has contributed to the theory that the killer had an accomplice, and Corona's attorney made an unsuccessful appeal based on the claim that another killer altogether had been responsible for the twenty-five deaths.

In Soledad prison, California, in 1973, Juan Corona was viciously attacked by fellow-prisoners who stabbed him thirty-two times, resulting in the loss of an eye.

Ten years after his conviction, Corona won a retrial at Hayward, California, a trial that cost the taxpayers $5 million, featured nine hundred exhibits and two hundred and twelve witnesses – in fact it was the most expensive single-defendant trial in California's legal history. The basis of the new trial was the allegation that it had been Juan's brother Natividad (conveniently deceased) who had committed the murders. The fact that Natividad was an acknowledged homosexual became one of the defence's strong points – countered by the prosecution's submission that the victims' trousers had been interfered with only in an attempt to rob the contents of their pockets.

The trial was something of a shambles, with unhelpful – even counterproductive – witnesses wasting much of the court's time; like the man who admitted that he was a practising Satanist and a drug addict, and anyway had only agreed to testify in return for a reduction in his own charges. In the end the result of the trial was as it had been the first time round and Juan Corona was returned to prison and his life sentences.

CORWIN, Daniel Lee   At the age of sixteen, Corwin was arrested and charged with the rape and attempted murder of a high-school student in Temple, Texas. Under a plea-bargaining arrangement whereby Corwin agreed to plead guilty to the lesser charge of rape instead of contesting the full charge, he was sentenced to forty years' imprisonment, but released on parole nine years later in 1984.

On Friday, 13 February 1987, Corwin attacked seventy-two-year-old Mrs Alice Martin, stabbing, strangling and sexually assaulting her before leaving her partially clothed body in a field near Normangee.

On 10 July, another Friday, police received a call that a gunman was holding up a shop at Huntsville; when they arrived, the armed robber was gone. Also missing was Debra Ewing, aged twenty-seven, employed by the shop as an optician. Two days later her body was found in a wood almost twenty miles from Huntsville; she had been repeatedly stabbed, then strangled and sexually assaulted.

Halloween at a car-wash in Walker County, thirty-one-year-old Mary Risinger was stabbed to death and her three-year-old daughter wounded. The child later described the attacker as a white man with white hair who had driven off in a brown truck.

A year later to the month, on 20 October 1988, a Texas University student sitting in her car was forced at knife-point to drive to a public park. There her abductor tore off her clothes and raped her before tying the girl to a tree and pushing a knife into her chest leaving her for dead. This was a mistake. Despite the unspeakable trauma that she had suffered, the girl managed to free herself and stagger to the road where a passing Samaritan drove her to hospital. Following an anonymous tip-off, Corwin was picked up, charged and pleaded guilty to attempted murder. This time he received a sentence of ninety-nine years.

Daniel Corwin's sordid history might have ended here but for changes in Texas state law that took account into sinister developments in serious crime; in short, the new 'serial murder law' which allowed an accused to be tried for more than one murder at the same time despite the crimes being committed at separate times and places. Previously each offence would require its own trial. Following interviews with psychiatrists and sociologists in prison, Daniel Corwin eventually admitted to the Martin, Ewing and Risinger murders, and in March 1990 was the first prisoner to be convicted of serial murder under the new statute. At the penalty hearing which followed, the jury voted for his death by lethal injection. Corwin was unlucky in his choice of states in which to commit a capital crime; Texas headed the 'league', in January 1991, with thirty-seven executions since the reinstatement of capital punishment in 1976. For those with a fondness for statistics, in the next highest position on the table is Florida, with twenty-five in the same period.

COTTINGHAM, Richard Francis Cottingham faced three trials on multiple charges of murder, attempted murder, kidnapping, rape, sodomy, aggravated assault, robbery and drug offences committed during his three-year reign of terror against prostitutes in the states of New York and New Jersey between 1977 and 1980.

The first victim of the series was twenty-six-year-old Maryann Carr, a radiologist who was abducted and later found dead outside the Quality Inn motel in Hasbrouck Heights on 15 December 1977. She had been either smothered or choked to death. In December 1979, firemen were called to a New York hotel to deal with a blaze, and in

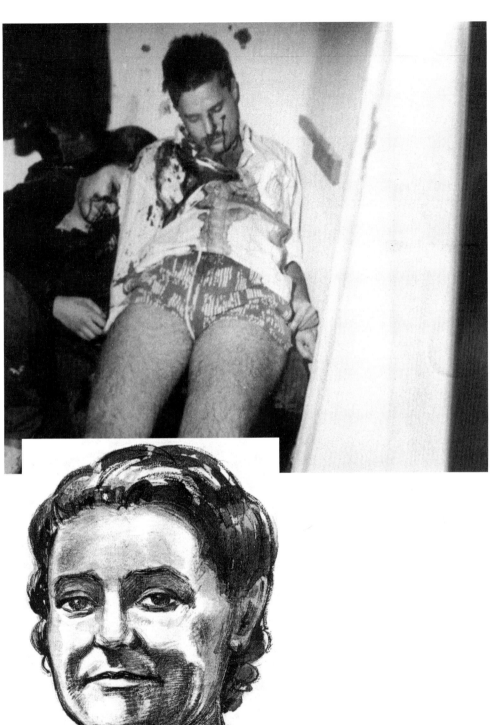

Above Adolfo Constanzo and his homosexual lover shot dead at their own request by members of the gang (*AP*). **Left** Mrs Juliana Lipke.

'Son of Sam' killer David Berkowitz (*AP*); **inset** the police artist's impression of the then unidentified suspect.

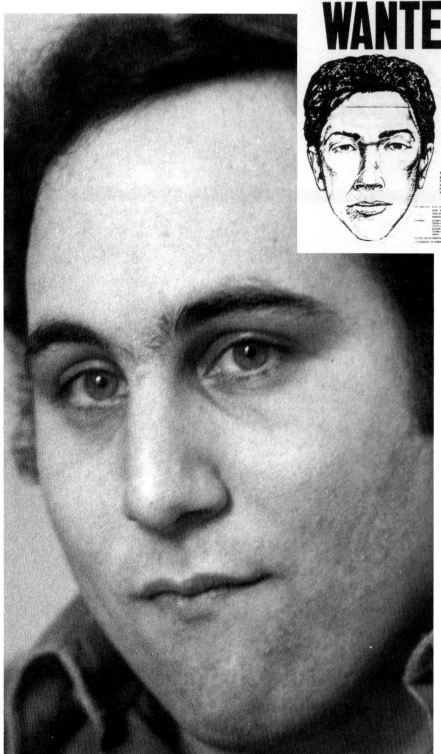

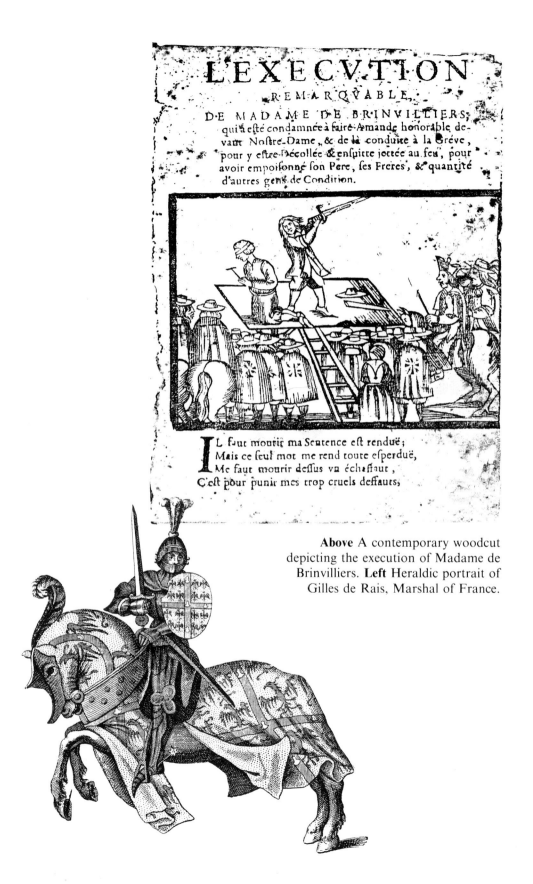

L'EXECVTION

REMARQVABLE,

DE MADAME DE BRINVILLIERS,
qui a esté condamnée à faire Amande honorable de-
vant Nostre-Dame, & de là conduite à la Gréve,
pour y estre Décollée & ensuitte jettée au feu, pour
avoir empoisonné son Pere, ses Freres, & quantité
d'autres gens de Condition.

IL faut mourir ma Sentence est renduë;
Mais ce seul mot me rend toute esperduë,
Me faut mourir dessus vn échassaut,
C'est pour punir mes trop cruels deffauts,

Above A contemporary woodcut
depicting the execution of Madame de
Brinvilliers. **Left** Heraldic portrait of
Gilles de Rais, Marshal of France.

Police artist's impression of Ted Bundy; **inset** some of the many faces of the charismatic man responsible for the deaths of as many as forty women (*AP*).

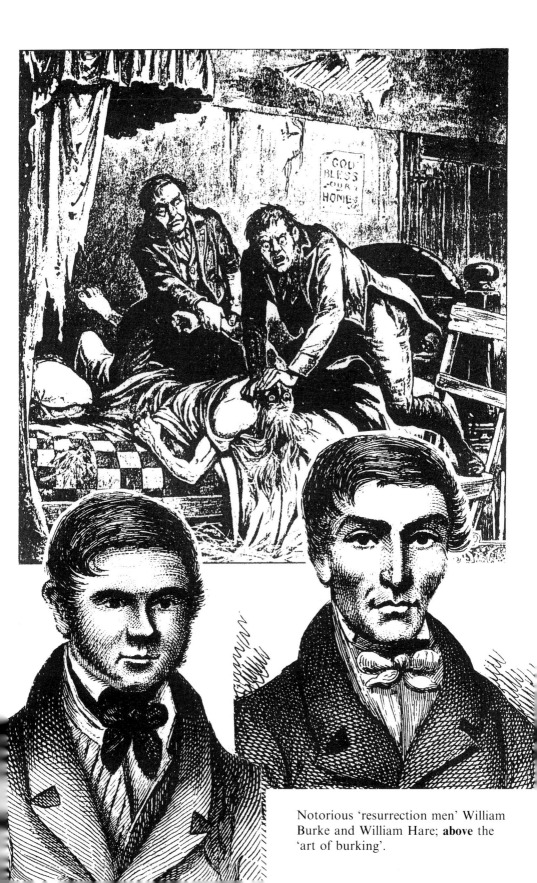

Notorious 'resurrection men' William Burke and William Hare; **above** the 'art of burking'.

The Artist's View. **Above** A caricature of Eugen Weidmann by Gea Augsbourg; **right** Philip Youngman Carter's pastel sketch from life of John Reginald Christie.

Donald Leroy Evans following a court appearance in Biloxi, Missouri, August 1991 to hear charges of kidnap, rape and strangling. He claims to have murdered sixty people over ten years (*Popperfoto*).

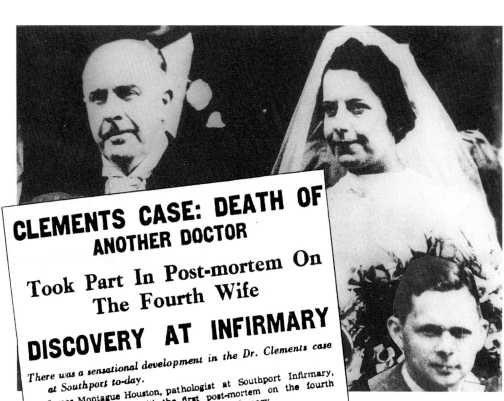

CLEMENTS CASE: DEATH OF ANOTHER DOCTOR

Took Part In Post-mortem On The Fourth Wife

DISCOVERY AT INFIRMARY

There was a sensational development in the Dr. Clements case at Southport to-day.

Dr. James Montague Houston, pathologist at Southport Infirmary, who was associated with the first post-mortem on the fourth Mrs. Clements, was found dead at the infirmary.

Dr. Houston, who was 39, married, with two children, was a native of Belfast. He had been at the Infirmary since last January, after serving in the R.A.M.C. during the war.

The inquest will be opened by the Southport coroner to-morrow.

Dr. Clements's Wife And £22,000 Estate

Daughter Of Liverpool Business Man Who Left No Will

The ECHO learned to-day that the fourth wife of Dr. Robert George Clements, of Southport—who died on Friday after his wife's funeral had been stopped — was the daughter of a well-known Liverpool business man, who left an estate valued at over £22,000.

Dr and Mrs Clements on their wedding day with superimposed at the bottom right, Dr James Houston. **Inset** Announcement of Dr Houston's tragic suicide.

Multiple poisoner Dr Thomas Neill Cream, with a view of
the portable medicine case which contained the lethal
strychnine pills.

John Wayne Gacy (*Popperfoto*).

Minnie Dean, the New Zealand baby farmer, and her trial judge Mr Justice Williams.

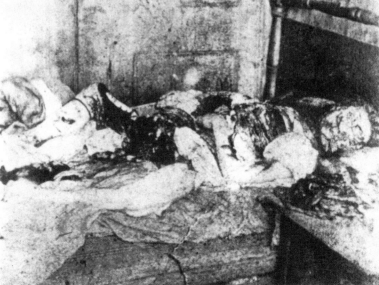

Right The mutilated corpse of Jack the Ripper's last victim, Mary Kelly, as police found it in her room in Miller's Court.

Paul John
Knowles (*AP*).

Above Fritz Haarmann returned to prison after sentencing.
Below The pathetic cry for help scrawled on the wall of his
victim's apartment by a very disturbed William Heirens.

The Cannibal Killers. **Above** Albert Fish (*AP*); **left** Edward Gein (*Topham*).

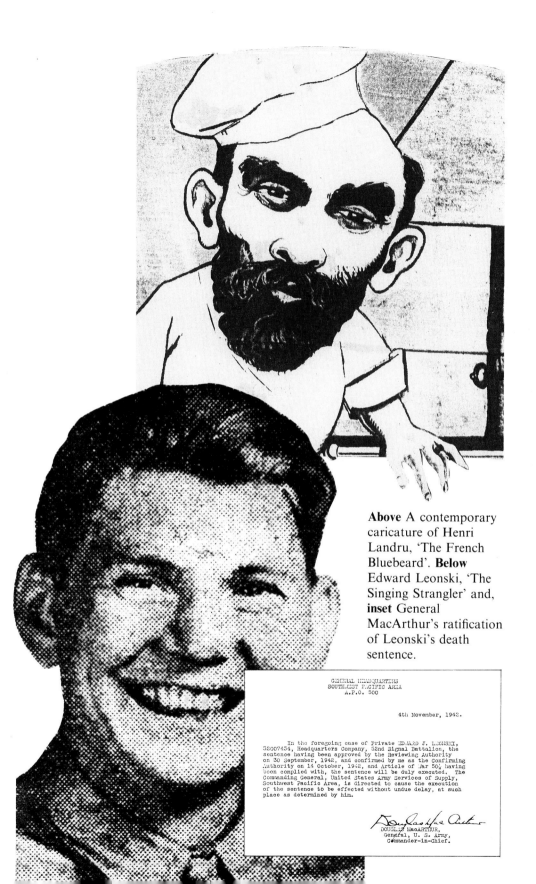

Above A contemporary caricature of Henri Landru, 'The French Bluebeard'. **Below** Edward Leonski, 'The Singing Strangler' and, **inset** General MacArthur's ratification of Leonski's death sentence.

GENERAL HEADQUARTERS
SOUTHWEST PACIFIC AREA
A.P.O. 500

4th November, 1942.

In the foregoing case of Private EDWARD J. LEONSKI, 32007434, Headquarters Company, 52nd Signal Battalion, the sentence having been approved by the Reviewing Authority on 30 September, 1942, and confirmed by me as the Confirming Authority on 14 October, 1942, and Article of War 50½ having been complied with, the sentence will be duly executed. The Commanding General, United States Army Services of Supply, Southwest Pacific Area, is directed to cause the execution of the sentence to be effected without undue delay, at such place as determined by him.

DOUGLAS MacARTHUR,
General, U. S. Army,
Commander-in-Chief.

Beauty and the Beast. Charles Manson (**above**) and actress Sharon Tate, victim of the Manson Family's first killing spree (*Popperfoto*).

one of the guest rooms found the badly mutilated torsos of two women. Although they were headless and handless, one of the victims was subsequently identified as Kuwait-born prostitute Deedeh Goodarzi; the name of the other woman has never been established. On 15 May, another hooker, Mary Ann Jean Reyner, was found stabbed and slashed to death in a hotel in the centre of New York near Times Square. Her breasts had been sliced off and her body set on fire. Valerie Ann Street, who worked under the alias Shelly Dudley, was found strangled in the motel at Hasbrouck Heights on 4 May and, on 22 May, police were called to the same motel to investigate reports of a woman screaming. When they arrived they arrested Richard Cottingham as he tried to escape. In Room 117 officers found a badly injured girl who alleged Cottingham had raped and sodomised her, forced her to have oral sex, and had beaten her and bitten her breasts.

Following further investigations, Cottingham was charged with all the above killings plus a mind-numbing list of related offences. His first trial in 1980 was for the New Jersey crimes comprising the murder of Valerie Street plus twenty other lesser charges. Forensic evidence in the form of fingerprints, semen stains, blood and fibres convincingly supported the testimony of several women who gave evidence of assault. Richard Cottingham was convicted on fifteen counts including the murder charge, and sentenced to from 173 to 197 years in the state penitentiary.

A year later Cottingham was again tried in Bergen County, New Jersey, this time for the murder of Maryann Carr. He was found guilty of second-degree murder and given twenty-five years to life with a minimum recommendation of thirty years to be served *consecutively* with the 1980 sentences. In 1984 Richard Cottingham faced yet a third trial in New York for the three prostitute murders in Manhattan; the verdicts were guilty of second-degree murder with sentences of another seventy-five years to life.

On the face of it, Richard Cottingham seemed an unlikely killer. Born on 25 November 1946, he had an above-average academic record, had been a distinguished high-school athlete, and had married in 1970 and fathered three children. He held down a well-paid job as a computer operator with Blue Cross-Blue Shield of Greater New York, who described him as one of their most productive and valuable employees.

It was certainly no coincidence that Cottingham almost invariably chose prostitutes as his victims – they were easily lured to hotel rooms on 'business', they were unlikely to report his excesses to the police, and if they ever got to court would make easily discredited witnesses. His *modus operandi* it later transpired was to pick the woman up (having first established his preference for 'rough sex'), drug her drink with barbiturates and then drive the victim unconscious to a motel. The lucky ones would wake up battered, bruised and bloody wherever Cottingham chose to leave them – in the motel, on the roadside, in a car park. The others did not wake up at all.

COTTON, Mary Ann Mary Ann Robson was born in 1822, in the pit village of East Rainton, near Durham. At the age of twenty, she became Mrs William Mowbray; after a couple of years in Newcastle-upon-Tyne, they moved south to Cornwall, where Mowbray worked as a navvy and Mary Ann devoted herself to producing five children. Of these, the four sons died in infancy, victims of 'gastric fever' so it was said. The surviving Mowbrays returned to Durham, where the fifth child, a girl, succumbed to the same 'gastric fever'. Then William Mowbray died unexpectedly of diarrhoea, not long after taking out a sizeable insurance.

Mary Ann made a fresh start at Seaham with a new husband, George Ward. Was it just bad luck that George died fourteen months later of 'gastric fever'? Within weeks, the widow Ward had taken up new responsibilities as housekeeper to John Robinson, a shipwright, and his five children. The scope of Mary's duties was obviously broad, for she quickly became pregnant and even more quickly became Mrs Mary Ann Robinson.

Tragedy, it seemed, still pursued this unfortunate woman. Already one of the Robinson children had contracted a fatal dose of 'gastric fever' and in 1867 three more children died. John Robinson, it must be recorded, was lucky. Like his predecessors, he too might have lost his life; as it was, Mary Ann simply helped herself to his savings and fled.

The next stop was Walbottle, where Mary met Mr Frederick Cotton and his sister Margaret. When, some months later, Mary was once again expecting a child she married Cotton (bigamously, for John Robinson was still alive) at St Andrew's church, Newcastle. She now bore the name which was to become notorious – Mary Ann Cotton.

Margaret Cotton, the sister, went down with 'gastric fever' and died shortly before her brother's wedding. She had thoughtfully left her savings to Frederick and Mary.

Now a significant number of pigs belonging to Mary Ann's neighbours mysteriously began to die, and those uncharitable farmers began to point an accusing finger in Mary's direction; indeed, such was the acrimony over the deceased pigs that the Cottons – Frederick, Mary Ann, two offspring of Cotton's earlier marriage and Mary's baby – found it wise to remove to West Auckland.

Once settled, the family rapidly decreased in number; Frederick was the first loss, on 19 September 1871. He was followed into the grave by Mary's ten-year-old stepson Frederick and her fourteen-month-old baby Robert. Joseph Nattrass, a lodger who had been imprudent enough to become Mrs Cotton's lover, and unwise enough to make a will in her favour, became the fourth victim of 'gastric fever', not inappropriately on April the First.

This left only little Charles Edward, a stepson, who had managed to survive the 'illnesses' to attain his seventh birthday. He would never see his eighth; on 12 July 1872 he died.

Mary Ann was arrested when a post-mortem on the body of this latest victim of 'gastric fever' revealed abnormal traces of arsenic. Exhumation was ordered for the four previous victims, and examination by Dr Thomas Scattergood, lecturer in forensic medicine and toxicology at Leeds Medical School, proved that they too had met their end through arsenical poisoning.

It was for Charles Edward's murder only that Mary Ann Cotton was tried at the Durham Assizes in March 1873. Her defence, advanced on her behalf by Mr Thomas Campbell Foster, was that her stepson had been accidentally poisoned by some wallpaper in his bedroom, the green pigment of which was derived from arsenic. And it is a defence that stood at least a chance of succeeding had not evidence of the four previous poisonings been deemed admissible in order to refute the proposition of accidental death (see also George Joseph **Smith**).

On the third day of the trial, the jury retired to consider their verdict. It was barely an hour before that decision had been reached and the judge, from beneath the black cap, had intoned the sentence of death.

Mary Ann Cotton died on the scaffold at Durham County Gaol at 8 a.m. on Monday 24 March 1873. Already her infamy was assured; already the children in the streets had immortalised her name in rhyme:

> Mary Ann Cotton
> She's dead and she's rotten
> She lies in her bed
> With her eyes wide oppen [sic].
> Sing, sing, oh, what can I sing?
> Mary Ann Cotton is tied up wi' string.
> Where, where? Up in the air
> Sellin' black puddens a penny a pair.

CREAM, Dr Thomas Neill Cream was born in Scotland in May 1850, the eldest of eight brothers and sisters; his family left its home in Glasgow four years later, bound for Canada. On 12 November 1872, Thomas Cream registered at McGill College, Montreal, as a student of medicine; little is recorded of significance in this period of Cream's development, except that he graduated with merit on 31 March 1876.

It was around this time that he met Miss Flora Elizabeth Brooks, the daughter of a prosperous Waterloo (Canada) hotelier. Miss Brooks shortly became pregnant, was aborted by Cream, and nearly died as a result. The furious Brooks senior would settle for nothing less than marriage, and on 11 September Thomas was dragged down the aisle; on the following day Cream walked out of the house bound for England, where he enrolled as a postgraduate student at St Thomas's Hospital, London, and rounded off his education with a qualification from the Royal College of Physicians and Surgeons at Edinburgh. Thus did Thomas Neill Cream become one of the few genuinely competent medics to turn murderer.

The killings began in a modest and clumsy manner. Cream had returned to Canada, and was acquiring a lucrative reputation as an abortionist. During this time a young chambermaid named Kate Gardener was found dead in the privy behind Cream's rooms; beside her body was a bottle of chloroform. The girl was known to have been visiting Cream for the purpose of securing an abortion, and despite the strength of evidence offered against him, the doctor avoided prosecution for murder. In Chicago, Cream's newly opened abortion surgery at 434 West Madison Street claimed its first fatality in August 1880. On the 23rd Cream was taken into custody on a charge of causing the death of Julia Faulkner; but luck was with him and the slippery rogue again escaped his just deserts.

A profitable sideline undertaken by Cream to supplement his earnings from abortion was the marketing of a quack remedy for epilepsy. Whether the treatment did any good or not is debatable, but it appeared at least to do no harm, indeed attracting a number of faithful 'patients'. One was a railway agent named Daniel Stott, who was so impressed with the improvement in his health that he sent his pretty young wife in person to Chicago for regular supplies. The inevitable happened and Cream availed himself of the favours of Julia Stott while taking her husband's money. When Stott became an inconvenience to the liaison his medicine was pepped up with an additional ingredient. On the 14 June 1881 Daniel Stott died in great agony, the sudden seizure being attributed to his epilepsy, so that Cream's nostrum would never have been suspected had it not been for the mad medic's inexplicable communication to the coroner of Boone County, claiming that Stott's death had been the result of a blunder on the part of the pharmacist, and demanding an exhumation. Although the coroner dismissed the letter as the fantasy of a madman, the District Attorney *did* order an exhumation, *did* find strychnine in the stomach of Daniel Stott, and *did* eventually send prisoner 4374 Thomas Neill Cream to spend the rest of his life at the Illinois State Penitentiary at Joliet.

With allowance for good behaviour, Cream was released on 31 July 1891 and, diverting to Canada only for as long as it took to collect an inheritance of $16,000, he boarded the *Teutonic* for England. On 7 October 1891, Cream took lodgings at 103 Lambeth Palace Road, in the heart of South London's slums, an area in which he was to commit a series of indiscriminate murders which were to rival Jack the Ripper's reign of terror in the East End three years before.

On 9 October Cream acquainted himself with the talents of Matilda Clover, a prostitute, and about this date purchased from Mr Priest's chemist shop a quantity of *nux vomica*, of which one constituent is the alkaloid poison strychnine. He subsequently bought a box of empty gelatine capsules and a further supply of *nux vomica*.

The evening of 13 October found James Styles standing outside the Wellington pub in Waterloo Road, when he saw a young prostitute who had been patrolling her beat stagger and collapse onto the pavement. Styles managed to carry her to the address she gasped out, whence her condition made removal to a hospital necessary. On the journey poor Ellen Donworth confided that a man she had met in the York Hotel in Waterloo Road, 'A tall gentleman with cross eyes, a silk hat and bushy whiskers', had given her a couple of draughts from a bottle of 'white stuff'. She died before reaching the hospital, of strychnine poisoning. Thomas Cream was away clear. On 20 October Matilda Clover met once again with the man she had been with on the 9th; on this second evening Matilda brought her client 'Fred' back to 27 Lambeth Road. Some hours later Matilda died, writhing and screaming with agonised convulsions. She was buried in a pauper's grave in Tooting, cause of death: *delirium tremens* as a result of alcoholism. Cream was in the clear again.

Dr Thomas Neill Cream now took a brief respite from the rigours of murder to fall in love and became engaged to be married. The object of these affections was Laura Sabbatini, a highly respectable young woman living with her mother in Berkhamsted. On 7 January 1892 Cream sailed for Canada, leaving Laura waiting. He returned to England aboard the *Britannic*, reaching London on 2 April. The brief respite was over.

It was over most specifically for twenty-one-year-old Alice Marsh and eighteen-year-old Emma Shrivell, two street girls up from Brighton, and currently lodging at 118 Stamford Street, south London. At about 1.45 a.m. on 12 April, PC George Cumley was on his Stamford Street beat when he saw a man being shown out of the door of No. 118 by a young woman. The picture was to remain in his memory, for not two hours later behind those same doors, two young women died with great suffering from strychnine poisoning.

Thomas Cream's madness must have struck him again now, for he lapsed into a series of unaccountable and slanderous attacks upon the reputation of one of his neighbours. There happened to be lodged at 103 Lambeth Palace Road one Walter Joseph Harper, a medical student at nearby St Thomas's and son of the respected Dr Joseph Harper of Barnstaple. To their mutual landlady, Miss Sleaper, Cream suddenly broke the news that young Harper was the author of the Stamford Street atrocities. Miss Sleaper's reaction was that Cream was a lunatic and the matter lapsed, until the 26 April, when Dr Joseph Harper received a letter (accompanied, inexplicably, by a newspaper cutting relating to Ellen Donworth's death) declaring that the correspondent, 'W.H. Murray', held incontestable proof that his son Walter had poisoned the Misses Marsh and Shrivell, and that for the consideration of £1,500 the writer was prepared to suppress it. 'Murray' further made it plain that if Harper was unwilling to find the money, the 'evidence' would be offered to the police on the same terms. Quite rightly, the doctor ignored this ludicrous threat and apparently Cream lost interest in the extortion.

Whether driven by clinical insanity or by a desperate, illogical desire to be associated with his own crimes, Cream began now to boast about his familiarity with the murders. To one man, John Haynes, he not only revealed far more than he should reasonably have known of the events, but actually took Haynes on a guided tour of the murder spots. To another acquaintance, McIntyre, Cream's uncommon knowledge proved of even greater interest – because his full title was Police Sergeant McIntyre, and he promptly set a watch on the doctor's movements. On 12 May, and quite by chance, Constable Cumley saw Cream and recognised him as the man leaving the scene of the Stamford Street murders, and he too put a tail on Cream. The attempt to blackmail Dr Harper came to light, and with Harper's cooperation in pressing charges, Cream was picked up.

At 5.25 p.m. on 3 June 1892, Inspector Tunbridge confronted him in Lambeth Palace Road and put him under arrest. Cream's response was typical of the irritating arrogance that was to tell so heavily against him at his trial: 'You have got the wrong man', he said, 'but fire away!'

By the time Cream was ready to be charged with attempted blackmail, Matilda Clover's body had been lifted from the soil and analysed. At the inquest on her death, the jury brought in the following verdict: 'We are unanimously agreed that Matilda Clover died of strychnine poisoning and that the poison was administered by Thomas Neill Cream with intent to destroy life.'

Cream stood for trial at the Old Bailey on 17 October 1892 before Mr Justice Hawkins, charged with the murder of Matilda Clover. Three days later the 'Hanging Judge' added another capital sentence to his long record.

Still unable to believe that he could be so badly used, Thomas Neill Cream stepped on to the scaffold at Newgate on 15 November to drop into eternal infamy.

By way of a postscript, Cream is said to have cried out as the hangman drew the bolt: 'I am Jack . . .' His eligibility for the identity of the Ripper is quite improbable, which is no doubt why the rumour has persisted (see **'Jack the Ripper'**).

CUMMINS, Gordon Frederick Cummins' murderous activities on the streets of London during 1942 have rightly earned him the title of the 'Wartime Jack the Ripper'. Like Jack, Cummins picked up women on the streets, killed them and inflicted terrible sexual mutilation on their bodies. Unlike the Ripper who terrorised Queen Victoria's London leaving no clue as to his identity, this twenty-five-year-old RAF cadet left enough evidence behind to ensure his arrest and certain conviction. He killed four times, and would certainly have continued, for he made a fifth and sixth attempt before he was captured.

The body of the first victim, a chemist's assistant named Evelyn Hamilton, was found in an air-raid shelter (this was during the Blitz) in the early hours of 9 February 1942; she had been strangled and her scarf had been wound tightly round her nose and mouth as a gag. Marks on the throat suggested that the killer was left-handed; a significant deduction as it transpired.

Cummins struck again the following night, Tuesday the 10th, and this time the victim was a thirty-five-year-old former Windmill showgirl Evelyn Oatley (otherwise known as Nita Ward). Mrs Oatley was murdered in her flat in London's Soho; she had been strangled like the previous victim, and her body was cruelly mutilated with a tin-opener. The fingerprints on the implement were those of a left hand, though not one known to the police since the Fingerprint Bureau could find no match on their files. The panic created among women at the thought of an apparently insane butcher at large on the streets of a city during the total darkness of a wartime blackout can only be imagined.

On 13 February the body of Margaret Lowe – or 'Pearl' as she was known on the streets – was found in her 'office', the small flat she used to entertain clients in Gosfield Street; one of her silk stockings was still tied tightly round her neck. Once again the corpse had been subjected to unimaginable mutilation and once again there were traces of the same left-hand fingerprints.

Within hours the police had another body on their hands, that of Mrs Doris Jouannet, the wife of a hotel manager. She had been strangled and slashed in her flat in Paddington. The attacks were getting to be uncomfortably frequent and for an unbelievable third time on the same night, this modern Jack the Ripper struck in the same small area of London's West End. Within hours of the murder of Mrs Jouannet, Cummins had imposed himself on a young woman in Piccadilly; when she gave him the cold shoulder, the Ripper followed, pushed her into a shop doorway and seized her by the throat. The woman collapsed unconscious and was saved only by the timely approach of a passer-by who scared the attacker off. In fact Gordon Cummins was in such a hurry to get away that he left behind his Air Force issue gas-respirator.

At the very time this fortunate victim was recovering from her ordeal, Cummins was on his way with another woman to her flat in Paddington where he later tried to strangle her. Perhaps he was losing his determination, or perhaps his luck had just run out, because the woman proved to be more than a match for her attacker, breaking free from his strangler's grip and arousing the best part of the neighbour-hood with her screaming. In his haste to escape, Cummins this time left behind his RAF uniform belt.

From the belt and the respirator – which bore the owner's Air Force number, 525987 – police routinely identified Gordon Frederick Cummins. Cummins, whose fingerprints proved a match for those deposited at the scenes of his crimes, was taken into custody and charged with four murders. Police officers had by this time recovered a number of items belonging to his victims from Cummins' billet in St John's Wood.

Gordon Cummins was tried at the Old Bailey only for the murder of Evelyn Hamilton (it was a common practice to select just one of a series of charges if a conviction was assured); he was found guilty by the jury and sentenced to death by Mr Justice Asquith. The 'Wartime Jack the Ripper' was hanged at Wandsworth Prison on 25 June 1942.

It is possible that Gordon Cummins was also responsible for two similar unsolved murders committed in London a year before the attack on Evelyn Hamilton. In October 1941, nineteen-year-old Maple Church was strangled and robbed at Hampstead, and Mrs Edith Humphries was bludgeoned to death at her home in Regent's Park – both locations are less than a mile from where Gordon Cummins had his billet in St John's Wood.

D

DAHMER, Jeffrey L. 'THE CANNIBAL', shrieked one London daily tabloid; the size of print was so large that it only allowed a cropped mug-shot of Dahmer alongside. The story opened, 'This is the face of cannibal killer Jeffrey Dahmer – the twisted beast who butchered, cooked and ate his victims.'

It had been on the previous evening, 24 July 1991, that the news broke. Thirty-one-year-old Dahmer had been taken into custody in Milwaukee, Wisconsin. Shortly before, police had been alerted by a terrified teenager, still in handcuffs, who had just escaped from a nearby apartment where he had been lured by a man offering him beer. When he reached the flat the boy had been manacled and, but for his lucky escape, was about to be slaughtered with a butcher's knife.

A search of the stinking flat at 213 Oxford Apartments in a run-down district of the city, revealed to investigating officers a sight more gruesome than any could remember seeing. Nine severed heads were found – two in the refrigerator, seven in various stages of having flesh boiled off the skull. Four male torsos had been wedged into a barrel, and several pieces of male genitalia had been stored in a pot. The apartment was littered with scraps of human bodies and limbs, and the smell of putrefaction was unbearable. One officer was reported as saying, 'You think you have seen it all out here, then something like this happens.'

After a blubbering apology: 'Please tell the world I am sorry for what I have done,' Jeffrey Dahmer settled down to make his confession. It had been his pattern to pick up his prey in shopping malls or around gay bars and take them back to Oxford Apartments. Here the victims would be drugged, strangled and gradually dismembered – some still alive. During the course of these dissections, Dahmer took photographs and video-tapes of his handiwork.

While Dahmer was confessing to eleven killings (the police estimated as many as eighteen over the previous two years), anxious relatives of missing young men began a vigil outside the apartment block where the cannibal had lived. Inside, forensic scientists in protective overalls and breathing apparatus continued to search among the rotting human debris for evidence of identity. Neighbours recalled for the benefit of anybody who would listen, how they had frequently been disturbed by the sounds of scuffling and banging and screaming from number 213; and how when they had complained about the foul smell coming from his flat, Dahmer had explained that his freezer cabinet had broken down and the meat was beginning to rot.

Meanwhile, details of this apparently 'harmless', 'quiet', 'polite' young man's background were beginning to emerge. Not unusually in cases of sex-oriented serial murder, Dahmer had arrived at the ultimate crime via a series of lesser sexual offences against children, including indecently exposing himself; he had been released from prison on probation in 1989 after being convicted of abusing a thirteen-year-old boy. At the time of the trial for this offence Dahmer's father had asked the probation service to provide Jeffrey with psychiatric treatment; and from as far back as his school days, fellow pupils remembered him as 'just generally one weird dude'.

On 26 July, Jeffrey Dahmer appeared before Judge Frank Crivello at Milwaukee County Court; he stood charged on four counts of murder, though the police had already identified no less than nine victims. Furthermore, the German police were anxious to interview Dahmer in connection with a series of seven brutal unsolved murders committed within a thirty-mile radius of his camp when Dahmer was serving with the US army at Mainz.

The fact that all Dahmer's victims came from among the ethnic minorities predictably fuelled accusations by the black and Hispanic communities that the police were less than rigorous when investigating reports of their missing and molested children; the family of one victim went as far as to file a $3 million lawsuit against the city and its police, charging them with racism and negligence.

Jeffrey Dahmer – already awarded the title 'Milwaukee Monster' – underwent psychiatric evaluation in the county jail and it was expected, at the time of writing, that he would stand trial late in 1991.

DEAN, Minnie   Born in Edinburgh, Scotland, in 1847, Williamina was an early immigrant to New Zealand. She arrived at East Winton, some nineteen miles from Invercargill, in 1865, and shortly after married Charles Dean. Minnie settled down to rural domesticity in a modest shack that the Deans had cobbled together themselves and called 'The Larches', with a flower garden that became the envy of Minnie's neighbours.

To supplement Dean's by no means reliable income, Minnie decided to take up the profitable side-line of baby farming – not always the sinister occupation that it became at the hands of such practitioners as Mrs **Dyer**. Whether through bad luck or inadequate care, one of her adoptees, young May Irene, died in her charge; as did six-week-old Bertha in 1891. Although the deaths were certified as due to 'natural causes', the medical authorities were far from happy about the squalid conditions in which the children were kept, and in her future advertising, Minnie thought it wise to use a number of aliases.

In April 1895, a reply to one of Minnie's advertisements (taken out in the name of Cameron), in the New Zealand *Timaru Herald*, left her in charge of a one-month-old baby, for the care of which she received £4 from a Mrs Hornsby. When the child disappeared after having been seen in Minnie Dean's arms in a railway carriage, awkward questions began to be asked, and Minnie denied ever having set eyes on the child – a lie quickly exposed by the discovery of the mite's clothing at 'The Larches'.

When Minnie and her husband had been placed under arrest, detectives began a more thorough search of the Dean household and 'estate' – in particular the newly turned patches of earth among Minnie's prize chrysanthemums into which cut flowers had been inexplicably pushed in imitation of their growing neighbours. Beneath the scented blooms, in a shallow grave, were two small bodies – one the recently missing baby's. From under the dahlia patch the almost skeletal remains of a third child was unearthed. An autopsy confirmed that one of the children had died from morphia poisoning and quantities of that drug were found about the house.

It had been established early on in the inquiry that Minnie's husband was forbidden to so much as cut a flower from the garden, let alone dig there, and it was a fair assumption that he was as genuinely concerned about the mysterious child-deaths as anybody else. So, on 18 June 1895, Minnie Dean faced her trial alone in the dock at Invercargill Supreme Court. She was found guilty of murder, and though protesting her innocence to the end, on 12 August Minnie Dean became the first and last woman to be hanged in New Zealand. A reporter for *The Times* described how Mrs Dean went to the scaffold: 'without flinch or falter; she died a brave, a wonderful woman'.

'DEATH ANGEL KILLINGS' *see* 'ZEBRA'

DEEMING, Frederick Deeming had been born in Liverpool around 1854, the youngest of seven children, and became a polymath among criminals, seeming to have left no crooked path untrod – bigamist, confidence trickster, swindler, thief and later multiple murderer. A broadly travelled rascal, Deeming, under a variety of aliases, plied his trade around Australia, South Africa, Aden, South America and Belgium.

In the year 1891, using the pseudonym 'Albert O. Williams', Deeming took up residence at Rainhill, a town to the east of his native Liverpool, celebrated as the location of the railway locomotive trials of 1829 won by Stephenson's *Rocket*. Deeming was posing as the agent of a 'Baron Brook' for whom he was seeking a suitable residential property. An arrangement was made with a Mrs Mather that 'Williams' should move into her empty Dinham Villa rent-free in order to prepare for the Baron's occupancy. He also began to court

Mrs Mather's daughter Emily. The latter diversion proved rather premature when Mrs Deeming and the four Deeming children arrived to stay. Nevertheless, Emily seemed prepared to believe that Maria Deeming was Frederick's sister who was about to 'join her husband abroad'. It was at about this time Deeming suggested that the floorboards at the villa would sit more evenly on a layer of cement; Mrs Mather saw no reason to object and Deeming got on with the job; this must have been the last time that Maria and the children were seen. Alive.

Still using the alias 'Williams', Deeming thought now to return to Australia, and having told Mrs Mather that the Baron no longer required accommodation, and having married her daughter, Deeming set sail for Melbourne with Emily. They arrived at the beginning of December 1891. By the 20th of the month poor Emily was lying in eternal rest beneath the newly cemented hearth of their furnished home in Andrew Street, and Deeming was on his way up to Southern Cross. It was here that he was arrested in March 1892 after the owner of the Andrew Street house had finally tracked down the offensive smell that seemed to be coming from the floor.

No sooner had the Melbourne police begun to look into Deeming's English activities, than their English counterparts began to piece together the trail that ended under the cement floor at Dinham Villa. For one lady at least this was all most timely, because Frederick Deeming (or 'Baron Swanton' as he now was) had just become engaged to Miss Katie Rounsefell.

At his trial in Melbourne in May 1892, Deeming was defended by Mr Alfred Deakin, later to be elected Prime Minister of Australia; on this occasion, though, the jury voted decisively against Deakin's defence that his client was insane.

Frederick Deeming stood on the scaffold calmly smoking his last cigar on 23 May 1892, watched by a large congregation of journalists and officials until he was eventually executed by the heavily disguised hangman and his assistant. Outside the prison gates a concourse of 10,000 people waited for news of Deeming's death.

DE MELKER, Daisy Louisa It was the obituary notice in the *Rand Daily Mail* in March 1932 that attracted Alfred Sproat's attention; and it was the reason why, after a little reflection, he wrote to the police authorities at Germiston, in the Transvaal.

The obituary was commemorating the death of Rhodes Cecil Cowle, only surviving child of Mrs Daisy De Melker, Sproat's former sister-in-law. In his letter, Alfred Sproat drew attention to the suspiciously bad luck enjoyed by Mrs De Melker in losing yet another close member of her family. His own brother Robert had been Daisy's second husband and had died five years previously on 6 November 1927. Her first husband, William Alfred Cowle (Rhodes' father), had also died suddenly in January 1923. In addition, counting Rhodes, all five of their children had also passed away long before their time.

The Johannesburg police commenced an investigation and discovered that Rhodes Cowle and his mother had regularly quarrelled over the question of his father's estate, which Rhodes thought he should inherit on attaining the age of twenty-one. He was a surly and deeply unpleasant youth, fond of threatening suicide to get his own way, and not above dealing his mother a few hefty blows during their increasingly frequent disagreements.

Detectives then questioned the doctors who had attended the deceased; they agreed that, although they had certified the deaths as due to natural causes, they could just as easily have been due to poisoning. In April 1932, a decision was made to exhume the bodies of Rhodes and William Cowle and Robert Sproat, and on the 19th all three were dug up and subjected to post-mortem examination. Arsenic was found in Rhodes Cowle's body and minute traces of strychnine in his father's and Robert Sproat's.

A warrant was immediately issued for the arrest of Daisy De Melker, and she was charged with murder even though at this time there was no evidence linking her with the purchase or possession of poisons. However, following extensive newspaper publicity a chemist named Spilkin, of Rose Henville, came forward and identified Daisy as having purchased arsenic from him six days before the death of Rhodes Cowle.

Mrs De Melker was tried before Mr Justice Greenburg and two assessors (in this instance Mr J.M. Graham and Mr A.A. Stanford, both experienced senior magistrates). The trial lasted thirty days (then the longest trial of a European in the legal history of the Union of South Africa) and Daisy spent a total of more than eighteen hours in the witness box. One man closely involved with her defence, Henry Harris Morris KC has described Mrs De Melker under cross-examination, 'She spoke rapidly and with animation; when in difficulties or on the defensive, her voice was raised in a whining pitch which gave the impression that she was not telling the truth . . . Her most striking feature was her mouth, which was strongly suggestive of a cruel disposition. She seemed almost incapable of emotion.'

Which is more than could be said for the general public, some of whom went so far in their disapprobation as to send Daisy De Melker letters threatening that if the hangman didn't get her, then unnamed assassins would. There was no need for lynch law as it turned out, for though the charges of poisoning her husbands remained unproven, Daisy was convicted of poisoning her son.

Mr Justice Greenberg pronounced judgement: 'Daisy Louisa Melker, this court has come to the decision that you are guilty of the crime of having administered poison to your son and murdering him. There is only one sentence I can pass. Whether that sentence will be carried into execution or not is a matter with which I have nothing to do; that rests with the Governor-General in Council, who will decide whether the sentence is to be carried out or not after having considered all the records in the case together with a report from the prosecutor and myself. But in the meantime the only sentence I can pass on you is that you be taken back to custody and that you be hanged by the neck until you are dead.'

It was a sentence which, in the case of a poisoner, was never commuted in South Africa. With what was reported as 'rare courage and fortitude', Daisy De Melker was hanged in Pretoria Central Prison on 30 December 1932.

And there the official story of Daisy De Melker ends, but there is a suspicion – and however strong, it can only ever be just that – that Daisy was responsible for a further seven deaths. Three of these were said to have taken place in Rhodesia, and officers from that country's police force were on hand at her trial to arrest Mrs De Melker in the event of an acquittal.

DENKE, Karl Except that he appears to have been one of the nastiest of a nasty bunch of German mass murderers and cannibals (see also **Grossmann, Haarmann** and **Kurten**) we know less of Denke's crimes than we might if he had been put on trial, and his whole life history paraded before the court.

We first encounter Denke as the landlord of a cheap lodging-house at Munsterberg in Silesia (now called Ziebice, in Poland). The Great War had come, for Germany at least, to an unsatisfactory conclusion a few years earlier, leaving the country in the grip of near-famine. According to one account, Karl Denke's little reign of terror came to an end in the December of 1924, when he was interrupted in the process of murdering a young traveller who had been staying over-night at the house. A search made by the police who had come to arrest Denke revealed a bag full of various identity papers, an assortment of clothing, and a ledger recording a succession of travellers, tramps and beggars who had entered the house as lodgers and never re-emerged. It was easy to see why, for in the cellar of the building were two great brine vats filled with pickled human cutlets, as well as several pots of 'dripping' and a collection of bones; in all, parts of thirty men and women – the rest had already provided nourishment for Denke and those of his guests who survived their night at the inn.

A religious man, who tended the organ in his local church, Karl Denke was perhaps overcome with remorse, which may be why he hanged himself with his braces in prison while awaiting trial.

DE RAIS, Gilles At the pinnacle of his power in the mid-fifteenth century, Gilles de Laval, Baron de Rais, Marshal of France, champion of the Maid of Orleans, was the wealthiest man in Europe. Sur-rounded by a bodyguard comprising the two hundred knights who had fought alongside him in the army of Joan of Arc against the

English, Gilles lived more lavishly than an emperor, perhaps than Charles VII of France himself.

To increase his wealth still further, and to replace that frittered away on a profligate lifestyle, Gilles embarked upon an alchemical search for the elusive 'philosopher's stone', which was believed to transmute base metals into gold. As he became increasingly bewitched by the Dark Powers, so Gilles began to sacrifice, in the time-honoured way, to his new gods and demons, building on an already notorious reputation.

And still the Baron might have remained free to continue a career of child sacrifice and sexual sadism, but for a small error of judgement, that of insulting a brother of the powerful Treasurer of Brittany, Geoffroi de Ferron, by beating and imprisoning him. Unfortunately, Jean de Ferron was also a priest and, in a civil suit, Gilles was brought before the Bishop of Nantes and the Inquisitor General of France, in September 1440, charged as a heretic. Of course, there was considerably more to the charge than met the eye – after all, Gilles de Rais had been living an heretical life for many years without interference. But here, with the watertight case of the maltreatment of a priest, was an opportunity to secure a conviction and in doing so allow all those concerned in the prosecution of the case to enjoy a share in the confiscation of Gilles de Rais' not inconsiderable wealth.

There were forty-seven charges made against Gilles de Rais arising from three categories of heresy: first, 'abuse of clerical privilege' (attacking de Ferron); second, 'the conjuration of demons'; and third, sexual perversions against children. For example, charge number fifteen read:

. . . according to the lamentable outcries, tears and wailings, and denunciations coming from many people of both sexes, crying out and complaining of the loss and death of children, the aforesaid Gilles de Rais has taken innocent boys and girls, and inhumanely butchered, killed, dismembered, burned and otherwise tortured them, and the said Gilles has immolated the bodies of the said innocents to the devils, invoked and sacrificed to evil spirits, and has foully committed the sin of sodomy with young boys and in other ways lusted against nature after young girls . . . while the innocent boys and girls were alive, or sometimes dead, or sometimes even during their death throes.

After six sittings hearing one hundred and ten witnesses, the court put Gilles de Rais and his servants to the torture to extract yet further incriminating evidence. One servant, Etienne Corillait testified that:

. . . to practise his debauches with the said boys and girls, against the dictation of nature, he first took his rod in his left or right hand and rubbed it so it became erect and sticking-out; then placed it between the limbs of the boys or girls, not bothering with the natural female receptacle, and rubbed his rod or virile member on the belly of the said boys and girls with much libidinous excitement until he emitted his sperm on their stomachs. . .

. . . after having had an orgasm . . . he had considerable pleasure in watching the heads of the children separated from their bodies. Sometimes he made an incision behind the neck to make them die slowly, at which he became very excited, and while they were bleeding to death he would sometimes masturbate on them, and sometimes he would do this after they had died and their bodies were still warm. . .

In order to stifle the cries of the children when he wished to have relations with them, he would first put a rope round their neck and hang them three feet off the floor, and just before they were dead would cause them to be taken down, telling them not to utter a word. Then he would excite his member and afterwards have an emission on their stomachs. When he had done this, he had their throats cut and their heads separated from their bodies. Sometimes he would ask, when they were dead, which of them had the most beautiful head.

Of course, even by the standards of the often ludicrous procedures of the Inquisition, the trial of Gilles de Rais was a farce. Most of the incriminating evidence was either elicited under torture or was given out of spite or self-interest. Eventually even Gilles de Rais himself succumbed to torture on 21 October 1440, and was prepared to admit whatever the court told him to admit. Two days later, at Nantes, Gilles was executed by garrotte and thrown on to a bonfire. As little could be serverd by this last indignity, his friends and family were allowed to remove his body from the pyre before it was lit.

Such truth as ever emerged from the trial of Gilles de Rais has in any case been embellished and distorted by time and fashionable prejudice. It is certain that Gilles was one of Europe's worst child rapists and killers; whether his death toll ever reached the often quoted 500 to 800 is doubtful.

DE SALVO, Albert   It ended on 4 January 1964. A reign of terror that had haunted the city of Boston since June 1962, leaving thirteen women dead, and the city with a modern legend. He would strike once more, ineffectually; but at least the killing had stopped.

Nineteen-year-old Mary Sullivan was found, like all the other victims of the killer who had become known as the 'Boston Strangler', in her own apartment. She had been stripped and bound, raped and strangled; and in a final sadistic gesture, Mary's killer had left a New Year's greeting card wedged between the toes of her left foot.

This maniac's first victim had been a fifty-five-year-old divorcee named Anna Slesers, back in June 1962. Mrs Slesers had been found by her son on the 14th, naked, raped and strangled with the belt of her own blue housecoat. The killer's method became unvarying. After targetting his victim, the Strangler gained admission to her home by posing as a workman. All his victims were women, all were sexually assaulted and all were strangled – usually with an item of their own clothing, often a pair of stockings or tights which he tied with a bow under the chin. In some cases strangulation had been accompanied by biting, bludgeoning and even stabbing. Despite the customary false confessions, and a blanket police response to the city's mounting panic, the Boston Strangler remained an enigmatic object of terror.

The Boston Strangler's thirteen victims

Date	Name	Age
14 June 1962	Anna Slesers	55
28 June 1962	Mary Mullen	85
30 June 1962	Nina Nichols	68
30 June 1962	Helen Blake	65
19 August 1962	Ida Irga	75
20 August 1962	Jane Sullivan	67
5 December 1962	Sophie Clark	20
31 December 1962	Patricia Bissette	23
9 March 1963	Mary Brown	69
6 May 1963	Beverley Samans	23
8 September 1963	Evelyn Corbin	58
23 November 1963	Joann Graff	23
4 January 1964	Mary Sullivan	19

After the murder of Helen Blake, the police enlisted the help of forensic psychiatrists to help profile the killer they were hunting. In the opinion of experts he was a youngish man, eighteen to forty, suffering delusions of persecution and with a hatred of his mother (so far only elderly women had been attacked). This 'portrait' was run alongside records of known sex offenders, and although a number of suspects emerged from the files and were interviewed, the Strangler remained free to kill Mrs Ida Irga on 19 August.

On 5 December 1962, the psychological profile of a 'mother-hater' collapsed when Sophie Clark was murdered; she was twenty years old, just three years younger than two of his next three victims. Just over a year later, after the death of Mary Sullivan, the 'father' of American psychological profiling, Dr James Brussel, provided a new 'psychofit' of a thirty-year-old man, strongly built, of average height, clean shaven with thick dark hair; possibly of Spanish or Italian origin – and a paranoid schizophrenic. It was to prove remarkably accurate.

Meanwhile another specialist used to working in the dark, Dutch psychometrist and psychic detective Peter Hurkos, had entered the investigation. After some remarkable demonstrations of intuition, Hurkos revealed that the man the police were after was slightly built weighing 130 to 140lbs, five feet seven or eight, with a pointed sharp nose and a scar on his left arm. The psychic added, 'And he loves shoes'. Unbelievably, there was just such a man on the suspect list, a perfect match down to his occupation as a ladies' shoe salesman. Unfortunately, he was not the Boston Strangler.

In the end it was for the Strangler to make himself known. On 27 October 1964 he entered, as he had done before, a young woman's apartment posing as a detective. The intruder tied his victim to the bed, sexually assaulted her, and then inexplicably left, saying as he went, 'I'm sorry.' The woman's description led to the identification of Albert De Salvo, and the publication of his photograph led to scores of women coming forward to identify him as the man who had sexually assaulted them. But De Salvo was still not suspected of being the Boston Strangler. It was only in 1965, while he was being held on a rape charge and confined to the Boston State Hospital that De Salvo confessed in detail to the Strangler's crimes. His knowledge of the murders was such that no doubt could be entertained as to the truth of his confession. Nevertheless, there was not one single piece of direct evidence to support these claims, and in a remarkable piece of plea-bargaining, De Salvo's attorney agreed that his client should stand trial only for a number of earlier crimes unconnected with the stranglings. Albert De Salvo never stood trial for the crimes of the Boston Strangler, but was instead convicted of robbery and sexual offences and sent to prison for life.

On 26 November 1973, Albert De Salvo was found dead in his cell, stabbed through the heart; he was forty-two years old.

DIAZ, Robert Robert Diaz had always wanted to be a doctor. Not a discreditable ambition for the sane, but in the fantasy world Diaz inhabited he need only pretend and he *was* a doctor.

In April 1981, the coroner of San Bernardino County, Los Angeles, received an anonymous telephone call from a woman alleging nineteen mysterious deaths occurring in the hospital at Perris. The coroner contacted the police and the police contacted the hospital. It was almost as the mystery caller had said, eleven patients had died there, and it was discovered later that a further patient had died in another hospital. None of the twelve were exactly young, their ages ranging between fifty-two and ninety-five years, but all had died suddenly, and all had exhibited an uncommonly high blood acidity. More suspicious still was the disappearance of the medical records of many patients in the intensive care unit. It did not take long for suspicion to fall on Robert Diaz. Diaz was a nurse at Perris, with access to the files kept by the hospital, and although it was by no means direct evidence other staff thought it uncanny the accuracy with which nurse Diaz could predict the deaths of patients even in the most stable condition.

Some even recalled seeing him administer unprescribed injections. It was enough to convince the police to make a search of Diaz's home, where they found quantities of the heart drug Lidocaine, some morphine and a number of syringes.

In November 1981, Robert Diaz was arrested and charged with twelve murders. The District Attorney announced that the indictment followed a number of exhumations and post-mortem examinations indicating that the deaths of the hospital patients had resulted from an overdose of Lidocaine administered during a twelve-day period in which Diaz was attending patients in the capacity of nurse.

In response, Robert Diaz, through his solicitor, issued a multi-million dollar legal suit against the authorities alleging defamation of character and violation of civil rights.

Not that it made any difference. At his trial in March 1984, there was sufficient evidence to find Robert Diaz guilty of all twelve murders and he was sentenced to die in the gas chamber. If California ever renews its programme of executions, Diaz will be found on Death Row waiting his turn; the attorney for the prosecution had already written Diaz's epitaph in court: 'He committed these murders for his own entertainment and amusement while playing doctor.'

'DOORBELL KILLER' *see* SZCZEPINSKI, Waldemar

DOSS, Nannie   A prolific familicide, Nannie Doss of Tulsa, Oklahoma, notched up at least eleven murders including five husbands, her mother, two sisters and two of her children.

Her first marriage was to George Frazer, in 1920, though Nannie's numerous affairs, conducted in the pursuit of 'Mr Right', did little to cement the union. The final straw for George was when he came home from work to find his two children lying dead on the floor – 'accidentally' poisoned. Not waiting around to see who might be next, Frazer wisely took a speedy leave of his wife. Husband number two, Frank Harrelson, died of 'stomach trouble' later the same year. Arlie Lanning lasted a bit longer – from 1947 until his death from 'stomach trouble' in 1952. A comfortable insurance of $1500 ensured that marriage to Richard Morton lasted no longer than necessary, and finally Nannie's fifth husband, Samuel Doss, contracted 'stomach trouble' after eating a bowl of his wife's stewed prunes. In this last case, Nannie came up against a more painstaking doctor, who not only refused to sign a death certificate but insisted on an autopsy and called in the police. When post-mortem examination proved without the least doubt that Sam Doss had died of a massive dose of arsenic, Nannie confessed all.

Nevertheless, the defiant Mrs Doss who had freely admitted her misdeeds, indignantly denied the prosecution attorney's suggestion at her trial that she had murdered solely out of greed. It had been, she insisted, a search for true love: 'I was looking for the perfect mate, the real romance of life.' Nannie Doss was convicted and sentenced to life imprisonment in 1964. She died in prison of leukemia the following year.

DRENTH, Herman (aka Harry Powers)   Drenth was an American 'Bluebeard' killer who is thought to have deceived and murdered around fifty women in a home-built, sound-proof concrete gas chamber.

During the late 1920s, Drenth was addicted to reading those newspaper classified advertisements in which middle-aged widows and spinsters sought husbands. Using a variety of *noms de guerre* Drenth built a thriving business courting (and if necessary marrying) these lonely hearts for the cynical purpose of self-enrichment. Having lured the prey to his hideaway, rustically named Quiet Dell, in West Virginia, Drenth would introduce them to one of his execution chambers. Much later, under arrest, he confided to the police that quite apart from the financial advantage, the thought of his victims' death agonies filled him with intense sexual gratification.

Drenth was courting under the name of Cornelius O. Pierson in 1931, and the lady's name was Mrs Aster Buick Eicher, a widow from Park Ridge, Illinois. Mrs Eicher had been blessed with three children during her marriage, daughters aged fourteen and nine, and a twelve-year-old son. Leaving the children with a friend, Pierson took his 'bride' on a honeymoon from which she never returned. Drenth picked the children up, paid the friend for her services and took the mites away. His cheque bounced, and the children were never heard of again, causing the friend such anxiety that she reported Drenth to the police.

Meanwhile Cornelius O. Pierson was engaged on his next amour. Mrs Dorothy Lemke of Worcester, Massachusetts. When the police searched Mrs Eicher's home and found a letter from 'Pierson' addressed from a post office box number in Clarksburg, West Virginia, the post office was put under surveillance and eventually Drenth was detained while collecting his mail. Under questioning he at first lamented that dear Mrs Eicher had deceived him and with her children had eloped with another man. A farmer living in the neighbourhood read of Drenth's arrest and reported the strange structure that their prisoner had built a couple of years earlier. When the building and surrounding land was searched, a ring identified as belonging to Mrs Eicher was found, and when the garden was turned over, there were the bodies of the lady herself and her three children; the children had been beaten to death with a hammer. Drenth admitted killing Mrs Eicher and her children and also Mrs Lemke, but confronted with a collection of items that clearly had more than one female owner, he would only say, 'You've got me now on five, what good would fifty more do?'

No traces of any more bodies were found, and Herman Drenth was convicted of murder, sentenced to death and hanged on 18 March 1932.

DUFF–SIDNEY CASE   The first to die had been fifty-nine-year-old Edmund Creighton Duff, a retired civil servant with the colonial office in Nigeria, then residing in South Hill Park Road, South Croydon. He had suffered a short illness and then passed away on the night of 27 April 1928. Mr Duff's death certificate attributed his decease to a failure of the heart muscle, and a post-mortem revealed nothing to contradict this conclusion.

Before another year had passed, Duff's unmarried sister-in-law Vera Sidney, who lived in nearby Birdhurst Rise, had also died, on 15 February 1929, after a brief illness. In Vera Sidney's case, the death was less explicable – she had been only forty years old, and was known to be very careful about her health. Death was, nevertheless, certified as due to 'gastric influenza'.

Three weeks later Vera's mother, Mrs Violet Emily Sidney, with whom she had lived, died suddenly and unexpectedly. This time the doctor refused to issue a death certificate which, in view of the lethal traces of arsenic later found in the old lady's medicine, was a wise decision – especially when the exhumation and a second autopsy on the remains of Edmund Duff revealed similar traces of poison.

The inquests on all three deaths were held consecutively over a period of five months, during which the sheer logistical problems of such a lengthy inquiry resulted in confusion and error. One quite extraordinary revelation concerned the original post-mortem carried out on Edmund Duff shortly after his death. It seems that the organs taken from Duff's body for analysis (a common procedure) had been mixed up with the viscera removed from another body, thus unwittingly delaying the ends of justice.

Although the inevitable conclusion of the inquest was that poison had most likely been administered in food and medicine, and therefore suspicion might fall on a member of the family or close friends, the case remains officially unsolved. Edmund Duff's widow, Grace, enjoyed brief notoriety when the finger of suspicion momentarily rested on her, but otherwise the once-celebrated 'Croydon Poisoning Mystery' was relegated to a dark corner in history.

However, there has never been any shortage of theories, and as recently as 1975 that incomparable armchair sleuth, Mr Richard Whittington-Egan, assembled his own very convincing case against Mrs Grace Duff. In a painstaking re-examination of the murders we learned of the love affair that Grace was having with a local doctor and her need to dispose of a now unwanted spouse. We learned also of her desire to inherit prematurely the estates of Vera and Violet Sidney – respectively Grace's sister and mother. It is unlikely, though, that this will be the last word on the mystery.

DUFFY, John Francis Known throughout the long investigation into his three murders as the 'Railway Killer', Duffy was the first criminal in English legal history to be identified by the procedure known as psychological offender profiling (POP).

A petty criminal described variously as 'weak', 'immature', 'lazy', 'lying', 'insignificant' and 'almost invisible', John Duffy nevertheless compensated for his inadequacies by throwing a blanket of fear over the activities of young women around north London and parts of the Home Counties. And far from describing him as 'insignificant', Duffy's wife told an Old Bailey jury how he had become 'a raving madman with scary, scary eyes' (he was also nicknamed by the press 'The Man with the Laser Eyes'), who used to tie her up before sex and frequently bragged, 'Rape is a natural thing for a man to do.'

The first attack that has been linked to Duffy was a rape in 1982, during which two men attacked a twenty-three-year-old woman in Hampstead, close to the North London Link railway line. It was the first of a four-year series of rapes, in eighteen of which Duffy worked with a so-far unnamed and uncharged accomplice. In July 1985 there were three violent attacks in a single night and the police, frustrated by lack of progress, launched 'Operation Hart', which was to develop into the most comprehensive manhunt in Britain since the search for the Yorkshire Ripper (see **Sutcliffe**), and involved officers from four forces – Scotland Yard, Surrey, Hertfordshire and the British Transport Police.

In the following month, August, John Duffy was arrested and charged with offences involving violence, but quite unconnected with the 'railway rapes'. Against police recommendations, Duffy was released on bail. Nevertheless due to the nature of the crimes he was routinely entered on the suspect file of Operation Hart.

Shortly after his release, Duffy attacked another young woman in north London, who in her confused 'rape trauma' condition was unable to bring herself to identify her attacker until December of the following year. By that time he had killed three times.

On 29 December 1985, John Duffy dragged nineteen-year-old secretary Alison Day off an east London train and took her to a squalid block of garages in Hackney where he garrotted her with what is known as a 'Spanish windlass', a kind of tourniquet favoured by carpenters (the trade Duffy once followed) for holding wood tightly together. Seventeen days later Miss Day's body was recovered from the River Lea.

The connection was not finally made with the 'Railway Rapist' until three months later, when a fifteen-year-old schoolgirl, Maartje Tamboezer, was killed on her way to the shops in West Horsley, Surrey. Duffy had tried to remove clues by burning his victim's body, but left semen traces and a set of uncommonly small footprints (it later transpired that Duffy had always been sensitive about his diminutive five feet four inches). At this point information on the two murders was included in the computer-based files of Operation Hart, and the hunt was accelerated.

On 18 May 1986, Mrs Anne Lock, who worked for London Weekend Television, disappeared on her way home from the studios; her body was not found until July.

In the meantime, forensic scientists had been working on eliminating suspects from the Operation Hart file by matching blood samples from Maartje Tamboezer's body with those on the suspect list. The register of more than 5000 was thus reduced to 1999 men, of whom John Duffy was No. 1505. Duffy was interviewed in July but refused (as was his right) to provide a blood sample, and after bribing a friend to 'mug' him, put himself voluntarily into a psychiatric hospital to recover from the trauma.

Psychological profiling was a relatively unknown technique, in Britain at least, in the arsenal of weapons being made available by the rapidly emerging science of forensic psychiatry. Increasingly concerned by their own lack of progress, the police enlisted the professional help of Professor David Canter, an expert in behavioural science and professor of applied psychology at Surrey University. Canter carefully built up a projectural profile of the Railway Killer based on statistical analysis of police witness statements. From these reports, Professor Canter was able to make deductions such as that the killer lived in the Kilburn/Cricklewood area of north-west London, was married, childless (this turned out to be a particular source of anguish to Duffy) and surrounded by domestic disharmony.

In all, Professor Canter's profile was to prove accurate in thirteen out of its seventeen points; he explained, 'A criminal leaves evidence of his personality through his actions in relation to a crime. Any person's behaviour exhibits characteristics unique to that person, as well as patterns and consistencies which are typical of the sub-group to which he or she belongs.'

While the police were awaiting David Canter's report, Duffy struck again. This time the victim was a fourteen-year-old girl who was blindfolded before her ordeal. During the struggle this mask slipped and she caught a glimpse of her attacker; why Duffy did not kill the girl is inexplicable on the basis of his former *modus operandi*. When the psychological profile was run alongside the computer file of Operation Hart it came up with the name that officers had been waiting years for: John Francis Duffy. After a short period of intensive surveillance, Duffy was arrested at his mother's home where scene-of-crime officers recovered sufficient forensic clues to build a watertight case against him.

John Duffy's trial took place during the first two months of 1988. He offered a weak and unsuccessful defence of amnesia, and on 26 February Mr Justice Farquarson, who described him as 'little more than a predatory animal who behaved in a beastly, degrading and disgusting way' sentenced Duffy to seven life sentences adding the recommendation that he serve at least thirty years. His Lordship added, 'You should not depend on that being the total amount of time you will serve.'

In the case of Anne Lock, Mr Justice Farquarson had directed the jury to return a verdict of not guilty on account of insufficient evidence.

DUMOLLARD, Martin and Marie As awful an example of the 'killer couple' as one could hope to find, Martin and Marie Dumollard farmed a patch of land near Lyons, capital of France's Rhône *departement*. They were helped in their endeavours by a succession of servant girls, none of whom lasted long in service and, as far as anybody could remember, most of whom were never seen again.

In 1855, the body of a girl who had been stabbed to death was found close to the Dumollards' cottage, and as she had been working for him, Martin Dumollard was a prime suspect. However, without the evidence even to make an arrest, the case quickly passed into local history and Dumollard was back at the employment agency recruiting a replacement. In fact, Monsieur proved to be an excellent customer, and between the end of the 1840s and 1861 upwards of twenty young women had crossed the Dumollards' threshold; at least ten of them died there, the rest made a hasty and lucky escape.

Once a girl had been installed in the house, Madame Dumollard would routinely inspect her modest possessions for any useful garments to keep back for her own adornment, making a note of the value of the remainder for future reference. Then it was Dumollard's turn, when the fancy took him, to dispatch the unfortunate girl, usually by a swift blow or two to the head, and to dispose of the remains – by burial if time and climate permitted, otherwise consigned without ceremony to the waters of the river Rhône. After removing any unsightly bloodstains, Marie Dumollard would distribute the victim's clothing between her own wardrobe and the bundle that was periodically sold off.

Events might have followed this pattern for many years to come had Martin Dumollard not decided to cut out the middle-man and go into recruitment on his own behalf. The object of this enterprise was Marie Pichon. While visiting Lyons, Dumollard approached the girl claiming to be employed at a nearby château and charged with the job of finding a suitable housemaid at a generous salary – she, lucky girl, would fit the requirements perfectly. As they hiked together out of town, Mademoiselle Pichon became increasingly apprehensive and after a few kilometres insisted on returning to town. Dumollard, by way of reply, took out a rope from his pocket and tried to lassoo the girl. Determined and cunning as she had previously been perceptive, Marie escaped the farmer's clutches and ran to a nearby farm from whence the authorities were alerted as to her recent and terrifying experience. Shocked as she was, Marie Pichon was able to identify

Martin Dumollard, not one of nature's more attractive offspring, and described as 'a strong and brutal peasant, with a large nose, thick lips, hollow eyes and bushy eyebrows, with a beard fringing his hard features' (his equally unlovely wife was 'thin and slight, with shifty eyes and a cunning face').

When the Dumollards' home was searched, and piles of female clothing found tied in bundles, Madame decided that self-preservation would be a stronger suit to play than loyalty, and immediately denounced her husband as a murderer. Dumollard later identified a number of makeshift graves and some remains were recovered for decent burial. The farmer and his wife were put on trial at Bourg in January 1862, with a howling mob baying around the court for their blood. To the sorrow, it seemed, of none, Martin Dumollard was executed on the guillotine on 8 March 1862, while Marie was condemned to a life serving on the galleys.

'DUSSELDORF DOUBLES KILLER' *see* BOOST, Werner

DYER, Amelia Elizabeth   Early spring 1896, and a barge is making its leisurely way up the Thames. The bargeman's lazy gaze takes in a brown-paper parcel lying on waste ground by the towpath, and stretching out his punt-hook to catch it up, the unfortunate man is treated to the unwelcome sight of a baby's leg protruding from the soggy wrapping.

In the more appropriate surroundings of a mortuary the parcel was peeled of its several layers, among which a sheet of paper was found bearing an address: 'Mrs Harding, 20 Wigotts Road, Caversham'. When this vital clue had been removed the body of a baby girl was revealed, a piece of tape knotted tightly round her tiny neck.

Inspector Anderson checked the Caversham address only to find that there was no Wigotts Road; however, there had been a Mrs Harding living at *Pigott's* Road and she had moved to Reading to live with her daughter Mary Ann and son-in-law Arthur Palmer. The Palmers had departed for London, though neighbours saw Mrs Harding leaving the house carrying a carpet bag on the morning following the bargeman's discovery; the detective also learned that Harding had been in the habit of adopting children.

Anderson now arranged for a young woman of his acquaintance to visit the Harding home with the story that she was looking to have a baby adopted. She was greeted on the doorstep by a crone of very advanced years calling herself 'Granny Smith'. The old woman was sure that Mrs Harding would be interested in the proposition, and a meeting was arranged two days afterwards.

Accordingly, Mrs Harding met the spy, and consented to take the child for a fee of £100, no questions asked. The transaction was to take place under cover of dark on the following evening.

But it was not a young woman and infant child that knocked at the door – it was Inspector Anderson and Sergeant James, who sufficiently intimidated Mrs Harding that she confided her real name was Dyer, Amelia Elizabeth Dyer. Anderson wrote later, 'In a cupboard under the stairs we found a quantity of baby clothing, and noticed a most unpleasant odour, as if some decomposing substance had been kept there. Doubtless, as subsequent events showed, the body of a little child had been concealed in this cupboard for some days before being taken out and disposed of.'

On 2 April Mrs Dyer was charged with murder, and despite two attempts to end her own life, once with a pair of scissors and once with her own bootlace, remanded to face trial.

By now the river was being dragged, and on 8 April the decomposing body of a male baby was pulled out; two days later a carpet bag was dragged up containing two more bodies. A ten-month-old baby was next to be taken from the river bed, and a week later, at the end of April, another boy was recovered.

Amelia Dyer, then fifty-seven years old, appeared before Mr Justice Hawkins at the Old Bailey on 21 and 22 March 1896. Through her attorney, Mrs Dyer acknowledged her guilt, but attempted to set up a defence of insanity. Dr Logan of the Gloucester Asylum testified that he considered her to be suffering from delusions (one of which was that birds spoke to her), and Dr Forbes Winslow agreed that she suffered delusional insanity complicated by depression and melancholia.

For the prosecution, Dr Scott said that as medical officer of Holloway Prison, where he had the opportunity of observing the prisoner, it was his belief that any delusions were feigned. The jury obviously agreed, since it took them a bare five minutes to find Amelia Dyer both guilty *and* sane; she drew her last breath on 10 June, on the scaffold at Newgate Gaol.

Mrs Dyer never revealed how many children she had murdered – if indeed she even remembered – but she did confide with some satisfaction, 'You'll know mine by the tape round their necks.'

A Note on Baby Farming

It is a fact that every period of history has its own characteristic forms of crime which develop out of the prevailing social and economic conditions. Our own time has, for example, been characterised by a vast increase in violent street robbery and housebreaking – reflecting in large part growing unemployment and the widening gap between small pockets of wealth and huge areas of poverty.

But in the time of Queen Victoria, many crimes had their origin in the repressive, often hypocritical, moral obligations towards the public image of marriage and the family. The consequence was some of the most notorious spouse-slayers – killers like Crippen, Armstrong, Florence Maybrick and later, Edith Thompson.

At the same time, the social disgrace of bearing illegitimate children led many women – particularly among the less advantaged classes – to dispose permanently of their 'embarrassment' at the earliest opportunity after birth. Indeed, the records are uncomfortably full of such cases, and provided the end was notably cruel, gruesome or tragic, they provided one of the most familiar subjects for popular broadsheets. However, this must be seen as a crime of fear and of poverty, and can at least be understood and perhaps sympathised with.

This was not the case with a more insidious product of these same moral taboos – the 'Baby Farmer', a breed of women prepared, for a price (and frequently a high one) to 'adopt' unwanted children. It was a service which obviously appealed to the better-off, better-class woman in trouble; a woman, say, outwardly living a virtuous life, probably married, who had had a child by a man other than her husband and was happy to ease her conscience with money. However, as most of the mothers in these circumstances were happy to turn their back on a child so 'fostered', and frequently had no intention of ever seeing their offspring again, the temptation was great for the unscrupulous baby farmer to neglect, starve and, as we have seen, even hasten the end of their young charges.

DZHUMAGALIEV, Nikolai Dzhumagaliev, known as 'Metal Fang' on account of his white-metal false teeth, created a reign of terror in the Soviet republic of Kazakhstan during 1980. He had already served one jail sentence for manslaughter when he began working on a building site in Alma-Ata; in his spare time, Dzhumagaliev enjoyed escorting women – he had a preference for tall, attractive ones – on strolls by the river. He was by all accounts the perfect gentleman, presentable, clean-shaven and neatly dressed, but with one appalling trait. Having lured his victim to a remote spot on the river bank, Metal Fang raped and then hacked the woman to death with axe and knife. As if this were not depredation enough, he would light a fire and cook his victims. It was always on the evening following one of these sorties that Dzhumagaliev's friends would be invited to join him in a supper of roast meat.

Metal Fang was eventually discovered when two drunks that he had invited back for a snack found a woman's head and intestines in the kitchen. He was charged with seven murders, but the court held that Dzhumagaliev was not responsible for his actions and committed him to a mental institution in Tashkent.

Nikolai Dzhumagaliev escaped from custody while being transferred to another institution in 1989; no public announcement was ever made of Metal Fang's escape lest it cause panic. He was recaptured at Fergana, Uzbekistan, in August 1991 after earlier being reported for trying to proposition women in Moscow.

E

ENGLEMAN, Dr Glennon E. Dr Engleman, a dentist from St Louis, Missouri, killed seven people over twenty-two years with the main objective of benefiting from their life insurance policies; though in the last case it was the expedient removal of a person who had dared to sue him for unpaid bills.

The first of the deaths occurred in December 1958, and was the shooting of James Bullock, at the time married to Engleman's former wife. She collected the life insurance, some of which she promptly invested in one of Engleman's business interests.

In September 1963, Eric Frey, Engleman's partner in the same business died in, of all things, a dynamite explosion. On receipt of the insurance money, Frey's widow invested a healthy portion in the business. On 5 September 1976, Peter Halm was shot in the back near the town of Pacific, where he had gone with his wife – one of Engleman's former dental assistants.

Arthur Guswelle and his wife were killed at their home near Edwardsville in November 1977, and their son Ron was murdered on 31 March 1979. These killings appear to have been a conspiracy between Engleman and Barbara Guswelle, Ron's wife and an old friend of the dentist. Subsequently, Barbara Guswelle was acquitted of murdering her in-laws, but convicted of murdering her husband and jailed for fifty years.

Mrs Sophie Barrera died in a car bombing in January 1980, after making the mistake of taking Engleman to court for non-payment of some bills. Ruth Bullock, widow of Engleman's first victim became understandably fearful lest she might be next on the dentist's ever-lengthening hit list, and took her story to the police. Mrs Bullock agreed to be fitted with a miniature microphone, and incriminating conversations which she had with Engleman were recorded and used as evidence against him at his trial.

On 19 June 1985, following a plea-bargaining arrangement, Glennon E. Engleman pleaded guilty to the murders of Mrs Sophie Barrera and Arthur Guswelle and his wife; he was sentenced to three life terms.

ERSKINE, Kenneth Called the 'Stockwell Strangler', Erskine was responsible for terrorising the elderly residents of South London during 1986.

Erskine's first identified victim was seventy-eight-year-old spinster

Nancy Emms, discovered on 9 April laid out on her bed as though for burial, in a basement room in Wandsworth. She had been strangled and subjected to a violent sexual assault. Mrs Janet Cockett, sixty-eight years old, was found naked and strangled on the bed in her Stockwell flat on 9 June; as in the case of Nancy Emms, there was no visible sign of a forced entry, though a palm print was found on a window ledge, and a thumb smudge on a plant pot.

On the night of 28 June, the staff of a home for the elderly in Stockwell disturbed an intruder, and following a close search of the house, Valentine Gleim, aged eighty-four, and his ninety-four-year-old friend Zbigniew Strabava, were found dead in their adjoining rooms. Gleim had been sexually assaulted, both had been strangled. As in the case of the previous victims Gleim and Strabava had been tucked up in their beds with no sign of a struggle.

The killer then moved out of his usual territory into Islington in North London, where on 8 July he strangled and sexually assaulted octogenarian William Carman. Neighbours found him lying on his bed, hands crossed over his chest with the bed clothes tucked up neatly under his chin.

Back in the south of the city, on his old killing grounds, the Stockwell Strangler struck again on 20 July. This time the victim was a seventy-five-year-old bedridden recluse named William Downes. Two days later Florence Tisdall, an eighty-year-old widow, was sexually abused and murdered in her bed in Putney.

The breakthrough in police investigations came when palm prints found on a wall and on a garden gate at the scene of the Downes killing were matched with that of a small-time crook named Kenneth Erskine. A homeless drifter, twenty-four years of age but with the mental capacity of an eleven-year-old, Erskine already had a record for burglary and was now living in squats and derelict buildings in the capital. His personal history was disturbing; he had spent much of his early life in schools for maladjusted children where he was frequently involved in assaults on other pupils and even on his teachers. Later becoming an habitual vagrant, Erskine had never been in regular employment, preferring to wait for his weekly stipend from the Social Security. It was while collecting his cheque from Southwark Social Security office that Kenneth Erskine was arrested. Questioned by police, he replied, 'I don't remember killing anyone. I could have done it without knowing. I am not sure if I did.' Later, he found no difficulty with his memory, and described in detail his technique of slowly squeezing his victim's throat with one hand, and at the same time suffocating them by clamping his other hand over their nose and mouth.

At his three-week-long trial at the Central Criminal Court, Erskine was charged with seven murders and one attempted murder. The unnamed victim of the attempt on his life was able to positively identify Erskine and forensic evidence sealed his fate. Sitting in the dock with a vacant grin on his face, Kenneth Erskine heard the judge sentence him to life imprisonment with a recommendation that he serve not less than forty years.

As a result of this conviction, police were able to close their files on a number of further indentical but unsolved cases, convinced that Erskine had been the killer.

EVANS, Donald Leroy   The world's press had barely regained its balance after the revelations of Jeffrey Dahmer's appalling cycle of murder, mutilation and cannibalism in Milwaukee the previous month, when in the middle of August 1991 Donald Leroy Evans confessed to the murder of 'at least sixty' people.

Evans had been held in Biloxi, Mississippi on charges of the kidnap, rape and murder of a homeless ten-year-old named Beatrice Routh. The thirty-four-year-old drifter from Galveston, Texas, told officers of the Mississippi police authority that the killing spree began when he was dismissed from the US Marine Corps in 1977. The fact that this coincided with the spate of prostitute killings in Washington State at first suggested that the notorious Green River Killer might have been apprehended. Evans initially admitted the rape and murder of six women in Florida, Illinois and Texas; he later expanded his claim to – as far as he could remember – around sixty men and women across Alabama, Arizona, California, Idaho, Colorado, Washington, Wyoming, South Dakota, Michigan, Pennsylvania, Kentucky, North and South Carolina, and Georgia. It seems that only his remorse at the killing of the Routh child persuaded Evans to confess. According to his legal adviser Fred Lusk: 'There is a strong possibility that [Evans] is telling the truth . . . the count could go higher.' To which Mississippi police chief George Payne added: 'He seems the type.'

At a brief preliminary court hearing following his arrest, Donald Evans promised to cooperate in locating the bodies of his victims in exchange for the death penalty. Lawyer Lusk explained: 'He said he lived by the sword and he wants to die by the sword, he does not believe in suicide so he wants to die by execution . . . I'll help him with everything, all his wishes, but it goes against my legal ethics to plead him to death.'

Within days of Evans' dramatic confession the country-wide police euphoria at the prospect of being able to clear up a significant number of unsolved homicides was more muted, and the possibility was being voiced that Donald Evans might just be trying to steal some of Jeffrey Dahmer's notoriety, and the case of Henry Lee Lucas was recalled; over the course of several years Lucas waxed and waned in the extravagance of his claims to multiple murder from more than three hundred deaths to just one. At the date of writing investigations into Evans' claims continue in advance of any charges being made against him.

F

'FEMALE BLUEBEARD' *see* GUNNESS, Belle

FERNANDEZ, Raymond *see* BECK, Martha

FIELD, Frederick Herbert Charles   The first time that Frederick Field came to the attention of the police and the courts had been over the matter of the death of twenty-year-old prostitute Norah Upchurch, whose strangled body had been found in an empty building in London on 2 October 1931. Field became involved because he had been working for a firm of signboard fitters who had asked him to remove a 'To Let' sign from outside the same building. According to what he told the coroner, Field was approached by 'a man in plus fours with gold fillings in his teeth' whom Field assumed to be the new tenant and handed over the keys when the man asked for them. There was no evidence on which to charge Frederick Field with the murder – though there was no lack of suspicion. Suspicion that seemed to be vindicated when, almost two years later, on 25 July 1933, Field walked into the offices of the *Daily Sketch* and made a detailed confession. He repeated this confession to the police, and it was read out to the Old Bailey jury. It was necessary to read it because by the time he got to court Field had retracted his admission. His preposterous explanation for the whole charade was that he had been dissatisfied with the 'finger of suspicion' that had been pointing at him since the inquest on Norah Upchurch's death, and he made up the confession in order to get the case to court and himself finally acquitted of any guilt.

As the only evidence against Field had been his own confession, and as he had now withdrawn it, there seemed little option but for Mr Justice Swift to instruct the jury to return a verdict of not guilty. Whatever happened now, of course, no matter if the police could make out a case against him, Frederick Field could not be tried for the same crime twice. He celebrated by joining the RAF as an aircrafts-man.

Then, on 4 April 1936, the naked body of Beatrice Vilna Sutton was found dead on her bed in her Clapham, south London, flat. She had been suffocated with a pillow. Shortly afterwards Frederick Field was placed under arrest as a deserter from the RAF, and while in custody, he did a most extraordinary thing – he made a full confession to the murder of Beatrice Sutton. Which is how Field came to be facing a jury at the Old Bailey for a second time on a charge of murder. Of course he adopted the same ruse of retracting his confession in the naive hope that it would work for him a second time. But in this case there was independent evidence, and besides, Field got so carried away that his confession was littered with pieces of information that would have been known only to the killer. By way of explanation, the best Field could offer was: 'I was just browned off. I don't even know who the woman was.'

Field's new defence – and one which he hoped would explain his special knowledge – was that he had been hiding in a cupboard under the stairs at the block of apartments in which Mrs Sutton lived. He heard a quarrel going on, and then saw a man coming out of the flat leaving the door open. Curiosity triumphing over good manners, Field walked in to see what was happening and when he found the occupant dead, fearing to become involved, he fled.

It took the jury only fifteen minutes to find the prisoner guilty, and he was hanged, at the age of thirty-two, on 30 June 1936.

FISH, Albert Born Hamilton Fish in Washington, DC, in 1870, 'Albert' came from a family dogged by ill luck and insanity. When he was only five, Albert's father died, and the boy spent an unhappy childhood in an orphanage from which he frequently absconded. At fifteen he became apprenticed to a painter and decorator and in 1898 he married.

Albert Fish was a rather meek, retiring man, known to be a good Christian and a good family man who adored his six children. In short, there was little indication of the monster which was to emerge and his sexual perversions remained comparatively latent until 1917 when Albert's 'eccentricities' were triggered by his wife's desertion. After this, according to the man who knew his mind best, Dr Fredric Wertham: 'There was no known perversion which he did not practise and practise frequently.' Obsessed with the religious concept of atonement through self-punishment, Fish abused his own body as cruelly as ever he did his victims, engaging in savage bouts of self-flagellation, burning and the insertion of needles into the pubic areas of his body. When he was finally taken into custody, an X-ray disclosed no less than twenty-nine metallic foreign bodies, some of which had been there for so long that they had begun to corrode.

Although Fish was known to the police as a minor nuisance – he was fond of writing obscene letters in reply to lonely hearts advertisements – and he liked swindling people, for which he had served several short terms in prison and mental hospital, nobody had the slightest idea of the scale of Albert Fish's activities as a torturer, murderer, necrophile and cannibal.

On 3 June 1928, Fish, calling himself 'Frank Howard', arrived on the doorstep of the Budd apartment in New York City. He was there in reply to young Paul Budd's advertisement in the newspaper; Paul was looking for a job, and Howard had come to offer him one on his fictional Long Island farm. The kindly, generous old man then remembered that his 'sister' was holding a children's party that very day, and suggested that while he was waiting for Paul to pack his grip, he could take the Budds' twelve-year-old daughter Grace to the party. It was the last time that Mr and Mrs Budd saw her – alive or dead.

Then in November 1934, Mrs Budd received an unexpected letter:

Dear Mrs Budd
Some years ago a friend of mine, Captain John Davis, shipped from California to Hong Kong, China, where at that time there was a great famine. It was dangerous for children under the age of twelve to be on the streets, as the custom was for them to be seized, cut up and their meat sold for food. On his return to New York, my friend seized two boys, one six the other eleven, killed, cooked and ate them.

So it was that I came to your house on 3 June 1928, and under the pretence of taking your daughter Grace to a party at my sister's I took her up to Westchester County, Worthington, to an empty house up there, and I choked her to death, I cut her up and ate part of her flesh. I didn't fuck with her. She died a virgin.

From an imperfectly erased address on the back of the envelope in which this letter was sent, police were led to Albert Fish's seedy room in a New York boarding house. For Fish, who became known as the 'Cannibal Killer' it was the end of a criminal career that included the violent assault of more than one hundred young girls and the murder of twelve of them.

On 12 March 1935, Fish was brought to trial at White Plains, New York, charged with the murder of Grace Budd, whose pathetic remains Fish had led police to. Although his defence attorney made a genuine and convincing case of Fish's insanity, the jury found him guilty of murder; one of the jury later confided, 'I thought he was insane, but he deserved to be electrocuted anyway.'

Which is what happened – despite appeals against the death sentence where Dr Wertham gave evidence that 'This man is not only incurable and unreformable, but unpunishable. In his own distorted mind he is looking forward to the electric chair as the final experience of true pain.'

Albert Fish was strapped into the 'Chair' at Sing Sing on 16 January 1936, looking for all the world as though he were going on a picnic.

' "FORCES OF EVIL" KILLER' *see* **HANCE, William Henry**

FRANKLIN, Joseph Paul   A rabid supporter of the extreme right-wing American Nazi movement, Franklin had a particular grudge against mixed-race couples upon whom many of his attacks were centred between the years 1977 and 1980. The first the world knew of

Franklin's obsession was on 7 August 1977, when Alphonse Manning and his white girl-friend Toni Schwenn were shot dead in a shopping precinct at Madison, Wisconsin. In a subsequent confession, Franklin claimed that this was a change of mind – his prime target was to have been a judge who had a reputation for leniency towards black defendants. On 21 October 1979, Jesse Taylor and Marion Bressette, another mixed-race couple, were shot to death in Oklahoma city. For lack of evidence, charges were dropped against Franklin in this case.

Again, in January 1980, lack of evidence allowed Franklin to evade the consequences of murdering two young blacks, Lawrence Reese and Leo Watkins, shot in two separate incidents in Indianapolis. Five months later, on 8 June, two black teenagers were shot dead in Cincinnati at a time when Franklin was known to have been in the city.

Salt Lake City was to be Joe Franklin's nemesis. On 20 August he shot David Martin and Ted Fields when he saw them jogging with white women. Extradited from Florida where he had fled, Franklin faced a Salt Lake City jury charged with the murder of the joggers and violating their civil rights. In March 1981, he was sentenced to four terms of life imprisonment. In February 1986, Franklin was tried and convicted of the Manning/Schwenn murders and collected a further two consecutive life terms.

'FREEWAY KILLER' *see* **BONIN, William**

'FRENCH BLUEBEARD' *see* **LANDRU, Henri Desiré**

FURLAN, Mario *see* **ABEL, Wolfgang**

G

GACY, John Wayne   At nine o'clock on the evening of 11 December 1978, fifteen-year-old Robert Piest went to a chemist's shop in his home town of Des Plaines, Illinois, to talk with a building contractor working on the shop about a holiday job. He was supposed to go straight back home afterwards where the family were holding a party for his mother's birthday. When Robert had not arrived by 11.30, Elizabeth Piest and her husband contacted the police.

Officers investigating the boy's disappearance learned that the man contracted to carry out the renovation work at the pharmacy was John Wayne Gacy – a name not unfamiliar to them. He had been reported earlier in the year by a twenty-seven-year-old man named Jeffrey Rignall. Rignall, according to his own story, had been approached by a plump man with a flashy car and invited to join him in the vehicle to smoke some marijuana. Once in the car the fat man had pushed a chloroform-soaked handkerchief into Rignall's face and driven him, unconscious, to a house where he was beaten with whips and raped; he had regained consciousness next morning where he had been dumped in Lincoln Park. In view of the fact that the victim could tell them little about his attacker, the police were unable to be of much help. In fact even when Jeffrey Rignall himself went on a trawl of the city and found the Oldsmobile it was still some time before the authorities went to arrest the owner; his name was John Wayne Gacy.

Even before this Gacy had been a familiar figure in law-enforcement circles – ten years at a correctional institution in Waterloo, Iowa, for various sex and violence offences against young men; arrested again in 1971 for trying to rape a teenaged boy; accused of forcing a man to have sex at gunpoint . . . Now there was the disappearance of young Robert Piest.

When investigating officers paid a visit to 8213 West Summerdale Avenue, Des Plaines, they followed the unpleasant smell to the trap door which led down to the crawl space under Gacy's house. Seven bodies in varying stages of decomposition were found there underneath the house, along with the parts of several others; eight more corpses were dug out of lime pits in the garden and in the garage. In all the remains of twenty-eight bodies were found around the house and five Gacy had thrown in the Des Plaines river – including that of Robert Piest. John Wayne Gacy admitted killing thirty-two teenaged boys, before, during or after sex; he had lost count – there were thirty-three.

Gacy had been born in Chicago on 17 March 1942. At the age of eleven he had been out playing when he had been struck on the head by a swing, and for the rest of his youth suffered fainting fits. He graduated from business school and became a star shoe salesman with the Nunn-Bush Shoe Company. Gacy married a colleague, Marlynn Myers, in 1964, but the marriage ended when he was imprisoned. He was married for a second time to Carole Hoff in 1972, and set up in business as a renovation contractor. This marriage also failed, not the least because of Carole's fear of her husband's violent temper. Nevertheless he was a man who made a great effort to be liked, was an enthusiastic member of the Junior Chamber of Commerce, and as 'Pogo the Clown' a popular children's entertainer. At the same time Gacy was using his contracting business to attract young men eager for work, many of whom were subjected to rape, and thirty-three of whom lost their lives. Curiously, Gacy always claimed that he was not a homosexual, and that indeed he hated homosexuals – a fact which if true would account in part for the conscience-free way in which he could kill his sex partners (even though they were not themselves homosexual).

Despite the several confessions that he made while in custody, John Wayne Gacy did not give evidence at his trial. On 12 March 1980, a jury rejected his defence plea of insanity and convicted him of murder with a recommendation for the death penalty.

GALLEGO, Gerald Armand, and **WILLIAMS-GALLEGO, Charlene**   Gerald Gallego was notable, though not unique, in keeping up the family tradition of facing death at the hands of an executioner. In 1955, Gerald Gallego senior died in the Mississippi gas chamber at the age of twenty-eight for the murder of a prison guard; junior managed to eclipse his father's record with a series of sex killings through California and Nevada that kept the states in panic between 1978 and 1980. Charlene Gallego, the most recent of Gerald's seven wives, played her part by enticing girl hitch-hikers into the car with a promise of marijuana, and kidnapping them so that her husband could rape, sexually abuse and then shoot them.

The first known victims were seventeen-year-old Rhonda Scheffler and sixteen-year-old Kippi Vaught, who vanished on a shopping trip to Sacramento on 11 September 1978. Two days later they were found raped, beaten and shot dead near Baxter. On 24 June 1979, Brenda Judd and Sandra Kaye Colley disappeared in Reno, Nevada, and Stacy Ann Redican and Karen Chipman-Twiggs, both seventeen, vanished while shopping in Sacramento on 24 April 1980. Their bodies were found later in Reno. Pregnant twenty-one-year-old Linda Aguilar was reported missing on 6 June 1980, and her body was found near Gold Beach. Mrs Virginia Mochel vanished from the Sacramento bar where she worked, and her body was not discovered until three months later. On 1 November 1980, Mary Beth Sowers and her fiancé

Craig Miller were kidnapped in Sacramento. Miller was found shot dead soon afterwards, and the body of Mary Beth Sowers was recovered later.

This last kidnapping had been witnessed, however, and the description of the car involved was identified as belonging to the Gallegos. Following an inter-state manhunt, Gerald and Charlene Gallego surrendered to the police in Omaha, Nebraska, where they waived extradition and were returned to California. Charlene made a complete confession and was the main witness for the prosecution at Gerald Gallego's trial in California in 1983. Here he was convicted of two counts of first-degree murder and two of kidnapping, relating to the Sowers/Miller killings. After a penalty hearing Gallego was sentenced to die in the gas chamber. He was then extradited to Nevada to face trial for the murders of Stacy Ann Redican and Karen Chipman-Twiggs. Again Charlene was the star prosecution witness, and again the court found Gallego guilty. At a penalty hearing, the same jury recommended death by lethal injection. Charlene Gallego pleaded guilty to the murders of Mary Beth Sowers and Craig Miller but, in return for testifying against her husband, received only two concurrent sentences of sixteen years eight months in jail. Gerald Gallego is on Death Row in Nevada state prison awaiting the results of the appeal procedure.

GARY, Carlton   Columbus, Georgia, was the scene of a series of seven rape-murders of elderly women by a killer called the 'Stocking Strangler', the investigation of which was complicated by the parallel activities of another killer in the same place at the same time calling himself the 'Forces of Evil' (see William **Hance**).

The first victim was Mrs Ferne Jackson, aged sixty, found dead in her home on 16 September 1977. Eight days later Miss Jean Dimerstein, seventy-one, was found in her apartment, raped and strangled with one of her own stockings. There followed a further five murders all exhibiting the same pattern and clearly with a common assailant. On 12 February 1978, a seventy-four-year-old widow successfully fought off an attacker trying to strangle her with a stocking, but the killer struck again on the same day not one hundred yards from the unsuccessful assault.

A jogger seen in the area of one of the murders was identified by a witness from a photograph of Carlton Gary. Gary had already served a prison sentence in New York for the assault and rape of an elderly woman found dead in her apartment. He evaded a murder charge by accusing a friend of the killing. With his arrest imminent, Gary went on the run and became involved in narcotics dealing, and it was not until 3 May 1984 that he was detained in Atlanta, Georgia. He was indicted for murder, rape and robbery in the cases of Mrs Scheible, Mrs Thurmond and Mrs Woodruff, and following a twelve-day trial, Carlton Gary was found guilty on all charges and at a penalty hearing was sentenced to death. He remains on Death Row in Jackson, Georgia, awaiting execution in the electric chair.

The Stocking Strangler's victims

Date	Name	Age
16 September 1977	Ferne Jackson	60
24 September 1977	Jean Dimerstein	71
2 October 1977	Florence Scheible	89
6 October 1977	Martha Thurmond	69
29 December 1977	Kathleen Woodruff	74
12 February 1978	Mildred Borom	78
20 April 1978	Janet Cofer	61

GASKINS, Donald Henry In 1975, police investigations into the disappearance of a thirteen-year-old girl revealed a neighbourhood paralysed into silence by fear of one man. The trail had led to a shadowy figure on the fringe of the South Carolina underworld, Donald Henry Gaskins – called 'Peewee' – and attempts to interview residents of the district in which Gaskins lived were met by frightened glances over the shoulder and sealed lips. But if the inquiry revealed nothing about their suspect, police were getting a clear indication that at least five more people were missing, and strong rumours about a 'cemetery' where they were all buried.

A quite separate line of inquiry had located an old cell-mate of Gaskins named Walter Leroy Neeley, who was clearly not intimidated by 'Peewee's' reputation. In fact Neeley offered to lead officers to the remote wood east of Prospect which served as the *ad hoc* graveyard. Here a total of six bodies were unearthed, three male, three female; four had been shot, two had their throats cut, and they had been buried two to a grave. Another 'cemetery' a mile away yielded up the remains of a woman and a baby. Gaskins obviously had a lot of explaining to do. He was arrested trying to cross the state line and indicted on eight counts of murder. When the investigation was completed, Walter Neeley had his name added to three of the charges, and another man, James Kony Judy, to one.

Gaskins stood his trial first, for the murder of David Bellamy, one of the first bodies found; he was convicted and sentenced to death. Neeley was tried on the same charge with a similar result. James Judy pleaded guilty to being an accessory to one of the other killings and received a ten-year sentence. Subsequent appeals by Gaskins and Neeley resulted in their death sentences being commuted to life imprisonment. But the courts had not heard the last of Peewee Gaskins. Continuing police inquiries had exposed the contract killings of three women and a man identified as Silas Yates. The contract had been taken up by Gaskins, for which he was given another life term to run consecutively. Arrangements were then made to put him back on the stand for another of the Prospect killings – that of John Knight. Perhaps 'Peewee' was tiring of the constant repeat performances, but in a bid to get everything out in the open to his best advantage he entered into a plea-bargaining arrangement and offered to plead guilty to seven murders in exchange for non-imposition of the death penalty. While in prison, Gaskins was questioned under the 'truth drug' sodium amytal. These drugs were a by-product of interrogation techniques developed during the Second World War; the effect is, quite simply, to inhibit that part of the brain which acts as a 'censor', rendering the subject incapable of anything but a spontaneous response to questions. Unfortunately, there is a chasm of difference between the flow of uninhibited speech produced by lowering the defences and what in legal terms would be considered 'truth'. However, for what it was worth, Donald Gaskins confessed to a total of thirteen murders. He later appeared in court and was sentenced to eight consecutive life sentences on top of the two he had already begun serving.

Nor was this yet the end of Donald Gaskins' villainy. While in prison, he accepted a contract put out by one Tony Cimo to assassinate Rudolph Tyner, another prisoner on Death Row. Tyner had been convicted of the double murder of Cimo's mother and stepfather in the course of a robbery. Gaskins told Tyner that he would rig up a form of intercom so that they could communicate between cells, all Tyner had to do was put the two leads of the device into an electrical socket. Which he did, and the side of his head was blown off by the dynamite contained in the 'walkie-talkie'. Once again Gaskins was in court charged with first-degree murder from which he could not escape sentence to the electric chair. Tony Cimo was subsequently sentenced to twenty-one years for conspiracy to murder, but was paroled after less than three years, most of which was served on a work-release programme.

GBUREK, Tillie (aka Tillie Klimek)   Tillie Gburek was celebrated for two outstanding qualities among the inhabitants of Chicago's Polish quarter – she was a superb cook and, on account of her uncanny accuracy in predicting the deaths of neighbourhood dogs, she was considered a seer.

It was after almost twenty-eight years of marriage that in 1914 Tillie confided to a neighbour that her powers of prediction bore sad tidings – her husband, John Mitkiewitz, would soon be passing into the next world, she would be a widow inside three weeks. Almost three weeks to the day later, Mitkiewitz died and Tillie collected one thousand dollars insurance.

Six weeks later, she was Mrs John Ruskowski. After three months, Tillie had another of her premonitions and, two weeks later, she became, quite suddenly, the widow Ruskowski.

The fact that Joseph Guszowski was disinclined to marry did not prevent Tillie moving into his house; indeed when it came to creature comforts he was treated to the same culinary expertise as her previous husbands. And when he suddenly died, he was buried next to them in the cemetery.

It was thirteen months after the death of John Mitkiewitz, about eight since Ruskowski's decease, and almost no time at all since Joseph Guszowski had handed in his dinner pail. Tillie was now about to marry Frank Kupczyk. At her wedding, a distant relative, Rose Chudzinski, asked Tillie how long the spirits gave her latest husband. The bride answered that she wasn't sure about that yet, but that Rose herself would give up the ghost in about six weeks; in six weeks she did.

Not until 1920 was Tillie privy again to the Grim Reaper's personal plans, and then it spelled sorrow for a couple with whom she had been quarrelling. Their three children died one by one – just as Tillie foretold they would! Then Kupczyk began to get on her nerves, and shortly afterwards died – fortunately the spirits had given Tillie plenty of warning and she was able to order his coffin well in advance. On the day of Kupczyk's death she told a friend that she hoped she had better luck with her next husband, Anton Klimek.

In fact, he brought her considerable ill-luck, for when he took seriously ill within months of the wedding, Klimek's brother went to the police and they launched an inquiry. An analysis of one of Tillie's famous stews revealed her secret ingredient – arsenic. With no more ado, the body of Frank Kupczyk was exhumed and a post-mortem established that he had died of arsenical poisoning.

At her trial for Kupczyk's murder, Tillie announced that her spirit guides had told her she would not be executed. And indeed she was not, she was sentenced to a lifetime's imprisonment, where her suggestion that she might be allowed to work in the kitchens was politely declined.

GEIN, Edward With a brother as weak and ineffectual as himself and a domineering mother, Ed Gein farmed the small family homestead at Plainfield, Wisconsin. The work was hard, the pleasures few; in fact the joy that was generated by the Gein household was nil. Women were most especially forbidden fruit to Ed and Henry, and when his brother died in 1944 and his mother the following year, a by now middle-aged sodbuster was left alone with his own morbid thoughts reinforced by the shade of his mother enshrined for ever in her room, locked and undisturbed since the day she passed away. But Ed had something else; he had a deeply unhealthy interest in the intimate anatomy of the female sex from whose company he had been so effectively excluded. It started with books; the sort of books mostly read by doctors, the sort of books which display for the student the human body in all its component parts. Like any emerging anatomist, Ed graduated on to the real thing, only in his case by way of nocturnal plundering of the local graveyard. In some cases Ed removed the corpse's skin and with intense gratification wore it about his own body. Or sometimes he draped it over a tailor's dummy; perhaps he was trying to recreate his mother.

If it had stopped there nobody might ever have disturbed 'ol' weird Ed', now a virtual recluse on the increasingly neglected and crumbling farm. But Ed Gein grew discontented with what he could harvest from God's little acre, and began to create corpses for himself. The first one had been that of fifty-four-year-old Mary Hogan, who disappeared from her isolated Hogan's Tavern in December 1954.

Three years later, on 16 November 1957, Bernice Worden, a woman in her late fifties who ran the local Plainfield hardware store, was reported missing by her son. Frank Worden was also a sheriff's deputy, so the pool of blood on the floor of his mother's shop and the missing till did not go unnoticed. Weird Ed had been in town that day too; his pick-up truck had been seen parked outside the Worden store.

16 November was a day the Plainfield Sheriff Office would never forget. They would never forget the ride out to the lonely Gein farm, already known by the local children as the Haunted House. They would never forget the headless body of Bernice Worden hanging by its feet from the rafters of the lean-to, or the ghastly array of artefacts fashioned from human corpses – lamp-shades covered with skin, the crown of a skull used as a soup-bowl, the refrigerator stocked with human organs.

As in the case of many other serial killers, the fantasies of sexual sadism that pervaded his inner world had grown in Ed Gein from the early teachings of an obsessive mother that sex was a sinful thing, serving only to make that sin a profound mystery that Ed would later explore so gruesomely. It is no surprise either that Gein's study of medical anatomy was heavily supplemented by pulp horror and pornography magazines. It was a world of fantasy that would erupt into necrophilia, cannibalism and murder.

Of course Ed was not 'weird', he was criminally insane; and it was some surprise that, in January 1968, he was found fit to face trial. Gein was found guilty but insane, and committed first to the Central State Hospital at Waupon, and then in 1978 to the Mendota Mental Health Institute. Always a model prisoner, Ed Gein died peacefully in the Mendota geriatric ward on 26 July 1984; he was seventy-seven.

It is said that Robert Bloch based his chilling novel *Psycho* (later transformed into film by Alfred Hitchcock) on the Ed Gein story. However, anybody with a knowledge of both may find it difficult to identify the schizophrenic transvestite Norman Bates with the farmer of Plainfield.

Gein's fondness for wearing human skin resurfaced in 1991 as one of the inspirations for the character of Buffalo Bill in Thomas Harris's novel *The Silence of the Lambs*.

GIBBS, Janie Janie Gibbs was a highly respected member of the small Georgia community of Cordele, where she ran the day-care centre for children of working mothers. Whenever a member of her family died (and nobody seemed to notice that it happened rather more frequently than in other families), Mrs Gibbs received nothing but kindness and sympathy – and insurance money. But she was careful always to donate part of each inheritance to the local church.

The first to die had been thirteen-year-old Marvin, Janie's son. Despite treatment at hospital he died from what was diagnosed as 'kidney disease' on 29 August 1966. Melvin, the sixteen-year-old, became seriously ill in January 1967, and died in hospital of 'hepatitis'. Janie Gibbs' eldest son, Roger, was already married, though the couple still lived in the family home and, in August 1967, Janie became a grandmother. Baby Ronnie Edward fell sick shortly after birth, and despite the best of care did not live beyond six weeks. An autopsy was performed, but results were negative.

Then two weeks after the infant's death, his father was taken ill with stomach cramps and nausea; two days later he too was dead. This time the doctor was unhappy with the results of the autopsy which displayed severe damage of the liver and kidneys, and he ordered tissue samples to be despatched to the Georgia State Crime Laboratory for analysis.

Following two months of exhaustive tests, the laboratory reported finding evidence of a large dose of arsenic. With the evidence of foul-play in Roger Gibbs' death, an exhumation order was obtained to subject the other deceased members of the Gibbs family to post-mortem examination. The results of the tissue tests were never fully released, though unofficially the police confirmed that all the deaths had resulted from poisoning.

Janie Gibbs was taken into custody and put under the care of a psychiatrist to whom she confessed the poisonings. Psychiatric evidence indicated that Mrs Gibbs was suffering from schizophrenia, and although she was capable of distinguishing right from wrong, believed the world to be a very bad place in which her loved ones should not be forced to live. Declared unfit to plead, Janie Gibbs was committed to the state mental institution.

In 1976, she was considered sane enough to stand trial and after conviction was sentenced to five consecutive life terms.

GIUDICE, Giancarlo Prostitution has always been a dangerous career; but never more so than in Turin between January 1984 and June 1986, when seven 'working women' were murdered after being flogged and tortured by a killer called by the press the 'Devil of Turin'.

Annunziata Paffunda was the first victim, found dead in a burned-out car on 10 January 1984; her hands had been bound together with electrical flex and she had been whipped. On 10 March 1985, forty-seven-year-old Addoralata Bienvenuto was found dead on the banks of the river Po, exhibiting signs of similar mistreatment; Signora Bienvenuto had been shot. Eight days later the strangled body of Giovanna Bicchi, sixty-four years old, was pulled from the waters of the Po.

More than a year passed, during which the activities of the Devil had been all but forgotten by the women of Turin; then, on 30 April 1986, forty-four-year-old Maria Gatre was found dead on the bank of a stream – her injuries left no doubt that the Devil was still abroad. By way of confirmation, he struck again, claiming the life of Maria Corda, and again, on 22 May, raping, torturing and whipping Clelia Mollo in her apartment. In addition, three other cases that had come to light during 1985 and 1986 had now been provisionally grouped with this series of killings. All three victims had been whipped and tortured, though only one had been bound with electrical flex.

On 29 June 1986, the body of Maria Rosa Paoli was seen thrown from a car passing over a bridge crossing the river Po, and an alert local police force immediately set up road blocks; the result was that later that night officers stopped the car driven by thirty-two-year-old truck driver, Giancarlo Giudice. In the car was the gun that had killed Addoralata Bienvenuto.

Following interrogation by the police, Giudice confessed to seven murders, and on 26 June 1987, he was sentenced by a court to prison for life.

GLATMAN, Harvey Murray Although he had never been a particularly naughty child, Glatman began to turn inward upon himself in early adolescence, and when he was imprisoned in 1945 for robbery, the authorities recognised immediately the need for psychiatric treatment.

When Harvey was released in 1951, he opened a TV repair shop in Los Angeles and took up photography as a hobby. Like many other amateur photographers, Harvey Glatman became interested in 'glamour' shots. Like many other amateur photographers with an interest in 'glamour' shots, Harvey hired himself a model. On 1 August 1957, nineteen-year-old Judy Dull arrived for the photo-session arranged by a man calling himself Johnny Glynn and masquerading as a professional photographer. Once in his 'studio' the girl was raped and then tied to the bed, helpless, while Harvey Glatman took his snaps. Fearful of the consequences, Harvey killed Miss Dull and buried her body out in the desert.

By this time the police already had Judy Dull listed as a missing person, and her description was circulated along with that of the enigmatic 'Johnny Glynn'. The description had been provided by Judy's flat-mate who had been at home when 'Glynn' called to make the appointment. Nothing more was seen or heard of the missing girl until her bleached skeleton was found protruding from the sand on 29 December 1957.

Shirley Bridgeford was a twenty-four-year-old divorcee whom Harvey had met through a lonely hearts club; she disappeared on their first date. On Sunday, 9 March 1958, Glatman (calling himelf George Williams) had taken her out to the desert where he raped her in the car, bound her and started clicking away with his camera. The next victim was a stripper and part-time model named Ruth Mercado ('Angela' to her clients) who had advertised her services in the newspaper. Glatman first forced his way into her home where he bound and raped her, then drove to the desert and for the best part of a day alternately raped and photographed her – she hoping the while to humour him, but being garrotted anyway.

Victim number four was amateur model Lorraine Vigil, and she had come to Harvey's attention through a modelling agency. On 27 October 1958, Glatman (or Frank Johnson as he was tonight) was driving her out to the desert when he pulled a gun on her. During the struggle which followed the weapon went off, wounding Miss Vigil in the leg; with uncontrolled fury, she wrested the gun from Harvey and held him captive at its barrel end until a highway patrol officer rescued her.

Taken into detention, Harvey Glatman admitted the attack on Lorraine Vigil, but claimed it was a sudden impulse. When his run-down home was searched, the real Harvey Glatman was revealed – walls covered with photographs of his trussed-up victims both alive and dead, and ominous lengths of rope.

Glatman was convicted of murder in San Diego in November 1958, and sentenced to death. Refusing to appeal, Harvey commented morbidly, 'It's better this way. I knew this is the way it would be.' He was executed on 18 August 1959, in the gas chamber at San Quentin.

GLAZE, Billy (aka Jesse Sitting Crow) It was by an old abandoned railway track in Minneapolis that they found the first of Billy Glaze's victims. Her body was only partly clothed and she had been raped, strangled and severely beaten – the three-foot pipe used to smash the girl's face lay across her throat. Nineteen-year-old Kathleen Bullman had been a prostitute, the same calling that was followed by Angeline Whitebird-Sweet, and like her Angeline was a Native American. Her body had been found in a park close to the Indian Center on 12 April 1987. Death was due to asphyxiation caused by the killer stomping heavily on her chest. The naked body had been sexually assaulted with a tree branch which lay beside it. Twenty-one-year-old Angela Green, also a prostitute, also a Native American, was battered to death with a stone on 29 April; she had been raped and her dead body discarded by some railroad tracks.

Enquiries around the bars used by the women as pick-up points led the police to Billy Glaze, who called himself Jesse Sitting Crow. Glaze was a Native American drifter who had been heard loudly proclaiming that all Indian women should be raped and killed – in the circumstances not the best thing he could have suggested. While Billy was in jail awaiting trial he put down his confession in a letter to another prisoner, and in February 1989, he was given one life sentence for each of the killings to be served consecutively.

GOHL, Billy The first stop for seamen arriving in the port of Aberdeen, Washington, was always the office of the Sailors' Union of the Pacific, where they could collect their mail and, if they had any sense, lodge some of their pay before squandering it – or having it squandered – in pursuit of the traditional night on the town. The man they usually dealt with was union official Billy Gohl, a friendly soul who would ask the men solicitously if they had any friends or family in Aberdeen; like as not they would just be passing through. Then the conversation would turn to cash and valuables; like as not, the hapless matelot would have just enough to make it worth Billy's while killing him!

As luck had it – for Billy Gohl at least – the 'Union' was in a building which backed onto the Wishkah River which in turn ran into the harbour. Conveniently, there was a chute descending to the river, down which Billy used to drop his corpses to be washed eventually out into the open sea. Of course, there were suspicions aired over the remarkably large number of sailors who had docked at Aberdeen and never re-embarked, but it was not until 1912, when a body was washed ashore which could be positively proved to be that of a sailor last seen alive entering Gohl's office, that any attention was directed to Billy or his official capacity as servant of the trade union.

So, in 1913, Billy Gohl was charged and convicted – but of only two of his suspected forty-one plus murders. And Billy's luck held out a little longer. Washington state had in the previous year suspended the death penalty, so he escaped what many considered an appropriate punishment. Not surprisingly perhaps, Billy always refused to give any details of his crimes, and so frustrated did the state prosecutor's office become that Billy Gohl achieved further notoriety by being cited as a very good reason for the reinstatement of capital punishment. He died in prison in 1928.

GONZALES, Delfina, and Maria de Jesus By the time the two Mexican sisters were brought to justice in 1964 they had been responsible for the deaths of a staggering eighty-plus young girls in ten years. The Gonzales sisters ran a brothel at their Rancho El Angel, to which the girls, many of them young teenagers, were abducted, forced into drug dependency and made to endure unspeakable humiliation and deprivation. Those who became ill, lost their looks, or became troublesome were killed.

It had been going on for heaven knows how long; it would have gone on for heaven knows how long if police had not finally caught up with the woman with a mole on her cheek. A familiar figure in the twilight world of prostitution, drugs and much else that is evil, Josefina Guttierez had been suspected for years of being behind the disappearances of so many young women from around Mexico's west-coast city of Guadalajara. In custody, Josefina proved willing enough to talk, though what persuaded her we can only guess – perhaps it was simply an uneasy conscience. The girls, it transpired – dozens of them – were destined for the Rancho El Angel, somewhere near the town of San Francisco del Rincon.

When police officers arrived at the ranch they found the Gonzales sisters had fled, leaving the pathetic dormitory of young girls, broken down by ill-use and narcotics, in the care of a handful of thugs. When investigators put a team in to dig over the ground around the ranch, they found the remains of more than eighty young women, plus the foetuses that had been forcibly aborted from those unlucky enough to fall pregnant.

But it was not only the enslaved and unwilling prostitutes who met a grim end; migratory workers returning from America with fat wage packets also fell victim to the insatiable greed of Delfina and Maria Gonzales when they stopped off at the ranch for a little 'recreation'.

The Gonzales sisters were tried and sentenced to forty years' imprisonment; some might say it was rather lenient – a few months each for all those miserable lives and horrible deaths.

GORE, David Alan and WATERFIELD, Fred   One July day in 1983, a fourteen-year-old boy was cycling towards his home in the Vero Beach area of Florida when he was startled to see a naked teenage girl running down the street pursued by a naked man brandishing a gun. Before the youth's horrified gaze, the man seized the girl, threw her to the ground, and shot her at point-blank range.

By the time the boy had rushed home and alerted the police, they had already received the same information from the occupier of a house in the street where the incident took place. The caller's name was David Alan Gore, already known to the police from his record of crimes against women.

Officers were despatched to Gore's house where, in a car parked outside they found the dead body of a nude girl later identified as Lynn Carol Elliott, aged seventeen. Inside the house was another teenage girl who described how she and Lynn had been kidnapped by David Gore and another man, taken to the house and subjected to sexual assault. Gore made no denial of the offences and named the second man as his cousin, Fred Waterfield. Under arrest, Waterfield refused to make any statement at all.

While he was in prison, Gore claimed that he had undergone a profound religious conversion as a result of which he wanted to clear his conscience by confessing to five other murders – thoughtfully implicating his cousin. The deaths had all taken place in Vero Beach, and all the victims had been female – Ying Hua Ling and her mother

Hsiang Huan Ling, Judith Kay Daley, Angelica Lavallee and Barbara Byer.

David Gore came to an arrangement with the state attorney that he would testify against 'anybody else' prosecuted for the rape-murders in exchange for immunity from sentence of death in the same cases. He was sentenced to five consecutive life terms instead. Gore was then put on trial for the murder of Lynn Elliott, and in the absence of any plea-bargain the prosecution demanded the death penalty. He was found guilty and sentenced to die in the electric chair.

In the case of Fred Waterfield, he was tried first for the murder of Lynn Elliott, but found guilty only of manslaughter and given the maximum sentence of fifteen years. He then faced charges of murder in the cases of Barbara Byer and Angelica Lavallee; Gore testified against him and Waterfield was found guilty. He was sentenced to two consecutive life terms for murder and two concurrent terms for kidnapping with the recommendation that he should not be considered for parole for fifty years. The charges of murdering Mrs Daley and the Lings were not proceeded with.

'GORILLA MURDERER' *see* **NELSON, Earle Leonard**

GOSMAN, Klaus   Gosman was born in Germany in 1941 in the middle of the Second World War. As a small child he had seen his father shot dead by American troops and this must, in part at least, have been responsible for his growing obsession with death.

If little else positive can be said for him, Klaus Gosman was at least a perfectionist, planning his killings down to the last detail – he always used a gun, and only ever shot people when Nuremberg's church bells masked the explosion with their noisy midday carillon; from this habit, Gosman became known as 'The Midday Murderer'.

In 1960, when Gosman was nineteen years old and a student of theology, he committed his first murder – the random shooting of a couple during a convenient noon break in his studies. Two years later he killed again, this time it was a banker; then there was a porter, a window cleaner, and in 1963 a widow and her grown-up son. Despite the free access to guns which it provided, the army did not agree with Klaus Gosman's temperament, and within six months of joining he deserted.

Gosman came unstuck in 1965, when he shot a customer in a busy Nuremberg shop, and was grabbed before he could reach the door. Clearly recognising the danger of letting a man like Gosman loose on the streets, his judge sentenced him to a life in prison without the least possibility that he would ever be released.

One curious detail to emerge from Gosman's confiscated diaries – which for the most part were fantasies masquerading as real life – was his plan to kidnap the popular film actress Elke Sommer.

GOTTFRIED, Gesina Margaretha   As a young woman Gesina was an attractive blue-eyed blonde, with no shortage of eligible suitors; from among them she happened to choose a man named Mittenberg, good looking enough but inclined to be prodigal. Despite warnings that the man was a drunkard, Gesina was determined to marry him and in 1815 she did. From the beginning the marriage was a disaster. Mittenberg drank increasingly large volumes of alcohol, and almost certainly as a result of this was unable to perform his marital functions. At first Gesina simply took a lover in the person of a young man named Gottfried, but finally she entertained a notion to dispose of her unwanted spouse permanently. Within the week the arsenic was in Mittenberg's beer, and Mittenberg was in his grave. His death was assumed to be the result of drinking – which in a way it was!

Although Gesina was now free to marry Gottfried, he declined to take on the responsibility of the two children fathered by Mittenberg. The solution was simple, and before long the mites were lying alongside their father. When Gesina's parents got to hear of the impending marriage they, with good reason or not, took against Gottfried and tried all they could to sabotage their daughter's plan. But by now Gesina had a ready answer to such minor irritations as these; she simply invited her parents to lunch at her home to discuss the matter and poisoned them. Their deaths were certified as 'inflammation of the bowels'.

Still Gottfried would not say, 'I do', and in a fit of pique Gesina decided that he should not only be her husband but also her next victim. Day by day she spiked Gottfried's food until he was confined to bed with only Gesina to nurse him. Feeling the chilly hand of death on his shoulder, Gottfried summoned a priest and a solicitor – the cleric to perform a sick-bed wedding, the lawyer to draw up the will that would transfer his every possession to Gesina. Within hours, Gottfried was dead and Gesina was rich.

The widow Gottfried's soldier brother was her next victim, for no other reason than that his habits 'disgusted' her. A doctor attributed his death to venereal disease. A love-lorn suitor followed him into the grave as soon as he had settled his worldly goods on Gesina. Then she travelled to Hamburg to visit one of her creditors – and settled her debt with arsenic.

In 1825 Gesina Gottfried took a large house in the Pelzerstrasse in Bremen, and when she could no longer afford to keep up the payments, the bank foreclosed on her and Gesina was obliged to sell the property to a wheelwright named Rumf. A generous man by nature, Rumf could not see Frau Gottfried on the streets, and asked her to stay on as his housekeeper. During the early months of this arrangement Mrs Rumf gave birth to a son, and only days later died; it was certified as 'complications of childbirth'. Then the Rumf children began to die one by one of mysterious illnesses, and by early 1828 nobody was left in the house except Gesina, a few servants, and Rumf. But although Rumf was himself chronically sick, he had not lost his powers of observation, was not entirely blind to the strange white powder that seemed to coat every meal his housekeeper prepared. In March 1828, he took a sample of meat to the police, tests were made, and the powder quickly found to be white arsenic. A magistrate arrested Gesina Gottfried and charged her with the murder of Frau Rumf.

Gesina offered no defence at her trial, during the course of which she proudly admitted to killing the Rumfs and *at least* thirty other people. The murders, she said, had given her great satisfaction, an ecstasy not unlike a sexual orgasm. Found guilty and condemned, Gesina was led up the steps to the scaffold where the executioner waited, masked and leaning on his heavy axe.

GRAHAM, Gwendolyn Gail, and **WOOD, Catherine**   The murders first came to light in 1987, when Catherine Wood confided to her ex-husband that she and her lesbian lover had been killing off elderly patients at the Alpine Manor Nursing Home, in Walker, Michigan. At first it had all been part of an elaborate game by which the first letter of succeeding victims' names would spell the word MURDER. This had proved too complicated an aspiration and so Wood and Graham settled for just killing the old ladies, most of whom were incapacitated with Alzheimer's disease, and stealing some trinket or other as a souvenir. The *modus operandi* had been for Wood to act as look-out, while Gwendolyn Graham suffocated the victims by pressing cloths over their nose and mouth. How long the series might have continued, how high the toll of deaths would have been, can never be known. But then Graham found herself a new lesbian lover and Catherine Wood became passionately vindictive.

Wood's former husband wasted no time getting the story to the ears of the police and the investigations commenced. Catherine Wood had fled to her native Texas, from whence she was extradited after agreeing to testify against her former partner in exchange for a reduced charge of second-degree murder for herself. For her own part, Wood confessed her part in six murders, the victims' ages ranging from sixty to ninety-eight; she was, it appeared, relieved to have everything in the open because she feared Graham was about to start murdering babies in the hospital which now employed her. According to Wood's evidence, her lover had expressed a feeling of 'emotional release' when they killed and afterwards when they washed the bodies down. She also confided that even talk of killing was sufficient to fill both of them with an uncontrollable desire for sex.

Both women were charged with murder, though on account of turning state's evidence Wood got away with the comparatively light sentence of twenty to forty years. Gwendolyn Graham, charged in December 1988, denied the killings, but was nevertheless convicted on six counts of first-degree murder and sentenced to six life sentences without possibility of parole.

GRAHAM, Harrison Residents of the slum district of North Philadelphia were used to a fairly raw standard of living, but the obnoxious smells emanating from a third-floor apartment during the hot August of 1987 finally became too much to take. Complaints were made and the tenant of the flat, a twenty-eight-year-old man named Harrison Graham – known in the neighbourhood as 'Marty' – was evicted. Before he left, Marty nailed up the bedroom door claiming that there was personal property still in the room which he would be coming back for. When he failed to come back and the smells got worse, the police were called in. As they entered the sealed room the stench hit the search team like a mallet; through the broken-down door they could make out the shapes of five bodies in various stages of decomposition. In a small closet a sixth victim was found. In each case putrefaction was so advanced that it was at first impossible to determine even the sex of the bodies, let alone the cause of their death. By the end of their painstaking search police had identified further remains distributed around the apartment indicating that in all they were looking at a possible seven suspicious deaths.

Although autopsies were carried out in all cases, only two revealed the cause of death – damage to the internal structure of the neck indicated manual strangulation. Nevertheless, the medical examiner ruled that although no precise cause of death could be established, all seven instances should be treated as homicide.

One week after the grisly discoveries Graham turned himself in to a police station, and when it became obvious that nobody was going to believe his claim that the bodies were already in the apartment when he moved in, Graham confessed to strangling all seven women, including his one-time girl-friend Robin DeShazor, while having sexual intercourse with them. Marty Graham was charged with seven counts of murder and seven counts of abuse of a corpse.

At his trial Graham pleaded not guilty by reason of insanity and waived his right to trial by jury; nevertheless, the judge sitting alone convicted him on all counts. At the penalty hearing (again without a jury) Graham was given one life sentence and six death sentences in the matter of the murders. However, the judge ruled that he should serve his prison sentences – seven to fourteen years for abusing the corpse, then his life sentence, before any death sentence could be carried out. This effectively commuted Graham's sentence to life imprisonment.

'GREEN RIVER KILLER' The death count for this unknown killer is reported to be as high as forty-nine, all the murders being committed in the area around Seattle's Green River between 1982 and 1984, since which date no further incidents have been recorded.

Sixteen-year-old Wendy Lee Coffield is thought to have been the first victim; her body was found where it had been washed up on shore close to the Peck Bridge, twenty miles south-east of Seattle on

15 June 1982. Since then bodies of further victims turned up regularly; all were young girls, many were full-time prostitutes.

A special Green River Task Force was set up to try to track the killer down, and over the years as much as $15 million has been spent on the effort, including $200,000 for the installation of a computer system to process in excess of 20,000 separate pieces of information. Botanists, anthropologists, psychologists and psychics have all been consulted without any positive results.

An FBI profile of the killer indicated that he had a deep hatred of women, was possibly a married man who came from a broken home and probably hated his mother. The profile suggested the man would be between twenty and forty years of age, white, a heavy smoker who likes to drink, and he could have a background of sexual crime. There is no information available as to what percentage of the population fits this profile.

Five prime suspects have been investigated by the Task Force but each one was eliminated from the inquiry. In December, 1984, Ted **Bundy** wrote to the Task Force from his cell on Florida's Death Row offering to help trace the Green River Killer.

A representative visited Bundy and listened to his theories, but felt that Bundy's interest was more in making himself indispensable to the police in order to avoid his date with the executioner. One cynic suggested that Bundy was anxious to ensure that the Green River Killer did not exceed his own death count.

While this book was at the editing stage, Donald Leroy **Evans**, a Texan, was arrested in August 1991 after confessing to a ten-year killing rampage over at least sixteen states. There was some optimism at the time that the Green River killings could be attributed to Evans, though subsequent information makes that unlikely.

GREENWOOD, Vaughn Orrin   Known during his reign of terror through Los Angeles and Hollywood as the 'Skid Row Slasher', this was an apt description of the man who preyed upon the vagrant population which inhabits the twilight underclass of the City of Angels.

From December 1974, the dead bodies of down-and-outs and alcoholics began to appear with more alarming regularity than usual. A few stiffs caught out by a cold snap, general debilitation or 'occupational hazards' are one matter; but these bums had been ritually slaughtered! In a single month seven corpses were found dotted around Los Angeles, and in the first month of 1975 two more were found in Hollywood hotels. They were what the police called 'weird' killings. All the victims had died from having their throats cut open, the killer had ceremonially scattered salt around the bodies, removed their shoes and left them pointing towards the victim's feet. Weird killings.

The inhabitants of Skid Row are not known for their reliability or accurate recall; which is probably why the police spent a while chasing their description of a young, blond-haired white man. In the end, on 3 February 1975, they arrested a thirty-one-year-old black man. His name was Vaughn Greenwood, and he had first attracted official attention by trying to murder two men in Hollywood. By March, the authorities announced that they were about to charge Greenwood with the Slasher murders. Even so, it was not until January of the following year that he was formally charged with an impressive eleven counts of murder – nine as the 'Skid Row Slasher', and two more from as early as 1964. On the recent charges, Greenwood was found guilty, on the other two a mistrial was declared. Exactly one year to the month after he was charged, on 19 January 1977, Vaughn Greenwood was sentenced to life imprisonment. The residents of Skid Row could go back to dealing with more manageable problems.

GRILLS, Caroline   Described as 'a kindly old lady to whom people looked in time of trouble', Mrs Grills nevertheless stood trial at the age of sixty-three in Sydney, Australia, facing four charges of murder and two of attempted murder by the administration of the metallic poison thallium.

In 1947, Mrs Grills' stepmother, Christina Mickelson died suddenly at the advanced age of eighty-seven; it was probably a relief to Caroline Grills because she had never really seen eye to eye with Mrs Mickelson since she married her son in 1908.

Shortly afterwards a family friend died, Mrs Angeline Thomas, also a venerable octogenarian. Sixty-year-old John Lundberg, a relative, was the next in Mrs Grills' circle of family and friends who fell ill; first his hair fell out and in October 1948 he died. Mary Ann Mickelson, taken ill with similar symptoms, was the next to die, then the late John Lundberg's widow and daughter began to lose their hair and feel a heavy deadness in their limbs.

They were nursed in their sickness by Caroline Grills, who seemed never happier than when soothing her patients with cups of tea. As the two women slowly weakened a relative began to put two and two together and arrived at the answer 'poison'. And when one of the cups of tea was analysed by the police chemist it was found to contain thallium – just in time to save the Lundbergs' lives.

Following a short investigation, Mrs Grills was arrested and charged with murder, though in advance of her trial, the prosecutor elected to proceed only on the charge of the *attempted* murder of Mrs Eveline Lundberg – who had now gone blind as the result of her experience with thallium. The prosecution contended that the pivotal motive for murder had been gain, but that there had been a secondary interest in Caroline Grills' clear desire to exercise the power of life and death over her victims. She was found guilty of the charge against her and sentenced to life imprisonment.

In jail, Mrs Grills became affectionately known as 'Aunt Thally' by her fellow inmates.

GROSSMANN, Georg Karl Grossmann was born in Neuruppen, Germany, in 1863, and had been a sadist and all-round degenerate from early youth, serving three terms of imprisonment for offences against children. In August 1921, Grossmann's fellow-residents in the apartment block overlooking Berlin's Silesian Railway terminal responded to the fearful shrieking coming from his flat by summoning the police. When they arrived, the noise had stopped – which was really no surprise, for officers found a young woman dead on Grossmann's bed, trussed up.

Grossmann had been in the same apartment since the year the Great War started (he had not participated in the conflict himself, being considered too undesirable even to serve as cannon fodder); and now that they came to think of it, his neighbours had been aware that a large number of street girls had passed in through Grossmann's front door to satisfy his lust, but could only remember a few of them coming out again. The answer was simple; Georg was butchering them, selling the flesh on the black market and dumping the useless bones into the river Spree. It is said that the 'Berlin Butcher' even had a hot-dog stand on the railway station from where he chose his next victim – while selling off the last.

Tried, convicted and sentenced to death, his last days in the condemned cell suited Georg Grossmann very badly, serving only to sever the already weak threads by which he was linked to sanity; in short, Georg went completely mad and decided to cheat the executioner by hanging himself. How many women he really killed will never be known, but some conservative estimates put Grossmann's toll higher than the fifty attributed to his contemporary Fritz **Haarmann**.

GUNNESS, Belle Bella Poulsdatter, as she was originally known, was born near Trondheim, Norway, in 1859, showing no early indication that she would enter history as one of America's busiest multiple murderers. She first set foot in the New World in 1883, marrying fellow-countryman Max Sorensen, and taking occupation of a homestead in Austin, Illinois, where Belle gave her time to farming and family. 1900 saw the turning point in Mrs Sorensen's life which would influence her whole future – Max Sorensen died.

Helped by the $100 that she realised selling up the ranch, Belle managed to put on a brave face and moved to Chicago to invest in a lodging-house. Within weeks a fire had destroyed her prospects as a hotelier, leaving Belle with no more than the huge insurance claim for comfort. This capital was put into a bakery business, and it too fell victim to the mysterious fire-bug.

The fact that her rooming-house had burned down before ever a guest's head had touched the pillow and her bakery was consumed before a single cookie had left the oven proved too much for the suspicious minds of the insurance investigators, and Belle was obliged to seek some less risky means of turning a dishonest dollar.

Marriage proved a satisfactory, if temporary, tactic, and Belle took herself to Laporte, Indiana, where she became Mrs Belle Gunness. Tragically, Peter Gunness did not long survive his wedding, a hatchet slipping from a high shelf dealing him a mortal blow on the head. Somewhat less tragically, he had taken out a sufficiently large insurance to permit his widow at least some solace.

Belle now realised that her future, and that of her growing children relied upon having a man about the house – or rather his money; and she must have heard that it pays to advertise:

Rich, good-looking widow, young, owner of a large farm, wishes to get in touch with a gentleman of wealth with cultured tastes. Object, matrimony.

Another specification, not entrusted to print, was that prospective husbands be without kith or kin. Surprisingly, there seemed no shortage of suitably unattached and friendless individuals, and Belle turned a tidy profit over the succeeding years:

I have been overjoyed by your answer to my advertisement, because I feel sure you are the one man for me. . . I have decided that every applicant I have considered favourably must make a satisfactory deposit of cash or security. I think that is the best way to keep away grafters who are on the lookout for an opportunity. I am worth at least $20,000, and if you could bring $5000 just to show you are in earnest, we could talk things over. . .

Of the many that arrived bearing money, none ever left, none was ever asked after. It was rotten luck then, when Belle chose a suitor named Andrew Holdgren, who not only had an undisclosed brother, but one to whom he had confided his marital aspirations.

After several months, Holdgren's brother was unimpressed to learn that Andrew had disappeared from Mrs Gunness's life and announced his imminent arrival.

Mr Holdgren was too late. On 28 April 1908, Belle's old adversary struck again. Police arriving at the conflagration found four charred corpses – one without a head was later identified as Mrs Gunness, the others as those of her children.

On 23 May, Roy Lamphere, employed by Belle to help out on the farm as well as other more 'personal' duties, was indicted on four counts of murder and one of arson. In the event, he was convicted only of arson.

Meanwhile the authorities were investigating the farm with picks and shovels. They solved the enigma of Andrew Holdgren – his dismembered body, wrapped in oil-cloth, was one of the first to be dug up. There were thirteen others, all cut up and neatly parcelled, there might even have been more had they dug further.

It was years before Roy Lamphere talked about that fatal night in 1908. He confided that he not only knew about the murders at Laporte, but had helped dispose of the victims. A more startling revelation was that the corpse identified as Belle Gunness was not his former employer and lover, but a female vagrant who had been lured to the farm.

And if this were true, where was Belle?

H

HAARMANN, Fritz The notorious 'Butcher of Hanover' who was responsible for the deaths of at least twenty-seven, possibly fifty, young men and boys between the years 1919 and 1924, Haarmann was also responsible for feeding a large number of families through his operations on the black market.

Like many whose crimes escalate to murder, Fritz Haarmann had spent many years serving his apprenticeship through petty theft and swindling, picking pockets and, more for pleasure, child molesting; he even gravitated to the despised activity of police informer – fingering other denizens of the murky world in which he lived. Not surprisingly, he was also familiar with the insides of a number of state prisons.

When the Great War ended in the crushing defeat of Germany, Fritz Haarmann was discharged from the jail in which he had sat out the conflict into a country broken by the ravages of four years' fighting, of families destroyed, of hundreds of homeless refugees from all over Germany, and a state of near famine. To a man as cynical and unscrupulous as Haarmann it was a business opportunity not to be missed. Posing as a policeman, Haarmann preyed upon the rootless young drifters who congregated around Hanover's main railway station, luring them to his grimy lodgings on the Kellerstrasse. Here Haarmann assaulted his victims sexually before biting his way through their throats until they were dead. Their clothing he sold; the meat from their bodies he sold; the bones and skulls he dumped in the river Leine.

In September 1919, Fritz Haarmann met a fellow homosexual degenerate named Hans Grans, and they transferred their expanding business to an apartment on Neuestrasse. Grans was clearly the dominant partner in the relationship, treating Haarmann little better than he would a servant, personally selecting their victims often because he coveted some small item of clothing for his own wardrobe, and making sure that it was Haarmann who took all the risks. During this period it has been calculated that they were disposing of two victims every week through the black market meat trade. Only once did a customer go to the police with her suspicions over the animal she was about to eat – only to be told that she should be grateful for finding so fine a piece of pork in such difficult times!

It might have gone on for years; German society was still desperately trying to re-form itself after the chaos of war; the victims were for the most part anonymous statistics; and the authorities were obliged to turn a blind eye to the black market.

Then the skulls started to be fished out of the Leine. On 22 June 1924, Fritz Haarmann was arrested trying to molest a boy in the street and a search of his apartment revealed piles of his victims' clothing awaiting sale. On 24 July, a pile of human remains was found by a group of children playing in a meadow, and the river began to yield up its collection of more than five hundred human bones.

Haarmann decided that now was the time to confess and by doing so implicated Hans Grans. Their trial at Hanover Assizes in December 1924, lasted fourteen days, during which Haarmann regularly interrupted the proceedings to shout some insult at witness or counsel. One particularly distressing exchange concerned a missing boy named Wolf, whose father was in the witness box to identify his pathetic possessions. Asking to see a snapshot of the boy, Haarmann held it aloft and shouted to the bereaved father that his son was far, far too ugly a creature to have interested him for one moment.

Haarmann and Grans's twenty-seven victims

Date	Name	Age
12 February 1923	Fritz Franke	17
20 March 1923	Wilhelm Schulze	17
17 May 1923	Hans Keimes	17
23 May 1923	Roland Huch	15
? May 1923	Hans Sennefeld	20
25 June 1923	Ernst Ehrenberg	13
24 August 1923	Heinrich Strauss	18
24 September 1923	Paul Bronischewski	17
? September 1923	Richard Graf	17
12 October 1923	Wilhelm Erdner	16
25 October 1923	Hermann Wolf	?
27 October 1923	Heinz Brinkmann	13
? November 1923	Adolf Hannappel	17
6 December 1923	Adolf Hennies	?
5 January 1924	Ernst Spiecker	17
15 January 1924	Heinrich Koch	?
2 February 1924	Willi Senger	20
8 February 1924	Hermann Speichert	15
6 April 1924	Alfred Hogrefe	17
? April 1924	Hermann Bock	23
17 April 1924	Wilhelm Apel	16
26 April 1924	Robert Witzel	18
9 May 1924	Heinz Martin	16
25 May 1924	Friedrich Abeling	10
26 May 1924	Fritz Wittig	?
5 June 1924	Friedrich Koch	16
14 June 1924	Erich de Vries	17

It was a puzzle to Haarmann why he was only being charged with twenty-seven murders, when to his own imperfect recollection the number must be more than forty. But the twenty-seven were sufficient to earn him a death sentence, and it was while he awaited decapitation that Haarmann produced a lengthy volume of lurid, rather fanciful confessions, in which he blames his sexual perversions for the lust to kill. As for Grans, he was sentenced to a more modest twelve years imprisonment.

HAERM, Dr Teet, and THOMAS, Dr Allgen Lars Dr Haerm, with the assistance of his colleague Dr Thomas, was responsible for the murder of eight prostitutes around Stockholm and Copenhagen between 1984 and 1986.

The dismembered body of Catrine da Costa was found in a plastic bag on a sports field in Copenhagen on 19 July 1984. A week later, Annika Mors was found in a similar condition dumped in a public park. On 1 August, Kristine Caravache's naked body was found in Stockholm's red-light district; she had been strangled. In addition, five more prostitutes disappeared and were assumed to be victims of the same killer.

A description of a man cruising in a car around the red-light district led to Dr Teet Haerm; ironically he was the surgeon who had performed the post-mortem examinations on the victims. There had already been suspicion over the death of Haerm's wife in 1982, but as in the present case he was questioned and then released from custody because of lack of evidence on which to proceed. The scandal, however, was enough to result in Haerm being discharged from his post as pathologist.

In March 1985, the bodies of two of the five missing prostitutes were found in a car dumped in the sea off Hamarby. On 7 January 1986, the body of Tazuga Toyonaga, a Japanese student, was found in Copenhagen; she had been mutilated in a similar way to the earlier victims.

It was not until 1987, when a welfare department began an investigation into the claim by a four-year-old girl that she had been molested by her father – Dr Allgen Lars Thomas – that the prostitute murders were solved. Under interrogation, Thomas confessed to having helped Dr Haerm commit the murders, explaining that Haerm was the leader of a secret society committed to elimination of prostitution, and the encouragement of cannibalism and necrophilia.

Haerm was charged with the murders of eight prostitutes, his wife and the Japanese student. Thomas was charged with the rape and murder of Catrine da Costa, and with molesting his own daughter. On 16 September 1988, both doctors were sentenced to life imprisonment.

HAHN, Anna Marie With her husband Philip and their young son, Anna Hahn emigrated from Germany to Cincinnati, Ohio, in 1929; and like so many immigrants before them, from so many countries, the Hahns made their home among their compatriots. They settled into the city's well-established German quarter, and soon Anna Hahn was recognised as the unofficial (and certainly unqualified) 'nurse' to the elderly gentlemen in the German community.

The wealthier these *alterer Herren* were, the more accommodating Anna was. And if their attentions sometimes passed beyond the merely paternal, then the gifts of money and promises of future bequests more than compensated.

In a matter of only a few years, Anna Hahn had been able to develop a most extravagant style of living, and by now some of her investments seemed to be paying off. Herr Ernest Kohler, for example, died in 1933 leaving Anna his large house. On 1 June 1937, Jacob Wagner was taken on as a patient and died the next day; later in the week another patient, seventy-year-old Georg Opendorfer suddenly died.

It had not gone unremarked, though, that both Wagner and Opendorfer had suffered acute stomach pains and vomiting in their final hours, and the deaths were suspicious enough to require the intervention of the police. In each instance the autopsy revealed that death, far from being natural, had been accelerated by a mixture of croton oil (a strong purgative) and arsenic. Autopsies subsequently carried out on Frau Hahn's other recently deceased patients indicated similar large quantities of various poisons. Unfortunately for her, Anna Hahn's house was also found to be well stocked with various poisons, and despite her claims to have been 'an angel of mercy' to her gentlemen patients, Anna was taken into custody.

Her case was hardly helped by her husband; when Philip Hahn reported that his wife had several times tried to persuade him to insure his life for large sums, and when he refused he began to suffer stomach cramps and vomiting, Anna's future looked bleak indeed.

At her trial, Anna Hahn's counsel admitted that his client had robbed and swindled the old men, but that charge, he suggested, was a very different matter from murder, which she absolutely denied. Anna was convicted nevertheless, and sentenced to death; she died in the electric chair on 7 December 1938. For all it might have cheered her last hours, Anna Hahn had the doubtful privilege of being the first woman in the state of Ohio to be judicially electrocuted.

HAIGH, John George   The notorious 'Acid Bath Murderer', Haigh successfully killed and disposed of five victims in vats of acid before being trapped by a combination of his own carelessness and arrogance.

In February 1949, Haigh was living at the Onslow Court Hotel, west London, and had become friendly with fellow resident Mrs Olive Durand-Deacon, a widow of independent means whose modest fortune Haigh had already earmarked for his own use. On the pretence of assisting Mrs Durand-Deacon in a scheme for marketing false fingernails, Haigh lured her down to his 'workshop' outside

Crawley, Sussex. Here he shot the unsuspecting woman through the neck and, having stripped it of any valuables, steeped her body in a forty-gallon oil drum of sulphuric acid.

In the course of the subsequent inquiry into the disappearance of Mrs Durand-Deacon, police interviewed Haigh on several occasions and formed a very poor opinion of his oily, ingratiating manner. A visit to his Crawley workshop revealed enough significant clues – not least a recently fired .38 Webley revolver and traces of blood – to have Haigh placed under arrest. Under questioning, Haigh made this startling announcement: 'Mrs Durand-Deacon no longer exists. I've destroyed her with acid. You can't prove murder without a body.' Of course Haigh was quite wrong, a number of significant cases *had* been proved without a corpse. But he was also wrong about Mrs Durand-Deacon no longer existing. It was true that the acid had succeeded in its grisly task of reducing Mrs Durand-Deacon's flesh and bones to a greasy sludge – but what Haigh had not taken account of was the longer time needed to destroy plastics. A set of acrylic dentures, custom-made for Mrs Durand-Deacon were positively identified by her dentist, and her red plastic handbag with many of its contents were positively identified by her friends.

Haigh's extravagant claim that he was a vampire who drank the blood of his victims was seen for what it was – a rather unsophisticated ruse to establish a defence of insanity – to exchange Broadmoor for the noose. As it was, John George Haigh kept his appointment with the hangman at Wandsworth Prison on 10 August 1949.

His account of the previous murders also makes interesting reading, because it provides a chilling insight into the cold, 'professional' approach that John Haigh had to murder – for him it was a job of work much like any other:

The Ration Books and clothing coupon books and other documents in the names of McSwan and Henderson [which police had found in his room at the Onslow Court Hotel] are the subject of another story. This is covered very briefly by the fact that in 1944 I disposed of William Donald McSwan in a similar way to the above [Mrs Durand-Deacon] in the basement of 79 Gloucester Road, SW7, and of Donald McSwan and Amy McSwan in 1946 at the same address. In 1948 Dr Archibald Henderson and his wife Rosalie Henderson also in a similar manner at Leopold Road, Crawley.

Going back to the McSwans, William Donald, the son, whose address at that particular time I can't remember, met me at the Goat public house, Kensington High Street, and from there we went to No. 79 Gloucester Road, where in the basement which I had rented, I hit him on the head with a cosh, withdrew a glass of blood from his throat as before and drank it. He was dead within five minutes or so. I put him in a forty-gallon tank and disposed of him with acid as before in the case of Mrs Durand-Deacon, disposing of the sludge down a manhole in the basement.

I took his watch and odds and ends, including an Identity Card before putting him in the tank. I had known this McSwan and his mother and father for some time and on seeing his mother and father explained that he had gone off to avoid his 'call up'. I wrote a number of letters in due course to his mother and father purporting to come from him and posted in, I think, Glasgow and Edinburgh, explaining various details of the disposition of properties, which were to follow. In the following year I took separately to the same basement the father Donald and the mother Amy, disposing of them in exactly the same way as the son. The files of the McSwans are at my hotel and will give details of the properties which I disposed of after their deaths. I have since got additional Ration Books by producing their Identity Cards in the usual way.

I met the Hendersons by answering an advertisement offering for sale their property at 22 Ladbroke Square. I did not purchase. They sold it and moved to 16 Dawes Road, Fulham. This runs in a period from November 1947 to February 1948. In February 1948 the Hendersons were staying at Kingsgate Castle, Kent. I visited them there and went with them to Brighton, where they stayed at the Metropole. From here I took Dr Henderson to Crawley and disposed of him in the same store room at Leopold Road by shooting him in the head with his own revolver, which I had taken from his property at Dawes Road. I put him in a tank of acid as in the other cases. This was in the morning and I went back to Brighton and brought up Mrs Henderson on the pretext that her husband was ill. I shot her in the store room and put her in another tank and disposed of her with acid. In each of the last four cases I had my glass of blood as before. In the case of Dr Henderson I removed his gold cigarette case, his gold pocket watch and chain and from his wife her wedding ring and diamond ring and disposed of all this to Bull's at Horsham for about £300. I paid their bill at the Hotel Metropole, collected their luggage and their red setter and took the luggage to Dawes Road. The dog I kept for a period at the Onslow Court Hotel and later at Gatwick Hall until I had to send him to Professor Sorsby's Kennels in the country on account of his night blindness. By means of letters purporting to come from the Hendersons I kept the relatives quiet, by sending the letters to Mrs Henderson's brother Arnold Burlin, who lives in Manchester. His address is in the Index book in my room. No. 16 Dawes Road, I acquired by forged deeds of transfer and sold it to the present owner, J.B. Clarke. The McSwan properties were also acquired in a similar way and disposed of and the particulars are in the file at the Hotel.

I have read this statement and it is true.
(Signed) John George Haigh

HANCE, William Henry Following the activities of the so-called 'Stocking Strangler' Carlton **Gary**, William Hance wrote a letter to a Georgia newspaper in March 1978, signing himself 'The Forces of Evil', and threatening to kill a black woman every thirty days unless the 'Strangler's' toll on elderly women ceased and the crimes were solved. Less public-spiritedly he also demanded a ten-thousand dollar ransom.

Within days of the letter being received, the decomposed remains of a black woman, later identified as Brenda Gail Faison, were found buried in a shallow grave outside Fort Benning army base; she had been bludgeoned to death. Two other women, Mrs Irene Thirkield and Private Karen Hickman, both black, were missing. At the very least it could be assumed that the Forces of Evil were serious in 'their' threat.

As they pieced together the last hours of the deceased Gail Faison, army CID officers made a breakthrough when they identified a soldier who had been seen drinking with her shortly before her disappearance. He was William Henry Hance, who was also believed to be behind the Forces of Evil letter.

Following a telephone tip-off, army police found the body of Irene Thirkield buried on an isolated and little-used rifle range at Fort Benning; like Gail Faison, Mrs Thirkield had been battered to death.

During an intensive interrogation, Hance confessed to three murders and led officers to the body of Private Hickman in a ditch inside the military post. He was initially indicted by the civil authorities for the murder of Gail Faison and charges of extortion arising from the ransom demand. At his trial, Hance was convicted and sentenced to die in the electric chair. He was then charged by the Army with the Thirkield and Hickman murders, and after an appearance before the court martial, Hance was convicted on both counts and sentenced to two terms of life imprisonment (the prosecutor had not asked for the death penalty). However, these findings were not ratified by a military review board which overturned Hance's convictions; in view of his already existing death sentence the Army decided not to retry Hance.

William Hance's defence counsel instituted formal appeals and the first two hearings against the civil conviction were dismissed. Nevertheless, a circuit court of appeal rejected the death sentence and ordered a new sentencing trial. At the end of the day it made very little difference, the jury at the new penalty hearing simply reinstated the death sentence.

HANSEN, Robert The skeletal remains of a woman later identified as topless barmaid Paula Golding were found in November 1981, buried in a shallow grave dug into a river bank near Anchorage, Alaska. In the same month another topless dancer, Sherry Morrow, disappeared, and her frozen body was found a year later in the same general area as the previous victim. Already, two girls had been found buried in 1980, and the signs were that these murders all formed part of the same series. One of these earlier victims was never identified, and the other was thought to be one Joanna Messina. Due to the extensive decomposition of the bodies, the cause of death could only be established in two out of the four cases – shooting with a high-powered rifle.

In what at the time seemed to be an entirely separate case, police were investigating the claim by a teenaged prostitute that she had been kidnapped, tortured and raped by well-known Anchorage resident Robert Hansen. When he was questioned, Hansen claimed an alibi and gave the names of two men who would support it; under interrogation the two alibi witnesses refused to incriminate themselves and admitted that Hansen had paid them to lie. His house was searched, and Hansen was found to be in possession of a rifle which ballistics experts later proved to have been used in two of the earlier murders.

What was more, a map was found in the house indicating the graves not only of the four known victims, but also sixteen other marked sites.

Hansen confessed to killing seventeen women after torturing and sexually abusing them. In some instances he had turned the naked girls loose in open country, given them a head start, and then tracked them down like animals with a high-powered hunting rifle.

On 28 February, Hansen pleaded guilty to four counts of murder and one each of kidnapping and rape. He was sentenced to life imprisonment on one count of murder, ninety-nine years on each of the others, and forty years for kidnapping and rape, all to be served without the possibility of parole.

HARE, William *see* BURKE, William

HARVEY, Donald   A hospital orderly, Harvey is thought to be responsible for the deaths of upwards of fifty patients in hospitals and nursing homes around Kentucky and Ohio.

The investigations started when John Powell, a patient at the Drake Memorial Hospital, Cincinnati, died suddenly in March 1987. An autopsy established that death had been due to cyanide poisoning, and under questioning Donald Harvey confessed to murder. Further inquiries showed that Harvey's nursing career had been punctuated by a succession of homosexual affairs and a far-above-average rate of fatalities in the institutions in which he was employed. Sudden deaths had also occurred among Harvey's lovers, friends and neighbours.

In June 1987 an Ohio television station reported that at least twenty-three questionable deaths had occurred in the last hospital at which Harvey had been engaged, and following a grand-jury investigation, a plea-bargain was made with Harvey's attorney to forgo the death penalty on any charges that might be brought. On 19 August,

Donald Harvey pleaded guilty to twenty-four murders and was sentenced to twenty years to life on each count, to be served consecutively. At a further trial, Harvey also pleaded guilty to murdering one of his neighbours, and was handed down another life sentence. This last murder had effectively disposed of Harvey's earlier claim that he had only killed terminally ill patients as an act of mercy. Free of the death penalty, Harvey now confessed to at least fifty-eight murders.

The action then moved to Kentucky where, at a further trial under a new plea-bargaining arrangement, Harvey pleaded guilty to eight counts of murder and one of manslaughter at Marymount Hospital; he was sentenced to eight more life terms plus twenty years. Even then, Harvey's ordeal was far from over; back in Ohio he was indicted on three more counts of murder and three of attempted murder. Donald Harvey had collected enough sentences to ensure that he will remain confined for the rest of his life.

HATCHER, Charles   Hatcher's first victim was a fellow prisoner in the Missouri State Penitentiary in 1961, and his final killing was that of eleven-year-old Michelle Steele at St Joseph, Missouri, in 1982. In between these crimes, Charles Hatcher claimed responsibility for at least fourteen other murders, including one for which another man was wrongly imprisoned for five years.

On 2 July 1961, Jerry Lee Tharrington, nearing the end of a prison term for burglary was stabbed in the back in the kitchen of Missouri State Penitentiary. He died instantly and it was reported that he had also been raped. The prison authorities isolated Hatcher, who was then serving time for trying to abduct a newspaper boy. An incorrigible bully who was generally feared by other inmates, Hatcher could not be accounted for at the time of the murder; however, in the absence of any direct evidence no charge could be brought against him.

In August 1969, after Charles Hatcher's release, he abducted twelve-year-old William Freeman and for no reason at all strangled him. Hatcher was later to claim that this was his sixth or seventh victim.

Later in the same month, Hatcher was arrested in San Francisco for sodomising a five-year-old boy. The trial was delayed by a series of psychiatric examinations until April 1973, and he was finally sentenced to one year to life. Released on licence in 1977, Hatcher almost immediately broke parole and left the city.

Four-year-old Eric Christgen was abducted and strangled in St Joseph, Missouri, in May 1978. In February 1979, Melvin Reynolds, a local man confessed to police that he had killed Eric, and was sentenced to life imprisonment. Prior to this, in September 1978, Hatcher had been arrested in Omaha, Nebraska, for sodomy, and briefly detained as mentally unstable. In May 1979, he was arrested for attempting to kill a seven-year-old boy, again declared mentally ill and detained in a secure hospital for a year. There followed a succession of arrests for various assaults, from all of which Charles Hatcher escaped imprisonment on account of his continuing psychological problems, and when institutionalised either escaped or was released prematurely.

On 20 June 1981, Hatcher stabbed to death James L. Churchill, aged thirty-eight, near Rock Island, Illinois. Back in St Joseph, he attempted to abduct children on successive days in July 1982, and on 30 July he kidnapped, raped and murdered eleven-year-old Michelle Steele. Arrested for this crime, Hatcher confessed to the murders of Eric Christgen, James Churchill and William Freeman.

For the murder of Eric Christgen, to which he pleaded guilty, Hatcher was sentenced to life imprisonment on 13 October 1982. The following day, Melvin Reynolds was released from prison. On 22 September 1984, Hatcher appeared in court again and was sentenced to a further life term for the murder of Michelle Steele. At the end of the trial, Hatcher pleaded for the death penalty.

What is remarkable about the case of Charles Hatcher is the almost criminal laxity of the mental health service in allowing this obviously dangerous, obviously sick man back on to the streets so many times following serious offences of violence. It can only be stated that, in the end, even Hatcher must have got sick of his own company, for on 7 December 1984, he hanged himself in prison.

HEATH, Neville George Clevely Margery Gardner, a thirty-two-year-old film extra, first met 'Lieutenant-Colonel Heath' in May 1946. Much the worse for drink, they booked into London's Pembridge Court Hotel, where Mrs Gardner was stripped, tied up and flogged by Heath; they were enjoying themselves.

On 15 June, nineteen-year-old Yvonne Symonds went to a WRNS dance in Chelsea, and there succumbed to the gentle manners and easy charm of the man calling himself Lieutenant-Colonel Heath. After spending the following Sunday in each other's company, and after Heath had proposed marriage, Yvonne Symonds consented to being booked into the Pembridge Court Hotel under the rather premature title 'Mrs N.G.C. Heath'. Sex, if it took place at all, was by Heath's standards disarmingly normal; Miss Symonds was not attracted to flagellation.

The second time that Margery Gardner shared Heath's room at the Pembridge Court Hotel, Thursday 20 June, was the last. The following afternoon a chambermaid found, on the bed nearest the door, covered by bedclothes, the shape of a person, a very still, stiff person. Beneath the covers Margery Gardner's naked body lay on its back, her feet tied together with a handkerchief; her wrists, judging by the marks, had also been bound, though the ligature had been removed. Her face had been severely bruised consistent with having been punched repeatedly. There were no less than seventeen vicious lash marks on various parts of her body – marks with a distinctive diamond criss-cross pattern. In addition the breasts had been bitten, the nipples almost bitten off. Finally, some rough object had been forced into her vagina causing excessive bleeding. The unspeakable savagery of the injuries was compounded by the fact that Margery Gardner had been alive when they were inflicted; death had come later, from suffocation.

That same morning Heath had gone down to Worthing to visit his fiancée. On the Saturday evening over dinner, Heath told Miss Symonds that a terrible murder had occurred in London at the Pembridge Court Hotel, in the room that *he* had booked; what was more, he had actually seen the body – 'a very gruesome sight'. Quite how this was affecting Yvonne Symonds' appetite we can only guess. Heath added that he met the victim earlier on the evening of her death, and that he had lent her his room to entertain a gentleman friend, and that on the following afternoon Inspector Barrett had personally invited him to view the body.

Next day Heath moved along the coast to Bournemouth from where he posted a preposterous letter to Scotland Yard's Inspector Barrett, in which he claimed to have met the late Margery Gardner and lent her his hotel room in order to accommodate a man friend with whom 'for mainly financial reasons' she was obliged to sleep . . . 'It must have been nearly 3 a.m. when I returned to the hotel and found her in the condition of which you are aware. I realised that I was in an invidious position, and rather than notify the police, I packed my belongings and left. Since then I have been in several minds whether to come forward or not but in view of the circumstances I have been afraid to. I can give you a description of the man. He was aged approximately thirty, dark hair (black), with small moustache. Height about 5ft 9in, slim build. His name was Jack and I gathered he was a friend of Mrs Gardner of some long standing . . . I have the instrument with which Mrs Gardner was beaten and am forwarding this to you today. You will find my fingerprints on it, but you should also find others as well.' The letter was signed 'N.G.C. Heath'. The alleged 'instrument' never arrived.

Neville Heath reached the Tollard Royal Hotel on the West Cliff at Bournemouth on 23 June, checking in as Group-Captain Rupert Brooke. On the morning of 3 July 'Brooke' met twenty-one-year-old Doreen Marshall along the promenade and later that evening entertained her to supper at his hotel. In a later statement to the police – when they finally caught up with him – Heath claimed: 'We dined at about 8.15 p.m. and sat talking in the lounge after dinner, moving into the writing room at about 10 p.m. The conversation was again general but she told me she was considering cutting short her holiday and returning home [she lived in Pinner] on Friday instead of Monday. The conversation continued until approximately 11.30 p.m. . . . the weather was clear and we left the hotel and sat on a seat overlooking the sea.'

When 'Group-Captain Brooke' returned to his hotel he 'decided to practise a small deception' on the night porter: 'as a ladder had that day been placed up against my window . . . [I] entered my hotel bedroom via the ladder'.

On 5 July the Norfolk Hotel's manager notified the police that one of his guests was missing – Miss Doreen Marshall. At the same time he informed his opposite number at the Tollard Royal, who asked 'Brooke' whether his guest might have been the missing Miss Marshall. 'Oh, no,' Brooke laughed. 'I've known that lady for a long while.' Nevertheless, the manager suggested, it might be wise to get in touch with the police.

And with amazing bravado Heath presented himself at Bournemouth police station at 5.30 that evening. He was shown a photograph of the missing girl, and with a great show of surprise and sorrow admitted that it was, after all, the same young woman with whom he had dined on the night of her disappearance. Throughout this exchange, Detective-Constable Suter had been scrutinising his guest carefully; he bore an uncanny resemblance to the photograph of the man Heath that Scotland Yard were anxious to interview. Finally, he gave voice to his thoughts: 'Brooke, is your real name Heath?' 'Good Lord, no!' he replied, 'But I agree it is like me.'

Nonetheless, the good detective detained his visitor until the Inspector arrived, at which point 'Brooke's' meagre belongings were brought from the Tollard Royal to the police station. Searched in front of him, Brooke's jacket pockets yielded a left-luggage ticket issued at Bournemouth West station, the return half of a first-class railway ticket issued to Doreen Marshall, and a single artificial pearl from a necklace. When the suitcase was redeemed from the station, a further damning array of evidence was revealed: clothing and a hat marked with the name 'Heath', and a blue woollen scarf and neckerchief, both stained with blood and bearing hairs later proved to have come from Doreen Marshall's head. At the bottom of the case was a leather riding switch; a riding switch with a distinctive diamond-pattern weave.

Early the following day Detective Inspector Reg Spooner arrived from London, and on Monday 8 July, Heath was removed to Scotland Yard, where he was charged with the murder of Margery Gardner.

Meanwhile, Doreen Marshall's mutilated body had been discovered at Branksome Dene Chine. Close by, police searchers found Doreen's torn stockings, a powder compact and a broken string of artificial pearls.

The trial of Neville Heath opened at the Old Bailey on 24 September 1946; he was charged only with the murder of Margery Gardner and pleaded not guilty.

There was never any question of Heath's guilt – he was quite patently a vicious and sadistic killer. The question was, was he insane? Mr Casswell's defence rested heavily on the fact that a man simply *had* to be mad to have committed such grotesque crimes; that though Heath may well have known what he was doing, he was so morally bankrupt that he had no conception at the time that what he was doing was wrong. For the Crown, two prison doctors, while allowing that Heath was both a sexual pervert and a psychopath, refused to agree that he was insane within the scope of the McNaghten Rules – which determined such matters in law.

As for the prisoner himself, he seemed throughout the three days of the trial to be quite indifferent to the proceedings – even bored. He said not one word in his own defence, nor exhibited the slightest remorse. After a retirement of one hour, the jury were unanimous in their verdict – guilty of murder.

Heath made no appeal and no last-minute confession; his sole gesture to decency was to admit, in a letter to his parents, that he had been 'damned unworthy of you both'. On 16 October he stood on the scaffold at Pentonville Prison. Before hangman Albert Pierrepoint carried out his public duty, Neville Heath is said to have asked the prison governor for a whisky, adding, 'You might as well make that a double.'

HEIRENS, William Born in Chicago in 1929, Heirens had impressed on him at an early age by a domineering mother that sex was a dirty and evil thing. So deeply had this cruel teaching affected him that Heirens claimed in later life that he was physically sick if ever he tried to caress a girl. Before he was even a teenager, Billy Heirens had already acquired an unenviably long record for burglary and arson which, following the repression of his sexual instincts, he saw as an alternative source of gratification. He had also collected an impressive arsenal of firearms and had a drawer full of stolen women's underwear which he enjoyed wearing in the privacy of his bedroom.

In 1942 Heirens broke into a storeroom and was sent to a reform school where he was reportedly of fairly good behaviour, but decidedly introverted. At the age of sixteen, Billy entered Chicago University where he was a below-average student; in June that same year, 1945, he slashed and stabbed to death Josephine Ross, the occupant of an apartment he was in the act of burgling. His haul amounted to a miserable $12.

In October he killed and mutilated Frances Brown in similar circumstances, using Mrs Brown's lipstick to scrawl on her wall: 'For heavens sake catch me before I kill more. I cannot control myself'; it was in the following year that the police learned just how little control Heirens had. Arrested while he was on a burgling foray at an apartment block in Chicago, Heirens confessed to three killings, including the kidnap, murder and dismemberment of six-year-old Suzanne Degnan. He subsequently disposed of the child's remains down a sewer grating.

Displaying neither regret nor remorse, Heirens proceeded to lay the blame for his crimes squarely on the shoulders of 'George Murman' – not a confederate, a partner in crime, but a sinister *alter ego* under whose malignant influence he had slain and robbed his way around Chicago: 'When I went out on a burglary, it seemed that George was doing it.'

On 4 September 1946, George and William were sentenced to three consecutive terms of life imprisonment in Joliet penitentiary with no possibility of parole.

HENLEY, Elmer Wayne *see* **CORLL, Dean Allen**

'HILLSIDE STRANGLER' *see* **BIANCHI, Kenneth Alessio**

HINDLEY, Myra *see* **BRADY, Ian**

HOLMES, H.H. *see* **MUDGETT, Hermann Webster**

HONKA, Fritz   The mysterious disappearances of women known to frequent Hamburg's 'Golden Glove' bar had already been occupying the efforts of the city's police department for some time when, on 17 June 1975, a fire broke out on the second floor of 76 Zeiss Street. In an attempt to prevent the fire spreading upwards, the fire brigade forced an entry into the attic flat of thirty-nine-year-old night watchman Fritz Honka. At the same time as controlling the blaze, they also found the remains of four of the missing women.

One of the corpses, consisting only of a torso and lower parts of the legs was identified as Ruth Schult; another torso, lacking arms, legs, head and breasts, was linked to Gertrude Braeuer. Fraulein Braeuer's head and limbs had been found thrown into a yard in November 1971. Another body which had been completely mummified was later proved to be Freda Roblick, and to compound the horror, the body of Anna Beuschel had been entirely dismembered and the parts put in a heap in the corner of the room.

When Fritz Honka selected a new lady-friend – and there seemed to be no shortage of willing consorts – he had very specific requirements; they should be no taller than himself (five feet four inches) and have no teeth. This last, uncommon requirement was explained by Honka's preference for oral sex, and his morbid fear of careless teeth damaging his sensitive parts. By and large this selection procedure seems to have worked very well; the exceptions, so police later learned, were those women who saw Honka's inability to indulge in 'normal' sex as a subject for ridicule. These he strangled, subjected their dead bodies to sexual indignities and dismembered. Of course the bodies began to smell after a while and Honka had joined his neighbours in puzzling over where the unpleasant odours originated – certainly not from his apartment he insisted!

After faking memory loss in the matter of the corpses in his apartment, Honka made a full confession, pleaded guilty at his trial and was sentenced to life imprisonment.

I J

'I-5 KILLER' *see* **WOODFIELD, Randall Brent**

'**JACK THE RIPPER**' For the three months from the end of August to the beginning of November in the year of 1888, the Whitechapel area of the East End of London was witness to a series of vicious – and still unsolved – murders. The slayings were characterised by an unparalleled savagery; each of the five victims – all prostitutes – had been attacked from behind and their throats cut; in four cases the bodies were afterwards subjected to such mutilation and dissection as to suggest a perverted sexual motive.

The enduring mystery of these, probably the world's most celebrated crimes, has resulted in a Ripper bibliography itself a bulkier tome than most of the volumes it lists, and this *Encyclopedia* is not the appropriate place for any more than a brief outline of the details.

The first victim was Mary Ann Nichols (called 'Polly') who perished on Friday, 31 August 1888, in Buck's Row. A report on the following morning claimed, 'No murder was ever more ferociously and more brutally done.' On 8 September, 'Dark Annie' Chapman, forty-seven years of age, was viciously slaughtered in Hanbury Street.

A double event occurred on Sunday, 30 September. The first body was found at around one o'clock in the morning by a carter about his lawful business in Berners Street: 'The body was that of a woman with a deep gash on the throat running almost from ear to ear;' she was later identified as 'Long Liz' Stride. It was at the south-west corner of Mitre Square that the second body, that of Catherine Eddowes, was found: 'In this case the face had also been so slashed as to render it hard for the remains to be identified, and the abdomen had been ripped up, and a portion of the intestines had been dragged out and left lying about the neck . . . The deed of blood had been the work of a practised hand . . .'

The last and most gruesome – because the Ripper had time to spare – was the murder in her room at Miller's Court of Mary Jane Kelly on 9 November:

The throat had been cut right across with a knife, nearly severing the head from the body. The abdomen had been partially ripped open, and both of the breasts had been cut from the body, the left arm, like the head, hung to the body by the skin only. The nose had been cut off, the forehead skinned, and the thighs, down to the feet, stripped of the flesh. The abdomen had been slashed with a knife across and downwards, and the liver and entrails wrenched away. The entrails and other portions of the frame were missing, but the liver, etc., it is said, were found placed between the feet of the poor victim. The flesh from the thighs and legs, together with the breasts and nose, had been placed by the murderer on the table, and one of the hands of the dead woman had been pushed into her stomach.

(*Illustrated Police News*)

And then the murders stopped; and the controversy that was to last a century and more began. Despite the huge effort put in by the Metropolitan Police no reliable evidence was ever found on which to bring a charge of murder, and such theories as there are regarding Jack's identity range between the improbable and the impossible – indeed, there are almost as many theories as there are theorists. A selection of some of the most prominent might be:

Montague John Druitt: failed lawyer who drowned himself in the river Thames in December 1888. The fact that his death coincided with the cessation of the Whitechapel Murders is seen by some as incontrovertible proof of Druitt's guilt.

Severin Klosowski (alias George **Chapman**): a triple wife-poisoner, there is little precedent for a killer to so sharply change his *modus operandi*. Nevertheless it is recorded that Detective Chief Inspector Frederick Abberline, in charge of the hunt for the Ripper, observed on the arrest of Chapman, 'You've got Jack the Ripper at last.' He later retracted this accusation, but it has become deeply embedded in Ripper mythology.

Dr Roslyn D'Onston Stephenson: esoteric author and magician who, it was suggested, performed the East End Murders as part of a Black Magic ritual. The 'mystery' deepened when Stephenson himself disappeared in 1904.

HRH Prince Albert Victor, Duke of Clarence (grandson of Queen Victoria): scandal in the Royal Family has always been popular, and Clarence surfaces in a number of theories which lay greater or lesser blame on the Duke himself. The most currently fashionable suggestion is of a conspiracy between *Sir William Gull*, the royal physician, the artist Walter Sickert and a royal coachman named John Netley; they apparently committed the murders in order to prevent a scandal involving Clarence, a shop girl, and an illegitimate child. A contrary theory names as the killer *James Kenneth Stephen*, the Duke's tutor at Cambridge, a homosexual and, so it is claimed, a pathological hater of women.

Dr Thomas Neill **Cream**: a multicide in his own right, Cream's only tenuous link with the Ripper is a self-perpetuating legend that on the scaffold he cried out, 'I am Jack . . . ' a confession sadly cut short by the tightening rope. Besides, Thomas Cream was in prison in America during the Autumn of Terror.

In addition it has been suggested that Jack may have been *Jill the Ripper*, possibly a mad midwife or an abominable abortionist; or was it a Jewish *ritual slaughterman*, a not-uncommon sight in the East End, who would reasonably be expected to wear blood-stained clothes and carry a bloody knife? Indeed, there were also references to another Jew, a Pole named *Kosminski* who lived in Whitechapel and was confined to an asylum in March 1889.

For what it is worth, it is the opinion of one of the authors that Jack was somebody quite other than these candidates; a killer who is so far, and likely to remain, unnamed and undetected.

'JACK THE STRIPPER' By the time her body was found on a patch of waste land near the Thames at Acton on 16 February 1965, twenty-eight-year-old Bridie O'Hara was the sixth prostitute to have been similarly killed and left naked in the space of one year. Bridie O'Hara had been asphyxiated after an unsuccessful attempt had been made to strangle her; her front teeth were missing and semen was found in the back of her throat.

The first victim of the killer who had become known as 'Jack the Stripper' was Hannah Tailford, found strangled on the foreshore of the Thames near Hammersmith Bridge on 2 February 1964; nobody could have foretold that the death of one member of that vulnerable profession was the overture to one of London's most notorious cases of serial murder. Bridie O'Hara was the finale. The police had eliminated two from an original list of eight possible victims, one as dying from natural causes, one as a suicide.

Investigating officers under Detective Superintendent Frank Davies had entertained their share of the publicity-seekers and lunatics who dog any such enquiry, including a believable fifty-four-year-old bachelor caretaker who confessed to one of the murders while in custody on another charge – Kenneth Archibald was eventually found not guilty and set free after a lengthy trial.

The breakthrough in the 'Nude Murders' case came when the Metropolitan Police Forensic Laboratory found particles adhering to the bodies of two later victims which were identified as flakes of paint of the kind used to spray cars. After exhaustive searching, officers located the paint-spray shop where four of the bodies had been stored prior to disposal in or beside the river; furthermore, it was located close to where Bridie O'Hara's body was found on the Heron Trading Estate.

The fact that the women were all abducted between the hours of 11.00 p.m. and 1.00 a.m., and dumped between 5.00 and 6.00 a.m., led police to make an educated guess that they were looking for a night-shift worker. Despite anticipation that an arrest was imminent, no charge was ever brought in the case. Nevertheless, one of the main suspects, a forty-five-year-old man whose name has never been revealed, killed himself during the investigation; his suicide note read, in part, that he was 'unable to stand it any longer'. Significantly, the man was a night-security guard whose rounds included the paint shop on the Heron Trading Estate.

JEGADO, Hélène   Following a most unpromising start in life as an orphan – and a particularly unattractive specimen at that – Hélène was, as were so many similar unfortunates, taken into domestic service to endure a future of endless drudgery followed by bleak old age. Revenge for the cruel lot cast for her passed through Hélène Jegado's mind when she was thirty years old. Within a period of three months, she had disposed of seven members of the household, including her own sister, through the simple expedient of poison. But such a pretence of devoted care had this cunning maid shown that even the local authorities could not bring themselves to think her capable of such infernal wickedness as murder.

It is clear that Hélène derived considerable pleasure from killing people, for no sooner had she found a new position, than the family 'upstairs' and her fellow servants began to drop like flies. Hélène Jegado was a committed and, one might almost say, 'professional' poisoner, for no matter how long her list of victims grew, by a judicious combination of hurt innocence ('Wherever I go, people die,' she would moan), and keeping on the move, she was never once suspected. When she tired of the rigours of the world, Hélène entered a convent and became Sister Hélène. It was a brush with the godly that did not last long, and she was thrown out for breaking that commandment which cautioned against stealing.

She was asked to leave her next convent for breaking that other commandment that forbids poisoning one's fellow nuns, and though in the interests of preserving the Order's good name no official inquiry was ever held, Hélène was once again looking for employment. It was 1833, and during her wanderings here and there during the next ten years, there can be traced a trail of corpses that number at least twenty-four, but almost certainly more – a fitting testimony to Hélène Jegado's grudge against the world.

Then in 1849 things began to go awry, and the world began to get its own back. Hélène was in service with a Monsieur Rabot at Rennes, and when the gentleman of the house found Hélène helping herself to a few trinkets he did not hesitate to give her notice. On the following day the entire family was stricken with nausea, vomiting and excruciating stomach pains – mercifully, none of them died.

Hélène seemed to be losing her touch, and it was at the home of Professor Theodore Bidard, also at Rennes, that she gave her farewell performance. Here, on 1 July 1851, Hélène Jegado poisoned fellow servant Rosalie Sarrazin, and the doctor, far from issuing a death certificate without question as she had become accustomed to, made the result of his very thorough examination known to the police – Mademoiselle Sarrazin had been poisoned with arsenic – murdered.

Still Hélène *might* have got away with it had she not made her first words to the visiting magistrate: 'I am innocent!' 'Of what?' questioned the magistrate. 'Nobody has accused you.' But they soon did; soon Hélène Jegado was on trial for her life. Despite the surprisingly scant amount of direct evidence that could be proved against her on most of the seventeen charges, in December 1851 the world had the last laugh when Hélène Jegado laid her neck upon the guillotine's lunette and heard the blade rushing down to meet it.

JOHNSON, Russell One of the most alarming cases in Canada's criminal history, Johnson literally got away with murder four times.

In the 1970s, the cities of London and Guelph in the province of Ontario, were hosts to four cases of women found dead in their homes with no suspicion of foul play. What transpired to be four undetected murders took place over a ten-month period, and in each case the victim apparently died peacefully in her sleep.

The first of the four was twenty-year-old student Mary Hicks, found dead in bed in London on 19 October 1973; she was in a natural sleeping position and there were no obvious marks of violence on her body. A pillow partly covering her face was not considered suspicious. As there was no sign of forced entry into her apartment, Miss Hicks' death was attributed to suffocation caused by a reaction to a prescription drug.

One month later, Alice Ralston, forty-two years old, was found dead in bed in her Guelph apartment; again there was no visible sign of violence. Miss Ralston was known to have suffered from hardening of the arteries, and this was thought to have caused her untimely death. On 4 March 1974, Eleanor Hartwick died at her home in London and, as in the case of Alice Ralston, her death was put down to a reaction to prescription drugs. It was not until August that the last of the deaths was reported, this time of forty-nine-year-old Doris Brown. On this occasion a pathologist found minor abrasions and some blood in her throat and rectum, but the police were not called in to investigate, and death was certified as from pulmonary edema.

Then a killing occurred about which there could be no doubt. On 31 December, Diane Beitz was found strangled with her own brassiere in her apartment in Guelph. She had been sexually assaulted after death. In April 1977, Louella Jeanne George was strangled and robbed of some jewellery and underwear which were later found dumped in a garbage can a few blocks away. Finally, twenty-two-year-old Donna Veldboom was found strangled in her apartment just a short distance from the previous murder site. This time the victim had been slashed in the chest with a knife.

When police investigating the killing of Donna Veldboom compared a list of tenants of the apartment block with details of sexual deviants on record, the name Russell Johnson emerged. Johnson had also once lived in the building where Louella George had been strangled. Further inquiries established a number of non-fatal sexual assaults on women by Johnson, both before and after he had been admitted to a psychiatric hospital diagnosed as a compulsive sex attacker.

At his trial in February 1978, Johnson was charged with the Beitz, George and Veldboom murders, and found not guilty by reason of insanity; he was committed to the maximum-security wing of the Ontario Mental Health Centre.

Following the trial, police authorities published a complete dossier on the crimes admitted by Johnson, including the four 'natural' deaths.

JONES, Genene   Babies admitted to the intensive care unit had begun dying at an alarming rate; between May and December 1981, the paediatric department of the Bexar County Hospital in San Antonio, Texas, had witnessed the loss of as many as twenty infants through cardiac arrest or runaway bleeding. In the majority of cases death had occurred while the babies were in the care of a licensed vocational nurse named Genene Jones; Miss Jones, though, was widely regarded as a paragon of her profession, and totally dedicated to the care of her small charges.

A series of internal inquiries were held without any positive recommendation, and eventually a panel comprising experts from hospitals in the USA and Canada was appointed to look into the deaths. The panel routinely interviewed members of the Bexar's staff and were surprised when one of her own colleagues bluntly accused Genene Jones of the infants' murder. The panel, as is so often the case, failed to reach any firm conclusion beyond the suggestion that the hospital dispense with the services of both Jones and the nurse who had accused her of killing babies. As a result, there was some acrimony during which Genene Jones resigned from the hospital.

Jones obtained her next appointment at the Kerrville Hospital, where within months of her starting work a number of children began experiencing breathing problems. As they all recovered, no special significance was attached to the incident and no suspicion was directed at Genene Jones. However, when fourteen-month-old Chelsea McClellan was brought to the hospital for regular imminisa-tion against mumps and measles, it was Jones who gave the child her first injection which resulted in an immediate seizure.

On her way to San Antonio for emergency treatment, the McClellan baby went into cardiac arrest and died. Other children receiving their treatment from Genene Jones while she was at Kerrville had attacks of various kinds though no more were fatal. But by now the health authorities had become troubled by the deaths at both hospitals and Jones was dismissed pending a grand jury investigation. News reports had begun to talk of as many as forty-two baby deaths under investigation. The grand jury finally returned indictments against Jones and she was charged with murder following the discovery of succinylcholine, a derivative of the drug curare, in Chelsea McClellan's body.

At her trial during January and February 1984, on a charge of murdering Chelsea McClellan, Genene Jones was found guilty and sentenced to ninety-nine years. She was subsequently put on trial for a second time charged with administering an overdose of the blood-thinning drug heparin to another child; this time she was handed down a concurrent term of sixty years. Although we are unlikely ever to really know what motivated Genene Jones to kill the babies entrusted to her care, there is general agreement that she took pleasure in creating life and death dramas in which she could play an influential role, so indicating a power motive.

JONES, Harold Fifteen-year-old Harold Jones of Abertillery, South Wales, stood in the dock at Monmouth Assizes on two occasions in the same year, facing two separate charges of the same crime – murder.

On the evening of 5 February 1921, eight-year-old Freda Burnell was sent on an errand by her father to a local oil and seed merchant; by late that night she had still not returned. Checks were made at the store and young Harold Jones who worked there as an assistant remembered that Freda had been in, that he had served her and that she had left straight away. On the following morning Freda Burnell's body was found in a back lane near the seed store. The cause of her death was certified as partial strangulation and a blow to the head; an attempt had also been made at rape. The girl's hands and feet had been bound, and on and around the body there were traces of corn chaff.

In a shed close by detectives found a chicken run in which chaff had been scattered, and on the ground a handkerchief belonging to Freda Burnell's sister. When questioned again, Jones insisted he had not been near the shed on the day of the murder.

Although the evidence was circumstantial, Harold Jones was charged with Freda's murder, and stood trial at Monmouth in June. His defence was an alibi, and he made a good impression on the jury – good enough anyway for them to find him not guilty – a verdict which was greeted with great jubilation by the local people, who put Jones on a bunting bedecked open-top bus and drove him home to a hero's welcome.

On 18 July of that same year, eleven-year-old Florence Little disappeared after having last been seen playing outside Harold Jones' home. Asked if he had seen her, Jones replied that she had been there, but then ran off. Police officers on routine house-to-house enquiries eventually reached the Jones family home, where a trail of blood led them up the stairs from the kitchen to the attic, where they found Florence Little; her throat had been cut.

This time the evidence pointed very directly to Harold Jones' guilt, and he confessed to Florence Little's murder. As he was still just under the age of sixteen, and therefore not subject to the death penalty, Jones was ordered to be detained during His Majesty's pleasure.

Harold Jones' confession to the earlier killing of Freda Burnell had been read out in court, prompting Mr Justice Roche to observe that the quite undeserved adulation lavished on him after his previous acquittal had almost certainly contributed to Jones' confidence in killing again.

K

KALLINGER, Joseph Kallinger was the kind of eccentric of whom one might expect almost anything. It was little surprise that the man who lived in a twenty-foot pit in the cellar of his house should also wear wedges in his shoes by which device he could adjust the list of his body to harmonise with his brain. And it would have seemed strange if he had *not* received direct instruction from God – and from the Devil as well. Indeed, it had become his conviction that God wanted him for a very special job – He wanted Joseph to annihilate mankind! In this prospective Armageddon he enlisted the help of his twelve-year-old son.

Perhaps it was in preparation for their higher calling that Kallinger and son spent 1973 and 1974 committing a series of robberies around Philadelphia, evading capture more by good luck than by smart planning. The crimes escalated with the abduction, on 7 July 1974, of a young boy who had been playing in a Philadelphia recreation ground; the child was killed and sexually mutilated. In the same month Joseph Kallinger took out a hefty insurance policy on his second son and on the 28th drowned him.

On 8 January 1975, during one of their robberies where the Kallingers were holding a number of hostages, Joseph killed one of the captives, a young woman. Kallinger fled and with scant effort made to cover his tracks soon found himself in custody. Joseph Kallinger and his son were charged with kidnapping, robbery and assault.

Joseph Kallinger was tried on these lesser charges in 1975 and convicted in spite of his obviously unbalanced state of mind. In 1976, still in daily contact with the Lord, Kallinger faced an earthly judge charged with murder. By now, he was blaming an *alter ego* named 'Charlie' for committing the murders, and even Kallinger's own defence counsel was finding it difficult to disguise the fact that his client was as mad as a March hare. Nevertheless, foaming at the mouth as he was and gibbering in 'tongues', Joseph the chosen one was judged to be able to distinguish right from wrong.

On 14 October 1976, Joe Kallinger was convicted at Bergen County Court of murder and given a mandatory life sentence. On 15 March 1977, he attempted to take his own life by setting fire to his prison cell and was removed to the state psychiatric hospital at Trenton, New Jersey, where he tried to commit suicide by choking himself with the plastic cover of his mattress. From 18 May 1978, Joseph Kallinger has been in Pennsylvania's Fairview State Hospital for the Criminally Insane.

KELLY, Kiernan By the age of fifty-four, Kiernan Kelly had developed some very strange obsessions; for a start he hated vagrants – which was odd because he was a vagrant himself. For another thing, he hated them so much he wanted to kill them; and as if this wasn't enough, he *did* kill them.

Kelly, originally from the Emerald Isle, was also an alcoholic, which couldn't have done much to help his problem. He had arrived from Ireland in 1953, and in 1975 had killed a fellow-drinker in an alcoholic brawl – this crime was not to be punished until 1983. However, by 1979, Kelly had collected some forty-odd convictions for offences arising mostly out of his inability to control his alcohol intake. He was about to move into a different league, for this was the year in which he was charged with killing a second tramp. The crime had occurred in Kennington Park, in south London, and, rightly or wrongly, Kelly was acquitted. In 1983 he was facing a jury for a second time, now charged with the attempted murder of a vagrant by trying to push him beneath an underground train. The jury failed to agree on a verdict, so Kelly was granted a retrial at which he was acquitted.

Shortly afterwards, in August 1983, Kiernan Kelly found himself in what must over the years have become a very familiar situation; he was drunk and in custody at Clapham police station in south-west London. His cell-mate at the time was another vagrant, forty-five-year-old William Boyd. Boyd was also drunk, but offended Kelly's sensibilities by raucous singing punctuated by copious foul language. Tying his shoelaces and socks together, Kelly fashioned a weapon with which he quickly strangled the last cracked note out of his noisy companion.

It was a crime which Kelly could clearly not deny, so he took the opportunity to make a lengthy confession to a series of nine killings over the previous thirty years. One of the murders was the so-far unsolved killing of sixty-seven-year-old Hector Fisher in a Clapham graveyard in 1975. It was with this offence that Kelly stood charged before an Old Bailey jury and for which he was sentenced to life imprisonment.

Just two weeks later, Kelly was again in the dock of the Old Bailey, again charged with murder, again about to be sentenced to life imprisonment. This time he was indicted for the killing of William Boyd in the Clapham police cell. Described by a psychiatrist at the trial as 'incorrigible in penal terms and incurable in medical terms', it is unlikely that it will ever be considered safe to release Kiernan Kelly from custody.

KEMPER, Edmund Emil The first murders took place on 7 May

1972; the victims were Anita Luchese and Mary Ann Pesce, two students from Fresno State College, Berkeley. The early seventies was still a time when it was comparatively safe to hitch-hike, and college kids all over the United States were using this traditional means of student transport. But it was an unlucky day for them if they were offered a ride by Edmund Kemper – the man who was about to give hitch-hiking a very dangerous name.

Held by Kemper at gunpoint, Anita and Mary Ann were driven into a wooded canyon, violently stabbed to death and their bodies violated before being driven back to Kemper's home in the boot of his car. On 14 September Aiko Koo, a fifteen-year-old Japanese high-school student was hitch-hiking; Kemper drove her to the mountains, a gun at her head, where he suffocated her, committed necrophilia, and then returned home with her body which he decapitated. After committing sexual acts with the headless corpse, Kemper dismembered it and took the pieces away to bury in the mountains near Boulder Creek. Cynthia Schall was Kemper's third 'Co-ed' victim, and after shooting her dead and abusing her body, he cut it up in the shower and threw the remains over the cliffs at Carmel.

The series that had become known as the 'Co-ed Murders' continued only a month after the death of Cynthia Schall, when Rosalind Thorpe and Alice Luis were picked up from Santa Cruz campus on the evening of 5 February 1973, after being offered a lift home by Kemper. On the way he pulled out a gun, and without the least provocation shot the girls through the head where they sat. Kemper stopped the car, transferred the bodies to the boot and drove home. Unfortunately Kemper's mother was in, so he was obliged to perform the decapitation while the bodies were still in the boot. Next morning he cut off Alice Luis's hands and then dumped the mutilated bodies in Eden Canyon, Alameda, where they were found more than a week later.

Easter Sunday 1973. His mother's presence in the house had obviously become an obstacle to Kemper's freedom to kill, abuse and mutilate; this was the day he crushed her skull with a mallet, cut off her head, and hid the rest of her body. Then he invited her friend Sarah Hallett over for tea, beat her over the head with a brick, strangled and decapitated her and had sexual intercourse with the remains before driving off in Mrs Hallett's car.

Edmund Kemper was clearly running out of steam; clearly coming to the end of his lust to kill. He made no attempt to hide, no attempt to disguise himself – a difficult task anyway for a man six feet nine inches tall and weighing twenty stone – or even change his name. And when they still failed to find him, Kemper telephoned the police in Pueblo, Colorado, and told them he was the Co-ed Killer. Of course, they didn't believe him, and it was only as a result of his own persistence that Edmund Kemper was eventually taken into custody.

At his trial in Santa Cruz in April 1973, Kemper faced eight counts of murder, and was adjudged sane – in a legal sense at least. It was nevertheless revealed that he had been possessed of a strong inclination to sadism even in childhood, when he practised for later life by torturing small animals; even his parents had described him as 'a real weirdo'.

At the age of fifteen, Kemper had shot his grandmother through the head ('I just wondered how it would feel to shoot grandma'), then his grandfather. Afterwards, Kemper telephoned his mother to tell her that they were dead. He was committed to Atascadero State Hospital and, much against the advice of his doctors, released in 1969 into the custody of his mother.

Found guilty, Edmund Kemper asked to be executed, but the best the court could do was sentence him to life imprisonment – in his case for *life*, with no possibility of parole.

KISS, Bela When Bela Kiss, a tinsmith from the Hungarian village of Czinkota, was called upon in 1914 to join his country's forces in the Great War, he left bars and padlocks on the doors and windows of his rambling villa on the outskirts of town. Not that such tangible deterrents were really necessary, for Kiss had an evil reputation as a sorcerer and few of his neighbours would venture close to the house on any pretext. So it was not until 1916 that anybody paid much mind to Bela Kiss and his heavily shuttered home; and then it was no gullible villager, but a pair of uniformed policemen, entrusted with the mission of seeking out illegally hoarded supplies of petrol for recycling into the war effort. When they arrived in Czinkota it was not long before the more garrulous locals informed the two officers of Bela Kiss and the metal casks. The casks had been part of village lore ever since the old crone who was Bela's occasional cleaner, and the only person ever to go into his house, had been dismissed for snooping. Kiss had caught the old woman peeping into the attic and thrown her out without ceremony – but not before she had seen the neat row of large metal barrels supported on trestles.

While the policemen officiously pulled the locks from the front door of the house a circle of wary villagers watched from a respectful distance, no doubt expecting an outrush of demons as the door was flung open. It was to be even worse.

Up in the attic, sure enough, there sat seven heavy metal casks, tightly lidded. As the first of the seals was broken and the top lifted the officers reeled backwards from the heavy fumes that billowed from the barrel – not the heady vapours of petrol but the stench of death and putrefaction. Propped up in each one of the casks was the dead and naked body of a woman, the marks of the strangler's cord still visible around her neck. Soon the building was swarming with policemen, uncovering items of female clothing and jewellery, and the pawn-tickets for hundreds more. When the surrounding land was dug over it yielded the remains of a further seventeen bodies – all females, all lured to this Bluebeard's castle by advertisements placed in the newspapers by Bela Kiss offering his services as matrimonial agent and fortune-teller.

According to army records, when Kiss had been called up he was posted to Serbia where he was later wounded and died in a military hospital. A check made with the hospital revealed that the man who had died was not in the least like the description of Bela Kiss – too young for a start, almost a boy. The cunning Kiss, it would seem, had exchanged identity discs with a dying patient and was thus free to disappear into the confusion of war with a new identity, his own bad name left to disgrace the memory of a fallen comrade. Nothing certain is known of Bela Kiss from this point; he may, as some have surmised, have become one of that war's millions of casualties. Or he may not, for there was rumour of him in Budapest after the war. He may have joined the French Foreign Legion, as others have claimed; and in 1932 there was even a sighting from New York. Only one thing is certain – Bela Kiss never faced an earthly judge for the slaughter at Czinkota.

KNOWLES, Paul John It is often only as the result of evidence given in a court of law that we can piece together the background and personality of a killer, and arrive at a rational assessment of his motive to murder. About Paul John Knowles we will never know the full story; during an attempted escape from custody he was shot dead by a law-enforcement officer. What is known follows.

After an inauspicious childhood spent mainly in foster homes, Knowles' youthful attraction to petty crime escalated through juvenile delinquency, through prison sentences for robbery, to multiple murder.

On 26 July 1974, just two months after his release from Railford Penitentiary, Florida, Knowles struck; his first victim was sixty-five-year-old teacher Alice Curtis, killed during the course of a robbery. This incident was followed by the killing of two young sisters, eleven-year-old Lillian and seven-year-old Mylette Anderson; their mother was a friend of the Knowles family. During the month of August Knowles claimed another three victims, and in the following month five more. 16 October found him in Marlborough, Connecticut, where Knowles raped and strangled a woman and her teenage daughter; three days later, in Woodford, Virginia, he shot Doris Hovey with her husband's gun.

At the beginning of November, Knowles was in Macon, Georgia, where he killed a man he had met in a bar and the man's daughter. The killings continued in Georgia until, on 8 November, he began an extraordinary relationship with an English journalist named Sandy Fawkes who was holidaying in the United States. They met in a hotel bar in Atlanta; Knowles was using the name 'Daryl Golden'.

For the next six days and nights they were almost inseparable, during which time Knowles was dropping hints that he might be a mass murderer, probably flattered by the possibility that Ms Fawkes might write a book about him, 'Daryl' hinted that he had recorded details of his activities on tape (in fact he had made a tape-recorded confession which was in the hands of his solicitor).

Despite the passionate overture, the relationship came to a halt partly because Knowles pulled a gun on his new friend. Among his last words to her were: 'I am going to be killed . . . Within a year I shall be dead.' In fact it was far sooner than that.

After committing two more murders, one of them of a police patrolman whose car Knowles had hijacked, he was arrested when his car skidded off the road trying to avoid a road-block. After a chase through woodland on foot Knowles was captured and taken into custody. On the following day, 17 November 1974, Paul John Knowles slipped his handcuffs and attempted to escape. As he tried to grab the sheriff's gun he was shot dead by an FBI agent.

So ended the short, wasteful life of Paul John Knowles, the man the press had christened the 'Casanova Killer'. He is known to have killed eighteen times over four months – his own estimate was thirty-five. Sandy Fawkes, *Killing Time* was published three years later.

KODAIRA, Yoshio   A former Japanese naval officer and employee of the United States government, Kodaira was tried for the rape and murder of ten women in the Tokyo area during 1945 and 1946. He confessed to seven of the killings but emphatically denied three others. In fact, soon after Kodaira was convicted another man, Shizu Koguchi, was arrested for the remaining three rape-murders and it was discovered that both men had used the same *modus operandi* to commit identical crimes. Taking advantage of post-war food shortages, the killers had lured their victims from home with the promise of black-market merchandise. Kodaira made, for him, the fatal mistake of giving his last victim his name and address, which she wisely passed on to her parents before setting out on her rendezvous with death. Shizu Koguchi was caught trying to sell his victims' clothing at a street market.

Tried before the Tokyo District Criminal Court in May 1947, Yoshio Kodaira was found guilty and on 5 October 1949, hanged. Koguchi, himself the son of a convicted murderer, was also sentenced to death.

KRAFT, Randy   During the 1970s and 80s, Randy Kraft combined a successful business career in computers in Southern California, with another more sinister life as a 'freeway killer'. He was operating around the region at the same time as William **Bonin** (convicted of ten murders), and Patrick Kearney (twenty-one murders, known as the 'Trash-Bag Killer'). Kraft was eventually convicted of sixteen murders, but was believed to have killed on sixty-seven different occasions between 1972 and 1983. All three killers preyed mainly on young homosexual men, but whereas Bonin's motivation was sexual, and Kearney's was power-oriented with a lust for necrophilia, Kraft received his gratification through torture and sexual mutilation.

The first established victim of Kraft's handiwork was a marine named Edward Daniel Moore, twenty years old, whose body was found in the Seal Beach area of California in December 1972. Moore had been sexually assaulted, strangled and traces of drugs were found in his body. In 1975, three more young men were found dead in similar circumstances. Another man disappeared in 1976, and was later found strangled and castrated. Four cases in 1978 were associated with the same serial killer and a further two in 1980. No further cases were reported until 1983, when in January and February three more marines were found strangled and emasculated.

On 14 May 1983, two Highway Patrol officers chased a car being driven erratically and ordered it to pull off the freeway. When it did, instead of remaining in the car as most people do under these circumstances, the driver got out of his car and walked towards the policemen. He identified himself as Randolph Kraft, aged thirty-eight, a computer programmer. In his car the officers found the dead body of marine Terry Lee Gambrel, who had died from an overdose of a stupefying drug. Both at the time and since Kraft has refused to make any statement or give any explanation.

During subsequent investigations, it was established that Kraft was homosexual, and the theory was advanced that his initial feelings of guilt over his sexual preference had compelled him to kill the men he had sex with. As in many cases the murders were accompanied by castration, the motive could be seen on a simplistic level as an attempt to destroy their maleness – for Kraft to make them into 'women' and thus normalise his sexual activities. An alternative explanation was simple sadism, which would account for the fact that some of Kraft's victims had been alive and conscious while being mutilated. In the course of his job, Randy Kraft had travelled extensively, and it could be seen in hindsight how murders across Michigan, Oregon, Ohio, Washington and New York could be fitted into the pattern.

Randolph Kraft has never confessed to murder; he was tried in Orange County, California, on sixteen charges of murder, nine of sexual mutilation and three of sodomy. He was convicted on all counts and on 29 November 1989, sentenced to die in the gas chamber at San Quentin.

It is over a quiet game of cards on the prison's Death Row that Randy Kraft feels most at home; his partners in bridge are Lawrence **Bittaker**, 'Freeway Killer' **Bonin**, and the 'Sunset Strip Killer' Douglas **Clark**. It has been observed by one reporter that not only did Kraft exceed his partners in the number of his crimes, but is also the better card player.

KUKLINSKI, Richard Kuklinski was called the 'Ice Man' by police, though whether it was because of his chilling personality or from his fondness for keeping victims in cold storage to confound estimates of the time of death is open to conjecture. Kuklinski was also a prolific confidence trickster with any number of deals on the go at the same time.

On 31 January 1980, George Malliband left his home in Huntingdon, Pennsylvania, to meet Kuklinski in Emerson, New Jersey. Malliband had twenty-seven thousand dollars about him and was owed a further thirty-five thousand by Kuklinski arising from a deal involving pornographic videotapes. Four days later, George Malliband was found in a large oil-drum in Jersey City; he had four bullet wounds in his chest.

Kuklinski set up a similar deal for 1 July 1981, with Louis Masgay, arranging to meet him in Little Falls, New Jersey, with ninety-five thousand dollars in cash; Masgay vanished and it was not until September 1983, that his body was found wrapped in plastic bags in Rockland County, New York. Masgay had been shot, but against all the rules of pathology the body had only just begun to decay. When the medical examiner autopsied Louis Masgay's body he found ice crystals in the tissues – Masgay had been kept in cold storage.

Paul Hoffman, a pharmacist, kept his appointment with Richard Kuklinski on 29 April 1982. He was carrying twenty-five thousand dollars to buy a supply of the prescription drug Tagamet. Like his fellow entrepreneurs before him, Hoffman was never seen again – alive or dead; but his car was found a year later in Kuklinski's warehouse. As in the case of Louis Masgay, police had been able to trace telephone calls between Hoffman and Kuklinski, but this did not amount to tangible evidence.

In December 1982, Richard Kuklinski and his associate Daniel Dappner killed a third accomplice, Gary Smith; first they mixed cyanide in his food, then strangled him for good measure. Smith's body was found in a motel room with a ligature round his neck and charred food remains in his burnt-out stomach. In May 1983, Danny Dappner's body turned up in West Milford, New Jersey – another colleague who had discovered that there is, after all, no honour among thieves.

The police now had five murders and a prime suspect in the person of Richard Kuklinski; but no hard evidence. Time now to beat the cheat at his own game. A police undercover agent made contact with Kuklinski with a proposition initially to purchase a large supply of cocaine. The plan later developed into stealing the drug and murdering the supplier, and by persuading Kuklinski to boast about his 'credentials', the officer obtained sufficient secretly taped information on the previous murders for Kuklinski to be arrested and charged on 17 December 1986.

Richard Kuklinski was tried for the murders of Smith and Dappner, was convicted and sentenced to life imprisonment; he agreed to plead guilty to the murders of Malliband, Masgay and Hoffman and received concurrent life sentences. Kuklinski has never revealed the whereabouts of Paul Hoffman's body.

KURTEN, Peter Kurten's reign as the 'Monster of Düsseldorf' began with the murder of nine-year-old Rosa Ohliger on 8 February 1929; he had led the child into the shadows around the city's Vinzenz Church and stabbed her to death with a pair of scissors. Kurten returned to the scene of his crime later that night and burned the kerosene-soaked body, thereby rearousing his sexual lust. On the night of 12 February, a drunk named Rudolf Scheer was stumbling his way home from a beer keller when he accidentally banged into Kurten who turned and knocked Scheer down and stabbed him repeatedly with the pair of scissors, at the same time sucking up the man's blood as it spurted from his wounds. For Kurten, blood had always been the object of his greatest sexual arousal, and the drinking of it a characteristic of many of his murders; like that of Maria Hahn on 11 August 1929. Fraulein Hahn was a loose-living domestic servant who was willing to offer Peter Kurten quite a lot of herself, but had certainly not expected their one-night stand to cost her her life and, as a final indignity, her blood as well. Between this killing and the next there were two attempted murders; then, on 24 August, Kurten lured two girls, thirteen-year-old Luise Lenzen and five-year-old Gertrud Hamacher, into a meadow where he strangled and stabbed Luise, and cut Gertrud's throat. Following the attempted murder of Gertrud Schulte, another domestic, Kurten bludgeoned Ida Reuter to death with a hammer in a wood just outside Düsseldorf on 29 September. His next victim was Elizabeth Dorrier, a young girl whom he battered to death on 11 October. After two more bungled attempts, Kurten's last victim was five-year-old Gertrud Alberman, whom he strangled and stabbed thirty-six times with scissors on 7 November.

By this stage the man called the 'Monster' or 'Vampire' of Düsseldorf was spreading a fear in the city that rivalled Jack the Ripper's 'Autumn of Terror'. It was no coincidence that Peter Kurten was a great admirer of the Ripper, and had made an extensive study of the case. It may even have been in imitation that Kurten decided to write a letter to the newspapers disclosing where the bodies of Gertrud Alberman and previous victim Maria Hahn could be found.

In May 1930, Kurten made the mistake that was to rid Düsseldorf of its Monster. Twenty-year-old Maria Budlies had taken a train from Cologne to Düsseldorf in the search for employment; at Düsseldorf station she was approached by a stranger who, under the pretence of helping her find her hostel, tried to lure her into the Volksgarten Park. She refused, and during the argument that followed a second man intervened and extricated the girl from her difficulties. Maria was grateful enough to the gallant stranger and comfortable enough in his company to accept the offer of refreshment back at his apartment on Mettmannerstrasse, before setting out, or so she believed, to find the girls' hostel. Instead, Maria found herself alone in a wood with the man she had only just met; his name was Peter Kurten. While Fraulein Budlies screamed and struggled, the Monster of Düsseldorf against whom she had been warned was closing his hands more tightly around her throat. Then as suddenly as he had started, Kurten released his grip and asked the terrified girl, 'Do you remember where I live in case you ever need my help?' Wisely, Maria said that she could not remember, with which Kurten politely escorted her out of the wood and set her in the right direction for her lodgings.

Maria Budlies never reported this incident to the police, but described her ordeal in a letter to a friend. By the wildest of coincidences, this letter had been incorrectly addressed and found its way to the post office 'dead letter' department where it was officially opened to discover the address of the sender. A quick-thinking clerk recognised the significance of what he read and passed the document on to the police, who in turn found Maria Budlies. Of course Maria *had* remembered Kurten's address and was able to lead detectives straight to the Monster's lair. In his forty-seventh year, Peter Kurten's perversions were at an end.

Kurten confessed in detail his sickening litany of rape, murder and mutilation, and was held in secure custody until his trial opened at Düsseldorf in April 1931. His plea of insanity was rejected by the court and after a lengthy trial, Peter Kurten was found guilty of all nine charges of murder. According to German procedure, he was beheaded; a prospect, he said, that gave him the most pleasing anticipation – the possibility that he might remain aware just long enough after the blade severed his head to hear his own blood gush from his body.

Peter Kurten had been born in Cologne-Mulheim on 26 May 1883, fifth of the thirteen children of an alcoholic sand-caster. Old Kurten was in the nasty habit of beating his wife and children mercilessly when in his cups, and young Peter's childhood was punctuated by these violent outbursts. In 1897, his father was imprisoned for attempting incest with one of Peter's sisters.

It is reported that at the age of five, Peter tried to drown one of his playmates by holding his head under water, and not long afterwards he began to help the local dog-catcher to round up and destroy strays.

In 1894 the family moved to Düsseldorf where Peter subsequently found work as a moulder's apprentice. At the age of fourteen he had his first sexual experience when he assaulted a girl in the woods at Grafenberger; he almost strangled her to death. From there, Kurten began with minor dishonesties, graduating to burglary and assault, accompanied by appropriate spells in various prisons. In all, he would spend more than twenty years behind bars. In 1904, Kurten added arson to his crimes – he claimed to find it sexually stimulating.

The first murder took place in 1913, when he robbed the house of a man named Peter Klein, and slit the throat of his eight-year-old daughter. Ironically, Kurten dropped his handkerchief embroidered with the initials 'PK', thus throwing suspicion upon the unhappy Peter Klein for killing his own daughter.

Kurten married in 1923, and as far as the neighbours were concerned, Peter was a quiet, modest man with decent standards, if a little vain. After the marriage, Kurten committed a series of sexual assaults, almost killing the victims by strangulation. Then on 29 February 1929, he attacked Frau Apollonia Kuhn and stabbed her almost to death with a pair of scissors; the arrival of passers-by attracted by her screams were all that saved Frau Kuhn from certain death. Less than a week later the first of the Vampire's killings was committed.

While he was in custody awaiting trial, Peter Kurten was examined by Professor Karl Berg, a leading psychologist of his day, who in conclusion of a lengthy study of his patient, described Kurten as 'a king of sexual perverts' and a 'narcissistic psychopath'.

L

LANDRU, Henri Desiré   Despite his eminence in the mythology of crime as the 'French Bluebeard', and the wildly exaggerated estimate of the number of his victims (some have said as many as three hundred), Landru was by no means unique among the 'Bluebeard' or 'Lonely Hearts' killers.

Murder came as an accompaniment to Henri's chosen profession of swindler – for which, in the first decade of this present century he was imprisoned several times. Although his short, stocky frame, bald head, and rather frightening long red beard made Landru an unlikely looking Don Juan, still his charm and mannered ways lent no small success to his relations with women – women for the most part who had responded to his advertisements in the newspaper matrimonial columns:

> Widower with two children, aged forty-three, with comfortable income, affectionate, serious and moving in good society, desires to meet widow with a view to matrimony.

His success was to a large degree a matter of timing. Europe, and France in particular, was currently engaged in the horrors of the Great War. It was a conflict that had made widows of many French women of middle years, lost without the comfort and companionship of a husband, and emotionally vulnerable to somebody like Landru with his implicit promise of a more secure future – what if he did have a long red beard? And he kept discreetly silent about the fact that he had *four* children – and a wife.

There were, of course, many whose savings and possessions Landru cynically plundered without the need for murder; but inevitably there were also those who were stubborn enough to want some control of their assets – and Landru had just the answer to this problem at the Villa Ermitage in Gambais. We know all this because Landru kept a systematic account of the financial prospects of his victims in the small notebook which was to prove so useful to the advocate-general who prosecuted him.

As for the tell-tale remains of those victims – whether simply the eleven for whose murder he was tried, or the fictional three hundred – they were disposed of in the villa's stove; and it too was an object celebrated for its introduction as a silent witness at the trial. It is surprising that such a regular nuisance as the oily black smoke and putrid smell of burning flesh should have gone so totally unremarked by his neighbours.

It was in 1919 that a Mademoiselle Lacoste wrote to the mayor of Gambais asking him to intercede in the matter of her sister. Madame Buisson had gone with a man calling himself 'Fremyet' to live at the Villa Ermitage and had never been heard from since. It was not the first such request that the mayor had received about missing relatives, though the man recently calling himself 'Dupont' had lately left the Villa. He was soon traced and discovered to be none other than Monsieur Henri Desiré Landru. A close examination of the stove that Landru had installed at the villa disclosed some two hundred and ninety fragments of human bones and teeth, and considerable quantities of his victims' clothing and possessions were found about the house.

Landru was tried at the Seine-et-Oise Assize Court in November 1921; he pleaded not guilty, but was nevertheless convicted, and on 25 February 1922, put to the guillotine. More than forty years later a story was circulating in the press that a confession had been found scribbled on the back of a drawing which Landru had given his defence counsel just before execution. The text: 'I did it. I burned their bodies in my kitchen stove,' was found by the lawyer's daughter when she removed the picture to clean the frame.

Henri Landru's victims

Date	Name	Location of disappearance
April or May 1915	Jeanne Cuchet	Vernouillet
April or May 1915	André George Cuchet	Vernouillet
25 June 1915	Thérèse Laborde-Line	Vernouillet
3 or 4 August 1915	Mme Guillin	Vernouillet
December 1916 to January 1917	Mme Heon	Gambais
27 December 1916	Anna Collomb	Gambais
12 April 1917	Andrée Anne Babelay	Gambais
1 September 1917	Celestine Buisson	Gambais
26 November 1917	Louise Jaume	Gambais
5 April 1918	Anne Marie Pascal	Gambais
13 January 1919	Maria Thérèse Marchadier	Gambais

LEHMANN, Christa Christa Lehmann was born in Worms, Germany, in 1922, and from her teenage years (when Christa's mother was confined to an asylum and her father lost interest in everything but drink) embarked upon the petty criminality that was to lead to murder and her own life imprisonment.

In 1944 Christa married Karl Franz Lehmann, a man with as few redeeming features as her father, and who drank even more. To nobody's surprise, he died in September 1952. The following January, Christa's mother-in-law Kathe Lehmann died and not long afterwards her father-in-law Valentin Lehmann simply fell off his bicycle in the street and after several agonised twitches, also perished.

12 February 1954 found Christa handing out cream-filled chocolate truffles to her neighbours. Seventy-five-year-old Eva Ruh took one and put it in the 'fridge for later; so much the worse for Anni Hamann, Christa's best friend and Eva Ruh's daughter. When Anni returned home from work and found the truffle she could not, poor woman, resist the temptation to take just the tiniest bite . . . It was more than enough, and minutes after spitting the bitter chocolate out of her mouth she died. The family dog, which lapped up the scraps was also found with its legs in the air. Of course, both Anni and the luckless canine had been poisoned, but with what nobody could tell. It was only after all the tests for all the known poisons had proved negative that analyst Kurt Wagner recalled that there was a new phosphorus compound known as E605 which had been developed as a chemical insecticide. It was also the deadly poison that had robbed Anni Hamann of her life.

Christa Lehmann, being the source of the poisoned confectionery, was the obvious suspect. But she was a suspect who had no hint of a motive to kill the person who was, after all, her best friend. But the case caused the police to remember the unexpected and remarkably similar death of Valentin Lehmann nearly two years before. Following exhumations and post-mortem examinations, not only Valentin, but his wife and son were found to have been poisoned by the same means – and presumably by the same hand.

Christa Lehmann at first defiantly protested her innocence; then, on 23 February 1954, she confessed to all four murders. The poisoned truffle was, of course, meant for Eva Ruh and not Anni. It seems that Frau Ruh had been guilty of criticising Anni's friendship with Christa.

Christa Lehmann was charged with murder in the three family poisonings and manslaughter in the case of Anni Hamann. At her trial in September 1954, Christa stubbornly refused to retract her confession, leaving her counsel to flounder along as best he could with a none-too-convincing defence that while Christa Lehmann was not insane in the legal sense she was, in the opinion of a psychiatrist, a 'moral primitive'. The jury just thought she was guilty, and brought in the appropriate verdicts, leaving the judge to sentence Frau Lehmann to life imprisonment – the maximum penalty for murder in West Germany.

Before Christa was taken to prison, she had these words for the waiting reporters: 'I don't suppose I should have done it. But with the exception of Anni, they were all nasty people. Besides,' she added, 'I love to go to funerals.'

Following the publicity that the case generated, more than twenty murders and seventy-seven suicides were reported in West Germany, all using the fashionable new poison E605.

LEONSKI, Edward Joseph   The third death was on 18 May 1942.

Gladys Hosking had followed Ivy McLeod and Pauline Thompson in the succession of strangled corpses to be found, where they had fallen, on the streets of Melbourne, Australia. It was to be the last in the series thanks to an observant sentry at the local US Army base who remembered challenging a shaken and dishevelled GI returning to camp late on the night of the murder. The description happened to match that of a soldier who had been reported for threatening violence to a young woman only a few days previously; both descriptions fitted Edward Joseph Leonski, a big Texan who had recently confided to a camp buddy the alarming news that 'I'm a Dr Jekyll and Mr Hyde! I killed! I killed!'

There was not much need to search for evidence against him, Leonski provided his own; sure he had killed all those ladies: 'It was to get their voices.' He recalled with particular affection that Pauline Thompson had sung to him as he walked her home, a soft, sweet voice: 'I could feel myself going mad about it.'

Nutty as a fruit-cake? The court-martial didn't think so, despite the prisoner's own best efforts to convince them and a long history of insanity in the family. The 'Singing Strangler', the 'Melbourne Jack the Ripper' was hanged on 9 November 1942, at Pentridge Gaol; it is said that in the hours before execution, Leonski sat in his cell singing softly to himself.

LEWINGDON, Gary James and Thaddeus Charles   On 13 February 1978, night-club owner Mickey McCann, his mother and live-in girlfriend Christine Herdman were found shot dead in their home in Columbus, Ohio. The following month Claudia Yasko, a twenty-six-year-old go-go dancer, walked into a police station and announced that she had been in the house with two men when they had committed the murders. So convincing was her description of the scene of the crime that Miss Yasko was arrested and charged with the killings. Later, the two men she implicated, her boyfriend and an associate of his, were also arrested and charged.

Following the arrests, four further murders were committed, in each of which ballistics tests established that the same .22 calibre gun had been used that killed the McCanns and Christine Herdman. Police also confirmed that this gun had been the weapon used in the murder of two girls in Newark in December 1977. All charges against Claudia Yasko were dropped, although why she should have confessed at all was at the time a mystery.

Joseph Annick was shot dead in the street and robbed on 4 December; the weapon had been a .22 automatic, though at the time the police were unable to make a connection with the earlier murders. Then, on 9 December, Gary Lewingdon was arrested for trying to use a stolen credit card, and property belonging to Joseph Annick was found in his possession. Lewingdon admitted the Annick murder, and it was recalled that Mrs Lewingdon had earlier informed the police that she thought her brother-in-law, Gary's brother, was the man responsible for the .22 killings. Under questioning Gary Lewingdon admitted his involvement in the killings, claiming that his brother was the dominant partner. Charles Lewingdon was arrested and made a full confession.

Charles faced two trials for a total of nine murders, and was given nine consecutive life sentences, plus further terms on lesser charges. Gary, at a single trial, received eight consecutive life sentences for murder, the jury failing to agree on two other counts. Gary Lewingdon subsequently became psychotic and was transferred to the State Hospital for the Criminally Insane.

Which left the enigma of Claudia Yasko. Some years after the '.22 Calibre Killings' had been solved, Daniel Keys conducted a series of interviews with Claudia and elicited the following information: she had overheard her boyfriend and Gary Lewingdon discussing the McCann murders, and on the night of the shootings was persuaded by the boyfriend to go with one of his associates to the scene of the murder to search for drugs. Claudia was a known schizophrenic and undergoing treatment; her strong recollection of the sight of the murder scene convinced her that she must have been responsible.

LIM, Adrian, *et al.*   A self-styled spirit medium Lim, with his wife Catherine Tan Mui Choo and his mistress Hoe Kah Hong, earned his place in the annals of infamy through the murders of two children at his apartment in Toa Payoh, Singapore.

The first victim, nine-year-old Agnes Ng Siew Heok, failed to return home from the religious school she attended in January 1981. On the 25th of the month her body was found stuffed into a bag beside a lift in the apartment block adjoining Lim's home; the child had been asphyxiated and the post-mortem examination suggested that she had been sodomised and that rape had been attempted.

While investigations were proceeding into the murder of Agnes Ng, a second corpse, that of ten-year-old Ghazali bin Mazurki, was found under a tree outside the same apartment block on 7 February. There was no indication of sexual assault, but there were three burns on the boy's back and a puncture mark on his arm which confirmed post-mortem findings of a tranquilliser in blood and tissue samples. Cause of death had been drowning.

Subsequent inquiry established that Ghazali had been enticed away from a playground by a 'Chinese' woman. Furthermore, small bloodspots were found leading from the young victim's body to the adjacent flats – the flats in which Adrian Lim lived with his menage of wife and mistress, and whose quarters were similarly spotted with Ghazali bin Mazurki's blood. Under questioning, all three confessed their participation in the two murders, supplemented by a catalogue of other unsavoury activities – rape, unnatural sex, blood drinking, child abduction and various practices of supernatural hocus-pocus and deception. Investigations were now reopened into the death twelve months earlier of Benson Loh Ngak Hua, who had been found 'accidentally' electrocuted in Lim's apartment; Adrian Lim and his wife were subsequently charged jointly with his murder.

During their forty-one day trial in 1983, the two women pleaded that Lim had forced them to help with the sacrificial murders aimed at invoking the goddess Kali's intervention so as to effect escape from an earlier charge of rape brought against him.

The proceedings were held, according to Singapore practice, before a panel of three judges without a jury, and concluded with convictions against all three defendants and death sentences accompanying each conviction. The two female prisoners made a desperate sequence of unsuccessful appeals, first to the Singapore Court of Criminal Appeal, then to the Privy Council in London and the President of Singapore; Adrian Lim did not bother to appeal at all. The result was the same; Lim, Tan and Hoe were hanged at Changi Prison on 25 November 1988. The *Straits Times* recorded that Adrian Lim went to the gallows with an inscrutable smile on his face.

LINEVELT, Salie   Salie Linevelt killed four times: all his victims were women, all were murdered in the suburbs of Cape Town and all had been savagely bludgeoned to death, sexually abused and robbed. Each of the attacks had taken place during daylight. That the police had so little success in trapping the killer may have been due, in part at least, to the unsettling effect of the first year of the Second World War. It may also have had something to do with the almost guileless way in which Linevelt went openly about the business of murder, and made no attempt to adopt a low profile after killing.

The first of his tragic victims was Ethel Marais, a serviceman's wife who was killed on the evening of 3 October 1940, close to her home in Lansdowne suburb. Although Mrs Marais was alive when she was found, the unfortunate woman died not long afterwards without regaining consciousness. Less than three weeks later in the suburb of Wynberg, Mrs Dorothy Tarling was murdered in her own home. This time the attacker had been careless enough to leave behind a clear palm- and thumb-print. But prints, as police the world over will testify, are only of any immediate use if their owner has a criminal record, or if there is a suspect with whose prints to compare them. In this case there were neither.

Wynberg was the scene of the third attack too. On 11 November, Evangeline Bird, twenty-eight years old, was murdered on her own doorstep. Although it was subsequently established that a young man on a bicycle had been seen near by, no suspect was forthcoming. The fourth murder occurred on 25 November at Rondesbosch. This time footprints and fingerprints were found in the house of the victim, Mrs Mary Hoets.

It was Salie Linevelt's last murder, but even so it was not until some weeks later that a young man was arrested as he stood in a queue outside a cinema. The charge was quite unconnected with the murders, but the prisoner *was* wearing a ring belonging to one of the victims on his finger.

Though his crimes had been brutal, vicious and pointless, it was in the bizarre personality of Salie Linevelt that the interest of the case lay. For a start, when he was taken into custody police noticed that twenty-year-old Linevelt was missing the tip of his left thumb. As part of an earlier plan to trap their quarry, police had issued the press with misleading information that the killer had deposited at the scene of the crime a left thumb-print. Linevelt had simply lopped his off in order to prove that it could not possibly have been him! When detectives searched his room, they found the bloody chopper and the tip of Salie's thumb. All in all Salie Linevelt seemed exceedingly pleased with the publicity that his crimes had generated, and confessed freely to murder while indignantly denying sexual assault – which on the forensic evidence was a clear lie. He accounted for the killings by explaining patiently that it was his *alter ego* – the one he called 'The Boss' – who had ordered him to commit murder.

Although he was obviously unbalanced, Linevelt refused to allow a defence of insanity to be entered at his trial. Despite a great deal of psychological evidence which was advanced to show mitigating circumstances, Mr Justice Davis in passing judgement told the court, 'I do not in the least suggest that any abnormality he may possess is such that it would prove a mitigating factor in this case. In the court's view it is rather the reverse.' Salie Linevelt was found guilty of murder and hanged at Pretoria.

LOBAUGH, Ralph, and **CLICK, Franklin** Between February 1944 and March 1945, four women were murdered around Fort Wayne, Indiana. The first incident occurred on 2 February 1944, when Wilhelma 'Billie' Haaga was found badly beaten, her clothes torn to shreds, on the steps of a farmhouse. Despite emergency hospital treatment she lapsed into a coma and died on 5 February.

On 22 May, the naked body of Anna Kuzeff was found strangled in a field. Close to the body was a black pocket comb and a belt buckle. On 4 August, Phyllis Conine, a seventeen-year-old student, was reported missing by her father – four days later, her body, too, was found beaten and strangled and left lying on the open space where the crime was committed.

Around four o'clock on the morning of 6 March 1945, Mrs Dorothea Howard, aged thirty-six, was found naked and badly beaten in an alleyway. It was at first thought that she might survive the ordeal, but a combination of trauma and exposure had led to Mrs Howard contracting pneumonia, from which she died on 17 March.

Progress, as far as the police investigation was concerned, was slow. In fact it led nowhere, and it was not for more than two years that there was any break. Then, on 9 June 1947, a man named Ralph Lobaugh confessed to the Kokomo, Indiana, police that he had killed Anna Kuzeff and Billie Haaga. He later added the name Dorothea Howard but, despite pressure, denied responsibility for the death of Phyllis Conine. Of course, any sensational crime – let alone a series of unsolved murders – attracts its share of cranks who, for reasons best known to their psychiatrists, want to confess everything, and there is a well-established police routine to eliminate these pathetic time-wasters; there are always small details, facts and features known only to the police and the killer, information not released to the media, knowledge of which reveals the true culprit. In this case, Ralph Lobaugh was asked if, by any chance, he remembered losing anything at the scene of the Kuzeff murder. Yes, he did. He lost a black pocket comb and belt buckle! Lobaugh then alternated between retracting and confirming his confessions until he stood his trial on three counts of murder to which he pleaded guilty of all charges, and was sentenced to the electric chair.

Shortly after Ralph Lobaugh's trial, an attempt was made to kidnap a woman from her home in Fort Wayne. Her abductor dragged the woman into his car, half-strangled her before driving off with her, and then seems to have thought better of it and driven her home. The car was traced to Franklin Click who was arrested, and while in custody admitted the bungled attack.

Then events began to take a decided step towards the burlesque. Click's wife produced a letter written by her husband in which *he* confessed responsibility for the murders of Billie Haaga, Anna Kuzeff *and* Phyllis Conine. He claimed to have committed the crimes alone and insisted that reward money totalling $16,500 for information leading to the killer should be paid to his wife for this confession. Further investigation revealed that, although he was remarkably vague about details of the location of the Haaga and Kuzeff murders (as, incidentally, Lobaugh had been), there was definite physical evidence linking him with the Conine case.

So Click was indicted for the Haaga, Kuzeff and Conine murders and for the attempted kidnap that led to his arrest. He pleaded guilty at trial to the kidnapping and was sentenced to life imprisonment.

The state prosecutor then elected to try Click for the Conine murder, for which he was convicted and sentenced to death. At this point Ralph Lobaugh also confessed to the murder of Phyllis Conine. It did not, however, prevent Franklin Click, his appeal already dismissed, being executed in the electric chair for the same murder.

Meanwhile, the Governor had been studying the reports by psychiatrists as to the mental state of Ralph Lobaugh, and decided that there were grave doubts as to the safety of the convictions in the cases of Haaga, Kuzeff and Howard. Lobaugh's death sentence was commuted to life imprisonment, and he was sent to the state prison for the criminally insane.

'LONELY-HEARTS KILLER' *see* **GLATMAN, Harvey Murray**

'LONELY-HEARTS KILLERS' *see* **BECK, Martha**

LOPEZ, Pedro Armando   Known in South America as the 'Monster of the Andes', Lopez has admitted to strangling 300 young girls over Ecuador, Colombia and Peru.

In hindsight perhaps we might be tempted to attach some supernatural significance to his being born a seventh son, to a prostitute in the Colombian town of Tolima. At the age of eight Pedro was discovered sexually fondling one of his younger sisters, and thrown out on to the streets to fend for himself.

Vulnerable and already sexually promiscuous, Pedro Lopez' early years were dominated by both heterosexual and homosexual experiences, and at the age of eighteen, on his second day of a sentence for car theft he was brutally raped in his cell by four fellow prisoners. Pedro's reponse was to make himself a crude knife, and within two weeks he had murdered three of his attackers. Such experiences had done irreparable damage to any normal development of the young Pedro Lopez; he had grown fearful of women and found social intercourse with them impossible, becoming, instead, addicted to sex through pornographic books and films.

Lopez travelled widely in Peru where he was responsible for the deaths of more than one hundred young girls, mostly from the Indian tribes, among whom he was finally visited by very rough justice. He had been caught by a tribe in Northern Peru while trying to carry off a nine-year-old girl; the Indians, after torturing Lopez, were preparing to bury him alive, and only the intervention of an American woman missionary convinced his captors that murder was ungodly. Luckier than he deserved, Pedro Lopez was deported back to Ecuador, where the killing spree continued. He would pick up young girls in the markets, deliberately seeking out those with a look of innocence. So successful was Lopez' reign of terror that the police in three countries began to think that an organisation was at work, kidnapping girls for sale as servants and prostitutes in the big cities.

It was in April 1980, that the inclement weather opened the eyes of the authorities to the true horror of the disappearances. A swollen river overflowed its banks near Ambato in Peru, and exposed the remains of four of the missing girls. A few days later a mother working in the Plaza Rossa market noticed that her twelve-year-old daughter was missing. She ran through the streets in search and caught up with the child leaving the market hand-in-hand with a stranger; she followed until they reached the edge of town and then called for help. Local Indians held Lopez until the police arrived; he had reached the end of his bloody road at last.

In jail awaiting trial, Lopez was tricked by the police into making a confession, in which he described first introducing his victims to sex and then strangling them. Convicted of murder in Ecuador, Lopez was sentenced to a life in prison, that country having abolished the death penalty even for monsters like Pedro Lopez.

LUCAS, Henry Lee   It was one of the most bizarre, one of the most grisly police 'conventions' that any of them could remember. The eighty-plus detectives representing twenty American states settled into a Holiday Inn in Louisiana to watch a videotape. Each one of these senior officers, like policemen the world over, had their share of unsolved killings and unidentified corpses, and as they sat in the screening room there was just a chance that some of these mysteries would be cleared up. On the screen was a short, ill-formed drifter of forty-seven, who, looking straight into the camera with his one good eye, was recounting what he could of the details of as many as two hundred murders committed in nearly every state of America. The show went on for forty-eight hours, a catalogue of sexual deviance, murder and mutilation unfolded that defied belief.

The number of Henry Lee Lucas's murders is unlikely ever to be known for sure – not surprisingly even Lucas has lost count – 'Once I've done it, I just forget it' – and since his arrest on 9 May 1983, he has changed his story a number of times. He claims that he committed his first murder at the age of thirteen after a female school teacher had snubbed his youthful advances. In January 1960, when he was twenty-four, Lucas stabbed his mother to death and was confined to the Ionia State Psychiatric Hospital after being sentenced to forty years for second-degree murder. To celebrate his release six years later, Lucas went on a murder spree that lasted seventeen years during which he drifted the length and breadth of America raping and killing. He met Ottis Elwood Toole, a pyromaniac, at a cheap diner in Jacksonville, and accompanied by Toole's thirteen-year-old, mentally retarded niece Frieda they travelled together for a year – Ottis burning, Henry killing, Frieda serving the animal needs of them both.

When Ottis Toole decided to withdraw from the partnership, Lucas and Frieda settled in the tiny Texan village of Stoneburg, where he worked as general handyman to eighty-year-old Mrs Kate Rich. Then Mrs Rich disappeared as did Frieda. Suspicious neighbours called in the sheriff and Henry Lucas was taken into custody. At the time, in the absence of any evidence that Mrs Rich was dead, Lucas was detained on a holding charge of illegally possessing a gun; he later led police to the remains of Frieda and Kate Rich. It was on the evening of his arrest that Henry Lee Lucas began the confession which was to take a nation's breath away: 'I've done some pretty bad things . . .,' he began.

The crimes were, as Lucas admitted, 'pretty bad', and from among the states that laid claim to charging him, Henry Lucas collected eleven murder convictions, one death sentence, six life terms, two seventy-five-year sentences and one sixty-year sentence. He is at present serving time on Death Row in Huntsville, Texas.

Predictably – for a psychopathic disorder most commonly originates with early childhood trauma – Henry Lee Lucas suffered the most appalling degradation as a child. According to his own recollections: 'I hated all my life. I hated everybody. When I first grew up and can remember, I was dressed as a girl by Mother. And I stayed that way for three years [in fact his mother sent Henry to his first day at school with permed hair and wearing a dress]. After that I was treated like what I call the dog of the family; I was beaten; I was made to do things that no human being would want to do . . .'

Lucas remained an outcast all his life, suffering frequent dizziness and blackouts as the result of all the savage head beatings he had suffered at his mother's hand; x-rays later revealed extensive damage to those areas of the brain which control behaviour and emotion. In childhood he also lost his left eye when a brother accidentally stabbed through it with a knife; and in early teenage he began to indulge in acts of sadism, homosexuality and bestiality.

At the end of his incarceration in the Ionia State Psychiatric Hospital where he had been committed for killing his mother and where he was diagnosed as a psychopath, a sadist and sexual deviant, Lucas almost pleaded with the hospital authorities to keep him inside; he knew, he said, that he was going to kill again. They released him anyway, and on that same day he murdered a young woman within walking distance of the hospital gates. Henry Lee Lucas was more perceptive than his doctors when he told them, 'I'm not ready to go.' If they had listened to him, two hundred people might still be alive today.

The 1991 film *Henry, Portrait of a Serial Killer* is loosely based on the life of Henry Lee Lucas.

LUDKE, Bruno   Ludke was born in Germany in 1909, and before he was out of his teens had already embarked on a career of rape, murder and necrophilia. The distraction caused by the Second World War provided a convenient cover for many of Ludke's activities, though it had its disadvantages when Bruno was rounded up by Himmler's SS and sterilised – partly because he was a suspected rapist, but mostly because he was an obvious mental defective. Which is how Bruno Ludke became a small part at least of the Führer's masterplan for a perfect race.

The sterilisation in no way impeded the progress of Ludke's sex crimes, though he did relocate his activities to a small village outside Berlin. On 29 January 1943, he was arrested in connection with the death of a woman who had been strangled not far from his home. Ludke readily confessed to that killing, and for good measure added eighty-five others between the end of the 1920s and the date of his arrest. His victims had invariably been strangled or stabbed, and sex had been the motivation, though Ludke admitted that intercourse usually only took place after the victim was dead.

Mentally deficient he certainly was, but Bruno Ludke was at least cunning enough when it came to self-preservation – pointing out to his captors that under Nazi law, prisoners deemed to be insane could not be indicted. And charged he was not; instead, Ludke was confined to hospital in Vienna and used as a human guinea pig in 'experiments'. On 8 April 1944, his participation in these experiments ended when an injection proved fatal.

'LUDWIG MURDERS' *see* **ABEL, Wolfgang**

LUPO, Michael It was about as much as either Brixton's gay community or its police could take. With relations between the two groups rarely better than a mutual suspicion, the murder of twenty-four-year-old Tony Connolly was looking set to tip the uneasy balance over into open hostility.

Connolly's body was found on 6 April 1986, by children playing in a workmen's hut on Brixton railway embankment in south London. It was clear that he had been taken there for sex and then strangled with his own scarf. The problems began when Connolly's body was taken to the mortuary at Southwark for post-mortem examination, and it was observed that the victim was a homosexual; furthermore, he had been sharing a flat with a fellow gay who was HTLV3 positive. Following guidelines laid down by the Department of Health and Social Security, mortuary staff declined to allow an examination until a test had cleared the body of being infected. The weeks of what police saw as unnecessary delay in making available forensic evidence, and the gay community interpreted as the police dragging their heels 'yet again' in the pursuit of a killer of homosexual men, led to angry exchanges. Police had already tentatively linked the death of Anthony Connolly to that of another man who had been strangled in west London, and another attempted murder in the same area. One informed commentator wrote at the time, 'It is far too early and far too dangerous to suggest a serial murderer is at large in the gay community.'

By May, less than six weeks after Tony Connolly's untimely death, it was clear that a serial murderer *had* been at large in the gay community. On the 18th, police arrested a thirty-three-year-old Chelsea fashion shop manager who doubled as a make-up artist; his name was Michael Lupo. Lupo was charged with the Connolly murder, that of thirty-seven-year-old railway guard James Burns, who was killed in a derelict flat in Kensington on 15 March, and the attempted murder of a man in Vauxhall Road, south London.

Three days later a further charge of murder was added to Lupo's sheet – Damien McClusky, twenty-two, a hospital worker found strangled in west London. By the time he reached the Central

Criminal Court, Michael Lupo's tally had risen to four murders and two attempted murders – the new murder charge was that of an unidentified sixty-two-year-old man who had been found strangled near Hungerford Bridge on 18 April.

Even before his trial,the tabloid press began piecing together what they called the 'bizarre world of a sex fiend'; the world of an Italian-born ex-commando, who had boasted that he would carry on killing until he was arrested; whose name, 'Lupo', means 'wolf', and who delighted in the nickname 'The Wolf Man'; a man who claimed to have had 4,000 homosexual lovers, who swore that he would attack again in prison.

At the Old Bailey on 10 July 1987, Lupo pleaded guilty to four counts of murder and two of attempted murder. The Recorder of London, Sir James Miskin, sentenced him to life imprisonment on each of the murder charges, and to consecutive terms of seven years on each of the attempted murder charges.

'LUST KILLER' *see* BRUDOS, Jerry

LYLES, Anjette   Well known around Macon, Georgia, as a practitioner of voodoo and Satanic rituals, Anjette Lyles nevertheless relied on the deadlier power of poison when it came to disposing of her family.

The sudden death of her husband Ben in January 1952, was a great disappointment to Anjette Lyles – or rather, the death was a success, but she had been sure he was insured for more than the measly three thousand dollars she got. Nothing ventured, she supplemented this modest sum by taking out a loan in order to open a restaurant which she called, not without a certain black humour, the *Gay Widow*.

One of the restaurant's regulars was an airline pilot named Joe Neal Gabbert who became as fond of Anjette as he was of her cooking, and after a whirlwind romance they married in June 1955. Three months after the wedding, Gabbert was taken seriously ill and Mrs Gabbert with the help of a hired nurse failed to effect any improvement. Joe Gabbert was hospitalised and died soon afterwards. Of course, he was insured.

And so was Anjette's former mother-in-law, Julia Young Lyles. She died on 29 September 1957, and eight months later nine-year-old daughter Marcia Elaine Lyles suffered an agonising death in hospital.

So alarming had the child's death been that an autopsy was ordered by the hospital, and the cause of death attributed to arsenical poisoning. A police search of Anjette Lyles' home uncovered six bottles of arsenic-based rat poison together with several empty poison bottles. Not surprisingly the Gay Widow was arrested and charged with murder.

It was stated in the evidence against her at trial that Anjette Lyles had altogether netted some $47,750 from the four deaths, including the estate of her mother-in-law which had been secured with a forged will. The money was spent mainly on men and supplies and equipment for her black-magic practices.

Although she was sentenced to die in the electric chair, Mrs Lyles was eventually declared insane and committed to hospital.

M

McDONALD, William   Between June 1961 and November 1962, the corpses of four vagrants were found in various parts of Sydney, victims of the so-called 'Sydney Mutilator'. The murders were characterised by an extreme of violence, and multiple stab wounds accompanied extensive mutilation of the genitals.

In one of the most bizarre episodes in the history of Australian crime, later dubbed 'The Case of the Walking Corpse', one of the bodies was identified as Allan Brennan – which came as a great surprise to the many people who had seen him alive, apparently well, and going about his business around the city.

Police investigations subsequently revealed that Brennan's real name was William McDonald, and that he had been born in England in 1926. When he was traced to Melbourne it became obvious that far from being a victim, McDonald was 'his own' murderer. In custody, McDonald attributed his grossly perverse sexuality to an incident in youth when he had been indecently assaulted by a corporal while serving in the Army. He had been diagnosed by the military pychiatrists as schizophrenic and treated. Obviously it had been only a temporary respite, for at his trial in September 1963 William McDonald's unbalance of mind, resulting in a compulsion to revenge himself through sexual mutilation was amply, if vainly, demonstrated to the court. In one of those thankfully rare acts of perversity the jury ignored the defence of insanity and found McDonald guilty of murder as charged. While he was serving a life sentence in Long Bay Penitentiary, William McDonald attacked and almost killed a fellow-prisoner. Now there were no more doubts and McDonald was confined to mental hospital.

MACKAY, Patrick David   A typical example of a child who grew up against a background of violence and abuse adopting the same characteristics in his own later life. Mackay's father, an aggressive alcoholic who regularly assaulted his wife and children when drunk, died in 1962, when Patrick was ten years old. From this point the boy seems almost to have taken over his father's role as the local bully. He was always in trouble at school, mostly for beating younger and weaker children than himself, and he became fond of torturing small animals, particularly the Mackays' long-suffering tortoise. This behaviour inevitably resulted in frequent visits both to mental institutions and to approved schools. Twice Mackay was released from Moss

Side Hospital – Liverpool's Broadmoor – against the strong advice of his doctors. When he was examined by a psychiatrist attached to the Home Office, fifteen-year-old Patrick was described as 'a cold psycho-pathic killer' – and this was even before he had begun to kill.

It is no surprise that Patrick Mackay enthusiastically embraced the outward manifestations of the German Nazis, developing an obsession with Adolf Hitler. Styling himself 'Franklin Bollvolt the First', he created crude uniforms by sewing and sticking various Nazi emblems on to his everyday clothes. Like his father, Patrick had also become dependent upon drink at an early age, and like his father reacted violently under its stimulus. He was also now a more-or-less fully employed crook, specialising in theft, street robbery and aggravated burglary – all his victims were elderly women.

On 14 February 1974, Mackay broke into the Chelsea, London, home of Isabella Griffiths, and in the course of robbing her, stabbed the eighty-four-year-old woman to death. Just over a year later, Mackay knocked at the door of Mrs Adele Price to ask for a drink of water; when he was invited in, Mackay strangled her.

Like many stranger-perpetrated homicides, these crimes were unsolved when Patrick Mackay made the mistake of killing somebody that knew him. Father Anthony Crean, a benevolent sixty-four-year-old Roman Catholic priest, had helped Mackay two years previously when he was having problems at home, and by way of thanks Patrick had robbed the priest's house. On 21 March 1975, Mackay attacked and killed Father Anthony at his home in Shorne, Kent. He stabbed his former benefactor several times, before splitting his head open with an axe; he then put him, still alive, in a bath of water and sat on the edge for an hour watching as his victim floundered and groaned, and then died.

Because of Mackay and Crean's previous acquaintance local police were very well aware of the relationship between the priest and the unworthy recipient of his generosity, and within forty-eight hours Patrick Mackay was under arrest. He was charged with a total of five murders, and questioned about six others. Improbable as it seems, Mackay was judged to be sane and fit to plead at his trial. He was found guilty and sentenced to life imprisonment.

MANSON, Charles, *et al.* Manson and his so-called 'Family' created shockwaves throughout California, a state not entirely unused to bizarre murders and serial killers. Those shockwaves would soon spread around the world.

An ex-convict and all-round drop-out, Manson dominated his equally unattractive disciples with a mish-mash of corrupted Biblical philosophy and mistaken interpretations of the lyrics of Beatles songs. This, combined with his magnetic sexual attraction for the female members of his 'Family', ensured Manson's complete physical and spiritual control of the group.

The first publicised murders took place in the summer of 1969, at which time the Family were occupying a disused movie-set ranch owned by George Spahn. While at the ranch, Manson organised the 'Land Armada', a fleet of armoured dune buggies that would protect the homestead during what he called 'Helter Skelter'. It is characteristic of Manson's retarded educational development that for him Helter Skelter was a simple misinterpretation of the words of a song written by the Beatles – he had no idea that the reference was to a fairground ride. Charlie had already decided that the Fab Four's earlier song 'Blackbird' represented a call to the blacks of America to rise up against the whites, and he now believed it was time to get the holocaust started which would lead to mutual annihilation of the races and leave the Family in control.

But all this military-style preparation needed financing, and Manson knew – or thought he knew – exactly where to get it: Gary Hinman, a musician friend of Manson's, was reputed to have recently come into an inheritance of $20,000. On 25 July 1969, Mary Brunner, Bobby Beausoleil and Susan Atkins arrived at Gary's house to try to beat the money out of him. When all the terrified youth could offer was his two cars, Manson ordered his death. As the Family trio left, they scrawled Gary's epitaph on the wall in his own blood: 'Political Piggie'. Atkins also attempted an inept drawing of a panther's claw intended to indicate that blame for the murder lay with the Black Panthers.

Just after midnight on Saturday, 9 August 1969, four shadowy figures were skulking about the grounds of the secluded mansion at 10050 Cielo Drive in Beverly Hills. At this stage, Manson was not doing his own killing; tonight it was the turn of 'Tex' Watson, Patricia 'Katie' Krenwinkel, 'Sadie' Atkins and Linda Kasabian to do their master's will. 10050 Cielo was occupied that night by actress Sharon Tate (her husband, the director Roman Polanski, was away on business), who was heavily pregnant, and four friends. In an orgy of overkill, the Family left all five victims horribly butchered. Voytec Frykowski alone was stabbed more than fifty times, slashed, shot and so savagely bludgeoned with the butt of a gun that the weapon shattered. On the front door to the house the word 'Pig' was painted in blood; not one of the murderous gang had had the slightest idea of whom they had killed – they were just random victims.

Only one person back at the Spahn Ranch was not pleased – Charlie Manson. When the news came through on television of the blood-bath it apparently offended Charlie's sensibilities that it had been such a messy job. He decided to show everybody how it should be done.

On 11 August, just two days after the Tate murders, after motivating themselves with drugs, Manson led a group consisting of 'Tex' Watson, Susan Atkins, Katie Krenwinkel, Linda Kasabian, Clem Grogan and Leslie Van Houten on a second murder spree. At shortly after 1.00 a.m. the Family invaded the Silver Lake home of businessman Leno LaBianca and his wife Rosemary; like the Cielo Drive victims, the choice was entirely random. After stabbing and slashing the LaBiancas to death, Manson and his disciples inscribed the mottoes 'Death to the Pigs', 'Rise', and 'Healter [sic] Skelter' in blood on the walls; as a final act of gratuitous violence, the word 'War' was carved into Leno LaBianca's abdomen.

Following these utterly mindless killings, the Family went to ground. Susan Atkins was later arrested on a prostitution charge and while she was in custody admitted her part in the Tate murders to a cellmate. The information filtered back to the prison authorities and, on 1 December 1969, the Family were rounded up and charges of murder were laid against the principal members. Manson, Krenwinkel, Atkins and van Houten were tried together and, on 19 April 1971, after one of the most extraordinary trials in California's history, they were convicted and sentenced to death for the Tate/LaBianca murders. At a later trial Manson, Bruce Davis and Clem Grogan were convicted of murder and conspiracy in the murder of Hinman and a cowboy actor named 'Shorty' Shea. Charles 'Tex' Watson was tried separately and found guilty on seven counts of murder and conspiracy; he too was sentenced to death. Susan Atkins pleaded guilty to Gary Hinman's murder and was sentenced to life imprisonment and Bobby Beausoleil was given the same sentence. Mary Brunner and Linda Kasabian turned state's evidence and no charges were brought against them. In view of the state of California's suspension of capital punishment, the death sentences were subsequently reduced to life imprisonment.

Although no further charges were brought, there is reason to believe that many other murders could be laid to the account of Charles Manson's Family, including several of their own members. Vincent Bugliosi, prosecutor in the Tate/LaBianca trial, in his book *Helter Skelter* does not dismiss Manson's own claim to have committed thirty-five murders – indeed, he now feels that it may have been an uncharacteristic understatement.

Charlie had been born illegitimately to a young prostitute named Kathleen Maddox in 1934. Shortly after the child's birth Kathy lived with a man named Bill Manson, whose name he was given. The imprisonment of his mother for armed robbery ensured that Charlie became even more of an outcast than he felt already and, after being fostered around various relatives, he was taken in by an obsessively religious grandmother who taught him the virtues of Christian meekness. From here he was dumped on an aunt and uncle in Maychem, Virginia, where in order to satisfy his uncle's ambition for him to be a 'man' Charlie had to unlearn all his Christian meekness. To help him, the family sent Charlie to school dressed as a little girl where the constant teasing of his classmates threw him into such fits of rage that the young Charles Manson became a formidable fighter (see Henry Lee **Lucas**, who was also dressed for school as a girl).

Manson spent a couple more years with his mother after her release from Moundsville State Prison, before being passed on to an alcoholic uncle who taught the boy how to drink. When he ran out of family, Charlie found himself at the Gibault Home for Boys – an institution run by an order of Catholic Brothers, where discipline was strict, pleasures were few and beatings were many. Of a naturally rebellious nature, Charlie Manson received more beatings than most.

Eventually, while not yet even a teenager, Manson escaped to a life of crime and further punishment. At fourteen he was in the Indiana School for Boys after conviction for car theft. Here Manson was beaten unmercifully by the guards and his fellow inmates and subjected to frequent sexual abuse. It was probably at this point that Charles Manson passed beyond salvation. He escaped from Indiana, was rearrested and incarcerated in the National Training School at Washington DC for more physical punishment and more sexual abuse; the difference was that by this time Charlie had been so brutalised that he was immune to anything authority or society could beat him with.

In March 1967, Charles Manson was released from Terminal Island reformatory, California, having spent all but months of the previous twenty years locked up; he was thirty-two years old.

If his life so far had taught Charlie anything it was how to survive against the odds. He was just ready for the new hippie revolution that was sweeping through America on the wafting aroma of pot and free love; and they were ready for Charlie. Within days of his release from custody, Manson was installed in the Haight-Ashbury district of San Francisco – world capital of Hippiedom. Here he became acquainted with the hallucinogenic drug LSD and with the hordes of other drifters and outcasts like himself, a 'tribe' inhabiting a twilight world on the fringes of society. Charlie started to use his modest musical talents to hustle small change on street corners and in the cheap bars of the Tenderloin, and became involved in Black Magic and Satanism.

By 1969, this charismatic, chameleon-like man was the centre of his own admiring group; as for a new messiah the Family would do anything for Charlie – even kill. Over the coming year they would act out Manson's blinding sociopathic rage against authority and all humankind.

Charles Manson has been eligible for parole for many years now. Serving his time in San Quentin, he applies for release at every opportunity, using his uncanny powers of psychological persuasion to convince the parole board that he is sane and safe. It is, however, unlikely that the person once described as the most dangerous man in America will ever be released.

MANUEL, Peter Peter Manuel was born in Glasgow in 1927, and from the age of twelve embarked on a life of crime which he pursued until he was hanged in 1958. Burglary, housebreaking, robbery and assault were all punctuated by greater or lesser periods as a guest of the Borstal or prison services until, in 1956, Manuel graduated to murder.

The first victims, three members of the Watt family were shot dead during a burglary. Two years later the Smart family died in identical circumstances. Manuel was also responsible for the sex-killings of two seventeen-year-old girls, Anne Knielands and Isabelle Cooke.

It was after the Smart killings that Peter Manuel and his father were both taken into custody. In exchange for his father's release, Peter Manuel confessed to the murder of Peter Smart, his wife Doris, and their eleven-year-old son, as well as five other incidents. After his trial and conviction in May 1958, Manuel confessed from the death cell to three more murders – two in Glasgow and one in London, and a coroner's inquest into the shooting of taxi driver Sydney Dunn in Newcastle in 1957 named Peter Manuel as his killer.

His readiness to confess, and his uncontrollable eagerness to 'help the police with their inquiries' earned Manuel the nickname of 'The Man Who Talked Too Much'; there follows a section of one of his many confessions:

I hereby confess that on January 1st, 1956, I was the person responsible for killing Anne Knielands. On September 17th, 1956, I was responsible for killing Mrs Marion Watt and her sister Mrs George Brown, also her daughter Vivienne. On December 28th, 1957, I was responsible for killing Mr Peter Smart, his wife Doris and their son. I freely admit and acknowledge my guilt in the above-mentioned crimes and wish to write a statement concerning them . . .

. . . On December 28th, 1957, I went to Mount Vernon about 7 p.m., going by bus from Birkenshaw to Mount Vernon. I walked up the road leading to the railway bridge that runs from Bothwell to Shettleston. Just over the bridge, I met a girl walking [Isabelle Cooke]. I grabbed her and dragged her into a field on the same side as Rylands riding school. I took her along with me, following a line going in the Bothwell direction.

I took her handbag and filled it with stones from the railway. Before going any farther, I flung it in a pond in the middle of a field. I then made her go with me along towards the dog track and she started to scream. I tore off her clothes, tied something around her neck and choked her. I then carried her up the line into a field and dug a hole with a shovel. While I was doing this a man passed along the line on a bike. So I carried her again over the path opposite the brickworks and into another field.

I dug a hole in the part of the field that was ploughed, and put her in. I covered her up and went back the way I had come. I went back to the road and got her shoes, which had come off at the outset. I took these and her clothes and scattered them about. The clothes I flung in the river Calder at Bromhouse, the shoes I hid on the railway bank at the dog track. I went up the same path and came out at Baillieston. I walked along the Edinburgh road and up Aitkenhead Road to Birkenshaw, and got there about 12.30 a.m. The first hole I dug, I left it as it was.

[After his arrest, Peter Manuel took police officers to this spot where he had buried Isabelle Cooke; he told them, 'This is the place. In fact I think I'm standing on her now.']

On the morning of January 1st, 1958, I left my home about 5.30 a.m., and went down the path to the foot of the brae crossing the road and into Sheepburn Road and broke into the bungalow.I went through the house and took a quantity of banknotes from a wallet I found in a jacket in the front bedroom. There was about £20 to £25 in the wallet. I then shot the man [Peter Smart] in the bed and next the woman. I then went into the next room and shot the boy.

I did not take anything from the house except money. I got the gun from a man in Glasgow at a club. I took the car from the garage and drove it to the car park at Ranco. Later that day I took the gun into Glasgow and threw it into the Clyde at Glasgow Green.

(signed) Peter Manuel

MAREK, Martha Extraordinary Austrian murderess who worked up to the 'ultimate crime' via a quite gruesome insurance fraud. After taking out an accident policy on her husband to the tune of $30,000, Martha chopped through one of poor Emil Marek's legs almost severing it below the knee. This, the couple claimed had been an accident sustained while felling a tree; the fact that there was evidence of *three* cuts, and all of them in the wrong direction to be consistent with the story, led the surgeon to offer another explanation – that the injury was self-inflicted in order to defraud the insurance company. After a brief trial the Mareks were acquitted of the fraud charge, but sentenced to a salutary four months' imprisonment for trying to bribe one of the hospital orderlies to malign the integrity of the surgeon.

On their release, Martha and Emil emigrated to Algiers and started up a business which almost as quickly failed, forcing the couple back to Vienna, destitute. So poor were they, that Martha was obliged to sell vegetables from a stall in the market.

In July 1932, Emil Marek died in a charity hospital from what was diagnosed as tuberculosis; soon after, their baby daughter Ingeborg also died, and Martha boarded out the elder child, Peter.

Later in the same month Frau Marek eschewed the market stall for the more ladylike occupation of housekeeper/companion to an elderly relative, Susanne Lowenstein. Frau Lowenstein lived only long enough to make Martha the beneficiary of her will.

The widow Marek next turned to letting out rooms in her house to a hand-picked group of lodgers. One of them was an insurance agent, another a Frau Kittenberger. Having persuaded the insurance man to make a $1000 policy in Martha's favour on the life of Frau Kittenberger, that lady became expendable, and died shortly afterwards.

Frau Kittenberger's son, Herbert, took the news very hard (perhaps because of the recent change of will, perhaps not), and suspecting foul play demanded a post-mortem. When his mother's body had been duly exhumed and examined it became clear that she had died because she had been given poison. And there was only one person who stood to gain anything by poisoning her.

So with Martha Marek under lock and key, the bodies of her husband, her daughter and Frau Lowenstein were also exhumed, autopsied and recertified as having perished from the effects of a fatal dose of the metallic poison thallium. Martha's son Peter, who though boarded out had been visited regularly by his mother bringing food, was certainly the next on her death list, for he was found to be in a very poorly state, and only immediate hospital treatment saved his life.

At her trial, the public prosecutor described Martha Marek as worse than Lucrezia Borgia, and a chemist from Florisdorf obligingly produced records of sales of thallium to Martha just before the death of each of the victims. She was found guilty on all four counts of murder.

Austria had by now been annexed by Adolf Hitler and the formerly discarded death penalty restored. Martha Marek was decapitated by one swift stroke of the executioner's axe on 6 December 1938.

MAZURKIEWICZ, Wladyslaw Mazurkiewicz had already been active on the fringe of the Polish underworld operating as a black-market trader and currency speculator when, in 1943, he made an unsuccessful attempt to add murder to his credentials by trying to poison and rob a man who was on the run from the Nazi occupation forces.

His second venture into murder was a great deal more successful, and Viktor Zarzecki never recovered from a cyanide-laced cup of tea, and certainly had no further use for the $1200 that Mazurkiewicz stole from him.

By the time the last shots of the Second World War had been fired in anger, Mazurkiewicz had graduated to a car and a gun, and put both to very profitable effect in July 1945, while driving Wladyslaw Brylski to negotiate a currency deal. He shot Brylski in the head, robbed him, and threw his body into the sparkling waters of Poland's major river, the Vistula. Three months later Mazurkiewicz killed Josef Tomaszewski. He was arrested for the crime after his car had been identified close to the field in which the victim's body was dumped but, thanks to an 'arrangement' with a corrupt police official, Mazurkiewicz was not long in custody.

In May 1946, he escalated the scale of killing to include families when he first killed and robbed Jerzy de Laveaux – again making use of the nearby Vistula as a convenient watery grave – and then in 1954 killed Laveaux's widow and her sister, burying the bodies under the concrete floor of his garage.

Wladyslaw Mazurkiewicz' next crime had the result of bringing about his downfall. He had attempted to shoot a fellow black-marketeer through the head, but the bullet miraculously lodged in the man's skull without any very serious consequences. Understandably rattled, the victim complained to the police and Mazurkiewicz was put in custody, where he made a statement in which he admitted all his crimes.

At a trial which started on 7 August 1956 and lasted fourteen days, Mazurkiewicz made a couple of attempts at offering a believable defence, first with the plea that he was suffering from schizophrenia and was therefore not to be held responsible for his actions, then towards the end of the trial when things seemed to be going against him, Mazurkiewicz withdrew his statement admitting guilt and claimed he had made the whole thing up and had never killed anybody in his life. Thoroughly bewildered by now, the court convicted him anyway – on all counts. Wladyslaw Mazurkiwicz was sentenced to death and duly executed.

'METAL FANG' *see* **DZHUMAGALIEV, Nikolai**

'MIDDAY MURDERER' *see* **GOSMAN, Klaus**

'MICHIGAN MURDERER' *see* **COLLINS, Norman John**

MIKASEVICH, Gennadiy   Reports in any depth of serious crime in the Soviet Union are rare even in the original language, and so it is with interest that we find the misdeeds of one Gennadiy Mikasevich recorded in Jay Robert Nash's *Encyclopedia of World Crime*. Few as they are, the details are set out below.

Between 1971 and 1985 thirty-six women had been found strangled in the Soloniki region of Russia – fourteen victims in 1984 alone. The killer was reported as picking up the women in his small red Zaparochet car and later strangling them with a scarf. Already with considerably more enthusiasm than sound judgement the police had arrested, and the courts had tried and convicted, four different men. In 1974 a man named Glushakov was sentenced to ten years' imprisonment for the murders; subsequently Oleg Adamov was sentenced to fifteen years in prison where, in utter despair, he killed himself; V. Gorelov spent six years in prison where he went blind; and a man called Tereniv was executed. Still the killings continued.

In 1984 the murder of a technical school student attracted the attention of Detective Nicolai Ivanovich Iquatovich, who ran a check on 200,000 cars – no less than 7000 of them Zaparochets. Handwriting on licence documents was compared with a letter that had been received by the police stating that the motive for the murders was 'revenge against adulterous women'; it had been signed 'Patriot of Vitebsk'. This letter was presumed to be genuine when the same message was found on the last two victims of the series in 1985. Detective Iquatovich further checked 312,000 inter-state passports which led finally to the arrest and confession of Gennadiy Mikasevich.

Mikasevich had been the chief of the State motor-vehicle repair works for the Soloniki region, and in his spare time was a police volunteer. Unbelievably, he had become very involved in the investigation of his own series of murders – going as far as to interview suspects and stop small red cars. Diagnosed as suffering from a sexual inferiority complex, Mikasevich was executed some time between 1985 and 1988.

MILLER, James William, and WORRELL, Chris The 'Truro Murders', so called from the location where the bodies were dumped in the hills outside Adelaide, South Australia, began on the day before Christmas 1976. An habitual criminal and frequent prison inmate, James Miller had taken to driving round Adelaide with a man named Chris Worrell. According to Miller – and by this time Worrell was in no position to contradict him – they had become close friends after a homosexual relationship. It seems, though, that Worrell was at least as strongly attracted to the opposite sex. On this fateful Christmas Eve, the two men picked up a young woman in Adelaide and drove her out into the Truro Hills. According to Miller, he left his companion and the young woman to engage in what he imagined would be a sexual encounter, but when he returned from a walk he found the girl dead. Miller claims that Worrell confessed to killing her after 'feeling violent', and together they buried the body. This same pattern was repeated six times before fate intervened.

On 19 February 1977, James Miller, Chris Worrell and Worrell's girlfriend were involved in a fatal car crash, which killed Worrell and his girlfriend and left Miller badly hurt but still alive.

It was more than two years later that the bodies in the hills began to be discovered; by this time the only witness to the deaths, James Miller, had merged back into the twilight world from which he had come. It took a large 'reward for information' for a member of the public to finally put the finger on him, and Miller, as one might expect in the circumstances, put the whole of the blame on to the late Chris Worrell.

It may well have been that the girls were, in a strictly physical sense, Worrell's victims alone. But the law quite rightly makes provision for imposing the strongest penalties on an accomplice who is said to 'act in concert' with the perpetrator. In other words, James Miller knew exactly what was going to happen when they picked girls up and drove them to the hills; he made no effort to stop it, nor did he inform the authorities. Furthermore, he assisted in the business of concealing the corpses. As a consequence Miller was tried on six counts of murder and sentenced to life imprisonment.

James Miller's attorneys entered an application for leave to appeal on grounds that the judge had misdirected the jury and that there was new evidence in the form of psychiatric reports on Miller. The appeal was turned down, but in 1984, while he was confined in the Yatala Labor Prison, James Miller wrote his autobiography, *Don't Call Me Killer!*, in which he continued to protest his innocence.

'MONSTER OF FLORENCE' An as yet unidentified serial killer, nicknamed by a press that seems to delight in such word exercises, the 'Monster of Florence'. The established victim pattern in all the murder/mutilations has been the killing of couples making love in cars (with one exception) in deserted streets around the Italian city of Florence. Sixteen couples were killed between 1968 and 1985, and the murders all took place at the time of the full moon. Victims were shot through their car window and in the cases where mutilation followed, the woman's sex organs were cut away, probably with a scalpel.

The first killing was in August 1968, when a man and his mistress were shot with a .22 automatic pistol in their parked car near an abandoned cemetery about fifteen miles outside Florence. In this instance, the woman's husband, Stefano Mele, was erroneously tried and convicted of their murder along with a further charge of perjury and, in March 1970, sentenced to thirteen years' imprisonment.

On 14 September 1974, a couple were shot in their parked car by a .22 handgun proved by forensic ballistics to be the same weapon used in the 1968 killings. The victims were naked and their bodies bore unusually shaped bruises which experts suggested were made with the handle of a scalpel. In addition, the woman had been violated with a vine stalk.

Another couple were killed on 6 June 1981, the first case in which the woman's sex organs were mutilated. Further murders took place on 22 October 1981 and, on 19 June 1982, there were two double murders on the same day, though neither was accompanied by mutilation.

Two homosexuals were shot dead while sleeping in their van on 9 September 1983, and two more couples were killed on 29 July 1984 and 8 September 1985. In both the latter incidents, the abuse of the women's bodies had included the removal of their left breast. In the last case, a local attorney was sent an envelope which contained two strips of skin removed from the breast of the victim.

To date, no further killings have taken place that are consistent with the 'Monster's' pattern, and no suspects have emerged from an understandably intensive police investigation.

'MONSTER OF MONTMARTRE' *see* **PAULIN, Thierry**

'MONSTER OF THE ANDES' *see* **LOPEZ, Pedro Armando**

'MOORS MURDERERS' *see* **BRADY, Ian**

MORS, Frederick   Mors arrived in New York from Vienna in June 1914 and in due course his native tongue enabled him to obtain employment as a porter at the German Odd Fellows Home in the Bronx. Shortly after starting work there, Mors began to exhibit signs of megalomania, manifested by his dressing up in white uniforms with a stethoscope round his neck, adopting an arrogant air and ordering the elderly patients to address him as 'Herr Doktor'. His manner instilled no little fear into the old, though for less explicable reasons he seemed to be liked by the child residents.

Mors took his masquerade a step further when he began purchasing items of pharmacy from a local druggist, including chloroform. During the four months from September 1914 to January 1915, the death rate in the Home escalated alarmingly, in all seventeen passed away. Fearing foul play, the administration called in the police who hearing of the elderly patients' terror of Mors decided to elevate him to the top of their suspect list. Mors could not have been more obliging if he had tried; of course, he calmly admitted, he was responsible for killing eight of those who had recently died. He had done it to put them out of their misery – besides they had become a nuisance to everybody: 'First I would pour a drop or two of chloroform on a piece of absorbent cotton and hold it to the nostrils of the old person. Soon my man would swoon. Then I would close the orifices of the body with cotton, stuffing it in the ears, nostrils and so on. Next I would pour a little chloroform down the throat and prevent the fumes escaping in the same way.' He had perfected this method, apparently, after encountering difficulties with the arsenic poisoning of his first victim.

Not surprisingly, Frederick Mors was certified a criminal lunatic and committed to the Matteawan Institution for the insane – which at the time was home to 'Mad' Harry Thaw, who had shot dead America's most famous architect, Stanford White, in a fit of jealousy.

Mors escaped from the institution some time in the late 1920s and was never heard of again.

MSOMI, Elifasi   In South African tribal folklore, the equivalent of the European *bogle*, or bogey-man is the 'tokoloshe'. From August 1953, for a period of twenty-one months, Elifasi Msomi embarked on a series of fifteen murders of men, women and children claiming that it was not he, but the tokoloshe that was responsible. Msomi was a native of Richmond, Natal, and carried on the profession of witch doctor – though how successful he was may be judged by his declining practice. Taking, so to speak, some of his own medicine, Msomi established that it would require the blood of just fifteen freshly slaughtered humans to boost his flagging fortunes and restore his business to its peak.

The first step in self-improvement was taken in August 1953, when Msomi, in the presence of his mistress, raped and stabbed to death a young girl. The woman, understandably shocked and disillusioned, reported her lover to the police and he was arrested. Perhaps Msomi was receiving a little advance reward from the tokoloshe, since he managed to escape from custody.

Soon afterwards, posing as a labour agent at a village in the Boston district, Msomi persuaded parents to let him take five children with him to work as servants for Europeans in the city. Having stabbed the unfortunate mites to death, Msomi had the audacity to return to the village, assure the parents that their offspring were well placed, and demand money to provide them with extra comforts. He seems to have continued to murder almost at will, frequently employing the 'labour agent' ruse to lure children from their families. The police, convinced that an unbalanced Zulu was responsible for the disappearances, could only advise the tribespeople in the area to be on their guard.

In April 1955, Elifasi Msomi was reported to the police for theft, arrested and placed in custody. Almost as quickly – and this may be attributed either to the power of the tokoloshe or the lax procedures of the native Natal police – he was away again.

Recaptured the following month, Msomi found himself in the embarrassing position of being in possession of some property formerly belonging to one of his victims, and the very knife with which he had committed his first murder. Not that Msomi was uncooperative; he was quite prepared to lead the police to the last resting grounds of all the victims – not of himself, but of the tokoloshe!

The court would entertain none of this mumbo-jumbo. As far as they were concerned Elifasi Msomi was a multiple murderer, and accordingly, in September 1955, he was sentenced to death for his crimes.

But there are powers abroad that transcend the judgement of a mortal court. So terrified were the local people that the tokoloshe would step in once again and lift Msomi from captivity to wreak further havoc that, to convince them that Msomi was dead, the prison authorities were obliged to arrange for a deputation of chiefs and elders to view Msomi before and after his appointment with the hangman at Pretoria Central Prison on 10 February 1956.

MUDGETT, Hermann Webster (a.k.a. H.H. Holmes) Born in New Hampshire in May 1860, Mudgett has been called America's worst mass killer, and whether or not he deserves this title he was certainly one of that country's most prolific and inventive criminals.

Bigamist, swindler and multicide, the final total of Mudgett's killings will never be known; remains of as many as two hundred corpses were found in the Chicago death-house known as 'Holmes' Castle', though he had only got as far as detailing twenty-seven of them before he was executed.

Hermann Mudgett studied medicine at Ann Arbor, and for a short while afterwards practised as a doctor in New York. After some misunderstanding with the law over the possession of corpses, Mudgett fled to Chicago where he entered employment with a drug company. The owner of the business, poor woman, disappeared mysteriously shortly after meeting Mudgett and he repaid her memory by taking over the company. Actually, quite a lot of people whose paths crossed Hermann Mudgett's disappeared mysteriously – including a succession of bigamous wives and mistresses.

In 1891 the man now calling himself H.H. Holmes gave up the drug business and moved in to manage the bizarre hotel which he had commissioned to be built on a vacant lot on the corner of Chicago's 63rd Street. He hired and fired his builders at such a rapid rate that none ever knew the exact layout of the building – which was how the labyrinthine series of torture chambers remained a secret for so long. The hotel was visited by hundreds of guests, particularly during the period of the Chicago World Fair, and many of them never checked out – at least not through the lobby. Particularly vulnerable were attractive young women, whom Holmes lured to his lair, seduced and after sexual intercourse drugged and despatched to the cellar via a specially constructed chute. Although the sequence varied according to whim or circumstance, most of the victims next found themselves in one of the air-tight gas chambers where they would choke to death while Holmes watched through a glass panel. When they were dead, the girls were transported to the dissection room where the deadly doctor performed his 'experimental' surgery, disposing of the unwanted remains in one of the many acid baths, furnaces and quicklime pits.

It was, nevertheless, a careless insurance fraud committed in Texas that first drew official attention to H.H. Holmes (or H.M. Howard as he then was). Thanks to a crooked lawyer he was soon free, but by then he had come to the unwelcome notice of a tenacious detective named Geyer, who pursued his quarry through Pennsylvania, New Hampshire and Massachusetts. During this period Holmes had disposed of a former partner named Pitezel and the three Pitezel children and run off with Pitezel's wife. When the corpses were found in an Indianapolis rooming-house, Holmes was taken into custody.

On 30 November 1895, Hermann Mudgett was sentenced to death for the murder of Benjamin Pitezel. Meanwhile, police had explored 'Torture Castle' and uncovered its grisly secrets. In the time that remained to him, Mudgett began a rambling memoir in which he was able to detail twenty-seven of his murders before being executed on 27 May 1896. Contrary to the last, Mudgett retracted his confession at the foot of the gallows, claiming that his previous admissions were simply for the purpose of publicity – to give the newspapers a good story.

MULLIN, Herbert The product of a devoutly, almost obsessively religious background, it was a surprise to almost everybody how well adjusted Herb turned out. He was academically successful at school, and both he and his best friend Dean Richardson were members of the school's prestigious 'Zeros' athletics team.

What seems to have triggered Mullin's mental degeneration was the death of Dean in a motoring accident in July 1965. He began to exhibit the outward symptoms of a schizophrenic disorder – he turned his bedroom at home into a shrine to his late friend, and broke off his engagement to his girlfriend because, so he said, he was a homosexual. He declared himself a conscientious objector in the face of imminent army call-up, and on his twenty-first birthday in 1969, Herb Mullin celebrated by announcing to his bewildered family that he was going to India to study religion. A spell in a mental hospital on the advice of his parents failed to shake Mullin's odd fixations, and by the end of the year it was clear he was suffering from paranoid schizophrenia. He began to indulge in hallucinogenic drugs and to hear disembodied voices; how much these two activities fed off each other is debatable, but his increasing dependence on narcotics can not have helped what went on in his head. Over the next two years Herbert Mullin was in and out of institutions where he underwent treatment and was declared cured only to relapse and be admitted to a different clinic. One of the more sinister developments was that the voices had begun to order him to kill.

The first time Herb carried out his orders was on 13 October 1972. He had been driving along a deserted road in the Santa Cruz mountains when he passed an old tramp, later identified as Lawrence White. Mullin stopped, got out of the car, and lifted the hood as if the vehicle had broken down. When 'Old Whitey' caught up and garrulously offered his help, Mullin beat the old man to death with a baseball bat.

On Tuesday, 24 October, he fatally stabbed Mary Guilfoyle, a college student from the Santa Cruz university campus, cut open her body and dragged out the innards with his bare hands, leaving the resulting shambles to be picked over by the vultures. And still there were the voices. Always there were voices.

Sometimes there were different voices – not the voices commanding him to kill, but the voices of people begging Herb to kill them. So in December 1972 he went out and bought a gun. At the end of the following month he shot five people dead in a single day.

Always there were the voices. Herb said, 'Satan gets into people and makes them do things they don't want to.'

On 6 February 1973, Mullin shot four teenage boys to death as they camped in the Cowell State Park at Santa Cruz. Less than a week after, the voices told him to shoot down Fred Perez as he worked in his garden; what they did not tell Herb was that Fred's neighbour was watching at her window and called the police.

Within minutes Mullin was under arrest and later confessed to thirteen murders.

At his trial in the Santa Cruz County Court in July 1973, Herbert Mullin's defence – not unreasonably one might think – was not guilty by reason of insanity; after all, he had been diagnosed paranoid schizophrenic. Perversely, a jury decided that Mullin was, by legal standards at least, responsible for his actions and therefore fit to stand trial. He was eventually indicted on ten counts of murder and found guilty on two counts of first-degree murder and eight counts of second-degree murder. He is at present confined in San Quentin, eligible for parole in the year 2025, when he will be seventy-eight.

Herbert Mullin is in many ways a stereotype 'visionary' psychotic killer. His reason for murder was that he genuinely believed that the voices and 'telepathic messages' were directed to him as a saviour of the world. Mullin believed that by killing people (the 'small disaster') he could avert the 'great disaster' – a cataclysmic earthquake and tidal wave that would destroy California.

The most alarming feature of this otherwise tragic narrative is that Herbert Mullin had been exhibiting symptoms of serious mental instability from youth, and it must in some part at least be laid to the responsibility of the California state mental health programme that a man so obviously disturbed should have been for so long without professional supervision.

MUMFRE, Joseph *see* **'AXEMAN OF NEW ORLEANS'**

N

NEILSON, Donald   His working uniform was always the same: black plimsolls, army camouflage suit, white gloves and the black hood which earned him his soubriquet of the 'Black Panther'.

The first victim of Neilson's series of murderous raids on the premises of sub-postmasters was Donald Skepper. On 15 February 1974, having terrorised Skepper's son, the mysterious intruder in search of keys to the safe confronted Donald Skepper and his wife as they lay in bed. With more courage than forethought Skepper shouted, 'Let's get him,' and was immediately shot.

On 6 September, sub-postmaster Derek Astin tackled an intruder in his post office at Higher Baxenden, near Accrington; he was shot dead in front of his wife and two children.

By mid-November the man, now popularly known as the Black Panther was in Langley, Worcestershire, where he shot Sidney Grayland, bludgeoned his wife Margaret, fracturing her skull, and stole £800 from the cash box.

Less than two months later the Black Panther committed the crime that moved the nation, and made him Britain's most wanted man.

Seventeen-year-old Lesley Whittle disappeared from the family home in Shropshire on the morning of 14 January 1975. Her abductor had left behind a number of messages pressed out of red Dymo-tape which demanded a £50,000 ransom and warned, 'If police or tricks, Death.' That same week, Gerald Smith, a security officer at the Freightliner container depot at Dudley, observed a man loitering by the perimeter fence. The man's behaviour when approached was so suspicious that Smith turned to call the police. The next thing he was aware of was the loud report of a gun and a searing pain in his buttocks; the attacker then emptied the gun into him and disappeared. Amazingly, Gerald Smith was able to crawl to a telephone and alert the police. Ballistics experts later confirmed that the gun was the same as that used in two earlier Black Panther crimes, and when police had traced the green Morris car that had been parked at the depot, they discovered a number of Dymo-tape messages – clearly pieces of a ransom trail and identical to those left at the Whittle home – and a taped message from Lesley Whittle to her mother. Soon Gerald Smith's description of his assailant had been transformed into a portrait drawing that was to become one of the best-known faces in the country.

Just before midnight on 16 January Ronald Whittle received a telephone call from a man claiming to be Lesley's captor. Following a trail marked by further Dymo-tape messages, Ronald arrived at Bathpool Park near the town of Kidsgrove, Staffordshire. Here the kidnapper was supposed to respond to Ronald Whittle's flashing car headlights with a torch. In the event there was no contact.

Following extensive publicity, a local headmaster remembered that one of his pupils had handed him a strip of Dymo-tape bearing the message 'Drop Suitcase into Hole' which he had found in Bathpool Park a couple of days after the kidnapping. A further clue was a torch found by another schoolboy wedged in the grille of a ventilating shaft to the sewage system that runs beneath Bathpool Park. Police and tracker dogs now began to search the underground culverts, and it was during this operation that the naked body of Lesley Whittle was found at the bottom of one of the ventilating shafts. Around her neck was a noose of wire attached to the iron ladder.

Almost a year passed, however, before the Black Panther was captured. On the night of 11 December 1975, two officers were on a routine Panda car patrol in the village of Mansfield Woodhouse. They stopped to investigate a suspicious-looking man with a black holdall when he produced a sawn-off shotgun and forced PCs White and Mackenzie back into the car. At gunpoint PC Mackenzie was ordered to drive on, but using a combination of verbal and visual signals (via the rear-view mirror), the two policemen conspired to disarm and capture the suspect. Jamming his foot on the brake at a T-junction Mackenzie sufficiently surprised the gunman for White to lunge at the gun now pointed away from his companion. With help from a public-spirited bystander, the two officers were able to subdue their prisoner and make an arrest. Although they did not know it yet, they had just terminated the career of the Black Panther.

When police searched his home in Bradford, they found enough evidence to bring four charges of murder against Neilson. He was tried for the death of Lesley Whittle at Oxford Crown Court between 14 June and 1 July 1975, and from 5 July to 21 July for the deaths of the postmasters. For each of the four murders Donald Neilson received life sentences; for kidnapping he was condemned to sixty-one years' imprisonment.

Gerald Smith died in March 1976 as a result of his confrontation with Neilson; but the laws of England allow a person only a year and a day in which to die if a charge of murder is to be brought.

NELSON, Earle Leonard Nelson was an odd-looking man, with the receding forehead, protruding lips, and huge hands that led to his nickname 'The Gorilla Murderer'. He had been born in Philadelphia in 1897, though his mother died of venereal disease contracted from his father when Earle was less than one year old, and he was fostered out to his Aunt Lillian. She was a devoutly religious woman, a trait which she instilled into her impressionable young nephew, with whom religion would become a Bible-thumping obsession. At the age of ten Nelson suffered a severe head injury when he was hit by a moving streetcar, and this trauma left him with physical and mental problems throughout his life. In fact as early as 1918, Nelson was admitted to a mental hospital after attempting to rape a neighbour's daughter. He absconded several times and was readmitted; the following year he contracted a marriage which was fated to last a mere six months; he was now calling himself Roger Wilson. Between February 1926, and June 1927, as the Gorilla Murderer, Nelson went on a rampage which left twenty-two known victims dead, all women, all boarding-house landladies, all raped and strangled.

The first victim was found in the attic of her rooming-house in San Francisco on 20 February 1926; sixty-year-old Clara Newman had been displaying a 'Rooms to Let' sign in her downstairs window, Earle Nelson had come to inquire about one.

Between this brutal attack and his last, in Winnipeg, Canada, Nelson managed to evade justice by continually moving around and changing his name.

Earle Nelson's known victims

Date	Name	Age	Location
20 February 1926	Clara Newman	60	San Francisco
2 March 1926	Laura E. Beale	60	San Jose
10 June 1926	Lillian St Mary	63	San Francisco
24 June 1926	Anna Russell	58	Santa Barbara
16 August 1926	Mary Nesbit	52	Oakland
19 October 1926	Beatrice Withers	35	Portland
20 October 1926	Virginia Grant	59	Portland
21 October 1926	Mabel Fluke	?	Portland
15 November 1926	Blanche Myers	48	Oregon City
18 November 1926	Wilhelmina Edmunds	56	San Francisco
24 November 1926	Florence Monks	?	Seattle
23 December 1926	Elizabeth Beard	49	Council Bluffs
? December 1926	Bonnie Pace	23	Kansas City
28 December 1926	Germania Harpin*	28	Kansas City
27 April 1927	Mary McConnell	60	Philadelphia
30 May 1927	Jenny Randolph	35	Buffalo
1 June 1927	Minnie May	53	Detroit
	Mrs Atworthy (a lodger)	?	Detroit
3 June 1927	Mary Sietsema	27	Chicago
8 June 1927	Lola Cowan	14	Winnipeg
9 June 1927	Emily Paterson	?	Winnipeg

* Nelson also throttled Mrs Harpin's eight-month-old baby.

On 8 June 1927, Nelson crossed over the border into Canada and hitch-hiked to Winnipeg, where he took a room in a boarding-house in Smith Street. Here Nelson broke his pattern and the landlady was unharmed; instead Nelson murdered fourteen-year-old Lola Cowan and, as part of a regular formula, hid her body under a bed in a spare room where it was found four days later.

In a separate incident on the evening following Lola Cowan's murder, William Paterson arrived home to find his wife Emily missing, and later to discover a suitcase rifled and money stolen from it. Fearing the worst, Paterson telephoned the police, anxious over his wife's whereabouts, but no accidents had been reported. A religious man, Paterson knelt by his bed to pray for strength before retiring, and that is when he found his wife, who had been raped and bludgeoned to death before being pushed under her own bed.

It was calculated that Mrs Paterson had been killed at approximately eleven o'clock that morning; shortly afterwards, Nelson walked into a second-hand clothes shop where he sold items stolen from the Patersons. Then he visited a hairdresser's for a shave where the barber noticed blood on Nelson's hair. Two days later he was heading back to the United States, but that forty-eight hours had given the Canadian police time enough to circulate a detailed description of Nelson which was recognised at a post office in Wakopa when Nelson himself walked in.

On 1 November 1927, Nelson was tried at Winnipeg before Mr Justice Dysart for the murder of Emily Paterson. Nelson pleaded insanity as a defence, in which he was greatly supported by testimony from Aunt Lillian and his former wife but, after a four-day trial, he was found guilty and, on 13 January 1928, hanged at Winnipeg.

Although the victims listed in this account were certainly attributed to Earle Nelson, there is some reason to suppose that he was also responsible for a triple murder committed in Newark, New Jersey, in 1926. Rose Valentine, Margaret Stanton and Laura Tidor were all landladies, all raped and strangled, and in two cases the body had been pushed under a bed.

NESSET, Arnfinn As befits Scandinavia's most prolific known multicide, the trial of Arnfinn Nesset was also the longest in Norway's legal history. At Trondheim in October 1982, Nesset's defence attorney Alf Nordhus submitted to the court that his client's so-called murders had in reality been 'mercy killings', though admitting that it was perhaps arrogance for Nesset to assume such god-like powers of life and death over other human beings.

Arnfinn Nesset stood charged with the murder of twenty-five elderly patients at the Orkdal Valley Nursing Home of which he was the manager; he may, however, have killed an even greater number. In fact Nesset is said by the police to have told them, 'I've killed so many I can't remember them all.' He later retracted this and other incriminating statements and pleaded not guilty to all charges at his trial.

The fourteen men and eleven women on the indictment were aged between sixty-seven and ninety-four, and died between 1977 and 1980. It was assumed that the cause of death was an excessive injection of the muscle relaxant curacit – a derivative of the drug curare used by South American Indians to tip their poison arrows. In a large dose it paralyses the respiratory system and causes painful death by suffocation. As curacit breaks down rapidly in the human body it is impossible to detect after a long lapse of time, and none of the alleged victims was exhumed for post-mortem examination. However there was ample evidence that unusually large quantities of the drug were being ordered by the nursing home, and it was this that initially caused the authorities to become suspicious and the police to arrest Nesset on 9 March 1981.

Despite his altruistic claim to have committed only euthanasia, Arnfinn Nesset was proved to have embezzled small sums of money from the deceased patients, of which crime he was also convicted at his trial. If he had really murdered for gain, then the profits were pitifully small – and besides, he had donated all the proceeds to missionary work. On 11 March 1983, forty-six-year-old Nesset was found guilty of twenty-two charges of murder and one of attempted murder – which attracted the maximum term of imprisonment under Norwegian law, twenty-one years.

'NIGHT STALKER' *see* RAMIREZ, Richard

NILSEN, Dennis Andrew   On 3 February 1983, residents of the flats at 23 Cranley Gardens, north London, were irritated to find that their lavatories were not flushing properly. It was not until five days later that a representative of the drain-clearage firm Dyno-Rod opened the manhole at the side of the house to check for blockages. Aiming the beam of his torch into the black hole, Mike Cattran could just make out a whitish sludge flecked with red. When he descended the twelve feet to the water line, he discovered lumps of rotting meat, some with hair attached, floating about in the slime.

Alerted by Cattran, the police made a fuller inspection of the manhole on the following morning, and although most of the flesh had been mysteriously fished out overnight, officers recovered fragments of flesh and bone later identified as having human origin.

Among the residents of No. 23, occupying the attic flat, was thirty-seven-year-old Dennis Nilsen, and when he arrived home from his job at the Soho 'Job Centre' on the evening of 8 February it was to be met by three detectives. Nilsen expressed surprise that the police should be concerned with blocked drains, and when told of the grisly finds replied, 'Good grief, how awful.'

It was an inspired guess, something that is as vital a tool to the experienced detective as any number of computers; Detective Chief Inspector Peter Jay rounded on Nilsen and said simply, 'Don't mess around, where's the rest of the body?'

'In two plastic bags in the wardrobe. I'll show you.'

When Nilsen had been cautioned, he was driven back with the officers to Muswell Hill police station. On the journey, Detective Inspector McCusker turned to Nilsen and asked, 'Are we talking about one body or two?'

'Fifteen or sixteen since 1978: three at Cranley Gardens and about thirteen at my previous address at Melrose Avenue, Cricklewood.'

During the course of the next eleven days Dennis Nilsen dictated thirty hours of unnervingly detailed confession, representing one of the most gruesome sagas of murder and dismemberment in the history of British crime. All the victims had been young men picked up by Nilsen on the street or from the public houses frequented by homosexuals in central London; many had been homeless vagrants, only too pleased at the prospect of exchanging sexual favours for food, drink and money. By the time Nilsen stood trial at the Central Criminal Court in October 1983, human remains of every description had been recovered from the two addresses and stored as evidence. There was never any question of Nilsen's guilt – he had after all admitted everything; what was in doubt was how accountable he could be held for those terrible crimes. At trial, Mr Ivan Lawrence, representing Dennis Nilsen, advanced the defence not that his client was insane, but that at the time of each of the killings he was suffering from such abnormality of mind that he was incapable of forming the specific intent to murder.

Predictably, much of the court's time was occupied in hearing the opposing views of a parade of psychiatrists called by both the defence and the prosecution to debate Nilsen's culpability. At the end of a complex trial the jury was able to agree only on a 10-2 majority that Nilsen was both sane and guilty of the six counts of murder and two of attempted murder with which he stood charged. He was sentenced to a mandatory life sentence, with a recommendation from Mr Justice Croom-Johnson that he serve no fewer than twenty-five years.

A remarkably articulate and introspective man, Nilsen has cooperated with journalist Brian Masters on a detailed analysis of his life and his crimes (*Killing for Company*, 1985).

NORRIS, Roy *see* **BITTAKER, Lawrence**

NORTHCOTT, Gordon Stewart Assisted by his mother Sarah and a teenaged nephew named Stanford Clark, Northcott made a business and pleasure from abducting children and holding them at his isolated ranch in Riverside County, California, for his own depraved purposes and those of unidentified clients from Los Angeles. The children were subsequently killed and their bodies buried in the surrounding desert.

In February 1928, the headless body of a Mexican boy was found in a ditch near Puent. Less than two months later two brothers aged eight and ten went missing after being seen in the company of Northcott at a boys club. Enquiries made at the Northcott ranch revealed that he had already fled to Canada. Searching the grounds police officers found the missing head of the Mexican child.

Under close questioning the boy Clark described how Northcott had sexually abused the two young brothers before beating them to death. Sarah Northcott had little option now but to confess her part in her son's crimes, including actively participating in one of the murders. When police intelligence had tracked Gordon Northcott down and extradited him back to California he was charged with just three murders. Although it was confidently believed that Northcott's total body count was as many as twenty, no further remains were found. Nor was the investigation much helped by Northcott's own many contradictory statements – finally settling on a self-confessed total of seventeen, and at the same time sending the police off on false trails when he 'remembered' where he had buried others.

Sarah Northcott, for her part, was sentenced to life imprisonment for the murder of the nine-year-old Mexican, and Stanford Clark agreed to turn state's evidence against his uncle.

During Northcott's hearing he dismissed his attorney and took responsibility for his own defence, emphasising that he was *not* insane – a conclusion upheld by the reports of two independent psychiatrists. So if he was not mad, then he must be bad, so Gordon Northcott was sentenced to hang. While he was awaiting sentence on San Quentin's Death Row, Northcott was taken ill, and firmly believing that he was about to die made a full confession to Assistant Warden Clinton Duffy. This statement, which Duffy described as a catalogue of mass murder, torture and sodomy was retained on his file when Northcott got over his far from fatal sickness. It was the sickness in his head that proved the death of him – Gordon Northcott was executed on 2 October 1930, in a state of abject terror.

O

'OGRESSE DE LA GOUTTE D'OR' *see* WEBER, Jeanne

OLSON, Clifford It had already begun to follow the familiar pattern of the recent nightmare of serial killings. The first mutilated victim was discovered on Christmas Day 1980, at Vancouver – she was twelve-year-old Christine Weller. In spring the following year, thirteen-year-old Coleen Daignault disappeared from her home in the same area, and at about the same time the corpse of Darren Johnsrud, aged sixteen, was found with a fractured skull in some woodland.

The crimes seemed unstoppable; on 19 May Sandra Wolfsteiner, also sixteen years old, hitched a ride in a car in a Vancouver suburb and was never seen again. In June, thirteen-year-old Ada Court vanished while walking home in Coquitlam, and nine-year-old Susan Partington disappeared after being seen talking to a man in a Surrey shopping centre. In early July, Judy Kozma, aged fourteen, went missing after being picked up by a man in suburban New Westminster – later in the month her stabbed body was found in Lake Weaver, near Agassiz, along with that of Raymond King who had disappeared two days before her.

Intense police activity in the Weaver Lake area eventually centred on forty-two-year-old Clifford Raymond Olson, an ex-convict with a previous record of ninety-four convictions ranging from fraud to armed robbery to rape. Olson lived with his wife and baby son on the outskirts of Vancouver and although he was put under surveillance, managed to slip away on a holiday to the United States shortly afterwards. On his return the surveillance was broken and, in late July, Louise Chartrand, Terri Lynn Carson, and German tourist Sigrun Arnd were all murdered. Olson was finally arrested attempting to pick up two girls, and a routine search of his van revealed a notebook containing Judy Kozma's address.

In custody, Clifford Olson outlined the deal he was prepared to make with the authorities: in exchange for information on the whereabouts of each of the bodies still missing he wanted $10,000, plus an additional $30,000 for the three which had already been found. The sense of this emotional blackmail was not lost on the police – it was obvious that victims' families desperately wanted to recover the remains of loved ones in order once and for all to bury the past, both actually and symbolically. On the other hand it was a preposterous situation which would almost amount to Olson being paid, per corpse, for committing murder. In the end, the Attorney-General overruled the refusal of the police to cooperate, insisting only that the bulk of the money be placed in trust for Olson's son. Clearly recognising a good trick when he held one, Olson offered a new 'cut-price' deal promising to disclose a further twenty graves for a bargain $100,000. This time the authorities stood firm, though not because they doubted that there were other victims still to be found.

On the third day of Clifford Olson's trial before the Supreme Court of Vancouver in January 1982, his defence attorney announced to the court that Olson was changing his plea to guilty in order to dispense with a full trial and so spare his own and his victims' families the further torment of having the details of the murders broadcast publicly. A formal plea of guilty was registered on each of the eleven charges and Olson was sentenced by Justice McKay to as many concurrent life sentences.

P

PALMER, Dr William Born in 1824 of what used to be termed 'bad stock', Palmer took readily to petty crime at an early age. By seventeen he had already been dismissed from one apprenticeship with a druggist (for embezzlement), and subsequently had to flee from another after 'grossly abusing his Master's hospitality' (Palmer was running a private abortion service, not least to cope with his own prodigious output). However, Palmer eventually qualified as a doctor at St Bartholomew's Hospital, London.

Notwithstanding his unruly past, Palmer set himself up in a modest practice in his birthplace of Rugeley, Staffordshire, and married. Now, as a leopard is said to have no control over its coat, so William Palmer found it impossible to settle down to a life of domesticity and honest toil. There was constant marital friction – not the least cause of which was the bastard child that Palmer had given one of the servant girls. His business began to suffer – almost certainly on account of his preference for horse racing and gambling over medicine.

To finance his ever-increasing gaming debts, Palmer engineered the decease of his mother-in-law, which in turn ensured his inheriting her fortune. As his debts and racing losses increased, so Palmer's family decreased. His wife Annie, who had been insured for £13,000, died mysteriously; his brother Walter, insured for a similar sum, quickly followed. And along the line four of Palmer's children had also died, plus an uncle, and several of his more pressing creditors.

None of these 'windfalls' ever did more than satisfy the smallest part of Palmer's financial needs, and by 1855 he was not only in deep debt but in the claws of the moneylenders. In November Palmer visited Shrewsbury Races with a gambling companion named John Parsons Cook. Cook won: Palmer, as usual, lost. Cook's celebration party, however, proved to be Palmer's golden opportunity. Cook was taken suddenly ill. Palmer generously offered to collect his winnings – and used them to pay off his own debts. Meanwhile, back at the Talbot Arms Hotel, John Cook was not responding to the treatment administered by his 'friend' the doctor. In fact, by 21 November he was dead.

The suspicious nature of Cook's stepfather proved Palmer's undoing, the worthy man insisting on an autopsy; an autopsy that revealed the traces of antimony that put William Palmer first in the dock of the Old Bailey in London, and then on the scaffold at Stafford Gaol on 14 June 1856, before an audience of fifty thousand.

Above left Harvey Glatman
(*Topham*); **above right** Peter
Thomas Anthony Manuel.
Right Wayne Williams, the
'Atlanta Child Killer'
leaving Fulton County
Gaol (*Topham*).

Scenes from the Life and Crimes of Hermann Mudgett (H. H. Holmes).
Above Child victims, realising their predicament, begin to beg piteously for
mercy. **Below** Mudgett arranges a tube attached to the gas tap into a hole in
the top of the trunk.

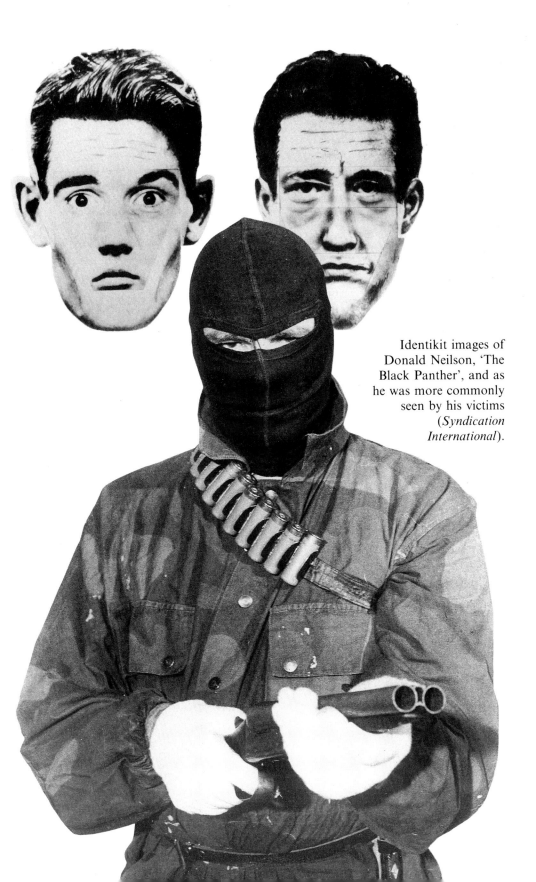

Identikit images of
Donald Neilson, 'The
Black Panther', and as
he was more commonly
seen by his victims
(*Syndication
International*).

Official police photographs of
Thierry Paulin 'The Monster of
Montmartre' (**above**, Rex), and
Dennis Andrew Nilsen.

Dr William Palmer, 'The Rugely Poisoner'.

Dr Marcel Petiot in court at the Seine Assizes (*Topham*).

EXECUTION

OF

Dr. PRITCHARD,

AT GLASGOW.

By ELECTRIC TELEGRAPH.—GLASGOW, Friday.

This morning, Friday, July 28th, the last dread sentence of the law was carried into effect on the body of Dr. Pritchard, for the wilful murder of his wife and mother-in-law. The prisoner since his condemnation has conducted himself with great calmness, and has, since his confession become more earnest in his religious duties, and paid marked attention to the exhortations of the Rev. R. S. Oldham and other worthy clergymen who have attended him.

The Sheriffs, with their usual attendants arrived at the prison, and immediately visited the wretched culprit in the condemned cell, when he thanked them for the kindness he had received at their hands. After the formalities had been observed of demanding the prisoner into their custody, Calcraft, the executioner was introduced to the prisoner, and the operation of pinioning having been gone through, and the mournful procession having been formed, began to move towards the scaffold, the chaplain reading the burial service for the dead. The prisoner ascended the scaffold with a firm step, and directly the wretched man appeared, loud murmurs was heard from the vast multitude assembled. Calcraft having adjusted the rope, and drew the cap over his eyes, the signal was given, the bolt withdrawn, and the wretched man, after struggling for a few moments, ceased to exist.

Contemporary 'gallows' broadsheet depicting the execution of Dr William Pritchard at Glasgow.

Two Dapper Men of Murder. **Above** Boysie Singh; **right** 'Acid Bath Killer' John George Haigh, as he liked to see himself.

'Brides in the Bath' murderer
George Joseph Smith, with his
three known victims (clockwise)
Alice Burnham, Margaret Lofty,
and Bessie Mundy.

Richard Ramirez, 'The Night Stalker'.

For the past four years a vicious killer has been at large in the North of England. There have been to date 12 horrific murders and four brutal attacks. The evidence suggests that the same man may be responsible for all of them. If so, he has struck 13 times in West Yorkshire, twice in Manchester and once in Lancashire. Large teams of police officers, including Regional Crime Squads, are working full time in West Yorkshire, Sunderland, Manchester and Lancashire to catch him. His original targets were prostitutes but innocent girls have also died. You can help to end this terror . . .

HELP US CATCH THE RIPPER

- ●**HAVE YOU SEEN** **HANDWRITING** **HAVE YOU H** **TAPE?**

IF YOU HA
TELEPHO
LEEDS (0
BRADFO

DO ANY OF THESE QUESTIONS
DESCRIBE SOMEONE YOU KNO

- Has a Wearside (Geordie) accent?
- Is physically fit and reasonably strong?
- Travels between, or has connections in, the Lancashire and Sunderland areas?
- Perhaps shows disgust of low moral standards?
- Is a manual worker or has access to tools?
- Possibly lives alone or with aged parents?
- Is prone to sudden outbursts of emotion?
- Owns a car of his own or has access to one?
- Sometimes stays out late at night?

- BUT DON'T DISCOUNT ANY SUSPICIONS BECAUSE
QUESTIONS. IF YOU HAVE ANY DOUBTS AT ALL, CONT
POLICE AND HELP CATCH THE RIPPER.

Above Part of the intensive newspaper campaign to trap the 'Yorkshire Ripper'. **Inset** Police Identikit of the man thought to be the Ripper.

Above 'Yorkshire Ripper' Peter Sutcliffe and his wife Sonia on their wedding day (*Topham*). **Right** A rare picture of the Australian multicide Arnold Karl Sodeman.

Head of a Convict, very
characteristic of low cunning &
& revenge!

'Head of a Convict', a self-portrait by
Thomas Griffiths Wainewright with the
portrait by Wainewright of his victim
Helen Abercromby.

This is the Zodiac speaking

I have become very upset with the People of San Fran Bay Area. They have <u>not</u> complied with my wishes for them to wear some nice ⊕ buttons. I promiced to punish them if they did not comply, by anilating a full School Buss. But now school is out for the summer, so I fanished them in an another way.

I shot a man sitting in a parked car with a .38.

⊕-12   SFPD-0

The Map coupled with this code will tell you whe-e the bemb is set. You have antill next Fall to dig it up. ⊕

C Δ J I ■ O K ⊥ A M ⊣ ◢ Ω O R T G
X ⊙ F D V ⊋ ◨ H C E L ◈ P W Δ

The notorious 'Zodiac' letters.

County Gaol, Durham
7th March 1873

Sir,

I beg to inform you that at
...Assizes holden in Durham
...Friday the 7th day of March
...3. Mary Ann Cotton was
...victed of Wilful Murder and
...nced to be hanged. Consequently
...accordance with the Rules laid
...in your Order dated 13th
...1868. Mary Ann Cotton
...be executed on Monday the
... Inst. at 8 o'clock A.m.
...I have the honor to be,
Sir,
...Your Most Obedt Servant
...

Glasgow March 18th 1865

Sir,

Dr Pritchards' Mother in law
died suddenly and unexpectedly
about three weeks ago in his house
Sauchiehall Street Glasgow under
circumstances at least very suspicion
His wife died to-day also sudden
ly and unexpectedly and under circum
stances equally suspicious. We think
it right to draw your attention to
the above as the proper person to
take action in the matter and see
justice done.

To Honbl Esqr

Yours &
Amor Justitiae

UNION GROUP ENGINEERING

CRAWLEY   CROYDON
PUTNEY   WIMBLEDON
GENERAL ENGINEERING, SMALL REPETITION.
GAUGE MAKERS TO M.O.S. and I.G.A.

THIS NUMBER MUST BE QUOTED

ORDER
FROM THE TECHNICAL LIAISON OFFICER
ONSLOW COURT HOTEL
LONDON, S.W.7.
TELEPHONE: KENSINGTON 6300

To Alfred White & Son Ltd,   16 Feby   1949
28 Dallington St
Goswell Road, E.C.1.

Please supply, Carriage Paid, to the address given below, the undermentioned goods:

1 Carboy Conc H₂SO₄.

18.6 @

Continuation of telephonic
order to Mr Brown today

UNION GROUP ENGINEERING

INSPECTION
DELIVERY   Collect
TERMS   Cash.

Three more incriminating
documents. **Clockwise from
top** Official notification of
Mary Ann Cotton's death
sentence; John George
Haigh's order for sulphuric
acid; Anonymous letter
accusing Dr Pritchard of
familicide.

Moscow

Dahmer . . . *his mum found bones in the bath*

Cannibal toll is 17 and rising

CANNIBAL maniac Jeffrey Dahmer has now confessed to 17 grisly killings as the police probe widens across the U.S.

Detectives say the trail of death may go back ten years or more.

Dahmer has admitted further murders on top of those at his squalid flat in Milwaukee, Wisconsin, which police raided this week.

Inside they found five whole corpses and an assortment of rotting body parts that added up to another six victims.

Brains

Altogether, there were 11 severed heads. Seven had been boiled to the bone and four others still had flesh on them.

Dahmer, 31, a convicted child molester, lured homosexual men to his apartment on the city's West Side, drugged them and then dismembered them with chainsaws.

He boiled the flesh from bones, preserved

LLER: Nikolai Dzhumagaliev ate his victims

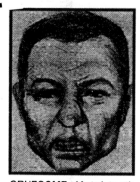

GRUESOME: Metal teeth

serial killer Dzhumagaliev is well-mannered and speaks without an accent.

"He is always clean-shaven and neatly dressed — his image is that of the perfect gentleman, though it has to be said the teeth are a bit odd," a police spokesman said. "He persuaded his dentist to fit them because

he reckoned they looked good."

Metal Fang was almost caught before his killing spree began, when he attacked a woman in her flat. Her screams alerted a neighbour, who chased off the would-be killer.

His next victim was invited to his home . . . and butchered.

"We suspect Dzhumagaliev is trying to establish a base in cheap accommodation," the police added.

Police also revealed that Metal Fang has been on the run for two years, but they have only just decided to alert the public.

"We have our reasons," the spokesman said. "We believe the danger to be far greater than when he first left the hospital."

STOP PRESS. As this book was being prepared for press two remarkable cases broke in the news. **Above** Cannibal killer Jeffrey Dahmer (*Popperfoto*); **right** the Russian Nikolai Dzumagaliev, called 'Metal Fang'.

Palmer's executioner (a contemporary portrait)

'Throttler' Smith, the man selected to execute the sentence of the law upon Palmer, was by trade a sailor, a great, coarse, brutal fellow, standing about five feet ten inches; he left his original trade to become hangman, and also pursues the precarious trade of a higgler. The earliest thing that is known of him is that he ran a race against time almost naked in a market town and was taken up immediately on accomplishing the disgusting feat, and sent to gaol. He was the Staffordshire hangman for sixteen years.

The rope with which Palmer was hung was made by a ropemaker of the name of Coates, who is also a porter at Stafford station. All the men employed at the station had a hand in making it; and Coates, having an eye to the main chance, made thirty yards, cut the surplus length up into small pieces of about two or three inches, and hawked them about Stafford. In one instance, half-a-crown was obtained for about two inches.

PANZRAM, Carl   Born of Prussian parents in Warren, Minnesota, in 1891, Panzram was engaged in petty crime before he reached his teens. At the age of twelve he was committed to a reform school which he burned down causing damage amounting to $100,000. Throughout his life Carl Panzram was to be either committing crimes or in prison paying for them. According to his autobiography written in jail, Panzram boasted, 'I have murdered twenty-one human beings, I have committed thousands of burglaries, robberies, larcenies, arsons, and last but not least I have committed sodomy on more than 1000 male human beings.'

It is quite possible that Carl Panzram's admission to twenty-one murders is uncharacteristically modest, and estimates vary – even his own. Panzram travelled widely in many parts of the world – in Africa and in Europe, and it is unlikely that these excursions should have been free from his murderous excesses. In August, 1928, as he was sentenced to twenty-five years at Fort Leavenworth for robbery and murder, Carl Panzram threatened, 'I'll kill the first man that bothers me.' In June of the following year he murdered Robert Warnke, the foreman of the prison laundry. For this he was tried, convicted and sentenced to death.

Predictably, Panzram had no time or patience for the liberal-minded civil rights groups who sought to have his sentence revoked. 'I wish you all had one neck', he told them, 'and I had my hands on it; I believe the only way to reform people is to kill them.' He even took the trouble to write a personal letter to President Herbert Hoover, demanding that he should be hanged without delay; after all had he not once defiantly declared, 'I don't believe in Man, God, nor Devil. I hate the whole damned human race, including myself.'

This human monster breathed his last on the scaffold at Leavenworth on 5 September 1930. Even that last breath was not free from a curse as he chid the hangman, 'Hurry it up, I could hang a dozen men while you're fooling around!'

PAULIN, Thierry   Paris – city of young lovers, romance and gaiety, of fine food and fashion and champagne's sparkle. But there is also another Paris; a city where one out of every two people lives alone, where solitary old ladies eke out their pensions in the tiny apartments of the poorer arrondissements. There are more than 250,000 women over the age of sixty-five in France's capital, and it is among this vulnerable group that the 'Monster of Montmartre' stalked his prey.

Between the years 1984 and the end of 1987, a succession of victims was reported – all women aged between seventy and eighty, all living alone in or near the Montmartre district, all found in their ransacked apartments with their hands and legs bound – either suffocated, strangled, stabbed or beaten to death; the only apparent motive in each case was a handful of francs.

As the death toll rose from ten to twenty (some estimates put the Monster's account as high as forty or fifty), so the panic grew among the solitary *vieilles de Montmartre*. Gendarmes escorted frightened pensioners to local shops; and the busy street markets of Pigalle, where in normal times the old ladies would linger to gossip were deserted before dusk. For it was said that the Monster would talk with an old woman in the street, and if for some reason he took against her . . .

In the three years of this reign of terror, the Sûreté had collected no less than 150,000 fingerprints from the scenes of the crimes, but it was not until December 1987, that they found a match – and then only by a narrow chance.

For once the Monster had blundered and left one of his victims, a seventy-year-old widow, still with a flicker of life in her. The old woman survived and provided the police with a shrewd and detailed description of her callous attacker. Within a remarkably short time, Thierry Paulin was taken into custody.

Paulin, a tall, athletic twenty-five-year-old originally from Martinique, was already known to the police through a record of petty theft and drug offences. Ironically, his fingerprints had gone missing from police files and so had never been run against the 150,000 suspect prints collected during the three years' carnage. Now there could be no mistake – Thierry Paulin *was* the Monster of Montmartre, and as he sat in the offices of the Sûreté, with chilling detachment he voluntarily confessed to the brutal murder of twenty-one women. So casual was his approach that even the most case-hardened detectives felt shock: 'It was sometimes as if he was talking about going out to buy some baguettes.'

During his confession, Paulin implicated Jean-Thierry Mathurin, a companion in the Parisian sub-culture of drugs, gay bars and seedy all-night cafés, in these and a score more killings; for his own part, Mathurin refused even to speak Paulin's name – referring to him instead as 'the other one'.

Confined to Fleury-Merogis prison to await his trial, Paulin was treated as a high-risk prisoner and put under constant surveillance. During the year after his arrest, Thierry Paulin's health deteriorated dramatically, leading the prison authorities to the inevitable conclusion that his life of homosexuality and drug misuse had put Paulin at risk from AIDS. On 10 March 1989, he fell into a coma and was rushed to Claude-Bernard de Paris hospital where he underwent emergency treatment for the tuberculosis and meningitis which his own impaired immune system could no longer combat. Transferred to the hospital at Fresnes prison, Thierry Paulin died of AIDS on 16 April; he was twenty-six years old.

Jean-Thierry Mathurin is still confined in the Prison de La Santé awaiting trial. But whatever the outcome of the charges against Mathurin, it is Thierry Paulin alone who will be remembered as France's most evil mass murderer of modern times – the Monster of Montmartre who condemned thousands of elderly women to solitary confinement during three terrifying years.

PETIOT, Dr Marcel A reluctance to keep his hands off other people's property (which began with pilfering trifling objects from his little schoolfellows) characterised the whole of Petiot's life, and resulted in his execution for the murder of at least twenty-seven people.

At the age of twenty-four, after an undistinguished career in the army where his most notable activity was the stealing of much-needed drugs to sell on the black market, Petiot qualified as a Doctor of Medicine from the University of Paris on 15 December 1921. It was to be Petiot's secret delight throughout his life that he had gained his doctorate at around the same time that he had been certified mentally unstable by the Army authorities.

In 1928 Petiot was elected Mayor of Villeneuve, the town in which he had been born in 1897. In this position of trust he was ideally situated for dipping his hand at regular intervals into the community chest to supplement his indifferent medical practice.

Although he may have known more about the pregnant servant girl who suddenly disappeared from his employ than he told the police, and although there may have been more than met the eye to the unexpected deaths of several of his patients, it was not until 1944 that official attention was focused on the activities of Dr Marcel Petiot.

Petiot had moved his practice to Paris in order to take advantage of the war raging in Europe, becoming involved in all manner of profiteering. One day a wealthy Jew approached Petiot in his capacity as his medical consultant, and asked if there was any way in which he,

Petiot, could help him, Monsieur Gubisnov, and his family to escape the excesses of the German occupation of France. This the doctor agreed to arrange, for a price; for a very high price. But there, what is wealth compared with freedom from fear?

The most that could be said for the arrangement that followed is that for the Gubisnov family the occupying Nazis would hold no more terror; they had found an enemy infinitely worse – the greedy little doctor who had spiked their 'typhoid injections' with strychnine.

Over the next three years Petiot similarly murdered at least twenty-seven more refugees, and no doubt would have continued so to line his pocket if the furnace in which he disposed of the unwanted by-products of his thriving enterprise had not set fire to the chimney.

On 11 March 1944, Petiot's neighbours in the Rue Lesueur, fearful of a conflagration, called the fire brigade. When they broke into the house via the cellar, the firemen, now joined by the gendarmerie, discovered the reason for the foul-smelling black emissions from the chimney. There was a pile of dismembered human remains waiting to be fed into the furnace.

When he was called upon to explain the carnage at his home, Petiot positively swelled with pride. They were, he explained, the bodies of pro-Nazi collaborators executed by the French Resistance and entrusted to the patriotic doctor to dispose of. Extraordinary as it may seem, the still-autonomous French gendarmerie accepted this preposterous story, at least for long enough to allow Petiot, his wife and son to flee Paris.

Things might, even so, have turned out better for him than he deserved, but Marcel Petiot possessed a streak of arrogance that would not leave well alone. During his flight from justice, Petiot had joined the forces of the Free French Army, and begun a correspondence with the magazine *Résistance*, the gist of which was that Dr Marcel Petiot was 'innocent'. The letters were signed 'Captain Henri Valery', but were clearly in the handwriting of Marcel Petiot. He was arrested in November 1944.

During his time in custody, Petiot confessed to killing no less than sixty-three people, all of whom – so he claimed – were either German soldiers or collaborators. However, it was for the twenty-seven established murders that were pieced together from the shambles at Rue Lesueur that Petiot was put on trial – the once-hopeful refugees whose bodies had been reduced to charred bones and melted body fat in the doctor's furnace; not forgetting the decomposing corpses found marinating in lime-pits in the stable.

The packed court at the Seine Assizes was stunned to silence by the wall of forty-seven suitcases stacked behind the dock – luggage containing clothing and valuables stolen by Petiot from his victims which included twenty-nine suits, seventy-nine dresses and five fur coats.

By turns abusive, violent, witty and sarcastic, Petiot proved to be good entertainment for the public gallery; with the judge and the jury his behaviour went down less well. At the end of an often-harrowing three-week trial, Marcel Petiot was found guilty of twenty-four of the twenty-seven charges of murder, and on 26 May 1946, he was executed on the guillotine in the yard of the Santé Prison.

PETRILLO, Paul and Herman *see* **BOLBER, Dr Morris**

PLEIL, Rudolf Pleil was at heart a thief, who really got into rape and murder as an accompaniment to robbing his female victims. Even so, his self-confessed record of fifty murders between 1946 and 1947 rivals any of his fellow German 'monsters'. He had first come to the attention of the police when he axed to death a salesman in 1947 and was sent to prison for twelve years. While he was in jail Pleil wrote a lengthy diary which, in tribute to Adolf Hitler in whose army he had served, he called *Mein Kampf*. It detailed a list of Pleil's sex murders, mostly committed during 1946 and 1947, while he was serving as a policeman patrolling the East–West border, where the opportunity for molesting refugees passing through to the Western zone was more than he could resist. He claimed that his first victim had been a woman named Eva Miehe, whom he had axed to death with a single blow in March 1946; he insisted that all his murders were for 'sexual gratification' – though why he should have felt that this was a more acceptable motive than robbery is anybody's guess.

A small, chubby, bespectacled man of twenty-six with a ready smile, Rudolf Pleil, once he had tried it, took to murder immediately, relishing every one and delighting in describing himself as 'der Beste Totmacher' ('the best death-maker'). He was at home with most weapons – knives, axes, mallets or bricks – and is recorded as saying, 'Every man has his passion; some like whist, I prefer killing people.'

At his trial in Brunswick in November 1950, Pleil stood charged with nine murders; it was an indictment which gave him constant cause for complaint. 'It's not nine, it is twenty-five', he frequently interrupted, 'I am the greatest death-maker in Germany.' In the dock with Pleil were two of his associates, Karl Hoffmann and Konrad Schuessler, accused variously of being accessories to some of the murders. Pleil, the court was told, had broken off his partnership with Hoffmann after the latter had decapitated their victim – an act of desecration which Pleil found in extremely poor taste.

Unfortunately – for from what little we know it was a bizarre event – the trial judge elected to conduct the greater part of the proceedings *in camera* on grounds of decency. One story that did emerge, however, was Rudolf Pleil's ambition to become a professional hangman. He wrote, it is said, to the authorities in the Soviet zone offering his services and pointing out that if they required evidence of his qualifications they need only look in a certain well; it contained a strangled corpse. Nevertheless, Pleil did get his big chance in a way –

in February 1958, he hanged himself in his cell.

POMEROY, Jesse   Clearly born to be bad, Jesse Pomeroy spent the two years between his twelfth and fourteenth birthdays at the West Borough Reform School at Boston. For the two years prior to his detention a series of attacks had been made on young boys in which they had been savagely beaten and then tortured with knives and whips before being left unconscious where they fell. The trail led, unbelievably, to twelve-year-old Jesse who was living with his widowed mother in one of the depressed slums of Boston. A most ungainly youth, Pomeroy's unnerving appearance with his hare lip and blind white eye was further complicated by mental retardation.

In March 1874, barely a month after Pomeroy's release from custody, ten-year-old Mary Curran went missing; in the following month, the horribly mutilated body of four-year-old Horace Mullen was found. All the evidence pointed in Jesse Pomeroy's direction, though even if it had not, Jesse was willing enough to confess – not only to the murder of the Curran girl and young Mullen, but to twenty-seven others, twelve of whose tortured and mutilated bodies were unearthed from the ground around his mother's house.

Despite the fact that Pomeroy was still only fourteen years old, he was tried, convicted and sentenced to death. In the end his sentence was commuted to solitary confinement for life – at first in prison and then, after a number of attempts on his own life, in an asylum. In all, Jesse Pomeroy spent fifty-eight years in solitary, until his death in 1932.

POMMERENCKE, Heinrich   Amply deserving his title, the 'Beast of the Black Forest', by the time Pommerencke was put on trial in Freiberg in October 1960, he had accumulated charges for four murders, twelve attempted murders, twenty-one rapes and sexual assaults, plus dozens of counts of robbery with violence, larceny and blackmail; and these represented only the tip of the iceberg. Among the crimes for which the Beast was not tried were at least six further murders. The state prosecutor encapsulated the feelings of a shocked nation when he declared, 'Human language is inadequate to describe the horror and misery Pommerencke had brought to so many people.'

Heinrich Pommerencke was born in the village of Bentwich, where he spent most of his childhood. He claimed to have had his first sexual encounter when he was only ten years old, but was later to confess, 'When I was a boy I never had a friend in the world.'

By the age of fifteen, Pommerencke's sexual frustration resulted in him hanging around outside the local dance hall propositioning young girls as they came in and out; if they objected he offered them violence and rape. In 1953 he went into voluntary exile in Switzerland to escape the consequences of a rape case, only to be imprisoned by the Swiss on another charge. In 1957 Pommerencke committed a number of rapes in Hamburg and spent a year in prison for robbery, and in

Austria in 1958 he assaulted two young English women.

It was in the following year, 1959, that Heinrich Pommerencke molested student Dagmar Klinek as she slept in an empty railway carriage and when she attempted to resist he pushed her out of the train door. Pulling the communication cord to stop the train, Pommerencke leapt off and ran back down the tracks to where his victim lay unconscious, raped the girl then stabbed her to death.

The rapes and murders continued, and despite a massive police search for the Beast of the Black Forest, it was pure chance that led Heinrich Pommerencke into the net.

It was the summer of 1960, and Pommerencke went into a tailor's shop in Freiberg where, after looking at several items of clothing, he forgetfully left a small package on the counter. The manager prodded the parcel, and when it felt suspiciously like a gun, he called for the police. It was, ballistics experts determined, the gun that had been used in an armed robbery the previous day. Pommerencke was detained after his description had been circulated, and during the course of questioning over the robbery, the rapes and murders were brought up. Pommerencke made no attempt to deny either robbery or murder, and following his conviction on multiple charges he was sentenced to a total of six life terms plus 140 years imprisonment; Pommerencke was twenty-three years old.

POWERS, Harry *see* **DRENTH, Herman**

PRITCHARD, Dr Edward William   Edward William Pritchard graduated from King's College Hospital, London, and the Royal College of Surgeons in 1846. Some years later he maried Mary Jane Taylor, and in 1859 bought a practice in Glasgow. In May 1863, a fire at the Pritchards' house at 11 Berkeley Terrace destroyed part of the attic floor, and during the subsequent investigation, the body of the Pritchards' maid was found naked and dead on her bed. When examined more carefully, the incident raised questions not entirely flattering to the good name of Edward Pritchard; for example:

1. Was there any significance in the fact that the girl, though unmarried, was pregnant?
2. Why, at the beginning of May and with no heating in the room, was she sleeping naked?
3. Was it coincidence that the fire started when the girl was alone in the house with Pritchard?
4. Why was the bedroom door locked – from the outside?
5. And most revealing, why was the girl lying straight out in the bed? Surely a conflagration in her bedding would at least have caused her to jump out of bed?

Could it have been Pritchard who had got the girl pregnant? Could he have murdered her in order to avoid a scandal? Given her a drug to make her more compliant before setting fire to the bed and locking the wretched girl in, lest she might recover her senses and have ideas of saving her own life?

Pritchard next moved the family to Clarence Place where his practice waned, and he began to face a series of embarrassing financial crises. By this time the doctor was up to his old tricks with the servants again – this time fifteen-year-old Mary McLeod, whom he first made pregnant and then aborted.

In October 1864, Mrs Pritchard was taken suddenly ill – a malady which her husband diagnosed as a chill. However, the symptoms of vomiting and diarrhoea became so acute that only a period of extended care in the capable hands of her parents in Edinburgh effected a recovery. She had not been back home with her husband for more than a couple of weeks before the symptoms returned. At the beginning of February 1865, she was in a critical enough state for her mother to cross Scotland to be at her bedside. The good lady's suspicions cannot but have been aroused when both she and her daughter and the cook all partook of a tapioca pudding, and all fell violently ill afterwards. By 24 February, the old lady herself was confined to bed – in fact, she was in a coma. Dr Patterson, a local man much intimidated by Pritchard, responded to a call to Mrs Taylor's sick-bed, and wrote later that she seemed to be under the influence of some narcotic drug. Mrs Taylor died, and three weeks later, on 17 March, her daughter also succumbed.

An anonymous letter to the Procurator-Fiscal finally exposed Dr Pritchard for the callous murderer that he was. It may have come from Dr Patterson, feeling guilt at not having voiced his misgivings over Mrs Taylor's condition more publicly. The police exhumed the bodies of Mrs Taylor and Mrs Pritchard, and the internal organs of both were found to contain high levels of antimony.

At his trial at the beginning of July 1865, Edward Pritchard was found guilty of two charges of murder, and sentenced to hang at Glasgow on 28 July. While awaiting sentence at North Prison, Duke Street, he made three separate and different confessions:

1. That he had murdered his wife with the willing collaboration of the servant Mary McLeod, his mistress.
2. The he had killed his wife with chloroform, and that McLeod was merely a witness to the act; but that he was not responsible for Mrs Taylor's death; and
3. That he had killed both Mary Jane and her mother, and that Mary McLeod was innocent of any involvement.

On the day of execution, a concourse of some 100,000 spectators came to see Pritchard hang – one of the largest audiences in Scottish criminal history. He also had the doubtful privilege of being the last man publicly hanged in the city of Glasgow.

The motive for Pritchard's murder of his wife remains a mystery.

When in good health she seems to have fulfilled all the requirements of a dutiful wife and was by all accounts a good mother to their five children. Indeed, Mary Jane Pritchard's constant stoicism in the face of her husband's infidelity and financial incompetence might be seen to put her a step or two ahead of the average partner. More extraordinary still, was the fact that her life was not insured for a single penny.

PUENTE, Dorothea Kindly, grey-haired Mrs Puente seemed to have just two preoccupations in life. First was the care of those less fortunate than herself, second her immaculately tended garden. Both Dorothea and the garden were sources of inspiration to her Sacramento neighbours, and to the local welfare department which boarded elderly and alcoholic mental patients with her in the sure confidence that they would enjoy the very best of care. And take care of them she certainly did! For though many passed through the doors of Granny Puente's boarding house, few were allowed to overstay their welcome – only their pension cheques remained to keep the old lady company.

For two years, until November 1988, the sixty-one-year-old widow opened her comfortable Victorian house to the homeless and the friendless at an irresistibly low rent. Surprising then that there should be such a rapid turnover of 'guests', so many deciding, as Mrs Puente phrased it, to 'move on'.

Then a persistent social worker arrived in search of a missing client; and rumours of disappearing boarders began to circulate, and tales of bad smells in the house. John Sharp recalled the night Granny Puente had taken 'Drunken Ben' upstairs to sober up, and how Ben was never seen again, only that same putrid smell hanging on the air.

Now the police took occupation of widow Puente's manicured lawn, and by the time they left little remained of the colourful flower beds and newly paved driveway; what there was instead were the decomposing remains of seven bodies each lying beside its shallow grave. The headless corpses had been covered with lime, presumably to hasten putrefaction. In the event, like so many amateurs whose knowledge of such matters derives from television gangsters and pulp fiction, Mrs Puente had not realised that in order to burn through flesh and bone, quicklime must be mixed with water. The effect here had been to *retard* putrefaction to an extent that autopsies were able to reveal cause of death as huge overdoses of the drug Benzodiazepine.

Meanwhile, sweet old Granny Puente had persuaded police officers to book her into a motel so that she need not suffer the heartbreak of seeing the precious garden wrecked. As soon as their backs were turned, the merry widow was on the first bus out of town.

It took a seven-day nationwide hunt to track Dorothea Puente to Los Angeles, where she had been recognised by the elderly gentleman she was trying to pick up in a bar!

R

'RAILWAY KILLER' *see* **DUFFY, John Francis**

'RAILWAY SNIPER' *see* **BLADEL, Rudy**

RAMIREZ, Richard   The recipient of no less than nineteen death sentences, Ramirez, who had become notorious as the 'Night Stalker', reacted according to expectation. 'Big deal,' he scoffed, 'death comes with the territory . . . see you in Disneyland.'

From June 1984 to August 1985, twenty-five-year-old Richard Ramirez, a drifter out of El Paso, Texas, and serious disciple of the Devil, terrorised the middle-class homes of suburban Los Angeles.

With skill and stealth, entering through an open window or an unlatched door, the Night Stalker crept through the sleeping houses: first to strangle or shoot the male occupants before turning his terrible intentions on to the women and children – brutal rape and vicious mutilation of victims of both sexes and all ages fuelled the fire of his demon-driven blood lust. Sometimes, as the representative of Satan himself, Ramirez would sign his handiwork with a pentagram in lipstick; sometimes he would compound the terror by turning child victims loose miles from home and family, barely alive, to wander in search of help.

Desperation and a belief that the Stalker was invincible were reducing the community to panic, when FBI officers at Quantico, checking out a getaway car, discovered the smudged fingerprint of a petty crook named Ramirez. Photographs were circulated to the media, and at nine o'clock on a Saturday morning in August 1985, a well-heeled LA suburb, as usual busy with its weekend shoppers became the scene of a drama that ended the fear. A man had been observed unsuccessfully trying the doors of parked cars, then he attempted to pull a woman out of her car and was attacked by her husband. Then everybody recognised the man whose face had been staring at them from the front pages of the morning papers; Richard Ramirez had come shopping for another victim and found himself the victim of the mob. Bruised and bloody, the Night Stalker was turned over to the police authorities for official identification.

Throughout his trial, Richard Ramirez was by turns sullen and explosive; at one moment flashing the Devil's pentagram scrawled on his hand to the eager press photographers, then falling silent for hours before placing his fingers to the sides of his head like a demon's horns and intoning, 'Evil, Evil . . . '

It almost seemed at one point as if his invocation of demonic help might be bearing fruit as two juries in succession had to be dismissed – one because a member, who was clearly unimpressed by the honour of sitting in judgement on the Devil's disciple, fell into a deep sleep, the other because one of the members was murdered in a quite unconnected incident.

As he was convicted of twelve first-degree murders, one second-degree murder, and thirty other major offences of rape and burglary, Ramirez summed up for himself. 'You maggots make me sick', he spat at the court, 'I will be avenged. Lucifer dwells within all of us!'

Richard Ramirez dwells on Death Row; and as California has not executed a prisoner since 1967, he is likely to dwell there for some years to come.

'RED SPIDER' *see* **STANIAK, Lucian**

REES, Melvin Davis On 11 January 1959, Carroll Jackson was driving his wife Mildred, and their two daughters, Susan, aged four, and Janet, eighteen months, to their home near Apple Grove, Virginia, when they were run off the road by another car which overtook, flashing its lights. The driver of the second car then forced the Jacksons out of their vehicle at gunpoint, tied them up, crammed them into the boot of his Chevrolet and drove away.

Later that same day Mildred Jackson's aunt, quite by chance, saw the family's abandoned car and reported them missing. It was not until 4 March that the bodies of Carroll Jackson and his eighteen-month-old daughter were found concealed in a ditch near Fredericksburg. Jackson had been shot in the head, little Janet had died of asphyxia under her father's body.

Over the state line in Maryland, police had already been investigating a similar attack since June 1957. An Army sergeant and his girlfriend, Margaret Harold, had been forced over by another car in a remote spot near Annapolis; when they stopped, the driver of the other car had got out, demanded first a cigarette and then money, and when he got neither shot Miss Harold in the face. With great presence of mind in the circumstances, the soldier jumped out of the car and ran as fast as his legs would move over the fields to a lonely farmhouse where he alerted the police. Near the scene of this incident had been an isolated breeze-block building which when searched by police revealed a large collection of pornographic pictures covering the walls, including mortuary photographs of women who had been brutally murdered.

It was almost ten months later when two boys out hunting squirrels close to that same hut found a newly-dug grave. It contained the decomposing corpses of Mildred Jackson and four-year-old Susan. The child had died from a fractured skull, Mrs Jackson had been raped, beaten and strangled with one of her own stockings.

Following a nationwide manhunt and the issue of a description given by the Army sergeant, police received an anonymous letter accusing a jazz musician named Melvin Rees of the murders of the Jackson family and Miss Harold, though even with this information the killer remained elusive. It was only when the writer of the incriminating letter himself walked into a police station and told officers where to find Rees, that he was eventually taken into custody in Memphis, Arkansas.

Rees was identified in the flesh by the soldier, and at the musician's home police found a .38 calibre handgun and notes describing the Jackson murders: 'Drove to select[ed] area and killed husband and baby. Now the mother and daughter were all mine,' including details of sexual offences against Mrs Jackson: 'then tied and gagged, led her to place of execution and hung her'. Rees concluded, 'I was her master.'

In February 1961, in Baltimore, Rees (christened by the press the 'Sex Beast') was sentenced to life imprisonment for the murder of Margaret Harold. In September a Richmond, Virginia, court convicted Rees of first-degree murder in the case of the Jacksons, and he was sentenced to death.

Rees appears to have become lost in the interminable system of appeal against sentence, as part of which the Supreme Court ordered psychiatric tests in 1966.

RENDALL, Martha Arguably Australia's most sadistic child killer, Martha Rendall murdered three children by swabbing their throats with hydrochloric acid.

In 1906, Rendall was living with Thomas Morris, a carpenter, and his five children. A strict disciplinarian, she insisted the children call her 'Mother', and frequently thrashed them unmercifully with little provocation. Neighbours had begun to notice that the formerly robust and well-nourished children were mere shadows of their former selves; still, it was 'none of their business', and so nothing was said.

The following year Morris's two daughters, whose debilitated state of health had made them vulnerable to colds and sore throats, had been prescribed throat swabs by the visiting doctor. Martha Rendall carried out the swabbing which, if the screaming and crying which accompanied the treatment were any indication, was extremely painful. Anne Morris died on 28 July and the cause was certified as diphtheria. Three months later Olive died of the same once-deadly bacterial disease. One year after his sisters' untimely deaths, fourteen-year-old Arthur Morris complained of a sore throat, and then complained even louder about the swabbing treatment meted out so unstintingly and with such obvious relish by 'Mother'. On 6 October he joined his sisters. This time the family doctor was suspicious, but although an autopsy was performed it revealed no signs of foul play, and diphtheria was once again certified as the cause of Arthur's death.

George Morris was the next recipient of Martha Rendall's nursing, though having been a keen observer of the consequences of the treatment received by his siblings, George preferred to run away from home rather than endure the agonising throat swabs. It happened that in trying to locate the fugitive boy the police began to question the neighbours, who by this time had a lot to tell and a great willingness to tell it. In short, there was sufficient suspicion present to apply for an exhumation order on the three Morris children. This time, a more exhaustive post-mortem examination established that their throats had been liberally washed with hydrochloric acid – little wonder they screamed; little wonder George took to his heels.

Rendall and Thomas Morris were jointly charged on three counts of murder. At their trial it was demonstrated that Rendall first laced the children's drinks with acid, and when they complained of a sore throat she swabbed their throats with more of the same. Only the inflammation of the mucous membrane of the throat, so characteristic of diphtheria, enabled her to continue so long undetected. Morris was acquitted of any complicity in his children's deaths, leaving Martha Rendall to face the full wrath of the law alone. She was hanged on 6 October 1909, the last woman to suffer capital punishment in Western Australia.

RIJKE, Sjef   Sentenced in January 1972 to double life imprisonment for killing two women in Utrecht. The first, eighteen-year-old Willy Maas, had been Rijke's fiancée. The second, Mientje Manders, died on 2 April 1971 and was also engaged to marry him. Both girls had succumbed to crippling stomach pains attributed at the time to some strain of food poisoning.

Three weeks after Miss Manders' funeral Sjef Rijke was married to Maria Haas, who almost certainly saved her own life by leaving her husband after only six weeks; she had become frightened by his pathological jealousy. However, Rijke's next lover was not quite so lucky, and suffered severe stomach pains until she stopped eating the peanut butter that Rijke had liberally laced with rat poison.

Police now interviewed the former Mrs Rijke who told officers that she had indeed suffered the familiar stomach cramps, which disappeared immediately she left her husband. The local health department isolated the rat poison, and a local shop-keeper identified Rijke as having bought quantities of it from him on a number of occasions.

Sjef Rijke confessed to the murders and attempted murders, explaining that although it gave him great pleasure to see women suffer he had not in either case intended his victims to die.

RIVERA, Miguel   During 1972 and 1973, young boys in the West Side and Harlem districts of New York were being mutilated and killed by a man christened by the local children 'Charlie Chopoff'.

The first known victim was an eight-year-old black boy named

Douglas Owens who was found in the East Harlem district on 9 March 1972; he had been stabbed thirty-eight times, but unlike later victims his penis had been cut but not severed from his body. Six weeks later a ten-year-old was discovered stabbed and emasculated in the hallway of a West Side apartment block; despite his injuries, which included being brutally sodomised, the boy survived.

On 23 October 1972, nine-year-old Wendell Hubbard was stabbed to death and mutilated on the roof of the East Harlem tenement where he lived, and on 7 March the following year a nine-year-old Puerto Rican child, Luis Ortez, was found dead in the basement of a building on the West Side.

The only lead that the police had at that time was a description given by the single survivor. He said that the man had looked like a Spaniard or an Italian, with skin neither dark nor fair, and he might have walked with a limp. Reports were now being received that a man answering this general description had been trying to persuade young boys into running errands for him. Then on 17 August 1973, eight-year-old Steven Cropper was found dead from a slashed artery in his arm and secondary chest wounds, but without the attendant sexual mutilation.

Following a failed attempt to kidnap a nine-year-old child in May 1974, a Puerto Rican named Miguel Rivera was arrested. Under questioning, Rivera exhibited acute signs of mental disturbance, claiming that he had been instructed by God to change little boys into little girls. Although the surviving child failed to recognise Rivera as his attacker, he had been seen in the company of Steven Cropper on the day he was murdered.

The police were quite satisfied that the evidence pointed to Miguel Rivera being 'Charlie Chopoff', however, his degree of mental instability made it unlikely that he would ever be considered fit to stand trial.

ROGERS, Dayton Leroy Rogers tortured, sexually abused and murdered seven women in the woods outside Oregon City during the summer of 1987. He had been raised in a strict home and was himself active in the Seventh-Day Advent Church; on the other hand he also had a conviction for an assault which had exhibited the early symptoms of a future preoccupation with hog-tying women and shedding blood as a source of sexual gratification.

In August 1987, he picked up prostitute Jennifer Smith and in his own unique way hog-tied her in the back of his van, and when she tried to break away, stabbed her to death. Dayton Rogers was arrested and charged with murder. When police searched his home metal fastenings from shoes and belts and hooks from brassieres were found among the ashes of a quantity of burned women's clothes. Rogers was found guilty of the murder of Jennifer Smith and sentenced to life imprisonment.

In the meantime, the naked bodies of six women, subsequently identified as known prostitutes were discovered in the wooded area close to the Molalla River; all the bodies showed evidence of having been tortured and sexually abused. In three cases the feet had been cut off, and in another severely gashed around the ankles. Broken lengths of shoelace were found tied in the same manner as the bonds which had constrained Jennifer Smith.

At Rogers' trial a woman witness testified to the court how earlier Rogers had hog-tied her in the back of his van and cut off her clothes with a sharp knife. Evidence was presented which indicated that Rogers had taken the women to the woods, bound their hands and feet together, and slashed their breasts and heels with a knife. He was found guilty on six counts of aggravated murder in May 1989, and at the penalty hearing which followed, the jury voted for death by lethal injection. At present Rogers awaits such time as the state of Oregon decides to exercise its right to implement the death sentence.

ROWNTREE, Mark Andrew As if it were not suffering enough from the activities of Peter **Sutcliffe**, the county of Yorkshire was at the very same time receiving the unwelcome contribution of a nineteen-year-old psychopath named Mark Rowntree. Rowntree killed four times in the space of just over one week, his victims chosen at random to fulfil what he called 'an urge to kill'.

The first attack took place on the evening of 31 December 1975, when Rowntree knocked at the door of Mrs Grace Adamson in Old Main Street, Bingley (the same town in which Sutcliffe had heard 'voices' in the graveyard ordering him to kill). Posing as a policeman, Rowntree forced his way into the house and stabbed Mrs Adamson seven times, two of the blows piercing her heart fatally. The urge satiated, Rowntree buried the weapon and bought himself a beer in the local pub.

Three days later when the urge rose in him again, Mark Rowntree bought another knife and cut down sixteen-year-old Stephen Wilson as he stood waiting at a bus stop in Wastburn. Stephen did not die immediately and was able to give this description of his attacker: about twenty-two years old with black shoulder-length hair, wearing a black jacket and carrying a shoulder-bag. As young Stephen Wilson lay dying in hospital, Mark Rowntree was in flight, swimming a freezing river then hailing a taxi home. It was the taxi driver who subsequently led police to Rowntree's home; but not before he had killed twice more.

Rowntree had previously made the acquaintance of Mrs Barbara Booth, a 'model', through the pages of a contact magazine, and on the pretence of wanting to hire her services, visited her house in Leeds on 7 January. There he stabbed Mrs Booth to death, and for good measure killed her three-year-old son in case he was able to recognise him.

Detectives were waiting for Rowntree at his home when he returned later on the same day; his only regret seemed to be that he had not had time to kill just once more – so that he could match the total achieved by his hero Donald **Neilson**, known as 'The Black Panther'.

A comparative rarity among serial killers, Rowntree, although he had been adopted as a baby, enjoyed all the love and privilege of a secure middle-class family. He was educated at a public school and was competent enough to have been offered a place at university. He chose instead to become a bus-driver. Sadly, Mark also suffered from schizophrenia, which in part was responsible for an unreasonable belief that women despised him. This seems to have originated from a single case of a girl rejecting his advances. At his trial at Leeds Crown Court in June 1976, Rowntree pleaded guilty to manslaughter on grounds of diminished responsibility; the plea was accepted by the prosecution empowering the judge to sentence Mark Rowntree 'clearly suffering from severe mental illness' to be confined in Rampton top-security psychiatric hospital without limit of time.

RUDLOFF, Fritz Fritz Rudloff, a male nurse employed in the East German hospital at Waltershausen, did not take kindly to being disciplined – especially when it was the hospital's director, Professor von Melchtal, who was handing out the discipline. Following a justifiable rebuke for the unauthorised administration of sedatives to patients, and the rather more questionable 'sin' of having an affair with one of the female nurses, Rudloff set about exacting his revenge by undermining the director's reputation through the simple, if drastic, expedient of killing off the Professor's patients.

In July 1954, von Melchtal performed major surgery on Werner Stauffacher. Stauffacher made good progress until, quite without warning, he died a few hours after drinking milk containing his nightly sedative; the drink had been brought to him by Fritz Rudloff. Although it was unexpected, there was nothing to arouse suspicion and the death was attributed to post-operative complications.

A month passed and Professor von Melchtal operated on Karl Furst, removing an inflamed appendix. The same pattern followed – good progress, and then in the early hours of the morning, sudden death. The night nurse was Fritz Rudloff. Again the loss was blamed on post-operative complications.

In the middle of August another of von Melchtal's patients died unexpectedly after an operation. Then a young man named Walter Strich was admitted to the hospital for only minor surgery. Nevertheless Strich died and his widow, understandably suspicious, insisted on an immediate post-mortem examination. Mrs Strich also informed the police that Fritz Rudloff had asked for her telephone number 'in case there was an emergency', which rather alarmed her in view of her husband's comparatively trivial complaint.

The post-mortem disclosed that there was enough arsenic in the body of Walter Strich to have killed three men. Investigations into the earlier patient deaths followed, and under police interrogation Rudloff confessed his guilt and confirmed that his motive was to ruin Professor von Melchtal's reputation.

In October 1954, Fritz Rudloff appeared before the People's Court of East Germany, where he was speedily convicted and sentenced to death. There was no appeal and Rudloff was duly executed.

S

SACK, George George Sack's first brush with death – other people's – came in 1923. At the time Sack was an undistinguished Chicago shopkeeper struggling to make his share of the proverbial 'almighty dollar', and the death was that of his first wife, Julia, in an inexplicable petrol fire at their home. Although there were a lot of unanswered questions and vague innuendoes, the coroner's jury returned a verdict of accidental death, and George Sack became five thousand dollars richer on the insurance money.

The following year George married again, and was again provident enough to insure his wife's life for five thousand dollars; a year later the Sacks' marriage was entering a rough patch. On 16 March 1925 the couple were on their way by cab to Sack's delicatessen, when Edna was shot dead and George wounded in the arm. Although no gun was found in the cab, George Sack was arrested and charged with murder. For his defence, Sack hired Clarence Darrow, arguably the most celebrated defence lawyer in the history of the American courts. The previous year, 1924, in one of the most famous murder trials in the annals of crime, Darrow had successfully saved Nathan Leopold and Richard Loeb from certain execution for the 'thrill killing' of fourteen-year-old Bobby Franks. George Sack certainly knew how to pick a winner.

Just as Darrow had not attempted to deny the guilt of Leopold and Loeb, only question the justice of the electric chair, so he made no attempt to convince the jury that George Sack had not fired the gun that killed his wife. Darrow's defence was that Sack was as mad as a hatter. The jury accepted this and he was committed to the State Hospital for the criminally insane in June 1926.

In 1932 Sack was released, in spite of the strongest objections from the hospital's superintendent. February 1939 found George living in Seattle, where he was arrested after the disappearance of a business associate, Joseph Young. No trace of Young or his body was ever found, and in May Sack was reluctantly released. Thinking it wise to move on, George Sack arrived in Portland, Oregon, in 1940 and purchased an apartment block. Eleven years later, one of the tenants, Roger Sherman, was found battered to death in his flat. As Sack was known to have been in dispute with Sherman he was closely questioned by police, but released and the entire matter was dropped for want of evidence.

Goldie Goodrich, a fifty-four-year-old spinster schoolteacher became Mrs George Sack in September 1952; and the late Mrs George Sack in early 1954. The marriage had been in trouble for some months when Sack reported his wife missing, and sure enough she was later found dead in the street apparently uninjured but for a small bruise on her temple. But appearances can be deceptive, and the post-mortem – obligatory in all cases of death in unusual circumstances – revealed traces of barbiturate poisoning and indications that Mrs Sack had died from being asphyxiated.

Once again George Sack faced a jury indicted for first-degree murder; this time he was found guilty and sentenced to death. In July 1957, the sentence was commuted to life imprisonment at the Oregon State Prison. Six years later, George Sack neatly rounded off his killing spree by committing suicide in his cell.

SANDWENE, Ntimane For a period of seven years in the late 1920s and early 1930s this Zulu became the scourge of Natal, committing eight murders and countless robberies while masquerading as a blameless servant on his master's farm.

Sandwene's first killing in the pursuance of theft took place on 17 May 1929. He had taken a shotgun from the farmhouse, blasted a storekeeper to death and rifled the till of the small amount that it contained. The gun was replaced, and the killer returned to the role of good and faithful servant until 27 January 1933, when Sandwene shot and robbed another shopkeeper: the pattern had been set. Robbery was about to become a way of life, at least, he told himself, until he had enough money to buy his own farm.

The police had concentrated their inquiries into the recent killing around the Midlands area of Natal and had on one occasion spoken to Sandwene, who expressed nothing but contempt for the callous killer, and pledged his help in any way he could.

The next victim was another storekeeper, and then on 13 June 1934, a triple murder at Heartsease – first the shop-owners Ismail Hajet and Hassan Mayat, followed by a fourteen-year-old-boy who was shot in cold blood after he had disclosed the whereabouts of his masters' money. In December, Sandwene shot and wounded a European while trying to rob him, and eleven months later at Hornesdale killed and robbed another shopkeeper, Abraham Hlatshwayo.

By now, understandably, the local Indian population – particularly those who followed the storekeeper's calling – were in a state of terror. Despite an attractive reward and one of the region's most intense police inquiries, no clues could be found as to the identity of the man known as the 'Killer of the White Mountain'.

The end for Ntimane Sandwene came indirectly from exhibiting an excess of emotion. He had managed cold-bloodedly to kill and rob his way around Natal without compunction, but in 1936, Sandwene journeyed to Bergville in pursuit of a man who was reported to have molested his wife. Perhaps this affair of the heart made him careless, for when he attacked two Zulus on the road to rob them, he killed one but left the other only wounded. This was the man who identified Sandwene as his companion's assassin.

Taken prisoner, Sandwene needed little persuasion to admit to his crimes, which he seemed to feel did not really deserve all the fuss that was being made over them – after all, it was not as though he enjoyed shedding blood, he had simply done it in pursuance of a more secure financial future. He went as far as to suggest he might be given another chance.

It was not an option taken seriously by the Native High Court when his case came before them, and far from release with a pat on the back, Ntimane Sandwene was sentenced to death and hanged at Pretoria Central Prison in May 1937.

SARRET, Maître Georges

French Murder Trial
'Bath of Sulphuric Acid'

The trial of eight people on charges of murder, defrauding insurance companies and complicity, opened on Saturday at the Aix-en-Provence assizes. The preliminary proceedings have lasted two years and in view of the considerable excitement pending the opening of the trial special precautions were taken to prevent disturbances. Soldiers with fixed bayonets as well as a strong force of gendarmerie guarded the approaches to the court, admission being refused to all but authorised persons.

The principal accused are Georges Sarret (otherwise Sarrejane), a lawyer, and two sisters, Catherine and Philomene Schmidt, of Bavarian origin, who were both formerly married to Frenchmen, having come to France in 1913. A long list of charges advanced by the prosecution includes the murder of four people, one of whom was an Englishwoman who went by the name 'Lady Annie Arnould'. The prosecution alleges that an unfrocked priest named Chambon was used by Sarret to impersonate a dying man (whom he had arranged for Catherine Schmidt to marry) for the purpose of defrauding an insurance company, and that Chambon was then murdered and his body and that of his mistress Madame Ballandreaux, also murdered, were dissolved in a bath of acid at Sarret's house. Sarret is alleged to have made 100,000 francs from the insurance company on this occasion. On another occasion it is alleged Sarret insured Catherine Schmidt for a large sum of money and that together they found a consumptive girl who, when she died of poisoning, was buried with the death certificate in the name of Catherine Schmidt. Philomene Schmidt, it is alleged, was paid the insurance money.

The Times, Monday, 23 October 1933

French Murder Trial

'Lawyer Sentenced to Death'

The trial of Sarret and his alleged accomplices on charges of murder and insurance frauds ended this evening. Sarret and the two Schmidt sisters were found guilty and the other accused were acquitted. Sarret was condemned to death [on the guillotine] and the Schmidt sisters to ten years' imprisonment followed by banishment for another ten years. The drama began on October 21st at Aix-en-Provence after a preliminary inquiry which had lasted for two years. Georges Sarret, the Schmidt sisters and three others were accused of the murder of four persons including an Englishwoman. Sarret was accused of having dissolved the bodies of two of his victims in a bath of sulphuric acid.

An unfrocked priest named Chambon and Madame Ballandreaux were both murdered at the villa occupied by the Schmidt sisters on August 19th, 1925. At the trial Sarret maintained that Madame Ballandreaux was killed by Chambon and that he, Sarret, accidentally shot Chambon when trying to disarm him at the villa to which Philomene Schmidt had called him. Sarret said that the sisters would not let him call the police so he dissolved the bodies in sulphuric acid. The defence of the Schmidt sisters was that they had been instruments of Sarret, acting under his influence.

The Times, Wednesday, 1 November 1933

It is reported that when Maître Georges Sarret was executed at Aix-en-Provence in April 1934, the blade of the guillotine became stuck, and his head remained clamped in the lunette for ten minutes while the apparatus was made ready again.

SCHMID, Charles Howard   As the state of Arizona's university town, Tucson is very much a young people's place. It is also where Charles Schmid, himself only twenty-three, set about reducing the student population. He was an unlikely Don Juan, and at five feet three inches tall used to pad the insides of his stack-heeled boots to give himself a bit more height. But what he lacked in inches, he made up for in dollars; son of a wealthy family, Schmid could afford all the little luxuries that made him popular among the girls of the local Palo Verde high school. His privileged upbringing – and perhaps his small stature – had conspired to turn Schmid into an arrogant, boastful youth, forever crowing about his romantic conquests and forever on the look-out for new ones. And if he wore rather clumsily applied foundation make-up and painted a beauty spot on his left cheek, it passed without much notice in the liberated campus life of 1960s America.

On 15 May 1964, Schmid persuaded his pal John Saunders, nineteen, and Mary Rae French to come along when he drove fifteen-year-old Alleen Rowe out to the desert where he raped and then bludgeoned her to death and buried her in the sand. Rumours spread like wildfire of course, helped along by Charles Schmid himself; but nobody seemed to think it worth reporting him.

In August 1965, Schmid was in the not-unfamiliar situation of trying to extract himself from an amour which had become tiresome to him. Unfortunately, seventeen-year-old Gretchen Fritz was clinging on like a limpet. On 16 August Charles invited Gretchen down to the shack at the bottom of his parents' garden and her sister Wendy tagged along too. In the solitude of his 'den', Schmid strangled both girls and later buried their bodies out in the desert. Charles Schmid, true to character, could not keep an impressive story like this to himself for long, and boasted of these latest killings to Richard Bruns – he even took Bruns out and showed him the bodies. As it turned out, Bruns was the wrong person to have told. An unstable and fearful youth, Richard began to suffer from nightmares, and became convinced that his own girlfriend was the next name on Charlie's hit-list. Bruns led the police to where Schmid had buried the Fritz sisters and there were the skeletons.

By the time Charles Schmid was arrested on 11 November 1965, he had just married a fifteen-year-old girl he had met on a blind date. One shudders to think what sort of life – or death – she would have had if Charlie had not been removed from decent society.

John Saunders and Mary French were arrested for aiding and abetting in the Alleen Rowe murder, but turned state's evidence against Schmid when he came up for trial.

Schmid was sentenced to death for the double murder, and later to a further fifty-five years for the murder of Alleen Rowe. He escaped execution under a US Supreme Court ruling which temporarily abolished capital punishment in 1971, but died in prison. Saunders was sentenced to life imprisonment and Mary French to four to five years.

SEARL, Ralph Ray   At the age of only nineteen, Searl confessed to the killing of five men over a period of two and a half months during the spring of 1964 in the states of Michigan, Nevada and Indiana.

Eventually Searl was indicted for just one murder, the last of his series. The victim was schoolteacher Earl Foote, who had benevolently picked Searl up when he was hitch-hiking in Kalamazoo, Michigan. During the journey, Searl held his good Samaritan up at gunpoint, forced him into the boot of the car, tied him up and shot the unlucky man through the head. Searl then drove the car on into Indiana, where at Elkhart he robbed and killed a gas-station attendant. Driving back to Michigan, Searl passed without hindrance through a police road block, the body of the late Earl Foote still in the boot of his own car.

Ralph Ray Searl was later arrested for being in possession of a stolen car and during routine questioning confessed to the murders of five men – two more petrol-pump attendants and another man who had been generous enough to offer him a lift while hitch-hiking, this time in Nevada. After a protracted trial Searl was convicted of first-degree murder and sentenced to spend his life in prison. A smart attorney earned Searl a retrial when it was revealed during his appeal that due to a procedural error his client had not been allowed access to a lawyer while in custody. In 1971 the Michigan Superior Court ordered the case back to the Circuit Court. Here Searl decided to abandon his previously unsuccessful defence of temporary insanity and entered into plea-bargaining negotiations offering to plead guilty on the understanding that he would be rehoused in a maximum-security reformatory for young offenders to serve his sentence, and be allowed to change his name to the rather more literary 'Luke Karamazov'.

While Searl had been awaiting retrial, the Kalamazoo area had been troubled by a spate of killings of young women. These culminated in the arrest of Searl's brother, Tommy, and for a short time they occupied adjoining cells in the county jail – a unique case of two brothers who, quite independently, and for entirely different motives became serial killers.

SEARL, Tommy In March 1972, while Ralph Searl was awaiting retrial, the body of Cynthia Kohls was found on the street in an outlying district of Kalamazoo; she had been raped and stabbed to death, and her eighteen-month-old baby was found nearby, covered with blood and crying.

Four months later, in July, two decomposing corpses were found in a car parked in a wooded area about twelve miles from Kalamazoo. They were later identified as two nineteen-year-olds from Chicago – Cornelia Davault and Nancy Harte; both had been strangled. And on 5 August, a student named Jennifer Curran disappeared while on a shopping errand.

In September, Tommy Searl, a twenty-eight-year-old service-station attendant was arrested in company with a fifteen-year-old boy. Searl was charged initially with the rape and murder of the Chicago women, and later with those of Cynthia Kohls and Jennifer Curran, whose body was found in October less than a mile from where the Chicago couple were found dead. Searl was put into maximum security cell No. 2 at the county jail; his brother was already in No. 1.

Unlike Ralph, Tommy Searl never admitted his crimes. At his trials, the main prosecution witness was the youth arrested with him, who described the way in which the women had been forced to undress and were then subjected to repeated rape before being strangled with a rope, stabbed or suffocated with a plastic bag over their head. Tommy Searl was found guilty of the murders of Cynthia Kohls and Jennifer Curran, and offered no defence in the cases of

Cornelia Davault and Nancy Harte. He was sentenced to life imprisonment.

'SEX BEAST' *see* **REES, Melvin Davis**

SHERMAN, Lydia The 'Queen Poisoner', as she was dubbed at her trial, was one of the greediest and most successful poisoners to emerge from the criminal records of nineteenth-century America. Always for profit, Lydia Sherman killed, according to her own detailed confession, at least eleven people, though there could, she added as an afterthought, have been a dozen or fifteen more.

In the early 1860s, Lydia was married to a policeman named Edward Struck, and had already borne him six children. It was obviously enough for Mrs Struck, who decided to put a stop to childbirth by the simple expedient of poisoning her husband; to earn a little money out of the venture she also insured his life for a modest sum. This murder seemed to work well enough, with the chemist having accepted without question her alleged intention to kill rats, so Lydia then insured and poisoned all six of her children. Thus she was rich and free both at the same time. It was as a compliment to her skill as an actress, that never once was the slightest suspicion cast on this tragic widow.

In 1868 Lydia was married to Dennis Hurlbrut, a moderately rich, elderly (some said senile) farmer from New Haven, Connecticut. By 1870, the widow Hurlbrut had squandered her way through the late Dennis's estate, and was looking for more. In April, Lydia became housekeeper to wealthy Nelson Sherman of Derby, Connecticut, and when he had agreed to marry her, showed gratitude by first poisoning his baby with arsenic, and then his fourteen-year-old daughter Addie. Nelson Sherman himself, grief-stricken over the loss of his beloved children, succumbed to a poisoned hot chocolate drink on 12 May 1871.

This time, the local doctor became suspicious and called in a second opinion, and then a third. Which was three too many for Lydia, who had fled to New York at the first hint of trouble. Proved correct in his diagnosis of arsenical poisoning by the exhumation of the Sherman children, Dr Beardsley made his findings known to the police who lost no time in ordering Mrs Sherman's extradition back to Connecticut to face trial.

Lydia Sherman was convicted of second-degree murder, which reflected the mainly circumstantial nature of the evidence. She was sentenced to life and died in prison on 16 May 1878.

SINGH, Boysie Boysie Singh terrorised the West Indian island of Trinidad from the 1930s to the 1950s as a robber, arsonist, pirate, vice and gambling king and multiple murderer. The son of full-blooded Indians, Boysie was born in Trinidad, drifting into crime at an early age when, rather than join a gang, he formed his own.

In 1932, Boysie was in deep dispute with David Leach, then considered to be – in the view of those who knew about such matters – the prostitution and gambling supremo of the capital, Port of Spain. In their frequent street confrontations Leach's gang had inflicted embarrassing defeats on Boysie's lads; in retaliation, Boysie disguised himself as an Indian beggar, which enabled him to get close enough to Leach to beat him to death. When he was detained by the police, Boysie's doctor stated that his patient could not possibly have attacked Leach due to the extensive injuries he himself had suffered at the hands of Leach's thugs. Besides, there were no witnesses so Boysie Singh was released.

Mr Singh now had the opportunity to expand his empire to include control of the Port of Spain gambling clubs and brothels, supplemented by profits derived from a fleet of fishing vessels used for smuggling between Trinidad and Venezuela. On the occasion of a dispute with the Venezuelan coast guard, Boysie and his crew felt obliged to take to piracy when, in March 1950, they took over a Venezuelan customs boat. All eleven men serving on board her were cast over the side, heavily weighted, to sink to the bottom of the Caribbean Sea. In the same year Boysie got word – rightly or wrongly – that one of his associates, the exotically named Philbert 'Bumper' Peyson, was 'talking' to the police. On 20 April, Bumper's body was found floating in the sea off the Trinidad Yacht Club. Boysie Singh and four of his 'business partners' were arrested and charged with murder.

The trial opened on 17 July and ended on 22 August when the jury failed to reach agreement on a verdict. A retrial took place during November and the beginning of December when convictions were returned against all five defendants. Under sentence of death, it looked as if Boysie Singh had finally been forced to relinquish his control over all things crooked on the island of Trinidad.

But that was to reckon without smart attorneys.

All the convicted men appealed against sentence, and in January 1951, the Court of Appeal overturned the verdicts, giving as its reason 'faults' in the judge's summing-up and what it termed the 'unreliable testimony' of several of the prosecution witnesses. Meanwhile, Boysie Singh was claiming to have undergone what he described as 'a religious experience' while in the death cell.

Despite his recent spiritual conversion, Boysie Singh still managed to stray from the path of righteousness often enough to earn several prison sentences for receiving stolen goods and for being implicated in an arson fraud. However, it was not until 1956 that he got into *big* trouble again. A lifeguard named Boland Ramkissoon had enlisted Boysie's help in the matter of a contract killing on an unwanted mistress. Boysie took up the contract and on 30 July Thelma Hayes disappeared without trace. Nobody's hero, Ramkissoon weakened under questioning and pointed his finger straight at Boysie Singh. Both men were put on trial on 4 February 1957, found guilty, and sentenced to death. Appeals went as high as the Judicial Committee of the Privy Council in London; none of which made the slightest difference and Ramkissoon and Singh were hanged at Port of Spain on 20 August 1957.

'SINGING STRANGLER' *see* LEONSKI, Edward Joseph

SMITH, George Joseph Notorious 'Brides in the Bath' killer, Smith disposed of three unwanted spouses in watery graves, and plundered the worldly goods of a further four bigamously married 'wives' who, though they lost their savings, were fortunate in escaping with their lives. Smith was a totally amoral killer, whose only motive was personal profit, and despite the services of the legendary Edward Marshall Hall as his defence counsel, a jury found Smith guilty and a judge sentenced him to death.

It had only been due to the luckiest of circumstances that Smith was stopped before he could kill again; indeed, we can never be sure whether the true total of Smith's murders is known now.

He had married, for the seventh time, to Margaret Lofty at Bath on 17 December 1914, and had taken rooms in Highgate, north London, on the following day. No sooner had Mr and Mrs Lloyd (Smith used enough aliases to fill a small directory) settled in than she was whisked off to the local doctor where Lloyd established that his wife suffered from 'black-outs', though the doctor could find nothing wrong with her. During the evening, John Lloyd suggested that Margaret should have a nice warm bath, and having got the landlady to fill the tub with water, he sat down to play the harmonium. Miss Blatch, the landlady, later recalled that it had been *Nearer My God to Thee*, but she was not paying a lot of attention until fifteen minutes later when there was a knock at the front door and there on the doorstep was her new lodger. 'Just stepped out to get some tomatoes for Mrs Lloyd's supper,' he announced. Lloyd inquired casually whether his wife was out of the bath yet, and seemed concerned when Miss Blatch confessed she had 'not heard a squeak'. Reminding the landlady that Mrs Lloyd was prone to fainting fits, he asked her to accompany him upstairs where, to her surprise at least, they found Margaret Lloyd lying dead in the bath of water.

After the inquest had found that Mrs Lloyd's death was due to a tragic accident, Smith collected his 'wife's' life insurance, emptied her savings account, and slipped quietly away.

Unfortunately for Smith (or whatever name he was using at the time), the father of his fifth 'bride' saw the account of the Margaret Lloyd inquest in the *News of the World* – it was identical to the death suffered by his own daughter, Alice Burnham, exactly a year before. And Burnham was convinced that this 'John Lloyd' was one and the

The history and fate of the seven brides of George Joseph Smith

Name or Alias	Bride	Place of Marriage	Date	Fate of Bride	Possessions gained by Smith	Inquest	Exhumation
Oliver Love	Caroline Thornhill	Leicester	17 Jan 1898	Emigrated to Canada 1900	—	—	—
George J. Smith	Edith Pegler	Bristol	30 Jul 1908	Survived	—	—	—
George Rose	S. A. Faulkner	Southampton	Oct 1909	Deserted at National Gallery	£300	—	—
Henry Williams	Bessie Mundy	Weymouth	26 Aug 1910	Separated 1910–1912 Drowned in bath at Herne Bay, 13 July 1912	£2,500	15 Jul 1912 Drowning in epileptic fit	18 Feb 1915 Herne Bay
George J. Smith	Alice Burnham	Portsmouth	4 Nov 1913	Drowned in bath at Blackpool, 12 Dec 1913	£140 plus Life Assurance for £500	13 Dec 1913. Accidental drowning	9 Feb 1915 Blackpool
Oliver James	Alice Reavil	Woolwich	17 Sept 1914	Deserted 23 Sept 1914, at Brockwell Park	£78, piano and furniture and clothes	—	—
John Lloyd	Margaret Lofty	Bath	17 Dec 1914	Drowned in bath at Highgate, 18 Dec 1914	£19 plus Life Assurance for £700	22 Dec 1914 and 1 Jan 1915 at Islington. Accidental drowning	4 Feb 1915 Finchley

same as the George Joseph Smith who had collected the insurance after Alice was drowned in her bath. And so a long investigation was launched into the activities of George Joseph Smith (alias Lloyd, Love, Rose, Williams, etc.).

At the end of their inquiry, Scotland Yard had added Bessie Mundy to Smith's list of 'Brides in the Bath', and on 22 June 1915, he faced a jury at the Old Bailey charged with her murder at Herne Bay, in Kent. Because Smith had advanced the defence of accidental death, it was, under English law, permissible for the prosecution to introduce evidence of the other drownings in order to prove what is legally called 'system'. In other words, the first time a new bride drowns in her bath it is tragic; the second time it is suspicious; the third time it begins to look as if *somebody* is trying to kill them off. Which is what the jury obviously thought when, on 1 July 1915, after a deliberation lasting just twenty-two minutes, they found Smith guilty.

Friday the thirteenth proved a very unlucky day indeed for George Smith – on that date in August 1915, they put him on the scaffold at Maidstone Prison and hanged him.

SOBHRAJ, Charles Gurmukh   Born in Saigon in 1944 to an Indian father and a Vietnamese mother. After his father had walked out of their home, Sobhraj's mother took up with a Frenchman who changed the boy's name from the Indian Gurmukh to the French Charles (after General de Gaulle it would seem). When his mother and uncle Jacques left Saigon for the rather safer and more cultured streets of Paris, Charles was initially left to the reluctant care of his natural father, only later to be dragged across continents to live with his mother in France. As he grew up, so Charles grew to despise European culture and long for the East. It is not surprising given such an emotionally unstable background that Charles should have been attracted to the life of other outsiders on the fringes of the criminal underworld. That he was not at first very good at it is testified by the increasingly lengthy prison sentences which Charles earned through the 1960s.

At liberty in 1970, Sobhraj took residence in the land of his father, in Bombay, and with some small success broke into local smuggling and black-marketeering. In 1972, after a bungled robbery, Charles was obliged to flee to Kabul where, unable to resist the pettiest of crimes, he was jailed for dodging his hotel bill. Although he was a pragmatist when it came to weapons, Charles Sobhraj made a particular trade mark of the use of drugs, which he employed in Afghanistan to great effect when he secured early release from prison by drugging the guards. At liberty again, but clearly anxious to put some distance between himself and the Kabul police, Charles hijacked a car. After drugging the owner he bundled the man into the boot of the vehicle, where he suffocated. Not intentional perhaps, but it was Charles' first unlawful killing.

In Tehran, Charles Sobhraj took up stealing again with the inevitable consequence that he became acquainted with the inside of an Iranian jail. Turkey was the next stop where, in November 1973, and with the now well-perfected method of drugging his victims' drink before robbing them, he managed to pay his way around the dives of Istanbul with enough left over to import his younger brother, Guy, to be his partner. In Greece he was less fortunate in that he was caught, but then lucky again in escaping from the prison on Aegina.

Back in India, Sobhraj tried his hand at various criminal capers before taking off for Kashmir. It was here that he met Marie Aimée Leclerc, and together they moved first to Hong Kong and thence to Thailand to rob and kill as a double-act. Leclerc lured a succession of drug-dealing hippies – of which there was no shortage seeking the spiritual enlightenment of the East – to the menage at Bangkok's Kamit House, where Sobhraj (now calling himself Alain Gautier) had been joined by an Indian crook named Ajay Chowdhury. When they had been drugged into a blissful unconsciousness and their modest supplies of narcotics and cash removed, the infinitely expendable hippies were despatched by knife or gun and their bodies burnt; it is said that some were still breathing when the match was lit.

By the beginning of 1976, Sobhraj was wanted on charges connected with eight murders – in Turkey, Thailand and India. When police eventually tracked him to Bangkok, Charles had already fled with a little help from a corrupt government official. A search of his apartment revealed not only a veritable pharmacy of drugs, but personal documents and property once the property of as many as twenty victims. Time was beginning to run out for the man whose name had risen to the top of Asia's 'Most Wanted' list. His most audacious crime was to be Charles Sobhraj's last.

Back now in India, in Agra, Sobhraj managed to ingratiate himself with a large party of French tourists staying at the Bikram Hotel. By the simple ruse of playing on the Europeans' fear of dysentery, Charles was able to administer doses of a soporific drug which he intended should put his victims to sleep for long enough to ransack their rooms while they lay unconscious in their beds. Unfortunately, he miscalculated the dose with the result that Frenchmen immediately started keeling over in the hotel lounge, while those that did not succumb so quickly accused Sobhraj of trying to poison them.

When he first came to trial in India, Sobhraj was charged with the murders of an American named Luke Solomon and a drug courier named André Breugnot. Though his one-time amour, Aimée Leclerc, testified enthusiastically against him, Sobhraj was convicted only of culpable homicide, and in July 1978 sentenced to seven years' hard labour. In 1982, Charles was again on trial for murder, this time of a young man who had been found drugged and strangled in Calcutta. Although he was sentenced to life imprisonment, Charles Sobhraj was still, unbelievably, able to drug his guards and once again escape captivity. After several weeks at large, Sobhraj was finally confined to Tihar Prison. And if he should ever be released from there, Thailand and Nepal have a number of outstanding murder charges for which they would like to try him.

SODEMAN, Arnold Karl In many ways, Arnold Sodeman typifies one of the basic requirements of a successful 'home-based' serial killer; that is, one who operates in the general vicinity of where he lives and/or works. The requirement is 'respectability'; a domestic and social life stable enough to blind friends, family and neighbours to any possibility of guilt. Who could believe the happily married man capable of sex-murder; or that every kid's favourite 'uncle' would kill a child?

That was Arnold Sodeman; a mild-mannered man who adored his wife, Doll, and lived for his daughter Joan. Well-liked at work, he was considered a general 'good guy' by his neighbours around the South Yarra district of Melbourne, Australia.

On 9 November 1930, Sodeman was strolling in Fawkner Park when he became attracted to twelve-year-old Mena Griffiths playing with her friends on the swings. The friends later told the police how the 'tall man' had sent them off to buy sweets while he kept Mena behind for a 'special' errand. She did not return home that night, and two days later her body was found gagged and strangled in an abandoned house six miles from the park.

Some weeks later a man named Robert James McMahon – identified by witnesses as being in the area of Fawkner Park on the day Mena Griffiths disappeared – was arrested and later committed for trial charged with her murder. A desperate McMahon pleaded that he hadn't even been in Victoria state that day; he had been in the outback of New South Wales. Despite unimpeachable witnesses to his alibi, McMahon remained in custody.

On 10 January 1931, the body of sixteen-year-old Hazel Wilson was found on wasteland near her home in the suburb of Ormond; her murder was a carbon copy of the Griffiths killing. So Robert McMahon *was* innocent, and with barely an apology he was released after spending seventy-six days in jail.

Ethel Belshaw disappeared on New Year's Day 1936. After nearly five years the deaths of Mena Griffiths and Hazel Wilson had been all but forgotten. When twelve-year-old Ethel vanished from the crowded seaside resort at Anderson's Inlet, apparently in company with 'a man on a bicycle' the old fears resurfaced. The fears were fully justified; next day Ethel Belshaw's body was found in scrubland – it was an identical murder.

This time around 11,000 people were interviewed – including Arnold Sodeman. Not surprisingly, Sodeman did not attract the least suspicion, though he had been a member of the large party from which Ethel Belshaw was abducted. Instead, suspicion fell on another member of the group, eighteen-year-old Gordon Knights; Knights was arrested and charged with Ethel's murder. Thankfully the mistake was recognised before he had spent too long in a cell.

The Melbourne Police Department was still trying to find a solution to the three murders a year later when the fourth of the strangler's victims, a six-year-old named June Rushmer was found dead at Leongatha township. Sodeman, a labourer by trade, had been working on a site barely a dozen miles away. Once again witnesses had seen the girl talking to a man on a bicycle.

It all began as a joke – the sort of leg-pulling that goes on over mugs of thick brown tea on construction sites the world over: 'Hey, Arnold, didn't I see you walking your bicycle down the street that day?'

Everybody grinned and looked at Arnold; they saw a man they hardly recognised. His face scowling anger, Sodeman threw down his mug and stormed off, shouting back over his shoulder, 'No, you bloody didn't! I wasn't there!'

Most of the gang just shrugged and forgot it – some of them had seen Arnold a bit peeved before, after he had been drinking heavily. One man didn't forget it, and perhaps a lot of little Melbourne girls owe him their lives. Whether out of good citizenship or a more personal reason, that man went to the police with his story. Two days later Arnold Sodeman was in a cell, with the police trying to keep a lynch mob at bay.

Finally, Sodeman made a full confession and resigned himself to the fate that his own uncontrollable actions had determined for him. Even so, the police had taken a lot of convincing. They had already suffered the embarrassment of charging two innocent men with the previous murders, they weren't about to be deceived by Sodeman. Then Arnold showed them how it was done. It had been a feature of the murders that the pathologists had never fully been able to explain – the strange configuration of bruises around the victims' necks; now Sodeman was demonstrating the way he had linked his thumbs together over their throats to give extra leverage. Besides, he had lured each of the girls with treats and could describe exactly the contents of their last meal – details known only to the post-mortem staff and police investigators.

Arnold Sodeman refused to give any justification for his crimes, and at his trial pleaded insanity. He was formally convicted and on 1 June 1936, hanged at the Metropolitan Gaol at Pentridge.

The explanation of Sodeman's almost 'Jekyll and Hyde' personality became clear only during the autopsy carried out on his body after execution (a standard formality). When his skull was opened, it was discovered that Sodeman had been suffering for many years from chronic lepto-meningitis, an inflammation of the tissue covering the brain which was activated by large intakes of alcohol.

SOLIS, Magdalena and Eleazor, and HERNANDEZ, Cayetano and Santos It was in the industrial city of Monterrey, in North-east

Mexico that Magdalena Solis eked out a risky living as a prostitute, engaging her homosexual brother Eleazor as pimp. In 1962 they were approached by the Hernandez brothers, Cayetano and Santos with a proposition so bizarre that it would defy the talents of a novelist to invent. The brothers had set up some kind of sex cult in Yerba Buena, and desperately needed a god and goddess – did Eleazor and Magdalena want the job? Of course they did.

The Hernandez brothers had been using the cult in order to squeeze money out of the gullible local farmers and, as an added bonus, had persuaded them that submitting to sexual molestation by the priests (themselves) was essential to the purging of demons. With the recruitment of the Solises, activities were expanded, and Magdalena satisfied the lesbian tendencies of the priestesses, while Eleazor and Cayetano Hernandez indulged their homosexual appetites with the farmers. Things could not be expected to continue in so idyllic a fashion for ever, sooner or later the peasants were certain to tire of giving body and soul as well as their meagre income to the cult. At this point Magdalena developed the idea of revitalising interest with a couple of human sacrifices, and ordered two men stoned to death and their blood collected for a kind of unholy communion. After the success of this venture, blood sacrifice became a regular feature of cult life, and before many months had passed eight members had given their lives in the interests of purification. Magdalena then offered the ultimate sacrifice and gave her lesbian lover up to be beaten to a pulp, accompanied by another member who had his heart cut out.

These last two ritual murders had been unwillingly observed by a teenage boy who took his horrifying tale as fast as his legs would carry him to officer Martinez, the local policeman. Martinez followed the lad back to Yerba Buena to investigate, and they themselves were hacked to death by devotees.

A few missing peasants were one thing, but when a policeman disappeared the authorities wanted to know why, and an armed police squad was sent in to investigate. During the battle that followed, members of the cult were routed, and after the shooting of Santos Hernandez they surrendered.

On 13 June 1963, eleven days after their arrest, Magdalena and Eleazor Solis together with twelve members of the cult were tried on charges of multiple murder, convicted and given the maximum sentence of thirty years in the state prison. One face notably absent from the court line-up was that of Cayetano Hernandez, founder of the cult. He had been murdered by a disaffected follower after the killing of officer Martinez.

'SON OF SAM' *see* **BERKOWITZ, David**

'SOUTHSIDE SLAYER' *see* **SPENCER, Timothy W.**

SPENCER, Timothy W. Spencer, the 'Southside Slayer' of Richmond, Virginia, committed four rape-murders in the autumn of 1987, having earlier (in 1984) killed a woman for which an innocent man spent five years locked in a prison cell.

The first reported victim of 1987 was Debbie Dudley Davis, thirty-five years old, whose raped and strangled body was found naked on the bed in her apartment in September. Two weeks later, thirty-two-year-old Dr Susan Hellams, a neuro-surgeon, was found gagged, partly clothed, raped and strangled in her bedroom wardrobe. Diane Cho, a teenage student was found on 22 November, bound and naked at her home fifteen miles south of the city; she too had been sexually assaulted and strangled. In December, forty-four-year-old Susan Tucker was reported missing and found a week later in the bedroom of her apartment in Arlington. The nature of her injuries left detectives in no doubt that this was the fourth victim of the 'Southside Slayer'.

On 16 January 1988, Rena Chapouris was found dead in her south Richmond apartment; she had been stripped naked, bound, strangled and bludgeoned; a bloody claw hammer was found beside the body. A few blocks away on the same day, twenty-nine-year-old Michael St Hilaire was found hanging from a wire attached to an overhead pipe. The absence of rape in the crime against Rena Chapouris combined with the St Hilaire suicide led the police investigation team to exclude the murder from the Slayer's record and list it as a copy-cat killing.

Timothy W. Spencer was arrested by police in Arlington, Virginia, in January 1988. He was charged with the most recent murder, that of Susan Tucker. Further investigation established Spencer's presence at the scene of the Davis, Hellams and Tucker murders through genetic profiling, the so-called 'DNA fingerprinting'. Although he was the prime suspect in the case of Diane Cho, insufficient semen had been recovered to provide a reliable test result. Using this same method of genetic testing, Spencer was proved to have been responsible for the murder of Carol Hamm at her Arlington home in January 1984, a crime for which David Vasquez had already served five years of a thirty-five-year prison sentence.

Timothy Spencer first went on trial in July 1988, charged with the murder of Susan Tucker; it was the first case to be heard in Virginia in which evidence of identity was established by DNA fingerprinting. Spencer was convicted and sentenced to life imprisonment. He was found guilty for a second time after facing trial for the rapes and murders of Debbie Davis and Susan Hellams; on this occasion the jury demanded the death penalty, though lengthy appeal procedures are likely to delay this sentence for some years.

STANIAK, Lucian Known as the 'Red Spider', Staniak stalked Poland like some modern-day **Jack the Ripper**, raping, murdering and mutilating more than twenty young women between 1964 and

1967. Like Jack's, the victims were disembowelled in such a manner as to suggest a sado-sexual motive, and most of the murders took place on Poland's public holidays such as All Saints or May Day.

Staniak's pride in his workmanship extended to writing letters to the police in red ink, the thin spidery appearance of the handwriting giving the media a convenient nickname. The letters took the form of braggardly challenges to stop him, followed by directions to the location where he had left the latest body. The Red Spider was also writing in a similar vein to the newspapers with such threatening mottoes as: 'There is no happiness without tears; no life without death. Beware, I will give you cause to weep.'

On 24 December 1966, the terribly mutilated body of seventeen-year-old Janina Kozielska was found aboard a train in Krakow; she was the sister of Aniela Kozielska, only fourteen years old, who had been murdered in Warsaw in 1964. Both girls, investigations revealed, had been members of the Art Lovers Club in Krakow. For the first time the police could see a lead – a small one, but a definite lead. Scientific analysis of the red ink used by the Spider had proved to be very thinned-down artists' paint. Officers interviewed all one-hundred-plus members of the Club, and settled easily upon Lucian Staniak, a twenty-six-year-old translator with the Government publishing house; he was a keen painter and an active member of the Art Lovers Club. Staniak's canvases were a revelation – painted predominantly in blood-red and depicting, among other subjects, a disembowelled woman with a bunch of flowers protruding from her split belly. Staniak was arrested on 1 February 1967, just after he had murdered student Bozena Raczkiewicz at the railway station in Lodz.

As might have been expected after his previous correspondence with them, the police had little difficulty persuading the Red Spider to talk. In fact he claimed to have committed his last murder because he felt he was falling behind in his publicity. By way of explanation for his crimes, Staniak revealed that both his parents and his sister had been killed in a hit-and-run accident and the woman responsible for their deaths had escaped conviction. His first victim had, so he said, been similar in appearance to the woman.

Although he was tried, convicted of six of his twenty confessed murders and sentenced to death, Staniak was later found insane and committed to an asylum in his home town of Katowice.

'STOCKING STRANGLER' *see* **GARY, Carlton**

'STOCKWELL STRANGLER' *see* **ERSKINE, Kenneth**

STRAFFEN, John Thomas Shortly after lunch on a quiet, early summer Sunday in 1951, a little girl was playing happily in the garden of her home; the date was 15 July, the child was Brenda Goddard, and the garden was in Camden Crescent, Bath. Because six-year-old

Brenda's mother was a widow and necessarily worked full-time, her daughter was fostered out to a Mr and Mrs Pullen. At about two-fifteen Mrs Pullen called Brenda to get ready for Sunday School. At three-fifteen, a worried Mrs Pullen informed the local police that Brenda was missing. At seven o'clock Police Constable Donald Drew found the child's body in a wood close to her home; she had been strangled and bludgeoned, but there was no indication of sexual interference.

As the heavy machinery of a murder hunt whirred into action, Mrs Pullen remembered that she had seen a tall man in a blue suit standing near the house when she looked out to check on Brenda. The description happened to fit a mental patient who had recently been released on licence from Hortham Colony in Bristol, and was known to the police for a number of minor offences and disturbances. His name was John Thomas Straffen. While he readily admitted that he was probably the man Mrs Pullen saw in the street, Straffen denied abducting Brenda, and there was no evidence to prove otherwise.

Just under one month after the death of Brenda Goddard, on the afternoon of 8 August, nine-year-old Cicely Batstone was walking purposefully towards the cinema near her Bath home eagerly anticipating the children's matinee. Cicely never reached her destination, but was later found strangled.

Identified by a courting couple as the man they saw talking to Cicely Batstone shortly before she disappeared, John Straffen was again taken into custody where he admitted the killings, adding, 'It didn't take long; about two minutes.' Straffen was committed to Taunton Assizes in October 1951, found unfit to plead and confined to Broadmoor.

John Straffen was no stranger to psychiatric institutions. In 1940, when he was ten, he was put into the care of a school for mentally defective children. At the age of seventeen he assaulted a thirteen-year-old girl, putting his hand over her mouth and saying, 'What would you do if I killed you? I have done it before.' He was committed to a mental institution from which he was released in February 1951; six months later he killed Brenda Goddard.

Straffen escaped from Broadmoor within months of arriving, and although he was only at large for four hours, it was sufficient time to murder another young girl, Linda Bowyer. Detained by the police, Straffen suddenly said, 'I didn't kill her.' To which an inspector replied, 'No one has suggested that anyone has been killed.'

Surprisingly, John Straffen stood his trial this time, his mental state being considered 'improved'. He was found guilty at Winchester Assizes of murder and in July 1952 sentenced to death; Straffen was later reprieved, but it is unlikely that he will ever be released.

'SUNDAY MORNING SLASHER' *see* **WATTS, Coral Eugene**

'SUNSET STRIP KILLERS' *see* **CLARK, Douglas**

SUTCLIFFE, Peter In November 1980, shortly after the brutal murder of Leeds student Jacqueline Hill, one national newspaper published its story under the headline 'Did one man really do all this?' It seemed incredible at the time, and no less alarming in retrospect, that one man – Peter Sutcliffe – *was* able, over a period of five years, to bludgeon, stab and mutilate an admitted total of twenty women, thirteen of whom died from this savage treatment. These tragic victims, aged between sixteen and forty-seven, with occupations ranging from student to prostitute, had only one thing in common – they were alone on the street after dark.

The investigation of the 'Yorkshire Ripper' case was a story of determination and frustration – of a police force desperate to put a stop to one of the worst mass murderers in Britain's history, but seemingly powerless to stop the carnage. Above all, it is the story of a county in the grip of terror, its women fearful of being out of doors at night. Thirteen of those women were to pay with their lives for that freedom.

Despite the largest manhunt ever mounted by British police, during which 250,000 people were interviewed and 32,000 statements taken, it was the very weight of all this paperwork that obscured the often obvious path through to Sutcliffe. He had been questioned on a number of occasions during the investigation, and as the result of one of these interviews a police officer had gone so far as to voice his suspicion that Peter Sutcliffe was the Ripper; his report was overlooked.

Another tragic complication of the case was the amount of time wasted by hoax letters, and by the tape recording sent to the police in June 1979, which was broadcast to the nation in the hope that the voice could be identified. Once again Sutcliffe's luck held out, and after yet another interview he was dismissed for not having a Wearside accent like the voice on the tape.

The five-year hunt for the 'Yorkshire Ripper' ended in an anticlimax on 2 January 1981, when a routine police patrol became suspicious about a car parked in a dimly lit driveway, and the owner, who gave his name as Peter Williams, was taken in for questioning; it was Peter Sutcliffe.

A multicide of the 'evangelical' type, Sutcliffe's declared mission was to rid the streets of prostitutes – as he explained to his younger brother Carl: 'I were just cleaning up streets, our kid. Just cleaning up streets.' He had, so he said, first become aware of his mission when working as a municipal gravedigger in Bingley cemetery, and heard the voice of God coming from one of the graves. There was, though, considerable doubt as to whether Peter Sutcliffe was truly psychotic or whether his 'voices' were a clever device to support his defence of diminished responsibility. In the end, Peter Sutcliffe was put on trial and on 22 May declared guilty on thirteen counts of murder and sentenced to serve not less than thirty years in prison.

The Yorkshire Ripper's victims

Date	Name	Age	Location
30 October 1975	Wilma McCann	28	Leeds
20 January 1976	Emily Jackson	42	Leeds
5 February 1977	Irene Richardson	28	Leeds
23 April 1977	Patricia Atkinson	32	Bradford
26 June 1977	Jayne MacDonald	16	Leeds
1 October 1977	Jean Jordan	21	Manchester
21 January 1978	Yvonne Pearson	22	Bradford
31 January 1978	Helen Rytka	18	Huddersfield
16 May 1978	Vera Millward	41	Manchester
4 April 1979	Josephine Whitaker	19	Halifax
2 September 1979	Barbara Leach	20	Bradford
18 August 1980	Marguerite Walls	47	Farsley
17 November 1980	Jacqueline Hill	20	Leeds

'SYDNEY MUTILATOR' *see* **McDONALD, William**

SZCZEPINSKI, Waldemar On 20 December 1983, the first murder was committed in a series of stranglings by the phantom who came to be known as the 'Doorbell Killer'. All the killings took place in West Berlin; all of the victims were elderly women.

The soubriquet had been coined when the newpapers learned the killer's *modus operandi*; police thought that he must just give a simple, but fatal, ring on the bell of an elderly woman's home, and when she answered the door, force his way in, throttling the occupant and stealing what he could find. There was never any sexual interference with the victims.

Following the December killing of eighty-two-year-old Frau Hedda Buekow, the next victim, a month later, was Elli Grybek, two years older than Frau Buekow, and murdered in the Wilmersdorf district to the south-west of the Tiergarten, where both of the women had lived.

The third victim was Frau Sigurd Bessener, aged eighty-one, found strangled in her flat in the Schoenberg district on 17 February. In all cases it was only small amounts of cash that had been taken. On this most recent occasion witnesses had seen a young man they described as tall and strongly built walking along the street behind Frau Bessener as she was returning home prior to the attack.

In March eighty-seven-year-old Erna Hoedicke was found dead in the entrance hall to her apartment in the Templehof district; as before, the flat had been ransacked for money.

Amid growing panic among the large population of elderly ladies in Berlin, Frau Caecili Hidde, aged eighty-three, lost her life to the

Doorbell Killer on 20 April 1984, in her flat in Neu Koeller. This time it would appear the murderer struck lucky, for Frau Hidde was known to keep large sums of money about the place. He had also been very careless, and during their examination of the scene of the murder, police officers found a sales receipt from a local clothes shop. Enquiries at the store established that it was the receipt for a pair of men's gloves; furthermore, an assistant at the store remembered the sale, and also having seen the customer's identity card when he accidentally dropped it while paying for the gloves. His name was Szczepinski.

A little research revealed that twenty-two-year-old Waldemar Szczepinski had recently lost his job and was having difficulty meeting the mortgage repayments on an expensive apartment. He was arrested and during police questioning admitted to the murders of Frau Hoedicke, Frau Hidde and Frau Kaethe Deidifuss, whose body had not yet been found where it lay in her flat in the Charlottenburg district. Szczepinski told officers that he had gained entry to the women's homes by showing a toy 'FBI Agent' badge. He denied the three other murders.

Waldemar Szczepinski was tried for those murders that he confessed to and was sentenced to life imprisonment on 7 June 1985. Since his arrest there have been no further 'doorbell' killings and the police have closed their files on the three outstanding murders.

T

TACKLYN, Larry Winfield *see* **BURROWS, Erskine Durrant**

TESSNOW, Ludwig   A very early triumph for the infant science of serology cut short the gruesome career of the man known alternately as the 'Monster of Rugen' and the 'Mad Carpenter of Rugen'. It was on the first day of July in the first year of the twentieth century that two young brothers, eight-year-old Hermann and six-year-old Peter Stubbe, failed to return to their home at Gohren on the island of Rugen in north Germany, after being out at play. It was not until the following morning that horrified villagers searching for the boys began to find the dismembered and disembowelled fragments of the Stubbe brothers scattered over a wide area of local woodland. Ludwig Tessnow, a journeyman carpenter from the neighbouring village of Baabe who had been working at Rugen and was seen talking to the children on the day they disappeared, was detained for questioning. During a routine search of his home, boots and clothes were found that bore dark stains, and others had obviously been recently washed. Tessnow's plausible explanation was that the stains were no more sinister than wood dye – a common material to craftsmen in his way of business.

Unfortunately for Ludwig Tessnow, the examining magistrate at Griefswald before whom he appeared, had a long memory. Three years earlier, Johann Schmidt recalled, there was a similar case in the village of Lechtingen, near Osnabrück, where seven-year-old Hannelore Heidemann and her friend Else Langemeier were found mutilated and dismembered in a wood near their home. A man seen hanging around the woods on the day of the murder had been picked up and his clothing was found to be stained. The man's name was Ludwig Tessnow, and when he told the police that the stains were simply wood dye from the job which they had just interrupted, he was absolved of any further suspicion. What if . . . thought Herr Schmidt. Then he remembered the sheep. Three weeks before the savage murder of the Stubbe brothers, on 11 June, a farmer had seen a man running away from one of his fields, and when he went to investigate found seven of his sheep eviscerated, hacked to pieces and strewn around the field. At an identity parade, the farmer picked out Tessnow as the man he had seen.

However, Tessnow was denying everything – and apart from the undefinable stains on his clothing (remember, this is 1901), there was no direct evidence on which to base a case against him. But that was to reckon without the persistence of magistrate Schmidt and his prosecutor Ernst Hubschmann. Hubschmann had just heard of the entirely new and remarkable test developed by a young German biologist, Professor Paul Uhlenhuth, which was able not only to determine the existence of blood stains, but also to distinguish human from animal blood.

On 8 August 1901, Uhlenhuth submitted his report: of the stains on Ludwig Tessnow's clothing the large number on the suit and shirt were human, others on the jacket were sheep's blood. Tessnow was executed at Griefswald Prison in 1904.

THOMAS, Dr Allgen Lars *see* **HAERM, Dr Teet**

TINNING, Marybeth   During a period of fourteen years while she and her husband lived at Schenectady, New York state, Marybeth Tinning gave birth to eight children and adopted another one; all of them died, few from natural causes. Although the marriage seemed an amicable enough one, despite their 'misfortunes', Marybeth was later to claim that all the while she had been trying to slowly poison her husband as well.

The first child to expire, in January 1972, was baby Jennifer, who had been born with meningitis and only lived for nine days. Fifteen days after Jennifer's death, Mrs Tinning took her two-year-old son Joseph to the hospital when he stopped breathing after what she described as a 'seizure'. The boy was kept in hospital for ten days receiving treatment for a suspected viral infection and sent home apparently recovered. Later the same day, Tinning rushed Joseph back to the clinic, but he was dead on arrival. Death was certified as due to cardio-respiratory arrest.

In March, Tinning admitted her four-year-old daughter Barbara to hospital, where she died shortly after arrival. Following an autopsy, death was attributed to Reye's syndrome. It should be said that up to this point there was no reason for hospital staff to suspect foul play. In November 1973, Marybeth gave birth to baby Timothy, whom she returned to the hospital nineteen days later where he was found to be dead. Timothy Tinning's death was assumed to be cot-death syndrome.

30 March 1975, saw the birth of baby Nathan, and three weeks later he too was in a clinic apparently suffering from pneumonia after having difficulty breathing and was secreting blood from his nose and mouth. After a month of treatment Nathan Tinning was returned to his parents, but by September had breathed his last, victim, it was certified, of acute pulmonary edema. Mary Frances, born in October 1978, underwent her first emergency treatment in January the following year; her second attack – on 20 February – proved fatal. Once again the child was assumed to be a cot death victim.

In 1978 the Tinnings applied to adopt a child, and rather than view their past history of baby losses as suspicious, the adoption agency approved the application from motives of sympathy. They went so far as to offer the explanation that previous deaths could have resulted from a genetic disorder. However far-fetched that may be, it did not help little Jonathan Tinning who was born after Michael's adoption in November 1979. He died on 20 February 1980, after encountering difficulty with his breathing. Michael was next to take sick, and in February 1981, he was rushed to the doctor but found to be already beyond earthly hope.

Tami Lynne, Marybeth's ninth child arrived in August 1985, and survived only four months, being found dead in her crib with blood on the pillow. Initially another cot death was suspected, but clearly such persistent misfortune could not go unremarked, and an inquiry was set up into the babies' deaths. The investigation concluded that little Tami Lynne had been suffocated.

Mrs Tinning was interviewed by police and admitted the murder of this latest child, adding that she was also responsible for the deaths of Timothy and Nathan. Despite her shock confession to trying to murder him too, Joseph Tinning remained loyal to his wife throughout her legal ordeal. Finally Marybeth Tinning was charged only with the killing of Tami Lynne, and after a six-week trial ending on 17 July 1987, she was convicted and on 1 October sentenced to twenty years to life.

'TOKOLOSHE MURDERS' *see* MSOMI, Elifasi

TOPPAN, Jane Jane was born Nora Kelley in 1854 in Boston, Massachusetts. Her mother died when she was young, leaving Peter Kelley to look after Nora and her three sisters. Kelley, either through overwork or a weak constitution, was not entirely right in the head, a fact that was amply demonstrated when one day he was found in his tailor's shop trying to sew his eyelids together. Kelley was sent to an insane asylum, and his daughters were cared for by their grandmother, and when this good lady found things too much for her, the girls were committed to an orphanage, from where Mr and Mrs Abner Toppan of Lowell, Massachusetts, adopted five-year-old Nora.

The Toppans changed the girl's name to Jane, and encouraged her to attend church. She did well at school, and grew into a popular young lady around the little town of Lowell. After an unfortunate engagement which ended when Jane's fiancé married another girl, she withdrew into herself, becoming a virtual hermit and twice tried to end her own life.

Suddenly, at the age of twenty-six, Jane informed her foster parents that she intended to take up nursing and immediately enrolled as a student in a Cambridge, Massachusetts, hospital where she was apparently an eager and well-liked trainee. If her fellow nurses had been asked to name any fault in Jane, they might have been tempted to refer to her unhealthy, almost morbid fascination with the activities of the post-mortem room.

One day a patient who had been in Jane's care, a man previously recovering well, unexpectedly died. Then another one, and Jane was called into the chief surgeon's office to answer a few questions. No official accusations were ever made against Nurse Toppan, but it did not go unnoticed that she was discharged from her post. Unbowed, Jane assured her foster parents, 'I will go to the old and the sick, to comfort them in their neediest hour.'

Between 1880 and 1901, Jane Toppan served as a private nurse in many New England homes – and what did it matter if a large number of her patients died? Illnesses, particularly at the turn of the century, were frequently fatal.

On 7 July 1901, Jane was among a group of mourners in the small cemetery in Cataumet. When the service was over, she participated in the age-old custom of scattering a handful of soil on to the coffin as it rested in the grave. Inside it was the late Mrs Mattie Davis, one of Jane's patients; it was touching, everybody thought, how the nurse was so loyally devoted even to the last.

So loyal and devoted, in fact, that the unfortunate woman's family begged Jane to stay on and look after the rest of them who had also unaccountably fallen sick.

Indeed, Mrs Annie Goodman, the deceased's married daughter, was so sick that on 29 July 1901, it was necessary to summon a doctor. Then, as her patient appeared restless, Jane obligingly gave her an injection. When the doctor arrived a few hours later, Jane told him, 'I think she is sinking.'

Dr Walters took the frail woman's wrist seeking a pulse, then gave his diagnosis: 'This girl is already dead.'

After the funeral Nurse Toppan again thought she ought to leave the house, after all she was becoming something of a jinx on the health of its occupants; the family would not hear of it. Next to suffer was Alden Davis. The regular funerals were proving depressing, and it was with gratitude that he accepted Jane's soothing nightcap. Next morning, Captain Davis was found dead in his bed. 'A stroke', Jane explained to the sole surviving daughter, Mary Gibbs. However, Mrs Gibbs had been unsettled by so many tragic deaths in her family, not least because her husband was far away on a sea voyage. Eventually she asked a cousin, Beulah Jacobs, to come and stay with her. However, despite the presence of Beulah's watchful eye, Mary Gibbs succumbed to the ministrations of her nurse within days. Thus the whole of the Davis family had been wiped out in just six weeks.

When Captain Gibbs returned from sea he found his wife dead, and a distraught cousin Beulah who informed him that Nurse Toppan had refused to allow an autopsy because 'Such practices were against the religious beliefs of the family.' Gibbs lost no time in sharing his suspicions with the police, and the body of Mary Gibbs was exhumed and found to have been murdered with an overdose of morphine.

By the time the police caught up with her, Jane Toppan had murdered her foster sister, Mrs Edna Bannister, at Lowell, and moved on to nurse the Nichols family in New Hampshire. On the night of 29 October 1901, Detective Whitney stood at the door in the rain and asked, 'Jane Toppan, the nurse?' 'Yes.' 'You are wanted in Massachusetts for questioning in connection with the deaths of Mrs Henry Gordon and Mrs Irving Gibbs.'

Jane went voluntarily back to Massachusetts, apparently amused by the thought that anybody should think her capable of murder: 'I have a clear conscience. I wouldn't kill a chicken, and if there is any justice in Massachusetts they will let me go.'

Police throughout New England began to disinter dozens of bodies – former patients of Nurse Toppan. Autopsies proved that all had died of morphine and atropine poisoning. Meanwhile, from the Barnstaple County jail, Jane was beginning a triumphant confession to as many as seventy murders: 'Yes, I killed all of them. I might have killed George Nichols and his sister that night if the detective hadn't taken me away. I fooled them all – I fooled the stupid doctors and the ignorant relatives; I have been fooling them for years and years . . . I read [the prosecutor's] statements about me poisoning people with arsenic. Ridiculous, if I had used arsenic my patients would have died hard deaths. I could not bear to see them suffer. When I kill anyone they go to sleep and never wake up. I use morphia and atropia, the latter to hide the effects of the former. It took days sometimes to kill them.'

On 25 June 1902, Jane Toppan was put on trial. Dr Stedman, the psychiatrist, gave evidence that 'Jane Toppan is suffering from a form of insanity that can never be cured.' At which, with an indignant cry, Jane shouted, 'The alienist lies. I am not crazy, and all of you know it. I know that I have done wrong. I understand right from wrong – that proves I am sane.'

Even so, Jane Toppan was confined to the Taunton State Asylum for the Criminally Insane. Her behaviour alternated between the docile, almost morose, and raging fits of paranoia, during which she would, ironically, accuse the nurses of trying to poison her. Jane continued to live a long and healthy life and on 17 August 1938, died of old age at eighty-four.

TORINUS, Metod Young girls kept disappearing from around the village of Dolenja Vas in central Yugoslavia. The first to be missed was eighteen-year-old Vida Menas, on 17 October 1977, and despite protracted inquiries no trace was ever found of her, alive or dead. On 4 May of the following year Ljuba Smarovas vanished, and on 21 August, the name of twenty-year-old Schipka Postalnyi joined the growing missing-persons file. Understandably the villagers were thrown into some panic, and the more imaginative went so far as to suggest a vampire was at large.

Lila Bratislav disappeared from the neighbouring village of Kocevsks Reka on 16 February 1979 and, on 5 December, Mira Kosecki went missing from the village of Starig Log.

Following the disappearance of Mira Kosecki, a German tourist named Klaus Hochbauer reported to the police at Kocevje that he had been beaten to the ground and robbed on the road between that town and Dolenja Vas. Hochbauer was able to give the police a description from which his assailant was tentatively identified as thirty-two-year-old Metod Torinus, who worked a small farm on the outskirts of Dolenja Vas.

A team of detectives paid the farmer a visit and searched his home; they noticed that Torinus became particularly agitated whenever an officer got close to a baking oven attached to the house, and automatically assumed that it was in this hideaway that Herr Hochbauer's money was stashed. When a move was made to open the oven, Torinus intercepted and confessed that it was he who had robbed the German, and that he would willingly lead the police to where the money was hidden. They opened the oven anyway; which is where they found the assorted charred bones and skulls. A forensic pathologist was able to identify the remains as those of young human females aged between sixteen and twenty-four. Dental work led to the identification of Ljuba Smarovas and Lila Bratislav; Mira Kosecki was identified from a reset collar-bone which she had broken as a child.

Metod Torinus confessed raping, torturing and strangling all five girls before incinerating their bodies in the baking oven. He explained to police that he was only capable of achieving sexual satisfaction through the rape of an unwilling partner.

Torinus was tried and found guilty of the five charges of murder on 10 December 1980, and executed four days later.

TORONTO HOSPITAL MURDERS The death rate among infants in the cardiac unit of Toronto's Hospital for Sick Children during the eight months between June 1980 and March 1981 was showing an alarming increase over the average. First reports quoted as many as between twenty-one and forty-three baby fatalities, and more worrying still were post-mortem indications of high levels of the powerful heart drug digoxin.

In March, a nurse at the Hospital, Susan Nelles, was taken into custody and charged with the murder of four of the infant patients. Exactly one year later, in March 1982, the charges against Miss Nelles were dismissed by the preliminary hearing, and the judge in that instance recommended that any future charges should cover the deaths of five babies which *he* felt had been murdered. His Honour explained that there was no evidence on which to charge Susan Nelles and that she was, in his opinion, an 'excellent' nurse.

Laboratory reports published in 1983 indicated that in twenty-eight of the dead babies, a high level of digoxin had been isolated, and a special inquiry numbered eighteen of the deaths as 'suspicious' while the remaining ten fatalities were at least consistent with poisoning.

In 1984, a nursing supervisor was accused by two of her nurses of injecting an unknown solution into the intravenous drip of one of the victims, but the allegation remained unconfirmed. The Royal Commission of Inquiry, set up under Mr Justice Samuel Grange of the Ontario Supreme Court, reported in early 1985 that at least eight of the deaths had been 'murder' resulting from overdoses of the drug digoxin, with another fifteen deaths falling into the 'highly suspicious' category. Mr Justice Grange had been ordered by the Ontario Court of Appeal not to reveal any names of suspects he might believe guilty; however, he did restate his opinion that Susan Nelles was innocent: 'Knowing what I do now, I would not recommend the arrest of Miss Nelles for the deaths of any of the babies.' Which was probably just as well, because Susan Nelles was already threatening civil action against the Toronto police for 'malicious' prosecution. In the wake of the report, the leader of the overnight nursing team on duty at the hospital when most of the deaths occurred resigned from the staff. The case remains unsolved.

TURNER, Lise Jane   Lise Turner was tried in the High Court at Christchurch, New Zealand, in November 1984, charged with the murders of three babies (two of them her own children) and three counts of the attempted murder of two other babies. On top of this there was evidence alleging four other incidents in which babies left in Turner's care had been found suffering serious breathing difficulties.

On 11 January 1980, eleven-week-old Megan Turner (who had already, it would be learned, suffered two attempts on her life) was rushed to hospital by her mother and a neighbour but found to be dead on arrival. A post-mortem failed to establish any serious disorder and the fatality was attributed to cot-death syndrome. Cheney Louise, Turner's second child was born on 31 January 1982. On 15 March, a neighbour visiting the Turner home was shocked to find that the baby had been vomiting blood and was now dead. This too was diagnosed as a cot death.

With such a record of 'bad luck' it is surprising that Mrs Turner was entrusted with the care of any more babies, but in October, a Mrs Packer left her four-month-old daughter Catherine while she went shopping. On her return she found the baby bleeding from the mouth and vomiting, though an emergency examination at the hospital revealed no abnormal symptoms and little Catherine Packer appeared to make a full recovery. However, the attacks recurred periodically over the next six months (in fact whenever Lise Turner was around) and on 1 April 1983, Catherine was again found unconscious with blood trickling from her nostrils. After further intensive treatment the child again recovered. This time, after Mrs Packer had visited Catherine in hospital in company with Lise Turner and the child had cowered into the corner of her cot screaming as she recognised Turner, the woman was never again let near the child and Catherine regained her health quickly with no further difficulties in breathing.

It was a pity that Mrs Packer did not know Mrs Hall, if she had five-week-old Katrina Hall might not have been found 'sick' after Lise Turner's offer to babysit. Despite her laboured breathing and vomiting, the baby recovered after hospital care. Michael Clark Tinnion was not so lucky. Michael had been left in Turner's charge by his mother on 28 May 1984, and when she returned her eight-month-old son was dead, a sticky fluid dribbling out of his nose and mouth. This time there was no difficulty in establishing the cause of death – asphyxia, and with Lise Turner's past record of disasters it was not long before she was facing some very searching questions. Clearly her answers did not satisfy the authorities; which is how Mrs Turner found herself facing three counts of murder and three of attempted murder.

At her trial the prosecution alleged that Turner had caused the deaths (and near deaths) by smothering the infants' faces, in many cases contriving to have another person in the house when the child was found. Lise Turner did not give evidence on her own behalf, though her defence attorney advanced a plea of diminished responsibility. The verdict, though, was a well-deserved 'guilty', and the habitual baby-killer was sentenced to life imprisonment for murder and further terms of five years' imprisonment on each of the counts of attempted murder.

V

VACHER, Joseph A vagrant who wandered the countryside of south-east France at the end of the last century, begging, stealing and killing. So vicious were Vacher's killings, so gratuitous the mutilations, that he quickly earned the name the 'Ripper of the South-East'.

Joseph Vacher escaped the deprivation of being born last of fifteen children of a poor peasant family by joining the army where, in a fit of pique brought on by slow promotion, he tried unsuccessfully to cut his own throat. In 1893 Vacher attempted to shoot a young woman who had rejected his unwelcome advances and again tried without success to commit suicide; the bullet lodged in his ear causing paralysis of the muscles on the right side of his face, damage to one eye, and mental instability. After spending some months in the asylum at Saint-Robert, Vacher was discharged in April 1894 and became a vagrant.

During the next three and a half years, Joseph Vacher butchered seven women and four young men, subjecting their bodies to the most appalling sexual mutilation. On 4 August 1897, he assaulted a woman collecting pine cones in the woods near Tournan, but was taken by the police after the woman and her husband, who had been working nearby, overpowered him. Even so, it was considered a comparatively slight offence, and the multiple killer was sentenced to three months for offending public decency.

Although there was never any more than a strong suspicion of the true extent of Vacher's crimes, like many criminals before him and since he proved his own worst enemy. For no apparent reason, Vacher wrote a letter to the examining judge confessing, 'Yes, I committed the crimes . . . I committed them all in moments of frenzy.' He explained that as a child of eight he had been bitten by a rabid dog and it was his belief that his blood had been permanently poisoned. Whether this seemed to him an adequate excuse for killing at least eleven people, and probably another fifteen besides, we will never know.

After prolonged investigation by a team of doctors headed by the eminent Professor Alexandre Lacassagne, Joseph Vacher was found, in their opinion, to be legally sane and fit to stand trial. At the Ain Assizes in October 1898, Vacher found himself facing charges connected with the killing of a young shepherd three years earlier. Clearly still determined to establish his insanity Vacher, uninvited, addressed the court, 'Glory to Jesus! Long live Joan of Arc! Glory to the great martyr of our time! Glory to the great saviour!'

Sane or mad, a reluctant Joseph Vacher was half-dragged, half-carried to the guillotine on 31 December 1898; he was twenty-nine years of age.

'VAMPIRE OF DUSSELDORF' *see* **KURTEN, Peter**

'VAMPIRE OF SACRAMENTO' *see* **CHASE, Richard**

'VAMPIRE RAPIST' *see* **BODEN, Wayne**

VAN ZON, Hans Van Zon's first murder was in many ways typical both of the man and his methods – cynical, intense and utterly without point. Elly Hager-Segor had been just an ordinary date, they had been out for the evening, and when van Zon pretended to have missed the last train, Elly, considerate girl, made him welcome at her apartment. They made love, then when she refused him a second bite of the cherry, he strangled her and cut her throat with a bread knife.

Hans van Zon was born on 20 April 1942, in the industrial city of Utrecht in the central Netherlands. He was a quiet, rather introspective child, prone to lose himself in fantasy. He was also unnaturally self-centred and had been impressed by his mother into a false belief in his own importance. An undistinguished education was followed by an equally undistinguished work record, dismissed from one job after another on account of the stubborn strain of dishonesty that marked his character. Not that it mattered overmuch, van Zon was in a world of his own most of the time – by turns a CIA agent, movie star, private detective, tycoon, fashion designer, even an orphan. Then in July 1964 he met and murdered Miss Hager-Segor, adding a new dimension to his life.

Always attractive to and attracted by members of both sexes, Hans next laid claim to the killing of homosexual film director Claude Berkely in Amsterdam in 1965; and in 1967, after his marriage to Caroline Gigli, she was obliged to go to the police and accuse her husband of trying to kill her.

Van Zon enjoyed greater success with his mistress, thirty-seven-year-old Coby van der Voort. After plying her with barbiturates by claiming they were an aphrodisiac, he bludgeoned her semi-conscious body to death with a length of lead piping, stabbed and sexually assaulted her. This same piece of lead piping became a favourite weapon, and featured in the motiveless murder of Jan Donse in May 1967 and in the killing of Heeswijk farmer Reyer de Bruin in August of the same year. It was, in fact, this crude but well favoured blunt instrument that would prove van Zon's downfall. In attempting to kill an elderly woman named Woortmeyer, the assassin failed to strike hard enough, and the startled victim came round, realised she had been attacked and robbed, and set up the hue and cry.

At his trial, the explanation emerged that many of van Zon's excesses were committed at the behest of an ex-convict called Old Nol, to whom he had, in an unguarded drunken moment, confessed the van der Voort murder, and had been blackmailed ever since. In fact the widow Woortmeyer turned out to have been a one-time lady friend of Old Nol.

One of the Netherlands' rare known examples of a serial killer, Hans van Zon was sentenced to life imprisonment with a recommendation that he serve no less than twenty years, and Old Nol ceased to be an ex-convict when he was returned to jail to serve a further seven years.

W

WAGNER, Waltraud, *et al.* In Austria's most sensational trial since the end of the Second World War, four nursing assistants at Vienna's largest hospital, the Lainz, stood accused of the murder of at least forty-two patients during 1988 and 1989. Waltraud Wagner, said to be the dominant force behind the 'death squad', Maria Gruber, Irene Leidolf and Stefanija Mayer sat in the dock of the Vienna District Court before Presiding Judge Herr Peter Straub. As the trial opened on 28 February 1991, state attorney Ernst Kloyber began to describe a series of murders which, he said, represented only the tip of the iceberg: 'How big the iceberg really is we will never know.' Recalling the awful recent past when Adolf Hitler and the Nazis had annexed Austria, Herr Kloyber said, 'It is a small step from killing the terminally ill to the killing of insolent, burdensome patients, and from there to that which was known under the Third Reich as "euthanasia". It is a door which must never be opened again.'

Although the four nursing auxiliaries were presently charged with responsibility for only forty-two deaths taking place over two years, it is generally believed that the true figure could be in the hundreds over as many as six years. All the defendants had made confessions at the time of their arrest, though claiming the most altruistic of motives – to end the interminable misery and suffering of their patients. Waltraud Wagner, thirty-two years old at the opening of the trial had confessed to starting her career as an 'angel of death' in 1983 (when she was just twenty-four); at that time it was an infrequent activity, though by her own admission in 1989 it had reached a rate of one killing a week.

The methods used to 'release' these patients to 'a place of peace' were overdoses of drugs and the fearful 'oral hygiene treatment', where one nurse held the patient's head back and mouth open, while another nurse poured water down the victim's throat until they literally drowned – a method which clearly had a great impact on the court when it was demonstrated.

The trial occupied the whole of the month of March and, on the 28th, judge Herr Peter Straub summed up the long and complicated case for the benefit of the jury, concluding, 'We must take note of all the possible extenuating circumstances: the bad conditions at the hospital at that time, the low level of staffing, the problems inherent in treating the very old, the defendants' previously good records and their cooperation with the police . . . Nevertheless, in each case above all was the horrifying brutality of some of their actions, the helplessness of their victims, and the gross abuse of the trust that had been placed in them.'

The jury returned their guilty verdicts at four o'clock on the following morning and sentences were passed that afternoon. Waltraud Wagner was convicted of fifteen counts of murder, seventeen of attempted murder and two of aggravated assault; she was sentenced to life imprisonment. Twenty-nine-year-old Irene Leidolf was sentenced to life imprisonment; Stefanija Mayer, aged fifty-two, received twenty years; and Maria Gruber, twenty-nine, fifteen years.

WAINEWRIGHT, Thomas Griffiths Born in October 1794, at Chiswick, west London, Thomas was orphaned early by the death of his mother in childbirth and his father shortly after. This left young Thomas to the care of his maternal grandfather, Dr Ralph Griffiths, who at the time was an editor on the influential *Monthly Review*, and living at Linden House, in what was then the village of Turnham Green.

Thomas could hardly have asked for a more stimulating upbringing; his grandfather's interests ensuring that the boy came into contact with some of the most exciting artistic and literary minds of the age. He attended the art academy where he showed talent as a draughtsman, though a certain shiftlessness of character was already beginning to show.

Wainewright took up a commission in the Guards, though he quickly tired of the life, leaving the service with no more than an uncommon appetite for whisky punch and a tendency to neurotic hypochondria. Back at Linden House he continued to paint, and to exhibit, and discovered he possessed a talent for art-journalism and literature, at which he enjoyed a modest success. He met Wordsworth and William Blake, who is said to have spoken generously of his paintings, though less indulgent contemporaries record an effeminate manner and a voice rarely rising above a whisper.

Writing and sketching, plus a bit of shady art dealing, provided Wainewright with an income of something around £200 a year – a scant sum with which to support his lavish entertaining; and his marriage in 1821 to Frances Ward, a sweet girl though penniless, merely contributed to the expenses.

By forging the signatures of the trustees controlling the small income he had from stock given by his grandfather, Thomas succeeded in laying his hands on a sum in excess of £2000 from the Bank of England. Even so, former debts and current extravagance quickly swallowed this windfall, and in 1828 Thomas and Frances managed to inveigle themselves an invitation to live under the roof of their uncle George Griffiths, the inheritor of Linden House.

Scarcely a year had passed when poor Uncle George suddenly died; in great pain, from a mysterious illness. Coincidentally, Wainewright inherited and once again the queue of creditors was marginally shortened.

Wainewright's next move was to invite his wife's mother, Mrs Abercromby, and her two step-sisters, Helen and Madeleine, to make their home at Linden House. In 1830, Helen's life was insured for £5000.

If only Mrs Abercromby could have seen into her future she might have allowed Thomas to go ahead and increase the value of the policies on Helen; as it was she obstructed the effort and died suddenly in August 1830, in great pain, from a mysterious illness. It must have saddened Wainewright's heart to have made no direct financial gain from his mother-in-law's demise, but he consoled himself by increasing the insurance on Helen to £18,000. On 21 December, in her twenty-first year, Helen Abercromby died suddenly, in great pain from a mysterious illness.

And mysterious was just the way the insurance companies chose to read it. In fact they refused outright to pay a single penny on the policies. Wainewright instituted proceedings in court, borrowed £1000 on the security of his claim, and disappeared to Boulogne before the ravening jaws of the wolves locked on to his temporarily full pocket.

Little is known of Wainewright's movements over the next five years, though he spent time in a Parisian prison. It is probably no coincidence that the man with whom Thomas lodged in France died suddenly, in great pain, from a mysterious illness! Or that his life was insured for £3000 in favour of Thomas Wainewright.

In June 1837 Wainewright returned to England and was arrested on a warrant relating to the forgery of ten years earlier. He also learned that his action against the insurance companies in the matter of Helen Abercromby's policies had been dismissed.

Although now openly known and referred to as 'Wainewright the Poisoner', his appearance at the Old Bailey was on the charge of forgery only. He pleaded guilty, and was sentenced to transportation for life to Van Diemen's Land.

Story has it that while in Newgate, Wainewright admitted poisoning Helen Abercromby because, he said, he was offended by her very thick ankles. He is also claimed to have told a visitor in the commercial way of business, 'Sir, you city men enter upon your speculations and take your chances of them. Some of your speculations succeed, and some fail. Mine happen to have failed.'

Unlike so many of his fellows, Thomas Wainewright survived his voyage on the transports, and died in the convict hospital at Hobart Town in 1852, to the last boasting of his famous connections.

'WANT-AD KILLER' *see* **CARIGNAN, Harvey**

'WARTIME JACK THE RIPPER' *see* **CUMMINS, Gordon Frederick**

WATERFIELD, Fred *see* **GORE, David Alan**

WATTS, Coral Eugene   Watts simply hated women, and although he killed at least twelve of them, and perhaps as many as forty, he was never prosecuted for murder.

Coral Watts first attracted police attention as a suspect in Michigan in 1974, when the body of Gloria Steele was found slashed to death near Western Michigan University. He was later released, but in December 1975, he was given a year in jail for an attack on another co-ed just prior to the Steele murder. On Halloween night in 1979 Mrs Jeanne Clyne was stabbed to death in a Detroit suburb, and once again Coral Watts was under suspicion.

In 1980, while Watts was living in Ann Arbor, he was taken into custody in connection with the activities of the so-called 'Sunday Morning Slasher' who stabbed three women to death in April, July and September of that year. In this, and in all the previous cases, no direct evidence was ever forthcoming to link him to the killings.

When Watts moved to Houston, Texas, in 1981, the Michigan police authorities advised Houston of their suspicions and for a period Watts was kept under surveillance as he had been while in Michigan. The watch was eventually relaxed, although at the time a new series of killings, reminiscent of those in Michigan had begun to plague Texas. The victim list was impressive if one man was responsible for all ten deaths in the space of little more than one year.

Possible victims of Coral Watts

Date	Name	Cause of Death
27 March 1981	Edith Ledet	Stabbed to death in Galveston.
12 September 1981	Elizabeth Montgomery	Stabbed to death.
13 September 1981	Susan Wolfe	Stabbed to death.
4 January 1982	Phyllis Tamm	Hanged with an article of her own clothing.
January 1982	Margaret Fissi	Asphyxiated and beaten in her car.
7 February 1982	Elena Semander	Found strangled in a trash bin.
March 1982	Emily LaQua	Aged fourteen, disappeared from her home in Brookshire.
15 April 1982	Carrie Jefferson	Failed to return from work.
15 April 1982	Suzanne Searles	Missing after going to a party.
16 April 1982	Yolanda Garcia	Stabbed to death.
23 May 1982	Michelle Maday	Strangled in her Houston home.

On the same date as the most recent killing, 23 May, Coral Watts was arrested and charged with burglary and attempted murder following an attack on two young women.

In advance of his trial, Watts agreed to plead guilty, and in return for a sixty-year jail sentence and immunity from further prosecution, to clear up many as yet unsolved murders and lead police to undiscovered corpses.

The deal was finally approved, and Watts admitted to all nine Texas murders plus that of Linda Tilley in September 1981 – previously attributed to accidental death. He gave detailed instructions for the recovery of the bodies of the three missing Texas women, and confessed to killing Mrs Jeanne Clyne back in Detroit.

On 3 September 1982, Coral Watts was sentenced to the agreed sixty years.

WEBER, Jeanne   A remarkable story of a compulsive child-killer who, despite two false acquittals, went on to murder again.

Jeanne Weber occupied an apartment in one of the many slums that were home to the impoverished and criminal in turn-of-the-century Paris. Jeanne had given birth to three children, of whom only seven-year-old Marcel was surviving. There has never been any evidence to suggest that these deaths were anything but 'natural', and it may be that the impact of these tragedies caused Madame Weber to turn to infanticide.

Despite her poor record with children, Jeanne Weber was nevertheless entrusted by her sister-in-law with the care of her eighteen-month-old daughter Georgette; the date was 2 March 1905. By evening the baby was dead, and despite the blue marks around the child's throat, a doctor certified the death as due to 'convulsions'.

It may have been family loyalty, it may have been stupidity, but within a fortnight Jeanne's brother and sister-in-law had left another of their children, toddler Suzanne, at the squalid apartment in the inappropriately named Passage de la Goutte d'Or. When the parents returned to reclaim the child some hours later, she was dying; in a few minutes, the unlucky infant joined her sister as a victim of 'convulsions'.

Incredible as it now seems, on 25 March, Jeanne Weber was to be found looking after another sister-in-law's child, Germaine; she was seven months old and, as things turned out, would get no older. Apparently ignoring the red marks around her throat, the doctor attributed Germaine's death to diphtheria. It was three days later, on the very day that Germaine's tiny coffin was consigned to the cemetery, that Jeanne's remaining child, young Marcel Weber, died. Cause of death, 'diphtheria' – and red marks around his neck.

The Webers were a large family, and on 5 April, Jeanne Weber was baby-sitting still another sister-in-law's offspring, one-year-old Maurice, while his mother went to the shops. When she returned, the boy was blue in the face, convulsed and foaming at the mouth. This time the victim's life was saved by prompt attention from the doctors at the Hôpital Bretonneau, and Maurice's mother promptly charged Jeanne with murder – family or not!

Madame Weber appeared before the Seine Assizes at the end of January 1906, and largely due to the sympathetic evidence given by Dr Leon Thoinot, the government pathologist in charge of the exhumations and post-mortems, Jeanne was acquitted. But her reputation had not gone unscarred and, childless, friendless, and recently deserted by her husband, Jeanne Weber moved out of the city to the village of Chambon. Here she became in quick succession first the housekeeper and then the mistress of a man named Bavouzet. Part of the attraction was no doubt Monsieur's three small children. The first tragedy to strike the house was the death of nine-year-old Auguste from 'convulsions resulting from an irritation of the meninges'. The second tragedy – for Jeanne at least – was that Auguste's sister was rummaging in Madame's handbag when she found a bundle of press cuttings covering the trial in Paris and showing a picture of Jeanne Weber titled 'L'Ogresse de la Goutte d'Or'. Discovery led to Jeanne's arrest for the second time and arraignment on another murder charge.

Again, despite extensive bruising of the neck, Dr Thoinot rejected death by manual strangulation in favour of 'typhoid fever', and Madame was, this time to the great approbation of a fickle public, acquitted for a second time.

During a short period of employment in a sanatorium, Jeanne was found with her fingers round the throat of a struggling small boy who was choking to death. The child recovered, but Madame Weber's career in nursing was at an end.

In 1908, the spectre of L'Ogresse appeared again before an astonished French public. Jeanne Weber was now living as the wife of a lime-burner named Emile Bouchery at Commercy, and they lodged at the inn kept by a couple named Poirot. The Poirots had two small children, and one night in May while Bouchery was away at work, Jeanne asked if seven-year-old Marcel might sleep in her room as she became anxious being alone at night.

In the dark of night, the inn was rent with screaming, and when an alarmed Monsieur Poirot burst into the Boucherys' room there was Marcel, his face discoloured and bloody, dead. Pacing the room was a highly agitated and incoherent Jeanne Weber, her hands and clothes smeared with the child's blood.

This final act had clearly loosened completely Madame Weber's already limited grip on sanity, and she was certified as a 'suitable inmate for close confinement'. Jeanne Weber was committed to an insane asylum where she died two years later, in 1910, as the result of injuries sustained trying to strangle herself.

WEIDMANN, Eugen Weidmann had been born at Frankfurt-on-Main on 5 February 1908, and his easy facility with other European languages enabled him to pass as English or French as well as his native German. It was a useful attribute for any international crook, and Weidmann travelled to Paris after an unsympathetic German court had obliged him to spend five years in prison for various currency swindles.

In July 1937, now calling himself Hunter and passing as a Swiss national, Weidmann ingratiated himself with a young American dancer named Jean de Koven, whom he persuaded back to his villa. Miss de Koven was never seen alive again, though her body was later found in the villa's cellar.

On 3 September of the same year, French police were investigating the apparent disappearance of a car-hire driver named Joseph Couffy, who had recently been hired by an American calling himself Dixon. Five days later Couffy's body was found beside the Paris–Orléans road shot through the nape of the neck and robbed of what modest possessions he had. In October, Jeanine Keller answered an advertisement offering a trip to South America and was invited by two men to meet them at Fontainebleau; it was an outing from which she never returned, her strangled corpse being pushed into a cave in the woods.

Later, on 17 October, a car was found abandoned outside a cemetery at Neuilly-sur-Seine, a suburb of Paris. Under a tarpaulin in the back was the body of theatrical agent Roger Le Blond. He had been shot through the back of the neck and robbed; he had last been seen in the company of two young men and a woman.

On 20 November, estate agent Raymond Lesobre took a client using the appropriate name of Schott to view a property at Saint-Cloud and was later found at the bottom of the cellar steps – a bullet in his neck and his wallet missing.

This last killing led police to investigate a local Saint-Cloud man called Siegfried Sauerbrey. When officers arrived at his home on 8 December they were met by a man calling himself Karrer who shot and wounded two policemen before being overpowered and placed under arrest. With little effort it was established that Karrer was Sauerbrey who was in reality Eugen Weidmann – alias Schott, Dixon, Hunter and various other names, nationalities and professions.

With a little more effort, Weidmann was persuaded to admit to the series of murders, obligingly adding a further victim, German compatriot Arthur Frommer. He also implicated his companions in crime, two Frenchmen named Roger Million and Jean Blanc and his girl-friend Colette Tricot.

Eventually, Weidmann was charged with six and Million two murders. Blanc was indicted for harbouring criminals and Mademoiselle Tricot for receiving stolen property. Their trial at Versailles in March 1939, resulted in death sentences for Weidmann and Million, twenty months' imprisonment for Jean Blanc, and Colette Tricot was acquitted of receiving. Million was finally reprieved, and Eugen Weidmann was guillotined on 18 May, having the doubtful distinction of being the last person publicly executed in France.

'WIDOW OF WINDY NOOK' *see* **WILSON, Mary Elizabeth**

WILLIAMS, Wayne B.   Not only was the whole of Atlanta caught
in a wave of terror, but at the rate of a quarter of a million dollars a
month the investigation into the series of killings that had become
known as the 'Atlanta Child Murders' was in danger of breaking the
municipal bank. So widespread had the fear become that from the
White House in Washington DC President Ronald Reagan had
pledged a government grant of one and a half million dollars towards
expenses; and celebrities including Burt Reynolds, Sammy Davis Jnr
and Frank Sinatra had dug into their pockets during fund-raising
events.

The first murders had occurred in July 1979, and the bodies were
identified as black youths Edward Smith and Alfred Evans. A third
teenager, Milton Harvey, disappeared in September, and on 21
October nine-year-old Yusuf Bell, son of civil-rights leader Camille
Bell, had disappeared while out on an errand. Afterwards the bodies
began to turn up – the decomposed corpse of Milton Harvey and then
the body of little Yusuf Bell, stuffed under the floor of an abandoned
school building. The disappearances began to accelerate. In March
1980, twelve-year-old Angel Laner was found raped and choked; in
May, Eric Middlebrooks; Christopher Richardson in early June – and
so on and on.

With all the victims black children, it was not an unreasonable fear
among the black community that this was the work of a white racist.
It was an unlikely theory for two reasons – first, all the children were
taken in the kind of black neighbourhood where a white face would
stand out; secondly, serial killers – indeed the majority of murderers –
tend to kill within their own ethnic group, black on black, white on
white.

After one year of killings – seven, with three more children missing
– there was not the glimmer of a breakthrough, and a genuine fear
existed among blacks that the police were less than 100 per cent
enthusiastic in their search because the children were not middle-class
whites. Still the count was rising, and with the panic, the theories
grew wilder – perhaps it was a *policeman*; after all, he would arouse
almost no suspicion.

By May 1981, twenty-six children were dead and one still missing.
On 22 May, a man was seen getting into a station wagon near the
Chattahoochee river just after a loud splash had been heard. The
driver of the car – a young black man named Wayne Williams – was
questioned and, short of any evidence to hold him on, released but
placed under strict surveillance. Two days later the body of Nathaniel
Cater was recovered from the water – the fifth to have been disposed
of in this way. Forensic tests established that dog hairs on Nathaniel's

clothing matched hairs taken from the rear of Williams's car; in fact they were also similar to hairs found on no fewer than ten of the victims' bodies. Now witnesses began to come forward claiming to have seen Williams and Cater together just before the youth's disappearance; others to testify that Williams had sexually molested them.

Wayne Williams was put on trial at the end of 1981 charged with two counts of murder. Although much of the evidence was circumstantial, the forensic evidence was impresive, and though it may not amount to scientific proof, it did not go unnoticed that since Wayne Williams had been in custody, the 'Atlanta Child Murders' had stopped. In February 1982, Williams was found guilty and sentenced to two terms of life imprisonment.

It would be comforting to think that the case ended there. But since Wayne Williams was incarcerated, considerable doubt has been expressed on the safety of his conviction. One allegation has been that there was evidence, suppressed during the investigation and trial, that linked the Atlanta killings – the 'Wayne Williams Killings' – with the activities of the Ku Klux Klan. In 1986, Williams' lawyers were granted permission to take depositions regarding statements made by some members of the Klan. There is no shortage of support for a re-opening of the case, and it is possible that there are still some surprises to come in the case of the 'Atlanta Child Murders'.

WILLIAMS-GALLEGO, Charlene *see* GALLEGO, Gerald

WILSON, Catherine   We can not be sure whether Catherine really did have any professional support for her claim to be a nurse, though it seems unlikely. At a time when few cared about such matters it was not difficult by offering a few kind words and bogus nostrums to win the confidence of the fearful and gullible. Between the years 1853 and 1862, first in Spalding, Lincolnshire, and then in Kirkby Lonsdale, Cumbria, Catherine Wilson made a very good living out of just that kind of 'service' – ingratiating herself with wealthy invalids until such time as they were prepared to express their gratitude through a hefty bequest – and then poisoning them.

Catherine almost went too far when she killed a drunken and quarrelsome husband by the name of Dixon. The problem was that the physicians insisted on carrying out a post-mortem, and it required one of the most desperate performances of her life when Catherine Wilson pleaded with the doctors not to open her husband up: 'For he was always horrified at the thought of his poor body being mutilated.' Say what you will, Mrs Wilson was nothing if not persuasive; and by the time the understanding doctors had allowed her to get the corpse under a good six feet of earth, Catherine was up to her old tricks again.

In 1862, she was living as resident nurse to a Mrs Sarah Connell and her husband. Perhaps Catherine was losing her touch, for no sooner had Mrs Connell made out a new will in her favour, and Kate had begun to feed her patient on poisons, than things started to go decidedly wrong. Perhaps it was Catherine's unsubtle choice of poison!

After taking a single mouthful of the 'herbal cup' Mrs Connell screamed, spat out the liquid and screamed again – even louder. When her husband reached the sick-room, the soothing broth with which Mrs Wilson had sought to ease her patient's discomfort had begun to burn holes in the floor coverings. It was, according to the analyst to whom Connell took it, sulphuric acid.

Though Catherine Wilson fled to London, it was not far enough to escape the long arm of justice. It is an irony that her plea that the chemist who made up Mrs Connell's prescription got it wrong prevailed – and the charge of murder was dropped.

However, by this time investigations into Catherine Wilson's past and the exhumation of a number of former 'patients' had revealed a further seven murder charges to answer. Mrs Wilson was tried first for the attempted murder of Mrs Connell and acquitted. She was re-arrested as she left the dock on 25 September 1862, and charged with the murders of two other women, and finally convicted of the murder of a Mrs Soames. Despite her emphatic denials, 'Nurse' Catherine Wilson gasped her last on the scaffold outside Newgate on 20 October 1862. It may or may not have gratified her that she attracted no less than 20,000 spectators to watch her hang.

WILSON, Mary Elizabeth   There was hardly a good thing to be said about Mrs Wilson, not least because of the cruel way in which, having inflicted the excruciatingly painful death of poisoning with phosphorus on her husband of forty-three years, she went on to dispose of a lover and two further husbands.

At the time of her trial for the two latter murders, Mary Wilson was sixty-six years old, plump, arrogant and grasping, and exhibited most of the least endearing characteristics of her working-class up-bringing – notably the inclination to seek recreation in heavy drinking.

Mary's first husband had been John Knowles, a labourer, and the son of the household to whom she was in service. Displaying an early greed for everything, Mrs Knowles took John George Russell, a chimney sweep who lodged with them at Windy Nook, as a lover. By 1957 both were dead, both certified as the victims of 'natural causes'; both leaving their worldly goods to Mary – all £46 of it!

During the summer of 1957, Mary met Oliver James Leonard; she was sixty-four at the time and he was seventy-five, a retired estate agent. As with her previous 'attachments', it was money to which Mrs Wilson was attracted, a fact that she made no secret of when enquiring of Leonard's landlady, 'Has the old bugger any money?' Apparently he had – or at least sufficient to satisfy Mary Wilson. In a trice, she was Mrs Leonard, the marriage being solemnised in September 1957 at Jarrow Register Office; almost as quickly, Oliver Leonard fell ill. Thirteen days after the wedding Mrs Russell, a neighbour, was called in during the night and found Leonard in such a poor state that she was constrained to comment that she believed he might be dying. 'I think so too,' Mrs Wilson replied, 'I've called you because you will be handy if he does.' By the following morning Oliver Leonard was, indeed, dead, and after a cursory examination the doctor accounted for his sudden demise as due to myocardial degeneration and chronic nephritis. His wife had bettered her lot by £50.

The next death to occur by Mrs Wilson's hand was that of her namesake, Ernest Wilson. Like Oliver Leonard, Wilson had also reached his seventy-fifth year; like Leonard, he was fated not to reach his seventy-sixth. Mrs Wilson saw the immediate advantage of marriage when Ernest confided that in addition to being provident enough to have a fully paid-up insurance policy on his life, he also had £100 invested with the Co-op. No sooner had Mary moved into the rather squalid bungalow which Wilson rented from the council than the old man suddenly died – of what the doctor diagnosed as 'cardiac muscular failure'.

It was only now that Mrs Wilson's 'jokes' – in poor taste even at the time – began to be seen in a decidedly sinister light. She had, for example, joshed with the undertaker that as she had put so much business his way, perhaps she was entitled to 'trade' price. Then at the modest reception after her marriage to Wilson, Mary had told the caterer, 'Save the left-over cakes – they will come in handy for the funeral,' adding later, 'Better not save them, I might give him a bit longer to live.'

Little surprise, then, that Mary Wilson came to the attention of the police; no surprise that the bodies of Messrs Leonard and Wilson were exhumed for post-mortem examination. The conclusion reached by pathologists Dr William Stewart and Dr David Price was that both men had died of phosphorus poisoning.

Mary Wilson was defended at her trial by Miss Rose Heilbron QC, who pointed out to the court that at that time phosphorus poisoning was relatively little known to forensic medicine – indeed, Dr Stewart had never seen a case previously – and that as the rate of oxidisation of phosphorus was then unknown, there was no reliable method of assessing how much of the poison had been ingested. It was advanced that both victims might have been taking sex-stimulant pills, one of whose ingredients was phosphorus. Miss Heilbron had also been wise enough to secure for the defence an expert medical witness of no less standing than Professor Francis Camps, destined to become one of Britain's most celebrated forensic pathologists. Whilst Camps had not examined the two bodies in question, he was familiar with several instances of phosphorus poisoning, and stated that, in his opinion, this was not necessarily the direct cause of death in the cases of Leonard and Wilson.

Mary Wilson did not give evidence on her own behalf, which prompted Mr Justice Hinchcliffe to remark, rightly or wrongly, 'Has she helped us all she could?' As to the preposterous notion of sex-stimulant pills, his lordship suggested that it should be given 'as much weight as it deserves'.

Found guilty as charged, Mrs Wilson was sentenced to death, though in the event her advanced years earned her the clemency she had done nothing to deserve. She served just four and a half years of a life sentence before dying in Holloway Prison, aged seventy.

It only remains to add that when the bodies of John Knowles and John George Russell were exhumed for pathological examination, they were found to contain appreciable traces of phosphorus.

'WOLF MAN' *see* **LUPO, Michael**

WOOD, Catherine *see* **GRAHAM, Gwendolyn Gail**

WOODFIELD, Randall Brent   It was at the beginning of 1981 that the press and television stations around Washington and Oregon first made an anxious population aware of the existence of a phantom killer who would soon be given the *nom de guerre* 'The I-5 Killer', and who would soon be distributing more victims along the Interstate 5.

On the evening of 18 January 1981, two twenty-year-old office cleaners, Lisa Garcia and Shari Hull, were leaving work in Salem, Oregon, when they were forced at gunpoint to remove their clothing and submit to a series of sexual indecencies; their attacker then forced the two young women to lie face down on the floor and shot them – Shari Hull three times, Lisa Garcia twice – in the head. Miraculously both victims were still alive when the man fled, though Shari Hull died later. In the meantime, with unbelievable determination, Lisa Garcia dragged herself, bleeding heavily from her wounds, to a telephone and summoned the police. Miss Garcia's description of Shari's killer materially matched that of a man wanted for questioning over a number of rapes and robberies committed in the same broad geographical area around the I-5 freeway.

By February no suspect had been apprehended when a man broke into a house at Redding, California, and raped and murdered the occupant's wife and stepdaughter. Less than two weeks later, at Beaverton, a suburb of Portland, a teenage girl was shot dead in her home. It was while detectives were checking out this last victim's friends and acquaintances that they turned up the name 'Randy' Woodfield. Although he knew the girl only slightly Woodfield did have a record of sex offences, and only two years previously had been released on parole after serving a sentence for robbery. A search of Woodfield's home revealed clues linking him with the attack on Shari

Hull and Lisa Garcia and, on charges arising from these crimes, he was arrested for murder and attempted murder, with positive identification provided by Lisa Garcia. Although Woodfield offered the alibi of being in a bar on the evening of the shootings, it was a weak and uncorroborated defence which in combination with his own admission that he had previously purchased a gun, convinced the jury to convict, and the judge to sentence Woodfield to life imprisonment. He was later convicted on charges arising from both the Redding and Beaverton incidents.

At the time of his arrest, 'Randy' Woodfield was thirty years old and working as a bartender in Beaverton. At college he had been an outstanding football player with every prospect of breaking into the full-time professional game. His problems seem to have begun when he was rejected by the Green Bay Packers team after only one tryout. Accustomed to 'hero' status, this apparent failure can be associated with his subsequent sociopathic behaviour and the need to recover the imagined loss of status by control-motivated crimes like rape – of which it is confidently estimated that he committed more than sixty – and murder, taking the need to dominate to the ultimate extreme. Indications are that Randall Woodfield was responsible for the deaths of between twelve and eighteen young women along the Interstate 5.

WORRELL, Chris *see* **MILLER, James William**

Y

'YORKSHIRE RIPPER' *see* SUTCLIFFE, Peter

YOUNG, Graham　Few killers, once convicted, get a second chance to commit murder; and those who do seldom take it. Graham Young was one of the exceptions.

In 1961, when he was fourteen, Young extended his youthful passion for chemistry, and in particular explosives, to embrace poisons and their effects on the human body. This piece of research culminated in the administration of small doses of antimony tartrate to members of his immediate family. His sister began to suffer regular stomach upsets, and in April 1962 his stepmother died. As the boy continued to lace his father's and sister's food and drink, they became increasingly ill, Winifred eventually being diagnosed suffering from belladonna poisoning. His father, by this time confined to hospital, was diagnosed as suffering from arsenic poisoning. Young's response was a disdainful, 'How ridiculous not being able to tell the difference between arsenic and antimony poisoning!'

When Graham Young was taken into custody by the police he was found to have several packets of antimony tartrate in his pockets and tucked in his shirt. Not that he would have dreamed of denying his guilt – indeed, Young readily confessed that although he had great affection for his family, they were, nevertheless, expendable. Not surprisingly, at his trial he was found guilty but insane and removed to Broadmoor.

Nine years later, in 1971, Graham Young, presumed 'cured', was free and working for Hadland, a photographic instruments firm in Bovingdon, Hertfordshire. In June – just weeks after Young had joined the company – sixty-year-old Bob Egle, the head storeman, was taken ill at work suffering diarrhoea, nausea, extreme backache and numbness in the tips of his fingers. After eight days of intense pain, Egle died in hospital of what was attributed to broncho-pneumonia and polyneuritis. Meanwhile, Ronald Hewitt, another employee, had been suffering similar symptoms which continued until he left the firm two days after Egle's death.

In September 1971 another of the workforce fell ill – sixty-year-old Fred Biggs. The symptoms were the familiar ones shared by Bob Egle and Ronald Hewitt. Later in the same month Peter Buck fell ill, and during the next month David Tilson, a clerk, and Jethro Batt, a storeman, also fell victim to what was now being called the 'Bovingdon Bug'. Both men grew gradually worse, and on 4 November Fred Biggs was admitted to hospital; the following day he was joined by Jethro Batt. On the 19th Biggs died.

Management now held a full medical enquiry into conditions at the plant in an attempt to defuse mounting panic. A medical team met with the entire workforce in the canteen, where Dr Arthur Anderson, head of the investigation, answered employees' questions. He was quite unprepared, though, for the barrage shot at him by one particular member of staff, in fact he was quite taken aback when Graham Young concluded his outburst with the question, 'Do you not think, doctor, that the symptoms of the mysterious illness are consistent with thallium poisoning?'

At this point, Hadland's management decided to check into the background of this smart-alec youth, and within hours of them learning that he had just been released from Broadmoor, Graham Young was again in custody.

'I could have killed them all if I wished,' Young told the police, 'as I did Bob Egle and Fred Biggs. But I allowed them to live.'

In July 1972 Graham Young was put on trial at St Albans for the murder of Egle and Biggs; he now pleaded not guilty. Throughout the trial it was evident that he was having the time of his life – an opportunity to show just how clever he was! Incriminating extracts from his diary were read to the court: 'October 30 [1971]. I have administered a fatal dose of the special compound to F[red Biggs], and anticipate a report on his progress on Monday 1st November. I gave him three separate doses.'

The diary entries, he claimed, were simply working notes for a novel that he was writing. The jury, however, were unconvinced, and Graham Young was once again removed from free society.

In August 1990, warders making a routine check on Young's cell at Parkhurst Prison found him lying crumpled on the floor. Rushed to the prison hospital Young was found to have died from a heart attack; he was forty-two years old.

Z

'ZEBRA KILLINGS' A terrifying example of black racism, the 'Zebra Killings', so called because all the offenders were black and all the victims white, took place during 179 days during the last months of 1973 and early 1974. In all, the five killers left a total of fifteen men, women and children dead – all of them selected totally at random and quite unknown to their assassins; their only 'crime' was to be white. A further eight victims were seriously wounded, several paralysed for life.

At the root of the slayings was the desire of five black ex-convicts, Jesse Cooke, Larry Greene, Anthony Harris, Manuel Moore and J.C. Simon, to earn entry into the elite force of assassins known as the 'Death Angels'. The Angels were backed by the Black Muslims of California, and committed to black supremacy and the annihilation of all 'white devils'. Qualification for membership of the 'Angels' was unvarying – the murder of at least nine white men, or five white women, or four white children. Already in California the police were looking into an alarming tally of unsolved murders – 135 men, seventy-five women, and sixty children, most thought to result from the activities of the Death Angels.

The new hopefuls, who had been indoctrinated into racial hatred at meetings of the Black Muslims, patrolled San Francisco in twos and threes, picking off people randomly at bus stops, in telephone kiosks, late-night launderettes, etc. One woman was additionally raped, and one still unidentified man was abducted, tortured and butchered alive.

Police response to public panic was a massive blanket operation in the black districts of the city, straining an already uneasy relationship between the ethnic minorities and the forces of law. Thousands of blacks were taken off the streets and interrogated, but in the end it was one of 'Zebra's' own members, Anthony Harris, who made a detailed confession and implicated his four collaborators.

On 1 May 1974, a squad of one hundred police officers stormed apartment blocks around the city and made seven arrests.

The resulting trial of four of the men responsible for the 'Zebra' murders – Anthony Harris not being tried at this stage because he had turned state's evidence – opened before Supreme Court Judge Joseph Karesh on 3 March 1975; it became the longest in California's legal history, lasting for one year and six days. One hundred and eighty-one witnesses were called, and Anthony Harris spent a total of twelve days on the stand giving evidence. Finally the jury returned unanimous verdicts of guilty on all four defendants, who were each given life sentences which they are now serving, two in Folsom Prison, two in San Quentin.

'ZODIAC' In California during the nine-month period 20 December 1968 to 11 October 1969, a still undetected killer took five lives and left two other victims wounded. The first murders occurred near Vallejo, outside San Francisco. In a 'lovers' lane' two teenagers, David Faraday and Bettilou Jensen, had been shot dead beside their station wagon. On 5 July 1969, a man with a 'gruff' voice telephoned to the Vallejo Police Department to report a double murder: 'If you will go one mile east on Columbus Parkway to a public park, you will find the kids in a brown car. They have been shot with a 9 mm Luger. I also killed those kids last year. Good-bye.' As they had been warned, the police found Darlene Ferrin dead of gunshot wounds, and Michael Mageau seriously injured.

Michael Mageau, when he had recovered sufficiently from his ordeal, described their assailant as about twenty-five to thirty years old, stockily built, with a round face and wavy brown hair. On 1 August, the *Times-Herald* of Vallejo and two newspapers in San Francisco received letters signed with a kind of cross superimposed on a circle which is the symbol of the zodiac. The letters contained sufficient detail to exclude anybody but the killer from being their author. At the bottom of each of the letters were lines of cipher which, the writer claimed, if the code was broken would reveal his identity. In fact it did not, but it was nevertheless a remarkable statement of what the killer thought was his motive: 'I like to kill people because it is so much fun. It is more fun than killing wild game in the forest, because Man is the most dangerous animal of all. To kill something gives me the most thrilling experience. It is even better than [sex]. The best part [will be] when I die. I will be reborn in Paradise, and then all I have killed will become my slaves. I will not give you my name because you will try to slow or stop my collecting of slaves for my afterlife.'

The man with the gruff voice telephoned the Napa Police Department on 27 September to report another double killing. It was almost as he had described it; in a parked car on the shore of Lake Verriesa Cecilia Shepherd and Bryan Hartnell, students at Pacific Union College, were lying bound and soaked in their own blood. The girl was dead, but Mr Hartnell survived and was able to tell the police that the man who had stabbed them was wearing a black mask with eye-slits and the zodiac sign painted on it in white. Through the eye-holes he could see a pair of spectacles, and the stocky build and light brown hair matched the description of 'Zodiac' given by Michael Mageau.

The last known victim was a taxi driver named Paul Stine, who was shot dead in his cab and robbed in San Francisco. On the following day the editor of San Francisco's *Chronicle* received a Zodiac letter threatening to kill a bus-load of children, and enclosing a piece of bloody cloth that had been cut from Paul Stine's shirt.

Zodiac now began to manipulate the media as never before. On 21 October he telephoned the Oakland police offering to give himself up if he could be represented by a famous lawyer – he suggested somebody of the distinction of Melvin Belli or F. Lee Bailey. Then he demanded air-time on an early morning television chat show. Ratings had never been so high as viewers tuned in to watch the Jim Dunbar Show. At 7.41 a man with what was described as a 'soft, boyish voice' came on the phone line and discussed the murders and his own health problems (it appeared he suffered from severe headaches, the implications being that they were the cause of his violence). He spoke at length with Melvin Belli who was in the studio, and whom Zodiac agreed to meet in a public place in Daly City. He failed to keep the appointment.

Although the few people who had heard Zodiac speak before could not identify him with the voice on televison, it is likely that any impostor would have been vigorously denounced by the real killer; Zodiac was clearly not the sort of man to share his limelight. Besides, Melvin Belli subsequently received an identifiable Zodiac letter containing a second piece of the taxi driver's shirt. Although the letter threatened to kill again, nothing more was heard from Zodiac until the *Los Angeles Times* received a letter in March 1971, commenting, 'If the blue menaces are ever going to catch me, they had better get off their fat butts and do something.' In 1974, the San Francisco Police Department received a Zodiac letter claiming a total of thirty-seven killings (almost certainly an exaggeration) and threatening to 'do something nasty'. All these letters were proved to have a common origin, and despite his self-publicity and that given to him by an eager media machine, Zodiac was never caught, nor, as far as we can know, did he kill again.

ZWANZIGER, Anna Maria   Born Anna Shoenleben in Buremberg, Germany, in 1760, she was courted by and eventually married a lawyer named Zwanziger. By the time he collapsed and died, Zwanziger had drunk his way through every last pfennig of their savings, leaving the widow nothing but debts and a bleak future as a domestic servant. After too many years of thankless, back-breaking, soul-destroying drudgery, the once beautiful, once vivacious Anna Maria had become a twisted, spiteful harridan, old before her years.

She was in service at the time of her first murder with a judge named Glaser who, though he had not yet altered his will, had nevertheless separated from his wife and was about to disinherit her. With the cunning born of hatred Anna Maria sought, and at least temporarily achieved, a reconciliation between Judge Glaser and his estranged wife. Within weeks the unfortunate woman was dead, and before anyone could say 'poison', the widow Zwanziger had moved on, into the service of a middle-aged judge named Grohmann. Although she proved a loyal and devoted servant, Anna Maria was not fated to share in her master's fortune, for he announced his forthcoming marriage, and the piqued domestic found no alternative but to dispose of her employer forthwith; and just for the fun of it she poisoned a few of her fellow servants as well.

Frau Zwanziger's luck nearly ran out when she tried to poison the already ailing wife of her next employer, another judge, named Gebhard. Although his wife complained that the housekeeper was trying to poison her, the judge dismissed the accusation as nonsense and Frau Gebhard shortly perished; she was followed into her grave by the Gebhards' baby. Even then it was not until the judge himself began to suffer uncommonly bad stomach upsets, which seemed to be connected with the strange sediment in the bottom of his brandy glass, that he parcelled up a number of suspect comestibles and sent them to the apothecary for analysis. The contents of the salt cellar alone proved to be almost pure arsenic, and when Frau Gebhard and her child were exhumed, they also contained uncommonly large quantities of the same poison.

Anna Maria Zwanziger was taken into custody in Bayreuth in October 1809. Of course, she denied all the accusations made against her, but when she was proved to be in possession of a number of incriminating packets of white arsenic the dour domestic broke down and confessed. She was put to the headsman's sword in 1811.

Select Bibliography

'ANGEL MAKERS OF NAGYREV'
The World's Worst Women, Bernard O'Donnell, W.H. Allen, London, 1953.

ARCHER-GILLIGAN, Amy
Famous American Poison Mysteries, Edward H. Smith, Hurst and Blackett, London, [no date: n.d. hereafter].

AXEMAN OF NEW ORLEANS
Murder in New Orleans, Robert Tallant, William Kimber, London, 1953.

BALL, Joe
Crimes of Passion, Edward D. Radin, Digit Books, New York, 1953.

BECK, Martha and FERNANDEZ, Raymond
Introduction to Murder, Wenzell Brown, Dakers, London, 1953.
The Honeymoon Killers, Pearl Buck, Sphere Books, London, 1970.

BECKER, Marie
The World's Worst Women, Bernard O'Donnell, W.H. Allen, London, 1953.

BERKOWITZ, David
Confessions of Son of Sam, David Abrahamsen, Columbia University Press, New York, 1985.
Son of Sam, George Carpozi, Manor Books, New York, 1977.
Son of Sam, Lawrence Klausner, McGraw Hill, New York, 1981.

BIANCHI, Kenneth Alessio, and BUONO, Angelo
The Hillside Strangler, Ted Schwartz, Doubleday, New York, 1981.
Two of a Kind, Darcy O'Brien, New American Library, New York, 1985.

'BIBLE JOHN'
Bible John, Charles Stoddart, Paul Harris, Edinburgh, 1980.

BILLIK, Herman
Famous American Poison Mysteries, Edward H. Smith, Hurst and Blackett, London, [n.d.].

BINGHAM CASE
The Trials of Mr Justice Avory, Bernard O'Donnell, Rich and Cowan, London, 1935.

BITTAKER, Lawrence and NORRIS, Roy
Alone with the Devil, Ronald Markman and Dominic Bosco, Doubleday, New York, 1989.

BOLBER, Dr Morris, *et al.*
Murder, Mayhem and Mystery, Alan Hynd, Barnes, New York, 1958.

BOOST, Werner
The Manhunters, Peter Deeley, Hodder and Stoughton, London, 1970.

BRADY, Ian and **HINDLEY, Myra**
Beyond Belief, Emlyn Williams, Hamish Hamilton, London, 1967.
Celebrated Trials, ed. Jonathan Goodman, David and Charles, Newton Abbot, 1973.

BRINVILLIERS, Marie Marguerite
Madame de Brinvilliers, Hugh Stokes, Thomas Nelson, London, 1912.
Enchanting Little Lady, Virginia Vernon, Abelard-Schumann, London, 1964.

BRUDOS, Jerry
Lust Killer, Andy Stack (Ann Rule), New American Library, New York, 1983.

BUNDY, Theodore ('Ted')
Bundy – The Deliberate Stranger, Richard W. Larsen, Prentice-Hall, New York, 1980.
The Only Living Witness, Stephen Michaud and Hugh Aynesworth, Linden Press, New York, 1980.
The Stranger Beside Me, Ann Rule, Norton, New York, 1988.

BURKE, William and **HARE, William**
Notable British Trials, ed. William Roughead, Hodge, London, 1948.
The West Port Murders, Anon, Thomas Ireland, Edinburgh, 1829.
Burke and Hare; The Resurrection Men, Jacques Barzun, Scarecrow Press, New Jersey, 1974.

BURROWS, Erskine Durrant and **TACKLYN, Larry Winfield**
Strictly Murder, Tom Tullett, Bodley Head, London, 1979.

BUTCHER OF KINGSBURY RUN
Torso, Steven Nickel, John F. Blair, North Carolina, 1989.

CARIGNAN, Harvey
The Want-Ad Killer, Andy Stack (Ann Rule), New American Library, New York, 1983.

CARPENTER, David J.
The Sleeping Lady, Robert Graysmith, Dutton, New York, 1991.

CARSON, James and Susan
Cry For War, Richard D. Reynolds, Squibob Press, San Francisco, 1987.

CHAPMAN, George
Notable British Trials, ed. H.L. Adam, Hodge, London, 1930.

CHASE, Richard
Alone with the Devil, Ronald Markman and Dominic Bosco, Doubleday, New York, 1989.

CHRISTIE, John Reginald Halliday
Notable British Trials, ed. F. Tennyson Jesse, Hodge, London, 1957.
Ten Rillington Place, Ludovic Kennedy, Gollancz, London, 1961.

CLEMENTS, Dr Robert George
A Scientist Turns to Crime, Dr J.B. Firth, William Kimber, London, 1960.

CLINE, Alfred Leonard
45 Murders, Craig Rice, Simon and Schuster, New York, 1952.

COLLINS, Norman John
The Michigan Murders, Edward Keyes, Reader's Digest, New York, 1976.

CONSTANZO, Adolfo de Jesus, *et al.*
Across the Border, Gary Provost, Pocket Books, New York, 1989.
Hell Ranch, Clifford L. Linedecker, Futura, London, 1990.

COOKE, Eric Edgar
Violent Australian Crimes, Michael Hervey, Cassell Australia, 1978.

CORLL, Dean Allen and HENLEY, Wayne Elmer
Mass Murder in Houston, John K. Gurwell, Cordovan Press, Houston, 1974.
The Man with the Candy, Jack Olsen, Talmy Franklin, New York, 1975.

CORONA, Juan Vallejo
Burden of Proof, Ed Cray, Macmillan, New York, 1973.
Jury, Victor Villasenor, Little Brown, Boston, 1974.
The Road to Yuba City, Tracy Kidder, Doubleday, New York, 1974.

COTTINGHAM, Richard Francis
The Prostitute Murders, Rod Leith, Lyle Stuart, New Jersey, 1983.

COTTON, Mary Ann
Mary Ann Cotton, Arthur Appleton, Michael Joseph, London, 1973.

CREAM, Dr Thomas Neill
Murder and Its Motives, F. Tennyson Jesse, Harrap, London, 1952.
Notable British Trials, ed. W. Teignmouth Shore, Hodge, London, 1923.

CUMMINS, Gordon Frederick
Cherrill of the Yard, Fred Cherrill, Harrap, London, 1952.

DAHMER, Jeffrey L.
The Milwaukee Murders, Don Davis, St Martin's Paperbacks, New York, 1991.

DEAN, Minnie
Famous New Zealand Murders, Dudley G. Dyne, Collins, Auckland, 1969.

DEEMING, Frederick
A Most Unique Ruffian, J.S. O'Sullivan, F.W. Cheshire, Melbourne, 1968.

DE MELKER, Daisy Louisa
Up For Murder, Benjamin Bennett, Hutchinson, London, 1934.

DE RAIS, Gilles
Gilles de Rais – The Authentic Bluebeard, Jean Benedetti, Peter Davies, London, 1971.
The Soul of Marshal Gilles de Raiz, D.B. Wyndham Lewis, Eyre and Spottiswoode, London, 1952.

DE SALVO, Albert
The Strangler!, Harold K. Banks, Mayflower-Dell, London, 1967.
The Boston Strangler, Gerold Frank, Cape, London, 1967.

DUFF-SIDNEY CASE
The Riddle of Birdhurst Rise, Richard Whittington-Egan, Harrap, London, 1975.

DUFFY, John Francis
Murder Under the Microscope, Philip Paul, Macdonald, London, 1990.

DUMOLLARD, Martin and Marie
Curious Trials and Criminal Cases, Edward Hale Bierstadt, Hutchinson, London, [n.d.].
Studies in Black and Red, Joseph Forster, Ward Downey, London, 1896.

DYER, Amelia Elizabeth
The Trials of Mr Justice Avory, Bernard O'Donnell, Rich and Cowan, London, 1935.

ENGLEMAN, Dr Glennon E.
Appointment for Murder, Susan Crain Bakos, Pinnacle, New York, 1989.

FIELD, Frederick Herbert Charles
Cornish of The Yard, G.W. Cornish, Bodley Head, London, 1935.

FISH, Albert
The Cannibal, Mel Heimer, Lyle Stuart, New York, 1971.
The Show of Violence, Fredric Wertham, Gollancz, London, 1949.

GACY, John Wayne
Buried Dreams, Tim Cahill, Bantam Books, New York, 1986.
Killer Clown, Terry Sullivan and Peter T. Maiken, Grosset and Dunlap, New York, 1983.
The Man Who Killed Boys, Clifford L. Linedecker, St Martin's Press, New York, 1980.

GALLEGO, Gerald Armand and **WILLIAMS-GALLEGO, Charlene**
All His Father's Sins, Ray Biondi and Walt Hecox, Prima Publishing, California, 1988.

GBUREK, Tillie
Some Like it Gory, John Kobler, Dodd Mead, New York, 1940.

GEIN, Edward
Deviant, Harold Schechter, Pocket Books, New York, 1989.
Edward Gein, Judge Robert H. Gollmar, Charles Hallberg, Wisconsin, 1982.

GIBBS, Janie
Satan's Assassins, Brad Steiger and Warren Smith, Lancer Books, New York, 1971.

GIUDICE, Giancarlo
Carnal Crimes, John Dunning, Arrow Books, London, 1988.

GLATMAN, Harvey Murray
Fallen Angels, Marvin J. Wolf and Katherine Mader, Ballantine Books, New York, 1988.

GOTTFRIED, Gesina Margaretha
Women Bluebeards, Elliott O'Donnell, Stanley Paul, London, [n.d.].

GREEN RIVER KILLER
The Search for the Green River Killer, Carlton Smith and Tomas Guillen, Onyx, New York, 1991.

GRILLS, Caroline
Famous Australasian Crimes, Tom Gurr and H.H. Cox, Muller, London, 1957.

GUNNESS, Belle
The Truth About Belle Gunness, Lilian de la Torre, Gold Medal, New York, 1955.
Belle Gunness, Janet L. Langlois, Indiana University Press, Bloomington, 1985.

HAARMANN, Fritz
Murder for Profit, William Bolitho, Cape, London, 1934.

HAHN, Anna Marie
The World's Worst Women, Bernard O'Donnell, W.H. Allen, London, 1953.

HAIGH, John George
The Acid Bath Murders, David Briffett, Field Place Press, W. Sussex, 1988.
Notable British Trials, ed. Lord Dunboyne, Hodge, London, 1953.

HATCHER, Charles
St Joseph's Children, Terry Ganey, Lyle Stuart, New York, 1989.

HEATH, Neville George Clevely
Notable British Trials, ed. Macdonald Critchley, Hodge, London, 1951.
Portrait of a Sadist, Paull Hill, Neville Spearman, London, 1960.

HEIRENS, William
Before I Kill More . . ., Lucy Freeman, Crown, New York, 1955.

'JACK THE RIPPER'
The Complete Jack the Ripper, Donald Rumbelow, W.H. Allen, London, 1975.
Jack the Ripper, Paul Begg, Robson Books, London, 1988.
Jack the Ripper in Fact and Fiction, Robin Odell, Harrap, London, 1965.

'JACK THE STRIPPER'
Found Naked and Dead, Brian McConnell, New English Library, London, 1974.

JEGADO, Hélène
Annals of Crime, W.H. Williamson, Routledge, London, 1930.
She Stands Accused, Victor MacClure, Harrap, London, 1935.

JOHNSON, Russell
Trail of Blood, Frank Jones, McGraw-Hill Ryerson, Toronto, 1981.

JONES, Genene
Deadly Medicine, Kelly Moore and Dan Read, St Martin's Press, New York, [n.d.].
The Death Shift, Peter Elkind, Onyx, New York, 1990.

JONES, Harold
The Life and Trial of Harold Jones, Lowden Macarthur, Burnside, Glasgow, [n.d.].

KEMPER, Edmund Emil
The Co-Ed Killer, Margaret Cheney, Walker and Co., New York, 1976.

KNOWLES, Paul John
Killing Time, Sandy Fawkes, Peter Owen, London, 1977.

KRAFT, Randy
Angel of Darkness, Dennis McDougal, Warner Books, New York, 1991.

KUKLINSKI, Richard
Unnatural Death, Michael M. Baden and Judith A. Hennessee, Random House, New York, 1989.

KURTEN, Peter
The Monster of Düsseldorf, Margaret Seaton Wagner, Faber and Faber, London, 1932.
Peter Kurten – A Study in Sadism, George Godwin, Acorn Press, London, 1938.
The Sadist, Karl Berg, Heinemann, London, 1945.

LANDRU, Henri Desiré
Famous Trials Series, F.A. Mackenzie, Bles, London, 1928.
The Ladykiller, Dennis Bardens, Peter Davies, London, 1972.
My Work at the Sûreté, Jean Belin, Harrap, London, 1950.

LEHMANN, Christa
The Power of Poison, Jurgen Thorwald, Thames and Hudson, London, 1966.

LEONSKI, Edward Joseph
Leonski – The Brown-Out Murders, Andrew Mallon, Outback Press, Victoria, 1979.
Leonski – The Brown-Out Strangler, Ivan Chapman, Hale and Iremonger, Sydney, 1982.

LEWINGDON, Gary James and Thaddeus Charles
Unveiling Claudia, Daniel Keyes, Bantam Books, New York, 1986.

LIM, Adrian *et al.*
Adrian Lim's Beastly Killings, N.G. Kutty, Aequitus, Singapore, 1989.
Unholy Trinity, Alan John, Times Books International, Singapore, 1989.

LINEVELT, Salie
The Noose Tightens, Benjamin Bennett, Howard Timmins, Cape Town, 1954.

LOPEZ, Pedro
The World's Most Infamous Murders, Roger Boar and Nigel Blundell, Octopus, London, 1983.

LUCAS, Henry Lee
The Confession of Henry Lee Lucas, Mike Cox, Pocket Star Books, New York, 1991.

LUPO, Michael
Murder in Low Places, Jonathan Goodman, Piatkus, London, 1988.
LYLES, Anjette
Satan's Assassins, Brad Steiger and Warren Smith, Lancer Books, New
 York, 1971.

McDONALD, William
Profiles in Murder, Oscar R. Schmalzbach, Hodder and Stoughton, Australia,
 1971.
MACKAY, Patrick David
Psychopath, Tim Clark and John Penycate, Routledge and Kegan Paul,
 London, 1976.
MANSON, Charles, *et al.*
The Manson Murders, Vincent Bugliosi and Curt Gentry, Bodley Head,
 London, 1975.
MANUEL, Peter
The Trial of Peter Manuel, John Gray Wilson, Secker and Warburg, London,
 1959.
The Hunting Down of Peter Manuel, John Bingham, Macmillan, London,
 1973.
MAREK, Martha
Crime Omnibus, Kurt Singer, W.H. Allen, London, 1961.
MAZURKIEWICZ, Wladyslaw
An International Casebook of Crime, H. Montgomery Hyde and John H.
 Kisch, Barrie and Rockliff, London, 1962.
MILLER, James William and **WORRELL, Chris**
It's a Long Way to Truro, Anne-Marie Mykyta, McPhee Gribble, Melbourne,
 1981.
MORS, Frederick
Famous American Poison Mysteries, Edward H. Smith, Hurst and Blackett,
 London, [n.d.].
MSOMI, Elifasi
Freedom or the Gallows, Benjamin Bennett, Howard Timmins, Cape Town,
 1956.
MUDGETT, Hermann Webster (aka H.H. Holmes)
The Girls in Nightmare House, Charles Boswell and Lewis Thompson, Gold
 Medal, London, [n.d.].
The Holmes-Pitezel Case, Frank P. Geyer, Philadelphia, 1896.
The Torture Doctor, David Franke, Hawthorn Books, New York, 1975.
MULLIN, Herbert
The Die Song, Donald T. Lunde and Jefferson Morgan, Norton, New York,
 1980.

NEILSON, Donald
The Black Panther Story, Steven Valentine, New English Library, London,
 1976.

The Capture of the Black Panther, Harry Hawkes, Harrap, London, 1978.

NILSEN, Dennis Andrew
Killing For Company, Brian Masters, Cape, London, 1985.

NORTHCOTT, Gordon Stewart
Some Like it Gory, John Kobler, Dodd Mead, New York, 1940.

PALMER, Dr William
Notable British Trials, ed. George Knott, Hodge, London, 1912.
The Life and Career of Dr William Palmer of Rugeley, George Fletcher, Fisher Unwin, London, 1925.

PANZRAM, Carl
Killer, Thomas E. Gaddis and James O. Long, Macmillan, New York, 1970.

PETIOT, Dr Marcel
The Great Liquidator, John V. Grombach, Sphere Books, London, 1982.
Petiot – Victim of Chance, Ronald Seth, Hutchinson, London, 1963.
The Unspeakable Crimes of Dr Petiot, Thomas Maeder, Little Brown, Boston, 1980.

PRITCHARD, Dr Edward William
Notable British Trials, ed. William Roughead, Hodge, London, 1906.

PUENTE, Dorothea
Human Harvest, Daniel J. Blackburn, Knightsbridge, New York, 1990.

RAMIREZ, Richard
Night Stalker, Clifford L. Linedecker, St Martin's Press, New York, 1991.

RENDALL, Martha
Infamous Australians, Andrew Dettre, Greg Keith and Penny Walker, Bay Books, Sydney, 1985.

RIVERA, Miguel
On the Track of Murder, Barbara Gelb, Morrow, New York, 1975.

RUDLOFF, Fritz
Detection Stranger than Fiction, Leo Grex, Hale, London, 1977.

SANDWENE, Ntimane
Famous South African Murders, Benjamin Bennett, Werner Laurie, London, 1938.

SARRET, Maître Georges
Crimes and Cases of 1933, Roland Wild, Rich and Cowan, London, 1934.

SCHMID, Charles Howard
The Pied Piper of Tucson, Don Moser and Jerry Cohen, Signet, New York, 1968.
The Tucson Murders, John Gilmore, Dial Press, New York, 1970.

SEARL, Ralph Ray
Luke Karamazov, Conrad Hilbery, Wayne State University Press, Detroit, 1987.

SEARL, Tommy
Luke Karamazov, Conrad Hilbery, Wayne State University Press, Detroit, 1987.

SHERMAN, Lydia
Instigation of the Devil, Edmund Pearson, Scribners, New York, 1930.

SINGH, Boysie
The Murders of Boysie Singh, Derek Bickerton, Arthur Barker, London, [n.d.].

SMITH, George Joseph
The Life and Death of a Ladykiller, Arthur LaBern, Leslie Frewin, London, 1967.
Notable British Trials, ed. Eric R. Watson, Hodge, London, 1949.

SOBHRAJ, Charles
The Life and Crimes of Charles Sobhraj, Richard Neville and Julie Clarke, Cape, London, 1979.
Serpentine, Thomas Thompson, Macdonald, London, 1980.

SODEMAN, Arnold Karl
Insanity and Injustice, J.P. Bourke and D.S. Sonnenberg, Jacaranda Press, Melbourne, 1969.

STRAFFEN, John Thomas
Notable British Trials, ed. Letitia Fairfield and Eric P. Fulbrook, Hodge, London, 1954.

SUTCLIFFE, Peter
Deliver Us From Evil, David A. Yallop, Macdonald, London, 1980.
. . . *Somebody's Husband, Somebody's Son,* Gordon Burn, Heinemann, London, 1984.

SZCZEPINSKI, Waldemar
Mindless Murder, John Dunning, Arrow Books, London, 1987.

TESSNOW, Ludwig
Dead Men Tell Tales, Jurgen Thorwald, Thames and Hudson, London, 1966.

TINNING, Marybeth
From Cradle to Grave, Joyce Egginton, W.H. Allen, London, 1989.

TORINUS, Metod
Madly Murderous, John Dunning, Hamlyn, London, 1985.

TORONTO HOSPITAL MURDERS
Death Shift, Ted Bissland, Methuen, Toronto, 1984.

VACHER, Joseph
Murder in France, Alister Kershaw, Constable, London, 1955.

WAINEWRIGHT, Thomas Griffiths
The Genteel Murderer, Charles Norman, Macmillan, London, 1956.
Janus Weathercock, Jonathan Curling, Nelson, London, 1938.
Suburban Gentleman, John Lindsey, Rich and Cowan, London, 1942.

WEBER, Jeanne
Dead Men Tell Tales, Jurgen Thorwald, Thames and Hudson, London, 1966.
WEIDMANN, Eugen
My Work at the Sûreté, Jean Belin, Harrap, London, 1950.
Comments on Cain, F. Tennyson Jesse, Heinemann, London, 1948.
WILLIAMS, Wayne B.
Evidence of Things Not Seen, James Baldwin, Michael Joseph, London, 1986.
The List, Chet Detlinger and Jeff Prugh, Philmay, Atlanta, 1983.
WILSON, Mary Elizabeth
The Laboratory Detectives, Norman Lucas, Barker, London, 1971.
WOODFIELD, Randall Brent
The I-5 Killer, Andy Stack (Ann Rule), New American Library, New York, 1984.

YOUNG, Graham
Obsessive Poisoner, Winifred Young, Robert Hale, London, 1973.
The St Albans Poisoner, Anthony Holden, Hodder and Stoughton, London, 1974.

'ZEBRA KILLINGS'
The Zebra Killings, Clark Howard, New English Library, London, [n.d.].
'ZODIAC'
Zodiac, Robert Graysmith, St Martin's Press, New York, 1986.
ZWANZIGER, Anna Maria
Narratives of Remarkable Criminal Trials, Anselm Ritter von Feuerbach, John Murray, London, 1846.
Women Bluebeards, Elliott O'Donnell, Stanley Paul, London, [n.d.].

General Reference Works

Crockett, Art, (ed.), *Serial Murderers from the Files of True Detective*, Pinnacle, New York, 1990.
Crockett, Art, (ed.), *Spree Killers from the Files of True Detective*, Pinnacle, New York, 1991.

Dickson, Grierson, *Murder by Numbers*, Robert Hale, London, 1958.
Douthwaite, L.C., *Mass Murder*, John Long, London, 1928.

Gaute, J.H.H., and Odell, Robin, *Murder 'Whatdunit'*, Harrap, London, 1982.
Gaute, J.H.H., and Odell, Robin, *Murder Whereabouts*, Harrap, London, 1986.
Gaute, J.H.H., and Odell, Robin, *The New Murderers' Who's Who*, Harrap, London, 1989.
Green, Jonathan, *The Directory of Infamy*, Mills and Boon, London, 1980.

Holmes, Ronald M., and De Burger, James, *Serial Murder*, Sage, California, 1987.

Levin, Jack, and Fox, James Alan, *Mass Murder*, Plenum Press, New York, 1986.
Leyton, Elliott, *Hunting Humans*, Pocket Books, New York, 1988.
Lindsay, Philip, *Mainspring of Murder*, John Long, London, 1958.
Linedecker, Clifford L., *Thrill Killers*, Paperjacks, New York, 1988.
Linedecker, Clifford L., *Serial Thrill Killers*, Knightsbridge, New York, 1990.
Linedecker, Clifford L., and Burt, William A., *Nurses Who Kill*, Pinnacle, New York, 1990.
Lloyd, Georgina, *One Was Not Enough*, Robert Hale, London, 1989.
Lucas, Norman, *The Child Killers*, Barker, London, 1970.
Lucas, Norman, *The Sex Killers*, W.H. Allen, London, 1974.

Mandelsberg, Rose G. (ed.), *Torture Killers from the Files of True Detective*, Pinnacle, New York, 1991.

Nash, J. Robert, *Bloodletters and Badmen*, Evans, New York, 1973.
Nash, J. Robert, *Murder, America*, Harrap, London, 1981.
Nash, J. Robert, *Compendium of World Crimes*, Harrap, London, 1983.
Nash, J. Robert, *Open Files*, McGraw-Hill, New York, 1983.
Nash, J. Robert, *Look for the Woman*, Harrap, London, 1984.

Nash, J. Robert, *Encyclopedia of World Crime* (6 volumes), Crime Books Inc., Wilmette, 1990.

Neustatter, W. Lindsay, *The Mind of the Murderer*, Christopher Johnson, London, 1957.

Newton, Michael, *Mass Murder: An Annotated Bibliography*, Garland, New York, 1988.

Norris, Joel, *Serial Killers*, Dolphin Doubleday, New York, 1988.

Scott, Sir Harold, *The Concise Encyclopaedia of Crime and Criminals*, Hawthorn, London, 1961.

Shew, E. Spencer, *A Companion to Murder*, Cassell, London, 1960.

Shew, E. Spencer, *A Second Companion to Murder*, Cassell, London, 1961.

Sifakis, Carl, *The Encyclopedia of American Crime*, Facts on File, New York, 1982.

Steiger, Brad, *The Mass Murderer*, Award Books, New York, 1967.

Thompson, C.J.S., *Poison Mysteries in History, Romance and Crime*, Scientific Publications, London, 1925.

Thompson, C.J.S., *Poisons and Poisoners*, Shaylor, London, 1931.

Tobias, Ronald, *They Shoot to Kill*, Paladin Press, Colorado, 1981.

Willcox, Philip H., *The Detective Physician*, Heinemann, London, 1970.

Wilson, Colin, *A Casebook of Murder*, Leslie Frewin, London, 1969.

Wilson, Colin, *Order of Assassins*, Hart-Davis, London, 1972.

Wilson, Colin, *A Criminal History of Mankind*, Granada, London, 1984.

Wilson, Colin, *The Mammoth Book of True Crime*, Robinson, London, 1988.

Wilson, Colin, *The Mammoth Book of True Crime 2*, Robinson, London 1990.

Wilson, Colin, *Written in Blood*, Equation, Wellingborough, 1989.

Wilson, Colin, and Pitman, Patricia, *Encyclopaedia of Murder*, Barker, London, 1961.

Wilson, Colin, and Seaman, Donald, *Encyclopaedia of Modern Murder*, Barker, London, 1983.

Wilson, Colin, and Seaman, Donald, *The Serial Killers*, W.H. Allen, London, 1990.

Wilson, Patrick, *Murderess*, Michael Joseph, London, 1971.

Wilson, Patrick, *Children Who Kill*, Michael Joseph, London, 1973.

Monthly magazines

Master Detective
True Crime
True Detective

Part Works

Crimes and Punishment
Murder Casebook

Alphabetical Index

ABEL, Wolfgang, and FURLAN, Mario (Italy)
'ACID BATH MURDERER', see HAIGH, John George
ALDRETE, Sara Maria, see CONSTANZO, Adolfo de Jesus
'ANGEL MAKERS OF NAGYREV' (Hungary)
ANN ARBOR HOSPITAL MURDERS (USA)
ARCHER-GILLIGAN, Amy (USA)
ARTIEDA, Ramiro (Bolivia)
'AXEMAN OF NEW ORLEANS' (USA)

BALL, Joe (USA)
BARBOSA, Daniel Camargo (Colombia and Ecuador)
'BEAST OF THE BLACK FOREST', see POMMERENCKE, Heinrich
BECK, Martha, and FERNANDEZ, Raymond (USA)
BECKER, Marie Alexandrine (Belgium)
BERDELLA, Robert (USA)
BERKOWITZ, David (USA)
BIANCHI, Kenneth Alessio, and BUONO, Angelo (USA)
'BIBLE JOHN' (Scotland)
BILLIK, Herman (USA)
BINGHAM CASE (England)
BIRNIE, David and Catherine (Australia)
BITTAKER, Lawrence, and NORRIS, Roy (USA)
'BLACK PANTHER', see NEILSON, Donald
BLADEL, Rudy (USA)
BODEN, Wayne Clifford (Canada)
BOLBER, Dr Morris, and PETRILLO, Paul and Herman (USA)
BONIN, William G. (USA)
BOOST, Werner (Germany)
'BOSTON STRANGLER', see DE SALVO, Albert
BRADY, Ian, and HINDLEY, Myra (England)
'BRIDES IN THE BATH KILLER', see SMITH, George Joseph
BRIGGEN, Joseph (USA)
BRINVILLIERS, Marie Marguerite (France)
BROWN, Debra Denise, see COLEMAN, Alton
BRUDOS, Jerry (USA)
'BTK STRANGLER' (USA)
BUNDY, Carol, see CLARK, Douglas
BUNDY, Theodore Robert ('Ted') (USA)
BUONO, Angelo, see BIANCHI, Kenneth Alessio
BURKE, William, and HARE, William (Scotland)

BURKITT, William (England)
BURROWS, Erskine Durrant, and TACKLYN, Larry Winfield (Bermuda)
'BUTCHER OF HANOVER', *see* HAARMANN, Fritz
BUTCHER OF KINGSBURY RUN' (USA)

'CANDY MAN', *see* CORLL, Dean
'CANNIBAL KILLER', *see* FISH, Albert
CARIGNAN, Harvey (USA)
CARPENTER, David J. (USA)
CARSON, James, and Susan (aka Michael and Suzan Bear) (USA)
'CASANOVA KILLER', *see* KNOWLES, Paul John
CHAPMAN, George (England)
'CHARLIE CHOPOFF', *see* RIVERA, Miguel
CHASE, Richard (USA)
'CHICAGO RIPPERS' (USA)
CHRISTIE, John Reginald Halliday (England)
CLARK, Douglas Daniel, and BUNDY, Carol (USA)
CLEMENTS, Dr Robert George (England)
CLICK, Franklin, *see* LOBAUGH, Ralph
CLINE, Alfred Leonard (USA)
'CO-ED KILLER', *see* KEMPER, Edmund Emil
COLE, Carroll Edward (USA)
COLEMAN, Alton, and BROWN, Debra Denise (USA)
COLLINS, Norman John (USA)
CONSTANZO, Adolfo de Jesus, ALDRETE, Sara Maria, *et al.* (Mexico)
COOKE, Eric Edgar (Australia)
COOPER, Ronald Frank (South Africa)
COPELAND, Michael (England and Germany)
CORLL, Dean Allen, and HENLEY, Elmer Wayne (USA)
CORONA, Juan Vallejo (USA)
CORWIN, Daniel Lee (USA)
COTTINGHAM, Richard Francis (USA)
COTTON, Mary Ann (England)
CREAM, Dr Thomas Neill (England and USA)
CUMMINS, Gordon Frederick (England)

DAHMER, Jeffrey L. (USA)
DEAN, Minnie (New Zealand)
'DEATH ANGEL KILLINGS', *see* 'ZEBRA'
DEEMING, Frederick (England and Australia)
DE MELKER, Daisy Louisa (South Africa)
DENKE, Karl (Germany)
DE RAIS, Gilles (France)
DE SALVO, Albert (USA)
DIAZ, Robert (USA)
'DOORBELL KILLER', *see* SZCZEPINSKI, Waldemar
DOSS, Nannie (USA)
DRENTH, Herman (aka Harry Powers) (USA)
DUFF-SIDNEY CASE (England)

DUFFY, John Francis (England)
DUMOLLARD, Martin and Marie (France)
'DUSSELDORF DOUBLES KILLER', *see* BOOST, Werner
DYER, Amelia Elizabeth (England)
DZHUMAGALIEV, Nikolai (USSR)

ENGLEMAN, Dr Glennon E. (USA)
ERSKINE, Kenneth (England)
EVANS, Donald Leroy (USA)

'FEMALE BLUEBEARD', *see* GUNNESS, Belle
FERNANDEZ, Raymond, *see* BECK, Martha (USA)
FIELD, Frederick Herbert Charles (England)
FISH, Albert (USA)
' "FORCES OF EVIL" KILLER', *see* HANCE, William Henry
FRANKLIN, Joseph Paul (USA)
'FREEWAY KILLER', *see* BONIN, William
'FRENCH BLUEBEARD', *see* LANDRU, Henri Desiré
FURLAN, Mario, *see* ABEL, Wolfgang

GACY, John Wayne (USA)
GALLEGO, Gerald Armand, and WILLIAMS-GALLEGO, Charlene
  (USA)
GARY, Carlton (USA)
GASKINS, Donald Henry (USA)
GBUREK, Tillie (aka Tillie Klimek) (USA)
GEIN, Edward (USA)
GIBBS, Janie (USA)
GIUDICE, Giancarlo (Italy)
GLATMAN, Harvey Murray (USA)
GLAZE, Billy (aka Jesse Sitting Crow) (USA)
GOHL, Billy (USA)
GONZALES, Delfina and Maria de Jesus (Mexico)
GORE, David Alan, and WATERFIELD, Fred (USA)
'GORILLA MURDERER', *see* NELSON, Earle Leonard
GOSMAN, Klaus (Germany)
GOTTFRIED, Gesina Margaretha (Germany)
GRAHAM, Gwendolyn Gail, and WOOD, Catherine (USA)
GRAHAM, Harrison (USA)
'GREEN RIVER KILLER' (USA)
GREENWOOD, Vaughn Orrin (USA)
GRILLS, Caroline (Australia)
GROSSMANN, Georg Karl (Germany)
GUNNESS, Belle (USA)

HAARMANN, Fritz (Germany)
HAERM, Dr Teet, and THOMAS, Dr Allgen Lars (Denmark and Sweden)
HAHN, Anna Marie (USA)
HAIGH, John George (England)

HANCE, William Henry (USA)
HANSEN, Robert (USA)
HARE, William, *see* BURKE, William
HARVEY, Donald (USA)
HATCHER, Charles (USA)
HEATH, Neville George Clevely (England)
HEIRENS, William (USA)
HENLEY, Wayne Elmer, *see* CORLL, Dean Allen
'HILLSIDE STRANGLER', *see* BIANCHI, Kenneth Alessio
HINDLEY, Myra, *see* BRADY, Ian
HOLMES, H.H., *see* MUDGETT, Hermann Webster
HONKA, Fritz (Germany)

'I-5 KILLER', *see* WOODFIELD, Randall Brent

'JACK THE RIPPER' (England)
'JACK THE STRIPPER' (England)
JEGADO, Hélène (France)
JOHNSON, Russell (Canada)
JONES, Genene (USA)
JONES, Harold (Wales)

KALLINGER, Joseph (USA)
KELLY, Kiernan (England)
KEMPER, Edmund Emil (USA)
KISS, Bela (Hungary)
KNOWLES, Paul John (USA)
KODAIRA, Yoshio (Japan)
KRAFT, Randy (USA)
KUKLINSKI, Richard (USA)
KURTEN, Peter (Germany)

LANDRU, Henri Desiré (France)
LEHMANN, Christa (Germany)
LEONSKI, Edward Joseph (Australia)
LEWINGDON, Gary James and Thaddeus Charles (USA)
LIM, Adrian, *et al.* (Singapore)
LINEVELT, Salie (South Africa)
LOBAUGH, Ralph, and CLICK, Franklin (USA)
'LONELY-HEARTS KILLER', *see* GLATMAN, Harvey Murray
'LONELY-HEARTS KILLERS', *see* BECK, Martha
LOPEZ, Pedro Armando (Ecuador)
LUCAS, Henry Lee (USA)
LUDKE, Bruno (Germany)
'LUDWIG MURDERS', *see* ABEL, Wolfgang
LUPO, Michael (England)
'LUST KILLER', *see* BRUDOS, Jerry
LYLES, Anjette (USA)

McDONALD, William (Australia)
MACKAY, Patrick David (England)
MANSON, Charles, *et al.* (USA)
MANUEL, Peter (Scotland)
MAREK, Martha (Austria)
MAZURKIEWICZ, Wladyslaw (Poland)
'METAL FANG', *see* DZHUMAGALIEV, Nikolai
'MIDDAY MURDERER', *see* GOSMAN, Klaus
'MICHIGAN MURDERER', *see* COLLINS, Norman John
MIKASEVICH, Gennadiy (USSR)
MILLER, James William, and WORRELL, Chris (Australia)
'MONSTER OF FLORENCE' (Italy)
'MONSTER OF MONTMARTRE', *see* PAULIN, Thierry
'MONSTER OF THE ANDES', *see* LOPEZ, Pedro Armando
'MOORS MURDERERS', *see* BRADY, Ian
MORS, Frederick (USA)
MSOMI, Elifasi (South Africa)
MUDGETT, Hermann Webster (aka H.H. Holmes) (USA)
MULLIN, Herbert (USA)
MUMFRE, Joseph, *see* 'AXEMAN OF NEW ORLEANS'

NEILSON, Donald (England)
NELSON, Earle Leonard (Canada and USA)
NESSET, Arnfinn (Norway)
'NIGHT STALKER', *see* RAMIREZ, Richard
NILSEN, Dennis Andrew (England)
NORRIS, Roy, *see* BITTAKER, Lawrence
NORTHCOTT, Gordon Stewart (USA)

'OGRESSE DE LA GOUTTE D'OR', *see* WEBER, Jeanne
OLSON, Clifford (Canada)

PALMER, Dr William (England)
PANZRAM, Carl (USA)
PAULIN, Thierry (France)
PETIOT, Dr Marcel (France)
PETRILLO, Paul and Herman, *see* BOLBER, Dr Morris
PLEIL, Rudolf (Germany)
POMEROY, Jesse (USA)
POMMERENCKE, Heinrich (Germany)
POWERS, Harry, *see* DRENTH, Herman
PRITCHARD, Dr Edward William (Scotland)
PUENTE, Dorothea (USA)

'RAILWAY KILLER', *see* DUFFY, John Francis
'RAILWAY SNIPER', *see* BLADEL, Rudy
RAMIREZ, Richard (USA)
'RED SPIDER', *see* STANIAK, Lucian
REES, Melvin Davis (USA)

RENDALL, Martha (Australia)
RIJKE, Sjef (Netherlands)
RIVERA, Miguel (USA)
ROGERS, Dayton Leroy (USA)
ROWNTREE, Mark (England)
RUDLOFF, Fritz (Germany)

SACK, George (USA)
SANDWENE, Ntimane (South Africa)
SARRET, Maître Georges (France)
SCHMID, Charles Howard (USA)
SEARL, Ralph Ray (USA)
SEARL, Tommy (USA)
'SEX BEAST', *see* REES, Melvin David
SHERMAN, Lydia (USA)
SINGH, Boysie (Trinidad)
'SINGING STRANGLER', *see* LEONSKI, Edward Joseph
SMITH, George Joseph (England)
SOBHRAJ, Charles Gurmukh (India and other Asian countries)
SODEMAN, Arnold Karl (Australia)
SOLIS, Magdalena and Eleazor, and HERNANDEZ, Cayetano and Santos
   (Mexico)
'SON OF SAM', *see* BERKOWITZ, David
'SOUTHSIDE SLAYER', *see* SPENCER, Timothy W.
SPENCER, Timothy W. (USA)
STANIAK, Lucian (Poland)
'STOCKING STRANGLER', *see* GARY, Carlton
'STOCKWELL STRANGLER', *see* ERSKINE, Kenneth
STRAFFEN, John Thomas (England)
'SUNDAY MORNING SLASHER', *see* WATTS, Coral Eugene
'SUNSET STRIP KILLERS', *see* CLARK, Douglas
SUTCLIFFE, Peter (England)
'SYDNEY MUTILATOR', *see* McDONALD, William
SZCZEPINSKI, Waldemar (Germany)

TACKLYN, Larry Winfield, *see* BURROWS, Erskine Durrant
TESSNOW, Ludwig (Germany)
THOMAS, Dr Allgen Lars, *see* HAERM, Dr Teet
TINNING, Marybeth (USA)
'TOKOLOSHE MURDERS', *see* MSOMI, Elifasi
TOPPAN, Jane (USA)
TORINUS, Metod (Yugoslavia)
TORONTO HOSPITAL MURDERS (Canada)
TURNER, Lise Jane (New Zealand)

VACHER, Joseph (France)
'VAMPIRE OF DUSSELDORF', *see* KURTEN, Peter
'VAMPIRE OF SACRAMENTO', *see* CHASE, Richard
'VAMPIRE RAPIST', *see* BODEN, Wayne Clifford

VAN ZON, Hans (Netherlands)

WAGNER, Waltraud, *et al.* (Austria)
WAINEWRIGHT, Thomas Griffiths (England)
'WANT-AD KILLER', *see* CARIGNAN, Harvey
'WARTIME JACK THE RIPPER', *see* CUMMINS, Gordon Frederick
WATERFIELD, Fred, *see* GORE, David Alan
WATTS, Coral Eugene (USA)
WEBER, Jeanne (France)
WEIDMANN, Eugen (France)
'WIDOW OF WINDY NOOK', *see* WILSON, Mary Elizabeth
WILLIAMS, Wayne B. (USA)
WILLIAMS-GALLEGO, Charlene, *see* GALLEGO, Gerald
WILSON, Catherine (England)
WILSON, Mary Elizabeth (England)
'WOLF MAN', *see* LUPO, Michael
WOOD, Catherine, *see* GRAHAM, Gwendolyn Gail
WOODFIELD, Randall Brent (USA)
WORRELL, Chris, *see* MILLER, James William

'YORKSHIRE RIPPER', *see* SUTCLIFFE, Peter
YOUNG, Graham (England)

'ZEBRA KILLINGS' (USA)
'ZODIAC' (USA)
ZWANZIGER, Anna Maria (Germany)

Geographical Index

(by location of murders)

Australia

BIRNIE, David and Catherine (1986)*
COOKE, Eric Edgar (1949–63)
DEEMING, Frederick (1891)
GRILLS, Caroline (1947–53)
LEONSKI, Edward Joseph, The 'Singing Strangler' (1942)
McDONALD, William, The 'Sydney Mutilator' (1961–2)
MILLER, James William, and WORRELL, Chris (1976–7)
RENDALL, Martha (1906–9)
SODEMAN, Arnold Karl (1930–6)

Austria

MAREK, Martha (1930s)
WAGNER, Waltraud, *et al.* (1988–9)

Belgium

BECKER, Marie Alexandrine (1930s)

Bermuda

BURROWS, Erskine Durrant, and TACKLYN, Larry Winfield (1972–3)

Bolivia

ARTIEDA, Ramiro (1930s)

Canada

BODEN, Wayne Clifford, The 'Vampire Rapist' (1968–71)
JOHNSON, Russell (1973–4)
NELSON, Earle Leonard, The 'Gorilla Murderer' (1926–7)
OLSON, Clifford (1980)
TORONTO HOSPITAL MURDERS (1980–1)

Colombia

BARBOSA, Daniel Camargo (1980s)
LOPEZ, Pedro Armando, The 'Monster of the Andes' (?–1980)

---

* Period during which the crimes were committed

Denmark

HAERM, Dr Teet and THOMAS, Dr Allgen Lars (1984–6)

Ecuador

BARBOSA, Daniel Camargo (1980s)
LOPEZ, Pedro Armando, The 'Monster of the Andes' (?–1980)

England

BINGHAM CASE (1910–11)
BRADY, Ian, and HINDLEY, Myra, The 'Moors Murderers' (1963–5)
BURKITT, William (1915–39)
CHAPMAN, George (1897–1902)
CHRISTIE, John Reginald Halliday (1943–53)
CLEMENTS, Dr Robert George (?–1947)
COPELAND, Michael (1960–1)
COTTON, Mary Ann (1857–72)
CREAM, Dr Thomas Neill (19th century)
CUMMINS, Gordon Frederick, The 'Wartime Jack the Ripper' (1942)
DEEMING, Frederick (1891)
DUFF-SIDNEY CASE (1928–9)
DUFFY, John Francis, The 'Railway Killer' (1985–6)
DYER, Amelia Elizabeth (19th century)
ERSKINE, Kenneth, The 'Stockwell Strangler' (1986)
FIELD, Frederick Herbert Charles (1931 and 1936)
HAIGH, John George, The 'Acid Bath Murderer' (1940s)
HEATH, Neville George Clevely (1946)
'JACK THE RIPPER' (1888)
'JACK THE STRIPPER' (1964–5)
KELLY, Kiernan (1953–84)
LUPO, Michael, The 'Wolf Man' (1986)
MACKAY, Patrick (1974–5)
NEILSON, Donald, The 'Black Panther' (1974–5)
NILSEN, Dennis Andrew (1978–83)
PALMER, Dr William (19th century)
ROWNTREE, Mark Andrew (1975–6)
SMITH, George Joseph, 'Brides in the Bath Killer' (1912–14)
STRAFFEN, John Thomas (1951)
SUTCLIFFE, Peter, The 'Yorkshire Ripper' (1975–80)
WAINEWRIGHT, Thomas Griffiths (1829–37)
WILSON, Catherine (1853–62)
WILSON, Mary Elizabeth, The 'Widow of Windy Nook' (1955–7)
YOUNG, Graham (1971)

France

BRINVILLIERS, Marie Marguerite (17th century)
DE RAIS, Gilles (15th century)
DUMOLLARD, Martin and Marie (1855–61)

JEGADO, Hélène (19th century)
LANDRU, Henri Desiré, The 'French Bluebeard' (1915–19)
PAULIN, Thierry, The 'Monster of Montmartre' (1984–7)
PETIOT, Dr Marcel (1930–44)
SARRET, Maître Georges (1920s and 1930s)
VACHER, Joseph (1893–7)
WEBER, Jeanne, 'L'Ogresse de la Goutte d'Or' (1905–7)
WEIDMANN, Eugen (1937)

Germany

BOOST, Werner, The 'Dusseldorf Doubles Killer' (1950s)
COPELAND, Michael (1960–1)
DENKE, Karl (1921–4)
GOSMAN, Klaus, The 'Midday Murderer' (1960–5)
GOTTFRIED, Gesina Margaretha (19th century)
GROSSMANN, Georg Karl (?–1921)
HAARMANN, Fritz, The 'Butcher of Hanover' (1918–24)
HONKA, Fritz (1970s)
KURTEN, Peter, The 'Vampire of Dusseldorf' (1913–31)
LEHMANN, Christa (1952–4)
LUDKE, Bruno (1927–43)
PLEIL, Rudolf (?–1950)
POMMERENCKE, Heinrich, The 'Beast of the Black Forest' (1959–60)
RUDLOFF, Fritz (1954)
SZCZEPINSKI, Waldemar, The 'Doorbell Killer' (1983–4)
TESSNOW, Ludwig (1898–1901)
ZWANZIGER, Anna Maria (18th century)

Hungary

'ANGEL MAKERS OF NAGYREV' (1914–29)
KISS, Bela (?–1914)

India (and various other Asian countries)

SOBHRAJ, Charles (1970s)

Italy

ABEL, Wolfgang, and FURLAN, Mario, The 'Ludwig Murders' (1977–84)
GIUDICE, Giancarlo (1984–6)
'MONSTER OF FLORENCE' (1960–85)

Japan

KODAIRA, Yoshio (1945–6)

Mexico

CONSTANZO, Adolfo de Jesus, ALDRETE, Sara Maria, *et al.* (1989)
GONZALES, Delfina and Maria de Jesus (1960s)

SOLIS, Magdalena and Eleazor, and HERNANDEZ, Cayetano and Santos (1963)

Netherlands

RIJKE, Sjef (1971)
VAN ZON, Hans (1965–7)

New Zealand

DEAN, Minnie (1891–5)
TURNER, Lise Jane (1980s)

Norway

NESSET, Arnfinn (1977–80)

Peru

LOPEZ, Pedro Armando, The 'Monster of the Andes' (?–1980)

Poland

MAZURKIEWICZ, Wladyslaw (1945–54)
STANIAK, Lucian, The 'Red Spider' (1964–7)

Scotland

'BIBLE JOHN' (1968–9)
BURKE, William, and HARE, William (1827–8)
MANUEL, Peter (1956–8)
PRITCHARD, Dr Edward William (1863–5)

Singapore

LIM, Adrian, *et al.* (1981)

South Africa

COOPER, Ronald Frank (1976)
DE MELKER, Daisy Louisa (1923–32)
LINEVELT, Salie (1940)
MSOMI, Elifasi, The 'Tokoloshe Murders' (1953–5)
SANDWENE, Ntimane (1929–36)

Sweden

HAERM, Dr Teet, and THOMAS, Dr Allgen Lars (1984–6)

Trinidad

SINGH, Boysie (1932–56)

Union of Soviet Socialist Republics

DZHUMAGALIEV, Nikolai, 'Metal Fang' (1980s)
MIKASEVICH, Gennadiy (1971–85)

United States of America

ANN ARBOR HOSPITAL MURDERS (1975)
ARCHER-GILLIGAN, Amy (1910–17)
'AXEMAN OF NEW ORLEANS' (1911–19)
BALL, Joe (1930s)
BECK, Martha, and FERNANDEZ, Raymond, The 'Lonely-Hearts Killers' (1948)
BERDELLA, Robert (1984–7)
BERKOWITZ, David, 'Son of Sam' (1976–7)
BIANCHI, Kenneth Alessio, and BUONO, Angelo, The 'Hillside Stranglers' (1977–9)
BILLIK, Herman (1905–6)
BITTAKER, Lawrence, and NORRIS, Roy (1979–?)
BLADEL, Rudy, The 'Railway Sniper' (1963–78)
BOLBER, Dr Morris, and PETRILLO, Paul and Herman (1932–7)
BONIN, William G., The 'Freeway Killer' (1972–80)
BRIGGEN, Joseph (1900s)
BRUDOS, Jerry, The 'Lust Killer' (1968–9)
'BTK STRANGLER' (1974–7)
BUNDY, Theodore Robert ('Ted') (1974–8)
'BUTCHER OF KINGSBURY RUN' (?–1938)
CARIGNAN, Harvey, The 'Want-Ad Killer' (1949–74)
CARPENTER, David J. (1979–81)
CARSON, James and Susan (1981–3)
CHASE, Richard, The 'Vampire of Sacramento' (1977–8)
'CHICAGO RIPPERS' (1981–2)
CLARK, Douglas Daniel and BUNDY, Carol, The 'Sunset Strip Killers' (1980–2)
CLINE, Alfred Leonard (1931–45)
COLE, Carroll Edward (1971–80)
COLEMAN, Alton, and BROWN, Debra Denise (1984)
COLLINS, Norman John, The 'Michigan Murderer' (1967–9)
CORLL, Dean, The 'Candy Man', and HENLEY, Elmer Wayne (1971–3)
CORONA, Juan Vallejo (1971)
CORWIN, Daniel Lee (1987–8)
COTTINGHAM, Richard Francis (1977–9)
DAHMER, Jeffrey L. (1989–91)
DE SALVO, Albert, The 'Boston Strangler' (1962–4)
DIAZ, Robert (1981)
DOSS, Nannie (1940s)
DRENTH, Herman (1920s)
ENGLEMAN, Dr Glennon E. (1958–80)
EVANS, Donald Leroy (1980s)
FISH, Albert, The 'Cannibal Killer' (?–1934)

FRANKLIN, Joseph Paul (1977–80)

GACY, John Wayne (1972–8)

GALLEGO, Gerald Armand, and WILLIAMS-GALLEGO, Charlene (1978–80)

GARY, Carlton, The 'Stocking Strangler' (1977–8)

GASKINS, Donald Henry, (1970–80)

GBUREK, Tillie (1914–21)

GEIN, Edward (1954–7)

GIBBS, Janie (1966–8)

GLATMAN, Harvey Murray, The 'Lonely-Hearts Killer' (1957–8)

GLAZE, Billy (1986–7)

GOHL, Billy (?–1912)

GORE, David Alan, and WATERFIELD, Fred (1981–3)

GRAHAM, Gwendolyn Gail, and WOOD, Catherine (1987)

GRAHAM, Harrison (1987)

'GREEN RIVER KILLER' (1980s)

GREENWOOD, Vaughn Orrin (1974–5)

GUNNESS, Belle, The 'Female Bluebeard' (?–1908)

HAHN, Anna Marie (1930s)

HANCE, William Henry, The ' "Forces of Evil" Killer' (1970s)

HANSEN, Robert (1980–1)

HARVEY, Donald (?–1987)

HATCHER, Charles (1961–82)

HEIRENS, William (1945–6)

JONES, Genene (1981–2)

KALLINGER, Joseph (1974–5)

KEMPER, Edmund Emil, The 'Co-ed Killer' (1964–73)

KNOWLES, Paul John, The 'Casanova Killer' (1974)

KRAFT, Randy (1972–83)

KUKLINSKI, Richard (1980–3)

LEWINGDON, Gary James and Thaddeus Charles, The '.22 Calibre Murders' (1978)

LOBAUGH, Ralph, and CLICK, Franklin (1944–5)

LUCAS, Henry Lee (1970s–83)

LYLES, Anjette (1950s)

MANSON, Charles, *et al.* (1969)

MORS, Frederick (1914–15)

MUDGETT, Hermann Webster (19th century)

MULLIN, Herbert (1972–3)

NELSON, Earle Leonard, The 'Gorilla Murderer' (1926–7)

NORTHCOTT, Gordon (1928–30)

PANZRAM, Carl (1920s)

POMEROY, Jesse (19th century)

PUENTE, Dorothea (1986–8)

RAMIREZ, Richard, The 'Night Stalker' (1984–5)

REES, Melvin Davis, The 'Sex Beast' (1957–9)

RIVERA, Miguel, 'Charlie Chopoff' (1972–3)

ROGERS, Dayton Leroy (1987)

SACK, George (1923–54)

SCHMID, Charles Howard (1964–5)
SEARL, Ralph Ray (1964)
SEARL, Tommy (1972)
SHERMAN, Lydia (19th century)
SPENCER, Timothy W., The 'Southside Slayer' (1984–7)
TINNING, Marybeth (1972–85)
TOPPAN, Jane (1880–1901)
WATTS, Coral Eugene, The 'Sunday Morning Slayer' (197?–82)
WILLIAMS, Wayne B. (1979–81)
WOODFIELD, Randall Brent, The 'I-5 Killer' (1980–1)
'ZEBRA KILLINGS', The 'Death Angel Killings' (1973–4)
'ZODIAC' (1969–74)

Wales

JONES, Harold (1921)

Yugoslavia

TORINOS, Metod (1977–9)